A LAB OF MY OWN

VIBS

Volume 212

Robert Ginsberg
Founding Editor

Leonidas Donskis
Executive Editor

Associate Editors

a volume in
Lived Values, Valued Lives
LVVL
Richard T. Hull, Editor

A LAB OF MY OWN

Neena B. Schwartz

Josie —
Thanks for helping
me buy a house
and sell a house
Neen

Rodopi

Amsterdam - New York, NY 2010

Cover art: Harriet Claire Wadeson, "Fall", watercolor,
used by permission of the artist.

Cover Design: Studio Pollmann

The paper on which this book is printed meets the requirements of "ISO
9706:1994, Information and documentation - Paper for documents -
Requirements for permanence".

ISBN: 978-90-420-2737-4
E-Book ISBN: 978-90-420-2738-1
© Editions Rodopi B.V., Amsterdam - New York, NY 2010
Printed in the Netherlands

Lived Values Valued Lives
(LVVL)

Richard T. Hull
Editor

Other Titles in LVVL

To my parents, Pep and Paul Schwartz, who encouraged their children to think for themselves, and to my sister Pearl Schwartz Imber and my brother Leon Schwartz (1928–2003) and their families, who have accepted cheerfully all of my identities—scientist, feminist, and lesbian.

To Harriet Claire Wadeson, artist and therapist, indefatigable travel companion, lover of life, who has worked ever so diligently to get me to have fun. What an amazing journey we are having!

I owe Rue Bucher (1928–1985), sociologist of professions, a debt of gratitude I can no longer repay. She introduced me to the world of the sociology of professions early in my academic career and I was never the same again.

CONTENTS

LIST OF PHOTOGRAPHS

LIST OF FIGURES

Dance evening at Society for the Study of Reproduction (SSR),North Carolina State University, 1992. Members l-r: Janice Bahr, Harold Spies, Phil Djuik, Anita Payne, Neena, Gordon Niswender.

EDITORIAL FOREWORD

The Lived Values, Valued Lives Series is composed of biographies, loosely defined, expressing and exploring how values appear in and shape human lives. The series aims to provoke readers to engage in reflection on the values expressed in the decisions, actions, and thoughts of philosophically reflective individuals. From one another's narratives we may learn much and come to consider possibilities that might otherwise never occur to us.

The series is intended for readers of all ages looking for inspiration not only for course papers but also for their lives. The value of thoughtful reflection, not conversion, is the goal. Neena Schwartz's *A Lab of My Own* is the fourth offering in this valuable series.

Schwartz's professional accomplishments are astounding ones, made all the more so by her being a woman in a male-dominated field. Yet even more astounding is how much she was able to accomplish despite battling life-long bouts of depression and being emotionally conflicted over being lesbian.

In this volume, Dr. Schwartz chronicles her experiences, professional and private, that mark her distinguished career in endocrinology. Those considering or pursuing a career in endocrinology, molecular biology, or any of the related fields will find the story of how her career developed fascinating and instructive. Scientists familiar with the work of this distinguished researcher will find the narrative of her life equally engaging. More than a few readers might be surprised to find her personal imprint on scientific techniques and discoveries that they took for granted without ever stopping to think about the individual persons behind the achievements. In particular, women bent on a career in science and some who may never have considered such a career will find Neena Schwartz's pioneering work on behalf of women in the sciences inspirational and encouraging.

With great pleasure, I am honored to have *A Lab of My Own* as the fourth volume in the series, Lived Values and Valued Lives. With this volume, the series now balances the stories of two women—one a world traveler, one a world-class scientist—with the stories of two men—one a student of classical and continental philosophy reflecting on academic culture, the other a student of classical literature grappling with the human issues of grief and consolation.

These four works pose questions that challenge us to become better persons: critically reflective and open to new possibilities.

Richard T. Hull, Editor
Lived Values Valued Lives Special Series
Tallahassee, Florida

PREFACE

I worry mostly, though, how having been made another person might have enabled me to do the Work better. As with the life, so ridiculously, with The work. But, after all, which of them is the enciphered version of the other one, and are we, after all, even supposed to know?

John Hollander
"Reflections on Espionage"
(Concerning a spy comparing basic spy "work" and cover "work")

My career in science started in September 1948, when I rode the train from Baltimore to Chicago to enter graduate school in the Department of Physiology at Northwestern University Medical School. My career ended when I retired in 1999 from my position as director of the Center for Reproductive Science at Northwestern and from teaching and conducting research in the Department of Neurobiology and Physiology in the College of Arts and Sciences.

This fifty-year span bracketed the beginning of the vigorous feminist movement in the United States, which partially opened up the workplace for women. I became very active in this movement at its beginning. Science has crucial potential for improving health and the environment, and for coping with the global energy crisis. We must encourage women and other previously excluded groups to engage in it. We need diverse ideas and viewpoints to save our planet from impending disaster. I believe that my contributions to enhancing diversity among practitioners of science have played an important role in making it possible for more women to contribute to science theory and practice.

In all, my life has been characterized by three passions: my activism in the struggle to gain equal opportunities in science for women, my love for reproductive science, and my love for women. All three are different ways of looking at the world.

I became a scientist and identified myself as a lesbian during the 1940s when few women were in science and the scientific community labeled lesbians "sick" or "sexually inverted."

Because of these personal struggles, I began to participate in the feminist movement in the sciences, which grew strongly during the 1970s. As a result of these political endeavors and my success as a scientist, I became the first president of the Association for Women in Science (1971–1972), the first female president of the Society for the Study of Reproduction (1977–1978) and the second female president of the Endocrine Society (1982–1983).

In 1998, I won the Distinguished Educator Award of the Endocrine Society and in 2003 I received the Lifetime Mentor Award of the American Association for the Advancement of Science. Both of these awards reflected my commitment to mentoring young scientists.

A few years ago, I decided *not* to apply for another research grant from the National Institutes of Health, which had supported my lab for fifty years, after my current five-year grant came to an end. That decision was a momentous one—essentially it meant that I was closing my lab and taking myself out of the research "business" I had been in since the end of graduate school. I made the decision because I was no longer as enthusiastic about lab experiments and the intricacies of my science as I had been for almost fifty years.

Frankly, I was also unenthusiastic about writing the "competing renewal grant" request for research money.

"Enough," I said, "I'll do something else."

I kept feeling the urge to write about my life in science. My research has investigated the endocrinology of reproduction. Science is important, pervasive, and it can be either a great boon to people or a terrible threat to life as we have known it, depending on your point of view. Much of feminist, gender-based scholarship has been focused on the humanities and the social sciences. It should also be dependent for analysis on understanding what biology can and cannot determine.

I wanted to address that issue from my point of view. For these reasons, I started working on this book. But something else intruded on this "straight"-forward narrative. My third side—not the activist or the scientist—needed to come out, literally and figuratively.

While I was acting dean of the Northwestern College of Arts and Science during 1997–1998, I personally interviewed every candidate for a tenured position. I enjoyed this part of being dean more than anything else. Each candidate and I sat in the paneled dean's office in comfortable chairs sipping tea or coffee, while I sized up the candidate and talked up Northwestern and Evanston. The high number of female candidates, particularly for the science positions, was exhilarating, after all my work nationally and at Northwestern to promote equal access of women to employment in universities. I had finally made it into a position where hiring was something I could influence directly. Never would I have predicted when I started graduate school, or during my first years in academe, that I might be in this position.

Another personal satisfaction stemmed from remembering that a previous dean at Northwestern had fired me from my position as chair of biological sciences twenty years earlier. How sweet it was to be in the dean's chair, albeit temporarily! But my biggest surprise came from something else completely. A number of candidates told me that we would need to find a position for someone else if we hoped to recruit successfully. Frequently, this someone else was a spouse—the regular kind—but for a surprising number it was a same-sex partner. We hired a number of both kinds of candidates.

I realized that I am lesbian at the age of sixteen while I was in high school, back during the 1940s, when secrecy was the only survival tactic for lesbians and gays who wanted to make their way in the professional world.

My whole life, until very recently, has been spent split in two with a coded alter ego. *Don't ask, don't tell.* Being in a situation where you are passing carries a terrible cost: self identity appears to be always in question, and self-esteem seems always shaky. Here were potential faculty members telling me about their homosexuality openly, without fear or embarrassment!

I wondered what it would have been like to have been able to be open about my own sexual preference, which I had tried, with varying success or failure, to keep hidden.

So this book completes what I have called my "microphone fantasy." This fantasy started at professional meetings when I would stand at a microphone and comment on a paper I had just heard presented, or even when I was giving a paper of mine. I would have to fight myself not to announce to the audience that I am lesbian. I never did it—until now.

All my life I have felt splits within me: between hiding my personal life from my professional colleagues; between separating my non-traditional activism from my "politically correct" applications for government grants and playing within the traditional academe rules of procedure; and between my allegiance to women in the field and my strong scientific activity in the "boy's club."

I have expended a great deal of energy keeping these three aspects separate. Gradually, I became angry with these splits and wanted to bring these aspects of my life together.

Now, while working on mending old splits, writing this book has aroused a new split within me. I want to write in hope that this book will provide young gay scientists or other professionals with a lesson of possibilities for success and happiness without such splits in their life.

But a possible downside frightens me and made me leery of writing at all. I have been successful as a scientist and have been accepted as a role model for other women—will my open admission of lesbianism erase my successes for homophobes? Will I be discounted as a female scientist because I am a lesbian, even in our more enlightened times?

I can still remember when Kate Millett was attacked at an early National Organization for Women (NOW) meeting because she appeared to have a "lesbian" agenda. The political climate for gays and lesbians in the United States, which had improved considerably since my own adolescence, suffered badly with the re-election of George W. Bush and the ascendancy of the religious right in our country.

But we also know that even the struggle to expand the role of women in science is itself still not won. The remarks of Larry Summers, then president of Harvard, at a conference in 2005 to the effect, "women are not the equal of men in math . . ." led to a furor in the media. This statement was not supported by any valid evidence, but was widely touted as the reason for the underemployment of female scientists at universities such as Harvard. My despair over these retrogressive events has spurred me to tell my story.

Most of my experiences as a scientist have been exhilarating and exciting; I hope to share some of these also. I suppose I could have done that without personally coming out, but that would have been incomplete and distorted. I feel the way Adrienne Rich has described herself in "Split at the Root":

> Sometimes I felt that I have seen too long from too many disconnected angles: white, Jewish, anti-semite, racist, anti-racist, once-married, lesbian, middle-class, feminist, exmatriate Southerner, split at the root— that I will never bring them whole.

This book is my attempt to "bring them whole" for myself.

ACKNOWLEDGEMENTS

Thanks to all of my undergraduates, graduate students, and fellows. It was so much fun to teach and learn and collaborate with you. The papers and chapters and research grants listed in the chronology section of this book attest to your dedication, hard work, and creative minds. My long time technicians, Bill Talley and Brigitte Mann, kept the lab going, going, and going for so many years with their fine attention to detail and methodology. Thanks to all of you.

Many people made it possible for me to have a quasi-administrative career. The late Bill Grove at University of Illinois gave me my first crack at administration very early, and it made a real difference in my subsequent career. The former Vice President for Research, Dave Mintzer, enabled me to start a Program, later a Center, for Reproductive Science at Northwestern University, which was the start of Northwestern University's presence in that research area. Adair Waldenberg, while Associate Dean at Northwestern, was a remarkable tutor in the myriad ways of academe. The late Larry Dumas, while he was Provost at Northwestern, appointed me as Acting Dean of the College of Arts and Science. What a privilege to end my career on that note.

I started writing this book when I retired from the Department of Neurobiology and Physiology in 1999. Thanks to my friends and colleagues in Portia who have listened to me read parts of this book countless times— especially to Ellen Wright who went far beyond the call of duty in helping this scientist write prose and to Fran Paden, good friend, critic, and neighbor.

Thanks to my friends Ellen Eslinger and Andra Medea for their very helpful comments about publishing. Various people have read chapters of the book and made helpful comments. I thank Judy Levy, Harriet Claire Wadeson, Marcia Gealy, Marianne Whatley, and Elaine M. Hull particularly. My former colleague and continuing friend, David Hull, heroically read the entire manuscript. My late brother, Leon Schwartz, and my sister Pearl Schwartz Imber, served me as a collective family resource, reminding me of old memories and providing me with new ones.

The material in Chapter Fourteen, "Don't Ask, Don't Tell," previously appeared in substantially the same form as "Genes, Hormones, and Sexuality," *The Gay and Lesbian Review Worldwide*, 15:1(January-February 2008).

The cover art is an original watercolor entitled Fall, by Harriet Claire Wadeson; © Harriet Claire Wadeson, used by permission of the artist.

Richard T. Hull, editor of the Lived Values, Valued Lives series, was persistent in keeping after me about what he called *"das Buch"* while I dithered around. Thank you, Richard, for your patience.

Emily Heckman and Nina Cantanese were very helpful in early editing. Elizabeth D. Boepple was my final editor with Rodopi. Not only is she a fine

XX

A LAB OF MY OWN

editor, but a great commentator and hand holder. Thanks for your patience and forbearance.

Our Chicago area Saturday Potluck group has now been meeting monthly for more than forty years. What can I say—you have been a support team when I needed it, confidantes when that was necessary. The food and company are spectacular and always fun. See you next Saturday!

One

BRINGING THEM WHOLE

Thy memory be as a dwelling place
For all sweet sounds and harmonies

William Wordsworth
"Lines Composed a Few Miles above Tintern Abbey"

Going to Omaha in the middle of a heat wave in July is insane. It's even crazier to go there to attend a professional meeting when I am retired and intended instead to go up to my house on Ellison Bay in Wisconsin to swim, hike, and read mystery stories. But I went to Nebraska in 2006 because Fred Stormshak, the Chair of the Senior/Emeritus Committee of the Society for the Study of Reproduction (SSR), wrote to me in January asking, "Would you be willing to come to the meeting to give a talk to the Emeritus group about Cornelia Channing? I saw your retrospective article in *Endocrine News* on your collaboration with her on inhibin."

My last trip to Nebraska had occurred in 1995, when I was asked to present a seminar at the University of Nebraska at Lincoln and at Clay Center, Nebraska, where a major lab is located, which focuses on reproduction in farm animals. I talked at both places about our research on the hormone inhibin, research I had started in collaboration with Cornelia Channing.

The Clay Center scientists had enticed me to prolong my trip to Nebraska with the prospect of seeing Sandhill Cranes migrating along the Platte River, near the lab. The day after my seminar, I was awakened at 3 a.m. and taken to a birding site with one of the lab guys. It was a birding experience not to be forgotten. As the day lightened, we could see hundreds of cranes dropping out of the sky and landing along the river shore. I have birded in many countries, but nothing has ever given me more pleasure than that morning along the river.

Cornelia Channing was a reproductive endocrinologist at the University of Maryland who died in 1985 at the age of forty-seven. In 1974, she had provided me with fluid from pig ovarian follicles, in which I had predicted we might find a hormone, inhibin. I hypothesized that inhibin might be playing a significant role in the regulation of the rat reproductive cycle and perhaps in the human menstrual cycle as well. This prediction sounded crazy, since endocrinologists had been looking for such a hormone in the testis for about forty years, but it had never been isolated.

Regardless, I turned out to be right, and this discovery led to the further discovery of a whole essential family of proteins and receptors with various functions, including development in humans.

I couldn't say no to Fred, since it was Cornelia who had made it possible for me to discover inhibin in the ovary, which became the pinnacle of my career as an endocrinologist—every endocrinologist wants to identify a new hormone! So I agreed to attend the meeting and give a talk.

ॐ

As I stood waiting for my suitcase to come off the carousel in the Omaha airport, I began to see other scientists I knew, who were also going to the convention, each looking as hot as I was feeling.

I had prepared a talk about Cornelia's science, interspersed with some pictures I had taken of her in front of the Taj Mahal, when we had attended a conference on pituitary hormones in Bangalore, India, in 1973. Unexpectedly, the few days I spent at the meeting in Omaha encompassed a kind of synopsis of where I have come from as a scientist, what I enjoy as a person, and what my life has been like as a lesbian.

ॐ

I am a charter member of SSR, having been at the meeting in Urbana, Illinois thirty years before, when a small group of reproductive biologists got together and in a noisy, raucous two hours, formed a new society to accommodate reproductive scientists of any persuasion (researchers, physicians, veterinarians) and provide a common forum for their research and a new journal (*Biology of Reproduction*). I remember our trying to name the society something that would give it the acronym "SEX" but "X" proved to be a difficult letter to associate with a relevant word.

Unlike most of the older professional societies, SSR welcomed women from the beginning. As a woman who has fought the battle for equality of opportunity and treatment of women in science, I have loved the openness and non-elitism of this society. I was its first female president in 1974, and I have been followed as president by many other women. Not surprisingly, the society has also welcomed trainees, giving them travel awards and prizes for excellent papers and places on the governing board. Before I retired and closed my lab, the annual SSR meeting was always the favorite yearly science event for me and my trainees.

Since I no longer have a lab of my own, I no longer have students who come with me to scientific meetings to present their science. I miss them. I had such fun watching them give papers, defending their science, and meeting other scientists whose names they had seen in their textbooks.

྾ঌ

As I stood in line at the hotel to register, a voice behind me said "Hello, Neena." It was a former graduate student, Ulrica Luderer, who is now an associate professor in the department of reproductive toxicology at the University of California, Irvine. "I'd like you to meet two of my students who are giving papers this week." She was beaming proudly, and while I felt a pang of regret and loss of things past, it was so heartwarming to feel her pleasure and pride in them. Ulrica and I kissed, and I shook hands with her two students, one male and one female, who told me eagerly about their research.

As I turned from the hotel registration desk to go up to my room, I bumped into Stan Glasser, who was looking disheveled and hot and was limping. Stan is the redheaded guy who had presented his first scientific paper at a meeting fifty-five years before, when I had presented my first paper. We were the last two speakers at a session of the physiology meetings in Rochester, New York, and we had stayed to hear each other as everyone else walked out to lunch. That forged an unbreakable bond.

So it went, as I drifted around the Statler Hotel, where most of the meeting participants were staying, and the Convention Center, listening to some science and saying hello to old friends. My talk, at a 7 a.m. breakfast, elicited a number of memories of Cornelia from other scientists. I talked about how she had shipped me the frozen fluid, which I had thawed and tested on my lab rats. Others told about what she was like as a postdoctoral fellow in England, and as a young assistant professor at Pittsburgh, before she moved to the University of Maryland as a professor, where she had a brilliant scientific career researching events in the ovary, before her untimely death from breast cancer.

྾ঌ

Despite having been retired for a number of years, I listened to a few science talks in Omaha to see how far my own field has gone, and even understood most of it. The heterogeneity of research subjects discussed at this meeting—with animal husbandry researchers talking about pituitary hormones in horses and sheep, physicians discussing genetic causes of infertility in humans, and biologists describing spermatogenesis in zebra fish—led to exciting discussions and enhances one's faith in the significance of evolutionary processes.

྾ঌ

My friends are always surprised when I describe the social events at a science meeting. "We didn't know scientists relaxed enough to party," they would tell me. Among the best aspects of the SSR annual meeting are the evening parties, dances, and dinners. On one such evening in Omaha, we were treated to a barbeque dinner and a dance. Instead of sitting down at a crowded table

with other past-presidents, I sat and drank and talked with one of the other female reproductive biologists for two hours, ignoring requests from other colleagues to join them,

❧

But "she" is yet another story from the past, which resurfaced for both of us
in Omaha. Thirty or so years before, during a SSR meeting on a college campus, she had edged up to me in the cafeteria and asked "How have you managed to be so prominent in science while being a lesbian?"

I had nearly dropped my tray of food. My secret (or so I thought) life as
a lesbian was something I kept apart from my professional life as much as I
could. We had talked then privately and, in fact, had a brief long-distance
affair. She is a good looking, very feisty woman, who also happens to be an
excellent scientist.

I had not encountered her for many years, and I was pleased to see her
sitting in one of the science sessions in Omaha, although I confess I was also
a little uneasy. It brought back for me the need I have felt for most of my life
to separate "Neena, the lesbian" from "Neena, the scientist and teacher." I am
dismayed that the prospect of my personal life intruding into a science meeting still frightens me. Has anything changed in thirty years in my view of
lesbianism or in the world's view? Lesbianism is certainly more openly talked
about these days, and is more acceptable to many, but the public nature of
arguments about it still makes me cringe. Still, it was good to see her again.
So we sat and talked a lot about the past and about our present lives and her
career, and we exchanged phone numbers.

My past and present were displayed before me as I walked around talking, talking, talking with friends in Omaha. For fifty years, I have been a
scientist, a teacher, a lesbian, a mentor, an administrator, a birder—usually
one at a time. All of them came together magically and unexpectedly, com-
pressed into three days in Omaha in July of 2006.

Study Questions

(1) What sorts of events or experiences trigger us to begin reviewing our
    lives? Postulate reasons.
- Is such review worthwhile? In what sense or to what purpose?
- Discuss whether an ideal age can be identified at which such life
  review would be more valuable than some other age; discuss your
  reasons.
- Discuss the differences in purpose of such life review as directed
  inward vs. directed toward others.

(2) Neena states, "the public nature of arguments about [lesbianism] still makes me cringe." Discuss the sentiment evinced by this statement within the context of writing a public autobiography that highlights the topic.
- Return to this question after you finish reading the book; discuss whether you believe the author's sentiments have changed during the writing, or because of writing the memoir.

(3) Discuss the persistence of personal identity. Was the Neena B. Schwartz who met Stan Glasser in Omaha during 2006 the same person she was when she interacted with him in the 1950s?
- Explain and discuss reasons for your answer.
- What elements of personhood, if any, remain the same over time; which change?

Neena, Dad, Pearl, Leon
Atlantic City, 1936.

Leon, at Bennett Pl. store, 1936
(Mom in windows).

Two

A BLANK SLATE

Try as I like to find the way
I never can get back by day
Nor can remember plain and clear
The curious music that I hear

Robert Louis Stevenson
"The Land of Nod"

Once riding in old Baltimore,
Heart-filled, head-filled with glee,
I saw a Baltimorean
Keep looking straight at me.
Now I was eight and very small,
And he was no whit bigger,
And so I smiled, but he poked out
His tongue, and called me, "Nigger."
I saw the whole of Baltimore
From May until December;
Of all the things that happened there
That's all that I remember.

Countee Cullen
"Incident"

How much of one's childhood needs to be known to understand where the adult comes from? As a woman unexpectedly in science, and a lesbian, what do I need to understand about my family, my upbringing, the events of my childhood, to understand how I got to where I am? As a biologist I have encountered nature vs. nurture controversies frequently. But within my own life, deterministic causes don't impress me. How much of life is a random response to everyday events, rather than an inevitable path taken after a cataclysmic or even an unnoticed happening?

The years I remember started when I was five years old, when my parents had a mom-and-pop grocery store in a predominantly black neighborhood in downtown Baltimore. During the entire time I attended school in Baltimore, grade school through college, the schools were segregated. That meant that while we lived with the store, my white schoolmates were not my neighbors and our neighbors did not develop into friends. As I look back on my life there, I see a child isolated from the rest of the world except my mother and father and brother.

Both my parents had been born in Russia in 1903. My dad, Paul Schwartz, came to the United States in 1912, with his parents and an older brother, my Uncle Norton. Their oldest brother, Ben Schwartz, helped bring his parents and brothers to Baltimore. Dad went through public school up to the second year at Polytechnic High School in Baltimore, leaving in his junior year to work in Norton's grocery store. I never asked him why he left school before graduating, nor did he ever tell me.

Dad played basketball in the Jewish leagues of Baltimore as he grew up. But his mother thought it was "foolish for boys to run around in short pants" so he hid his uniform in the back shed where their outdoor toilet was. I am sure that the reason Dad encouraged my brother Leon to play basketball and football in high school and college, in spite of our mother's misgivings, was because he had missed out on this as a teenager.

I loved those stories Dad told of his early life growing up in Baltimore. It seems funny to me now that he never talked to me about his years in Europe. I think he put that all behind him and became the consummate American. He really bought the American dream—he worked hard, loved sports, and enjoyed this country for its free and easy way of doing things.

My uncles on both sides were openly cynical and critical about the American focus on sports and business. But all his life, my father enjoyed sports, taking my brother Leon and me to watch the Baltimore Orioles play when they were in the International League. He was obviously proud of my brother's talent as a runner, football player, and basketball star in high school and college.

∾

Mother (Ethyl or "Pep" Shulman Schwartz) was born in 1903 in a small town—Mlynov, a *shtetl*—in what is now Ukraine. In contrast to Dad, she told me many stories while I was growing up about her life on the farm and in Warsaw where she attended the "gymnasium."

"While I was in Warsaw I lived with a gentile family, so I ate only vegetables and fish."

I remember being impressed with that since I didn't like either fish or vegetables while I was growing up. Although Mom's family had a farm, her father also worked outside running a logging camp. She liked to read so much that her family worried that her eyes would become "weak." So she read up in a tree or in the attic of their barn. One book she particularly liked was Stowe's *Uncle Tom's Cabin*, which she read in Russian translation.

"I cried so much when Little Eva died, my family took the book away," she told me.

As I grew up and began going to the Baltimore Public Library myself, Mom asked me to pick up books for her, best sellers or sometimes Russian books in translation. Once I brought her *Uncle Tom's Cabin* in English. She read it, but I do not remember her crying.

Mother's family left Russia for America in 1921. They rode by train to Belgium to board the boat for America. She was in her late teens. She and her parents, a brother and his wife, and her two sisters, along with the fiancé of one of them, traveled together to New York. They left her two oldest sisters, Lisa and Nechumah, who were already married and settled with families, behind in Russia.

Mom developed measles just before they were to board *The Lapland* in Antwerp. Her face was flushed and severely broken out, so my grandmother Pearl powdered her face to hide the rash and she was able to board. Once the boat took off, she was sent to the ship's hospital, where she spent the rest of the voyage below decks. They arrived at Ellis Island on 5 June 1921. Mother wasn't allowed to leave with the others for Baltimore; she was kept in the infirmary to make sure she had only the measles.

"While I was in the hospital one of the doctors fell in love with me and wanted to marry," she told me.

"Why didn't you?" I asked, excited at the thought that I might have had a different father and grown up in New York City! I have often wondered how different her life might have been had she stayed with him in New York. But instead, after she recovered, she took a train to Baltimore to join her parents and siblings.

Every day, Mother took the streetcar to work in a factory that made union suits—probably a "sweat shop." She was the typical immigrant working in a factory and taking two-week summer vacations in the Catoctin Mountains of the Blue Ridge Range at Camp Louise, run for young Jewish women. Dad took the yellowing photographs we have of her climbing a tree there; he was courting her while she was at the camp. Everyone in the family went to night school to learn English and to prepare for citizenship in this country that they loved.

Somehow, they got along; her two sisters married, and she began dating my Dad. But Mom's mother, Pearl Shulman, and Dad's mother, Yenta Schwartz, were sisters. The family opposed their romance, but they had fallen in love and threatened to elope. They were married in January 1926—"on the same day as Irving Berlin married" Dad always said—and they went to New York City for their honeymoon.

కురోౖ

I was born in December, 1926. My first memory of a house was above the mom-and-pop grocery store they bought in the early 1930s, on Bennett Place in downtown Baltimore, in a neighborhood changing from white to black. I was about five when we moved there and my brother Leon was a year and a half younger than I. We lived next to an Irish family, the Dolans. Their daughter Nancy was destined to become a schoolteacher. She practiced on me; she taught me to read before I started kindergarten.

Mother spent a good deal of time working in the store, especially when it was busy on Saturdays. We had an African American woman, Lily, who worked for us, doing laundry, some of the cooking and cleaning, and taking us for walks in a nearby park. I have a vivid memory of that park; it was so small and had so many kids playing in it that the entire rim of it was ground down to dust or mud depending on whether it had been raining recently.

Mom's cooking was quite Russian to begin with: cabbage borscht, boiled chicken, and soup with *knadels,* but Lily taught her to make fried chicken and hamburgers.

Mom bought rye bread at the bakery, but as we began to grow up and see the lunches our classmates brought to school, my brother and I began to want sliced white bread. Later, after we moved to the suburbs, Lily continued to come to our house, but I started doing the cleaning up after dinner so that she could take an earlier streetcar home.

Being the child of parents who owned, lived on the premises of, and ran a small grocery store was like being in a family living and working together on the farm or in a home where a trade was conducted, like a blacksmith or a tailor, baker, or artisan. We felt very close to what our father did to support the family.

The house/store was a large, three-story building. The store, of course, was on the first floor; behind the store was the entrance hall to our living quarters. The first floor had only three rooms in our living space: an entrance hall, a very large kitchen and a living/dining room area.

Strangely, I have only a few memories of the last room, which is where the family spent most of its time when the store was closed.

I can still remember Dad buying the parts for a crystal radio set and putting them together. Leon, Mother, and I sat close to him, all of us oohing and ahing as the first wonderful crackling sounds emerged.

I can also still picture sitting at the table with Dad at my side, going over my arithmetic homework, working through a formula. I can remember sitting and fidgeting in the morning before school while Mother tried to get me to eat a soft-boiled egg. I was so worried that I would be late for school.

As I think about those times, I realize how compulsive I have always been about being "on time"—a necessary attribute for a lab scientist as it turned out!

Finally, Pearl was born in 1935; Leon and I both remembered seeing her when she came home, lying in a portable carrier.

Those are the only memories I can dredge up of a room where I must have played and eaten and read for hours over six or seven years. That seems odd to me—why are those years so blank?

ॐॐ

On the second floor of the house were a bathroom, three bedrooms, a laundry room, and a back porch. The third floor was spacious but empty when I remember it. Members of our extended family lived there when they were between businesses. When our cousins came on Sunday to visit, we would all go up to this floor and play tag or tell ghost stories to each other.

I slept in a small room in the back of the second floor; the room contained a bed, a nightstand with a lamp, and a chair. The room was hardly private since it had three doors, one leading from the bedroom shared by Leon and my grandfather, one to the back stairs and laundry room, and a third to the only bathroom in the house except for an outdoor toilet in back of the store. This meant everyone in the family had to go through my room to the bathroom. I do not remember feeling a lack of privacy; maybe I enjoyed all the movement.

The fourth wall of the room had a window looking out on Fremont Avenue and a tall tree grew outside the window; a saloon was across the street. A streetcar ran past at regular intervals, and a street lamp shone through my window. Sometimes I would see the lamp go on as I sat at the window. I would feel secure and recite softly to myself, *"I wish when I am stronger and can choose what I'm to do, O Leerie, I'll go round at night and light the lamps with you."*

The room and street were noisy with the rattling of the streetcar, people passing under the window, and the occasional loud conversation as the patrons of the bar emerged into the street. But I slept soundly and had no problems until we moved to the suburbs when I was ten. There the silence at night was oppressive in the beginning. A couple of months passed before I stopped waiting for noise other than crickets and began sleeping soundly through the night.

ॐॐ

But in many ways the store was the most important "room" in the house. I knew this was what supported us and I liked the clerks who worked there. The butcher Phil, would occasionally cut me a piece of cheese. Arthur was the African American general man about the store who put away groceries and helped keep things cleaned up; he named his kids after me and Leon. We loved him; he took us to school in the car occasionally and talked about his family with us. Then there was Murray, who was also a butcher and Dad's chief clerk. Finally, there was Jim—an ancient African American who shuffled about with a broom. Dad didn't really need his help, but had "inherited" him with the store. He let Jim continue to work there so he could get his groceries free along with a small salary. I remember Dad quietly adding to Jim's shopping bag when he had forgotten to put a loaf of bread in it. The guys who worked in the store were like part of our family to me.

At the age of seven, I said I wanted to work in the store, so Dad let me come out and sell candy. In those days, while some candy was wrapped, a lot of it was loose; people bought it by the ounce or piece. I remember going to my father with five pennies and telling him, "I made a nickel." He took them and explained that I had not really made a whole nickel.

"I paid a penny and a half for that, and I have to pay for electricity and salaries for the clerks." My first lesson in economics!

As I got a little older, I would sometimes sell cigarettes. People could buy six cigarettes from an open package for a nickel. One day, I was selling cigarettes to a man, and another man standing by said to me, "In Canada, it's illegal for an underage person to sell cigarettes." This really scared me—I was afraid that my father and I would be arrested. I told Dad about what the man had said. He told me not to worry about it, as I wasn't really employed by him to sell in the store. But it worried me, and I stuck to candy, bread, and canned goods after that on the occasional times I "worked" in the store.

≈•≈

My mother was anxious about the safety of her family, particularly her kids. She had come from a country that had just gone through a war and then a revolution. She was living in a neighborhood surrounded by unfamiliar African Americans, who were not as soft spoken as she was. She was self-conscious about her Russian accent and felt socially inferior because she was living with her family in back of and atop a store in the center of the city instead of in a suburb. Yet with all of her anxiety, she had great confidence in her intellectual ability and that of her kids. She always assumed we would not cheat, steal or be disrespectful of our elders. My parents assumed that their kids were honest and would behave well, and for the most part they were right. But I clearly also caught her discomfort about where we lived.

≈•≈

When I started kindergarten, Baltimore schools were segregated, which meant that I had to go about six blocks to a "white" school. I loved school and still remember Miss Carey, my homeroom teacher, and Miss Jennings, who taught geography. When I was very small, Dad or one of his clerks would drive me there, but by the time I was nine, I was walking and taking my brother Leon with me.

It is a tribute to the way a southern border city like Baltimore used to be that I walked through black and poor white neighborhoods without fear. However, I did not become close enough to any of my classmates to invite them home or to see them outside of school in their homes. I have wondered since then why this was so.

If I felt lonely, I would read a book. I know that my mother felt diminished because of where we lived, and I guess I picked up from her a sense of not belonging or not being "good enough," or maybe, heaven forbid, I felt better than my classmates! What a terrible thought! It occurs to me because Mother frequently gave me the feeling that "we are superior." I think it came from her sense that her father, a very educated man, made the family special.

Mother enrolled me at the age of six at the Peabody Institute for piano and a rhythm class. I didn't want to practice, and I resented the dark hallway in the house on the second floor above the store where the second-hand upright was installed. I also hated the rhythm class where we had to move in time to the music. I was very uncomfortable with my body and was uncomfortable with myself physically.

But a picture of me at about two or three running around on the grass exists. I think it was in Patterson Park, when we had gone there to see the fireworks. I look so carefree and spontaneous, as though I was having fun! So what went wrong for me? Perhaps it was the constraints I felt from my mother about where we lived.

Twice later in life I returned to playing the piano—while I was in college and years later in Chicago. I loved playing but was frustrated by the discrepancy between what I heard in my head and what I played. When I started attending yoga class during the last twenty years, I found I had lost my self-consciousness about moving in front of people and remembered the young awkward, self-conscious me.

My rejection of the piano while we were living in Baltimore seems indicative of all that was wrong for me in the city. Music is now such a major factor in my life; it has been since I first listened to the Metropolitan Opera on Saturdays after we moved to the "'burbs."

❧

Dad helped me with homework, particularly with arithmetic and later with more advanced math. My mother always felt self-conscious about her English and hesitated to correct my grammar and syntax. My memories of that early schooling are scattered and I do not remember my classmates well. This contrasts with my brother, who continued to know his school friends as they grew up—even after we moved to the suburbs. Since I also essentially broke off with my Baltimore friends after I left for graduate school, my pattern seams to be that I was not to feel connected. Certainly this was true after I came out as a lesbian when I began to feel very much the outsider.

But I loved school itself; I caught on very early to the pleasure of learning new things. My memories of the elementary school are dim, but I was avid for learning history and geography. I do not remember learning any science, but I read every novel I could get my hands on. In fact, unlike many female scientists, I was not particularly an animal lover, nor was I interested in plants or natural habitats as a child. The science I turned to years later was a total surprise and seemingly a real break with my past. As an adult, however, I have become a birder, a dog and cat aficionado, and the owner of a house in the woods.

❧❦

On some Saturday mornings, at around 4 or 5 a.m., I would go with Dad to the wholesale market to buy fruit and vegetables, or down to Baltimore Harbor to meet the watermelon or cantaloupe boats up from the south. I watched him sound the watermelons, thumping them and holding them up to his ear, and bargaining over the price. I learned to tell how ripe cantaloupes were by pressing them on the ends and smelling their fragrance. These trips seemed like great adventures to me and much more exciting than traveling by streetcar with my mother to downtown Baltimore to buy clothes or go to a movie.

❧❦

During the time my parents had their store on Bennett Place, they were visited one day by an inspector from the city of Baltimore. He came late one Saturday afternoon, when the store was crowded and had been busy all day. They had not yet cleaned up. The Inspector said the store was dirty and he would report them to the city, which would force them to close. They protested that they had not yet had the time to clean up after the Saturday rush, but he left on a threatening note and said he would be back. My mother was scared, remembering Czarist Russia with its Cossacks and a Communist Russia with its stringent controls.

But Dad said, "He's just trying to get me to pay a bribe. He has done it with other stores in the neighborhood."

Mother was shocked—"I didn't come from Russia to pay bribes to a crooked government official." On her own, without telling anybody, she boarded a streetcar that week and went to City Hall to see the mayor! According to her, she saw him and he said that he could see that she would not keep a dirty business. "You and your husband will never be visited again by an inspector," he said, and they were not.

Was the story true? It felt true to me, and it delivered a clear message that I have, for better or worse, never forgotten: if someone is being abusive or unfair or dishonest, don't let it go–do something about it. Leon and our sister Pearl also integrated this message into their lives.

❧❦

My sister Pearl was born in 1935 and did not get to do many of the things Leon and I did. Partly this was because my mother's mother died (my sister

Pearl was born shortly after and was named for her), and Mother was quite depressed for some years. Then the Second World War with gas rationing intervened; this meant we could not take our weekend trips to the beach or the hills of Pennsylvania, or drive to Washington D.C. on Sundays to visit the Smithsonian Museum, or to see Lincoln's tomb. Soon after my grandmother died, my grandfather, Tzadik Shulman, came to live with us, which he did until he died in 1948.

My brother Leon was my closest playmate when we were very little. Since I was older, I was the leader in games. Dad brought us boxing gloves and I apparently knocked Leon down and out the first time we fought. This was easy then since I was taller and heavier at that time. We would act out books I had read, adventure stories where we were shipwrecked or adrift in a boat or camping in the north woods. All of these adventures we acted out on the porch behind the laundry room or in the empty third floor rooms. Until the move to the suburbs, none of them took place away from our house.

かくゟ

When I was about ten and a half, our family doctor told my mother that I would soon begin to menstruate. She was apparently too embarrassed to talk with me about it, so she asked one of my older cousins, who was about fourteen at the time, to talk with me. Betty was shy, but she managed to get me a booklet, which gave me the right information. Later, I learned about sex from my classmates and friends. But as my sister approached her menarche after we moved to the suburbs, I decided to tell her about it myself. So at the age of sixteen, I went to the library, checked out some books, and gave them to her to read—and then we *talked* about it. I was the academic even then! Perhaps it comes as no surprise that when I taught a freshman seminar years later at Northwestern ("Menstrual Cycle: Fact and Fiction") the first essay I assigned to the students was "How I Learned about the Menstrual Cycle."

かくゟ

My father was quite busy in his store in downtown Baltimore—but on Wednesday afternoons, he took time off while my mom worked in the store. He was the one who took me to the library. Since we lived in downtown Baltimore (Fremont near Mulberry), he would drive me to Baltimore's main library located on Eutaw Street. The children's section was in a kind of basement that could be entered separately from the adult library. There was a fishpond at the entrance. I still remember vividly when he took me to get my first library card. I cannot express what a major event that was for me, because it gave me unlimited access to books. Each week, he would take me back to return books I had read and get new ones.

In 1986, when I went to my niece Nancy's wedding, which was held near the Peabody Institute in downtown Baltimore, I walked after the wedding down to the library where I had not been for forty years or so. I was shocked to see the fishpond drained and the separate children's entrance looking shabby and derelict. Even though Baltimore has gentrified its downtown harbor area, it appears to have forgotten about its central library.

ॐ~ॐ

Dad also sometimes took my brother and me fishing on Chesapeake Bay on Wednesdays. Then, every Wednesday evening, my parents went out to dinner and a movie or to a play without the kids. In the summer, Sunday was the day for the beach. The store was open on Sunday until around 1 p.m. Then we bundled into the car, Daddy and Mother, Leon and me. Mother made a salad and carried rolls, hamburgers, and pickles for a picnic in the park. We would drive out with the crowds to Bay Shore beach on Chesapeake Bay.

I still remember the salt air, the smell of lotion in the dressing rooms, the women with their thick bodies yelling at their children, who dressed as fast as they could since they only wanted to run out on the beach and into the water. We would go into the water also, but we never learned to swim, although both my parents swam. So we could go into the water, but only with them. I don't know why they never taught us; was it my mother's anxiety about our safety? In the days of the polio epidemic when we were kids, public swimming pools were considered dangerous, so Pearl, Leon, and I all learned to swim in college.

For several years, in the summer while we lived downtown, Mother took Leon, Pearl, and me to Atlantic City. Her two sisters and their kids joined us. We would stay for several weeks, using the beach, walking the boardwalk, and sitting and watching passersby.

All of us would go to the Steel Pier to watch the horses dive into a tank. Mother and her two sisters did not drive, so we had to wait for one or more fathers to drive north from Baltimore if we were going home.

Dad sometimes stayed with us from Monday to Thursday or Friday and then he would head back for the busy weekend in the store. When he came back on Sunday evening, he always carried one small paper bag each for Leon, Pearl, and me—with five shiny pennies in each. We would take a long time to spend them, stretching it out throughout the next week. It seemed wonderful to me then, and still does now, that he took the time not just to hand us a nickel, but to get the pennies, always new.

On Sundays, when we were not going to the beach or driving to spend the day at Loch Raven Falls or Washington, D.C., the aunts and uncles on Mom's side got together for a poker game. Grandfather Tsadik loved Penny Ante poker, and we kids would sometimes hang around to watch the game. Other times, we would put on plays, borrowing "costumes" from closets from whoever's house we played the game. But poker stayed with me; I have always loved the game. While I was living with Rue, a medical sociologist, in Chicago during my early days of teaching at the University of Illinois, we would sometimes play poker with friends.

My mother came to Chicago every year by the overnight B&O train, even though she disapproved of my living arrangements. She arrived to spend her usual week one Saturday morning, and I picked her up at the station. "We are playing poker tonight with friends," I said; "would you like to join in?" "I might play for a little while," she said. When our friends arrived, they looked somewhat bemused by this mild looking woman with a Russian accent, about 5'1" in height. The game started, and within an hour, my mother had all of the money and announced she was tired and going to bed.

❧

Mother and I would take the streetcar downtown to shop for clothing for the family. Eating lunch together in the Read's Drug Store was my treat—I always got a tuna fish sandwich and a milk shake—and sometimes we would go to a movie. As we sat one day watching a movie, she remembered a day she had been in that theater with her mother seeing a live group of Jewish drama actors doing a play when suddenly a cry of "Fire" broke out. Mother was sitting in the cheaper seats in the balcony, above where her mother sat in the orchestra. Mom says she saw people begin to panic and run. She called down to her mother to sit still. A number of people were injured from being trampled and she always felt she had saved her mother.

Once, Mother and I saw Molly Picon in a Yiddish language movie. In 1960, on my first trip to London, I saw Molly Picon in a play with Robert Morley and I bumped into her on Haymarket Street. Like a groupie, I gushed that I had seen her "years ago with my mother." She was gracious but probably not pleased at the reminder of the years between our "meetings."

I would also go with Mother to the Lexington Market to buy horseradish for grating and fish for chopping for gefilte fish for Passover. After we moved to the suburbs, I was trusted to go downtown alone to the market by streetcar for the horseradish; I was only eleven and felt very responsible and grown up.

Mother kept an orthodox kosher home. Every Friday at sundown, she lit the Sabbath candles and we always stood around to watch. Until I was a teenager, I had never knowingly eaten anything that was not kosher.

We walked to the old synagogue downtown on holidays, and Mother was the sisterhood secretary. I don't remember being bothered as a kid by the separation of men and women during the Orthodox services, but later, when I was a teenager, it began to bother me. As I began eating out with friends in high school and college, I started eating unkosher food. My grandfather taught us to read Hebrew and Yiddish, but he did not focus much on religion per se.

෧෩

Dad was quite good at making a living in a retail store, but he wanted to get out of the business. In 1937, he went into a partnership with a man who owned a wholesale meat business. But just after he had sold the store, when we had already bought a house in the near suburb of Liberty Heights but before we had moved in, disaster struck.

I still remember waking in the middle of the night to hear Mom talking to my grandfather in whispers in the next room. I heard her say, in Yiddish, "Paul's brother, Ben, was shot and killed by robbers in his grocery store."

My uncle, Ben Schwartz, left two daughters and a wife, my Aunt Hannah. He also left some debts for loans, which Dad had cosigned. So, just as Dad was starting in a new business, with a new home, he was saddled with having to pay off a rather large amount debt. The death and the debts overshadowed our first years in the suburbs. Dad's new business did not do well, and he eventually went back for a few years into partnership with my uncle, Paul Shulman, in a retail grocery store in a white Catholic neighborhood.

Leon worked in the grocery as a delivery boy on Saturdays. As Dad would tell his customers, "I want Leon to see how tough this business is so that he will do something better with his life." Later, Dad again left the retail grocery business to go into a wholesale grocery business as a partner; he worked there until he retired.

෧෩

It seems clear to me, looking at my early childhood, that I felt loved by both of my parents, whom I respected, and I picked up their assertiveness. But I unfortunately picked up my mother's uneasiness about our living situation.

On the last day at the elementary school, which I had attended since kindergarten, I stood on the corner waiting for Arthur to pick me up. Two of the girls in my class came over to say goodbye. We knew it was goodbye because I was moving all the way up north to the suburbs. I had never visited their homes, and they had never come to mine. I don't remember their names, and I don't feel connected now. But they must have felt connected to me—they brought me two tops to perfume bottles in gold-colored metal. I kept them for years.

Why did I not acquire and keep friends? Did I not feel good enough, or did I just really prefer my books? I felt very constrained physically, somehow afraid to do things on my own, away from home.

During the last summer we lived downtown, Mother signed me up for a day camp north of Baltimore. I did a little hiking there, but I didn't want to learn to swim or play softball. After two days, I begged Mom to let me stay home. My brother loved the camp and stayed for the week.

But then we moved and my world opened up.

Study Questions

(1) Neena opens this chapter with the question, "how much of one's childhood needs to be known to understand where the adult comes from?"
  - Discuss your answer and reasons upon which you base your conclusions.

(2) After describing a paltry few memories of the living/dining room area in her first home where she lived for eleven years, she asks "why are those years so blank?"
  - Based on the first person account offered in this chapter, discuss whether Neena's memory of those early years or only her memories of that room appear to be blank.
  - Discuss reasons for your answer.

Grandfather, Tzadik "Zadie"
Shulman 1925.

Dad and Mom in front of their new
house, Forest Park, Baltimore, 1939.

Three

LIBERTY HEIGHTS

And I have known the arms already, known them all . . .
Arms that are braceleted and white and bare
(But in the lamplight, downed with light brown hair!)
Is it perfume from a dress
That makes me so digress?

T. S. Eliot
"The Song of J. Alfred Prufrock"

I was in the sixth grade in November 1937 when we moved from the center of the city of Baltimore to a new house in the nearby suburban area called Forest Park, which opened off Liberty Heights Road, of Barry Levinson's movie, *Liberty Heights* fame. The following eleven years spent in that area made a crucial impact on the rest of my life. I learned the rudiments of being "social," I discovered that I was lesbian; I enrolled in college as an English major and graduated as a nascent scientist.

❧

The house we moved into was on Callaway Avenue, in a row of stand-alone brick houses, which had been newly constructed in this older, predominately Christian (and, of course, white) neighborhood. Strangely, I don't remember seeing the house before the day we moved in. Is it possible that my parents never showed it to us kids?

When I walked up the steps to the house and opened the door, I saw all new living room and dining room furniture that I am sure I had not seen before. A couple of paintings I had never seen were hanging on the walls. I felt as though I was stepping through the looking glass with Alice. In fact, in the living room, a looking glass did hang over the mantel; when I saw myself reflected in it for the first time, I was not sure who I was. Had I changed magically to go with our new house? It felt like that to me—in a way I had.

❧

I started attending elementary School 65, about half a mile from home, walking with my brother. At first I was placed in the second class of grade 6A probably because the school assumed that since I was from an inner city school I was not well prepared. But in February, the principal switched me to the first class of grade 6B.

I graduated from my new elementary school with excellent grades in June of 1938. I was offered the chance to go to School 49, where I could complete junior high school in two instead of three years. Getting into "49" was highly competitive, since it drew from all of the elementary schools in Baltimore. My family and teachers assumed I would attend, so I signed up. This meant that in September, I would not be walking to Garrison Junior High School, four blocks from home, but would be taking a streetcar to downtown Baltimore.

All summer I kept thinking about 49, and decided not to go there. Since my decision meant I had to transfer to the nearer junior high, I had to justify this decision to the principal of the school I was not attending, as well as to the principal of the school I wanted to attend. I did both on my own. Both principals tried to change my mind, telling me what a privilege I would be missing, but I stuck to my guns. Both my parents accepted my decision.

What moved this eleven-year-old kid to make this rather heavy decision on her own?

Life in the city had felt closed in to me, filled with concrete pavements, Baltimore's white stoops, and lots of traffic noise except when we had gone to the park or the zoo, away to the Chesapeake Bay, or the ocean in Atlantic City. But the books I read were filled with space: secret gardens and mysterious forests. That the suburbs seemed like a dream came as no surprise.

At night I could sit on the side porch listening to crickets and hearing other night noises. A couple of blocks away, was a small wooded area, about an acre, where I could walk among the trees, by myself. The world had opened up for me. No wonder that I did not want to go back into the heart of the city for junior high school!

But I had another reason. I felt, without ever being able to express it in words, maybe not even to myself, that I needed the social life of the neighborhood and I saw no reason to skip the year. Life had suddenly opened up for me.

This decision proved to be very important to the breadth of education and leisure activities I began to acquire. It was a good choice for me. Garrison gave me a chance to learn to play volleyball and tennis and to write for the school newspaper. It changed me from the loner I had been before into a more social, more comfortable teen. I even began to walk to school every day, stopping to walk with classmates as I went past their houses. It was a major transition. I must have picked up my mother's relief at being in the suburbs. She felt it was more fitting for her than living with a store downtown. She was now "okay," and so was I.

While the new neighborhood meant the real beginning of a social life for me, as well as for Pearl and Leon, it also meant for my brother the initiation of his life as an athlete, which partly dominated his life in high school and college. For my sister, who was three when we moved, it was the start of many friendships still meaningful to her after sixty years.

Although I made friends with schoolmates and neighbors, I have not kept up many contacts, partly because I have been away from the city for fifty years and, as well, because I began to feel estranged from them after I realized I was lesbian.

❧❦

After our move, Leon and I asked for two-wheel bikes, which we had not had in the city. Our parents agreed after telling us that it would not be easy for them to find the money. Years later, I was going through a drawer in Mother's dresser looking for something and came across a canceled contract Mom had signed for the time purchase of the bikes; she and Dad had paid a quarter for each bike weekly until they were paid for! Leon and I had not pushed them hard and had accepted their initial reluctance, but obviously they had talked it over and agreed we should have them.

The second day I had the bike, I fell in the gravel up the street and seriously tore up my left knee. Mom wasn't home when I limped in, bleeding badly. Leon was mad at me because he was afraid our parents would take our bikes away. Lily cleaned me up a bit, and I sat through supper with my knee hidden under the table. The next day, Mother discovered what had happened and took me to our doctor. He removed some of the gravel, cleaned my knee up, and gave me a tetanus shot. We kept the bikes, which I finally learned to ride, but for many years, bits of gravel kept coming out of my knee.

❧❦

While I was in my early teens, Mother developed an occasional very rapid heartbeat and was told to go to bed when her heart began "fluttering." I later learned it was called paroxysmal atrial tachycardia. I wound up learning to make simple meals for the family during this time—sandwiches, hamburgers, potatoes, and vegetables. Dad was quite tolerant of the food I provided and bawled my brother and sister out if they complained. The responsibility was good for me and started me on a lifetime of enjoying cooking. But sometimes when I came home from school and found my mother lying in a dark room in bed, I felt sad and down. Maybe this marked the beginning of the intermittant depression I have experienced over my lifetime.

Our grandfather, Tzadik "Zadie" Shulman, continued living with us until his death in 1948. We kids loved and respected him.

Our new house had three bedrooms. My sister and I shared one, and Leon and Zadie shared the second, with my parents in the master bedroom with an en-suite bathroom. Zadie continued telling us stories into our teens of his time in the army and his life in Russia. He taught us Hebrew and we learned to read and speak Yiddish. When Leon was thirteen he had a Bar Mitzvah; Tzadik wrote the following letter to him in Hebrew:

"*Mazel Tov*"*

April 26, 1941, Baltimore, Maryland

Today is the 5th day of the Parshah Acharai-Kedoshin in the year 570. My Dear Grandson, Moshe Leib!

Son of my beloved son–in–law Peretz and my beloved daughter Ethel Schwartz. Today my dear child, you have become a Bar Mitzvah, you have thus become a responsible person for yourself and like all the elders, you have the fortunate opportunity to observe all the rules of the Torah, the true torah of Moses which I have the joy of presenting to you, the Tanach which was the Bible, five Books of Moses and nineteen prophets.

Study the sacred writings and review them, review and study. There you will find everything.

And when you will ask wisdom of God, obey the words, and God will grant you wisdom. Fear God for this is the first love and binding yourself to him, is the beginning of belief. When you pray use a pure Hebrew, not like the fashion to read like a parrot.

Love your neighbor as yourself! Think not that only you are entitled to life's blessings. Help him when it is possible. Envy him not when he is wealthier than you. Respect older people. Honor your Father and Mother. This applies to both of them. Honor your Father and you will enjoy long life. With your lips and with your heart, honor your Father and your Mother, and then blessings will come to you.

Therefore my beloved child, my heart is filled with blessings but unfortunately I cannot find the vocabulary, neither the words to express my feelings nor the space to include everything.

Therefore, I wish you, my beloved child, a long happy life. Your life should flow in peaceful waters and not be troubled. This is the wish of your loving grandfather.

Tzadik Shulman

*Translated by Rabbi Martin Halpern, Shaari Tfila Congregation, Silver Spring, Maryland, 7 April 1971.

This letter says everything there is to say about this man. His influence in the household was enormous. Somehow we always understood that our Dad was the head of the house, but I believe that having our grandfather live with us was a major determinant of how we three turned out. He was tolerant, humorous, warm, and loving. He liked to walk around our neighborhood. He had a beard, and on his walks before Christmas, he was frequently approached by young gentile kids who thought he was Santa Claus. He would stop and listen to them tell him what they wanted and would nod and pat them on the head as he walked away.

こうど

When I was about twelve, a new and overwhelming set of emotions entered my being. I began to have fantasies about becoming intimate with girls at the same time that my mother was encouraging me to take care of my appearance and to "dress up" to attract boys.

All my friends were talking about sex and dates, while I developed a crush on my Latin teacher in the seventh grade in junior high. She was a young blonde woman whom I thought was very attractive. (Later, during high school, when I worked at the department store in downtown Baltimore, she came in to buy her trousseau. I remember being pleased to see her but disappointed about her upcoming marriage!)

I was also very taken with a girl who lived down the street from our home, and I hung around her house talking with her. I don't know if she felt the same longing for closeness that I did, since we didn't talk about it. But we rode our bikes together and went to the movies together, and I felt warm and happy in her company. One of the neighbors with whom my mother played Mahjong began being friendlier to me, and I crossed the street many times to go to her house to talk about "deep" things. In retrospect, I realize that she was coming on to me, but I never recognized it, and nothing ever happened between us.

My fantasies about women started out as rescue stories. I would go to the rescue of someone (girl or woman) trapped by a natural disaster or by someone wicked. Certainly, I myself was never trapped, only to be rescued by a prince or a frog or even by another woman.

We are in the mountains, an avalanche occurs, and SHE is missing. We had met at the ski lodge and talked over the fire about our lives and our futures. I race out to the mountain to find her and she is unable to walk. I help her to a derelict little cabin in the woods, light a fire, and make some hot milk—I have no idea where I found the milk!—we sit close together, and I hold her hand.

Other fantasies of mind revolved around an illness, undefined, which left me weak and in pain. A female figure would come and give me food, love, and tenderness. These fantasies were not openly erotic, although they involved physical closeness and tender feelings.

The closest I ever came to living that fantasy was in a cabin in Western Pennsylvania with a lover and a fireplace and a copy of my uncompleted doctoral dissertation: No avalanche—just a bottle of wine, *La Boheme* on the portable record player, and, for a crisis, the dissertation, which I needed to finish writing. I didn't that weekend.

৶৶৶

On Sunday, 7 December 1941, when I was fifteen, we heard on the radio that the Japanese had attacked Pearl Harbor. The following day, we students in the Forest Park High School, which I had entered in the fall, were called into the auditorium to hear the radio broadcast by President Franklin Roosevelt declaring war on Japan and Germany. The army classified my father 3A: in good health with three kids. As an alternative to being drafted, he trained as an air raid warden, the chief for our geographic sector.

I was old enough to take a Red Cross emergency course and a course to become an air raid messenger. After the courses, I was fingerprinted, and I received an armband, a helmet, and a gas mask. Thus, when the sirens sounded, I picked up my helmet and mask, first aid kit, and arm badge and went off to meet my warden, who was a woman who lived one block away. She and I patrolled several blocks together, in complete darkness, all streetlights and house lights being turned off. We checked to make sure all houses were completely blacked out.

Walking in the silent darkness felt exciting; I felt patriotic, brave, and important. Occasionally, an "incident" occurred: a flare was dropped with a note, fictional but plausible, about damage or injuries and I would have to carry messages back to sector headquarters, our basement. All the alarms proved to be practice sessions, although we did not know it at the time the sirens sounded. My mother was quite anxious about my doing this, but for me, it was a way to be independent, and I absolutely loved it. My thirteen-year-old brother also had a responsibility; the street lights in our neighborhood were still lit by gas, and he shinnied up the poles to shut off the gas in our block when the sirens blew.

৶৶৶

In spite of the ongoing war and the draft, which began to affect the fellows in our high school, I entered the dating game, which felt awkward, uncomfortable, and unreal. It was strange from the beginning. It felt as though I was just playing a part, observing myself speculatively from a distance.

I had not been a tomboy, whatever that is. I had not played boys' sports; I wasn't brave about getting into mischief, and I never played with boys' toys. (These traits were standard criteria in the psychosocial set during the 1940s and 1950s for defining tomboys.) But I also had never played house or cared about dolls. I never fantasized about being married. My unformed dreams of the future were of living in or near a forest, of being out of doors, of traveling. The only reason I dated was that I was expected to, but it always felt faked.

During the war, I volunteered at the USO at the Young Women's Hebrew Association (YWHA) in downtown Baltimore, where lots of guys could be found to "make out" with. I danced and dated some of them, and I even drove out to Fort Belvoir with my parents to see one of them. He and I corresponded while he was overseas. Poor guys—they went to Europe during the worst part of the fighting, and I was doing my best to make them feel better about it, but it was a charade for me and I began to know it.

❧

When I was sixteen, one of the girls in my high school class loaned me a copy of *The Well of Loneliness* by a British woman, Radclyffe Hall. I don't remember talking with my classmate about the book; I guess I understood that this was forbidden stuff, not to be discussed. I still don't know what instinct led her to give it to me; it's too late to ask now since she died several years ago. The book stunned me—I was not the only person in the world with feelings about other women and it was possible to do something about it, although I learned from the book that happy endings were not to be expected. The story was about a young "masculine"-looking British woman named Stephen, who fell in love with a more feminine-looking woman, and went to live with her in France. Eventually, the other woman married a man and Stephen went on "alone."

The book was banned in England for a number of years because of its focus on lesbians, but by the time I read it, the book was available in most bookstores. In fact, it was the only serious fiction available on the subject as far as I knew. The book started me thinking about unexplored possibilities, even though the thoughts made me feel guilty and I kept them to myself.

After all these years, I find it hard to remember why I started with a sense of guilt about all this. Was it a general attitude about sex and "naughty bits" that I had picked up from my family or society in general, or was it more specifically related to homosexuality? I do not know. One has to remember that during the 1940s, the movie censors did not even allow married couples to be shown together in a double bed; open discussion of even conventional sex was not common, much less "deviant" sex.

At the beginning of the semester, in the eleventh grade, one of my classmates, Alicia, walked into our homeroom and smiled shyly at me. She was feeling self-conscious because she had had a nose job during the summer. It didn't make a lot of difference; her face was not conventionally "pretty." I had scarcely talked with her during the year in tenth grade. But I looked at her, maybe really for the first time. My bowels stirred. I had fallen in love for the first time, and with a woman.

We talked for a while after school. Alicia had a car to get between Forest Park and upper Park Heights Avenue, where she lived in a big, expensive house. We started going to the movies together and rode our bikes together across town to Gwynn Oak Park or down to Druid Hill Park in Baltimore. Alicia was a dancer, and a violinist, and I loved looking at her when she danced, her body was so beautiful. Our conversations became more and more intense, and I began wanting to touch her, oh so much! But we did not talk about *it*; it seemed taboo— sick and wicked.

One weekend, Alicia's parents went out of town, leaving her and her younger sister at home. She asked if I would like to sleep over to keep them company. I had never done anything like that before. I had slept over at my cousins' houses, but not at a friend's house. In fact, I had never been to or given a pajama party. I nervously asked my mother if I could go. She was thrilled at the idea of a developing friendship with this wealthy Jewish family. So one Friday afternoon after school, I put some clothes in a sack (I didn't have a real suitcase) and boarded a streetcar and then a bus for Alicia's house. We talked for hours, trying to keep away from her kid sister, who was thrilled to be there alone with two practically grown up women.

On Sunday morning, Alicia picked up the *Baltimore Sun* newspaper from the front stoop and invited me to share her single bed to read the funnies together. We had pajamas on, but our hips and legs touched. I felt feverish and we finally dropped the paper and began touching each other shyly but in earnest. Thus, I had finally openly declared that I had sexual feelings about women. I had "come out" at least to myself and to one other person.

Alicia and I were able to make out to a certain extent in her car. We traveled to New York City to see some plays, staying with her uncle's family. We experienced the joy and freshness of walking up Broadway together, touching hands every once in a while, and sitting in the theater holding hands. That feeling is still with me. God, I loved her and I still do. She was sweet, warm, sensual, and caring.

During the war, Alicia's older sister lived in Atlantic City, where her husband was a psychiatrist at the veteran's hospital. She and I would go up to New Jersey to spend time at their home—walking on the beach together, reciting poetry, and gazing out at the Atlantic Ocean in an adolescent paroxysm of love and intensity. We both decided to stay in Baltimore for college, me out of financial necessity and she because she wanted to stay near me.

In 1946, my mother discovered a letter Alicia had written to me. (I was living at home while going to Goucher College.) She was traveling with her parents and wrote about what she was seeing, and she told me how much she missed kissing and touching me. Stupidly, I had left the letter near the front table where our telephone was. Did I want to be discovered? Perhaps.

Mother confronted me and asked, "What does this mean? Do you know that this is wrong?" She went on.

"You must stop this relationship. It will ruin your life and you will never be happy."

Mother started me on a life-long guilt trip I still have to fight. My lover's family, as well as my mother, blamed *me* for this *unnatural* behavior, much to Alicia's chagrin. But they couldn't keep us separated, since we attended college together and both had access to cars and a little money. I remember a magical Thanksgiving dinner out in a country inn in Maryland with candlelight and wine. By our senior year, she began dating a guy and I drifted away, but we stayed best friends, even occasionally double dating.

ॐ⊷✿

By now, many people have written about what the 1940s were like for homosexuals. All I could find to read then, besides the Radclyffe Hall book, were the Richard Freiherr von Krafft-Ebing books in the Goucher College library about "sexual inversion," as it was called then, and the paperback novels I examined covertly in the drugstore. As I look back at these novels so many years later, I am appalled, albeit somewhat amused, by the sub-titles which appeared on the covers of books I read or looked at furtively when I was seventeen. "*The gripping story of Hilda, whose twisted desires led her to the brink of degradation,*" or, "*It is like a beautiful spider's web waiting to lure innocent strangers into the perverted worlds from which there is no possible escape,*" or, "*One twist of fate—must it keep a woman forever chained to forbidden deviation?*" or, "*Twisted passions in the twilight world.*"

Unquestionably, I felt guilty and ashamed about my sexual feelings. One of the toughest things in my life has been trying to defeat that sense of shame. I spent years and a lot of money in psychotherapy after graduate school trying to "change." The current trend of the Christian right conservatives to get homosexuals to change is laughable—and tragic. I know lots of people out there feel guilty and will try to change, and some will get married. How happy will they be? Well, I have not always been happy, but this is the only way I can be.

ॐ⊷✿

I was also doing other things with my time, aside from carrying on an intense love affair. An important part of junior high school for me had been joining the staff of my school paper, writing news and special features. I also became increasingly captivated by English literature, becoming quite the Anglophile. After I had entered Forest Park High School in September 1941, I continued writing and editing for the school newspaper.

When I had started on the paper, we had a male advisor who believed in allowing the student staff to run things pretty much on their own. He left a year later to work in a factory associated with the war effort. Angela Broening, head of the English Department, took over. She immediately called a meeting of the staff at the beginning of our senior year. In her autocratic way, she announced that she would run the paper the way *she* wished saying, "anyone who disagrees can get up and leave." I immediately rose and left, assuming everyone else would follow. No one did, and so I found myself off the newspaper staff. This incident became one of many during my life when I have found myself swimming against the current, many times by myself.

Despite this, I very much enjoyed Forest Park High School. I had many friends, played tennis, read a lot, really enjoyed my English and history classes, and took science only when required. I did well in tenth grade math, but I elected not to go on to algebra and calculus. My teacher told me I would be sorry later, and as it turned out, she was right. But I was still only focused on literature.

෨෴෨

The greatest gift my mother gave her children was a love of reading books; Leon, Pearl and I were all voracious readers. When we moved to the suburbs, we walked or cycled about half a mile to the local branch library. When I was young, my friends' mothers would try to get them to stop reading and go outside to play, but my mother never did, because she hated to be interrupted while reading. In the evening, we would all be in the living room reading, stretched out on the sofa or floor, and if we laughed aloud, we had to read the passage aloud.

෨෴෨

On my sixteenth birthday, my first cousin, Mel Shulman, presented me with three books as a birthday present: the *Standard Book of Verse* (an anthology), a complete Shakespeare, and Dorothy Sayers' anthology of mystery short stories. For some years as I was growing up, when my family visited Mel's parents (his father was my mother's older brother Simon), I would go up to Mel's room to talk with him about art, literature, and philosophy, and watch him carve a chess set. He had started Johns Hopkins University already and was sharing what he was learning with me—and I was an ardent listener.

Mel took me to my first symphony concert at about the same time. He was remarkably sensitive to my need to expand my life. He was a wonderful older brother I never had. Reading poetry and mystery stories and listening to the Chicago Symphony Orchestra have remained in my life, fortunately. Mel went on to Medical School, eventually becoming a psychoanalyst.

෨෴෨

As soon as I could get a driving permit at the age of sixteen, I started working to save money for college. My first job was as a sales clerk at a department store in downtown Baltimore. I reached the store by streetcar from our home in Northwest Baltimore. During the school year, I worked on Thursday evenings from 5 to 9 p.m. and on Saturdays all day. During the summer, I worked six full days a week. As a part-time worker, I was shuffled from department to department, wherever extra help was needed. I worked selling inexpensive summer hats, candy, and boy's clothing.

One incident from the summer when I sold cheap women's summer hats stands out in my mind. A woman came by with her daughter, who was about my age. The daughter picked out a small white piqué hat which was designed just to sit on top of the head and needed to be kept in place by a hat pin. As I put it on her head and stuck the pin in, I pricked my finger and involuntarily said "Ouch."

The woman looked up, asking in a concerned voice "What happened?"

"I pricked my finger," I said.

"Don't get any blood on the hat," she replied.

The job was a real learning experience for me—I had discovered that some people treated their perceived "inferiors" badly, which had not struck me before, since I had never heard my parents talk that way to anybody.

Although I kept asking to be put in the book department, it never happened. After I had worked there for a while, one of the female managers in personnel asked if I would like to continue after college in a managerial training position. I knew I did not want to do this. (It is interesting that our father was a terrific salesman and none of his three children went into sales as a life's work.)

During the war years in college, I switched to selling on Thursday night and Saturday in a small variety shop owned by our neighbors, the Levins, and enjoyed that much better. They paid me more and trusted me to run the store myself when they needed to do other things.

At Christmastime during high school and early in college, I worked additionally at the post office sorting mail, a job I hated, but it paid good money, particularly at night. I would do it with friends from school, and we would talk while sorting. We felt contemptuous of people who did something as routine as a career, with all the arrogance of youth. Then in 1945, the summer between my sophomore and junior years at college, I worked for the federal government in a nursery school for children of men and women in the armed forces or working in defense plants in the Baltimore area.

The kids came at 6 a.m. and many stayed until 6 p.m.; we caretakers worked 8 hour shifts. It was tough, but it paid very well. As the youngest caregiver, I was given responsibility for the two- and three-year-olds—getting them to eat lunch, showing them how to tie their shoes, following them around on the playground.

I remember sitting on the edge of the sandbox reading the *Baltimore Sun*, on a warm day in August 1945, while watching the kids playing, on the day after we dropped the A-bomb on Hiroshima. The news stories overwhelmed me and I started shivering in spite of the hot sun. By that time, the American army had also entered all of the concentration camps in Germany and discovered the stacks of unburied bodies and the terribly emaciated prisoners. The pictures of the starving prisoners and of the survivors of the A-bombs haunted me and contributed to the slowly growing anxiety and depression I began to experience.

৵৽৾

While Leon and I were growing up, our parents always said. "Neena will go to Goucher, and Leon will go to Johns Hopkins." These were the two "prestige" colleges in Baltimore. At the time, Goucher admitted only women and Hopkins only men, and that is what happened. I received a partial scholarship and with the money I had saved, I was able to pay my way to Goucher College starting in September 1944. (Leon went to Hopkins on a four-year athletic scholarship two years later.)

I intended to major in English and immediately joined the staff of the *Goucher Weekly*. In my English classes, I enjoyed reading nineteenth-century novels, Chaucer, *Beowulf*, and American and English poetry. But I was never comfortable reading with a critical eye. It became tiresome for me and began to interfere with my enjoyment of reading. A course on Shakespeare proved to be the final straw. I loved the plays but hated the droning, endless interpretations made by my classmates. Professor Beatty told me that I was not doing well in the class; he asked whether I knew I was making a C.

"Do you usually get C's?" he asked.

"No," I said, "I do not."

Internally I was bored and felt trapped. I knew this was not what I wanted to do for the rest of my life.

So I knew I did not want to be a critic of literature or drama, nor did I want to analyze the meaning of literature. This was well before postmodernism, political correctness, and feminist analysis. But something else happened; in one of the writing courses, my teacher told me that she felt my writing was not very imaginative or highly creative. Secretly, I agreed with her, but I felt devastated anyway. I had done well as a reporter and features writer for school newspapers when I had a specific assignment, but I knew that constructing stories from the beginning was tough for me. I felt awkward at it. I thought about journalism, which I enjoyed doing, but it wasn't what I wanted to do as a career.

৵৽৾

I enrolled in the basic physiology and hygiene course at Goucher, to satisfy a distribution requirement in science. I was turned on by the textbook, A. J. Carlson's simplest text. What hit me suddenly was that the ideas and explanations in physiology were *creative*; maybe this could satisfy the urging inside me to do something creative.

I was particularly hooked by learning about feedback controls. For example, if a person goes to high altitude, say Denver or the Andes, where the oxygen content of the air is lower than it is at sea level, the heart rate speeds up and breathing rate increases. This permits more air to be brought in to the lungs and blood stream, and thus more oxygen can be delivered to the brain and muscles. Physiologists discovered that detectors (receptors) for oxygen level in the blood stream detect the low oxygen and send neural signals to the brain, which causes signals to be sent to the heart and rib cage muscles, which then speed up breathing and heart rate, thus taking in more air and delivering the oxygen faster to the organs where it is needed. I learned that this was not a conscious process but a reflex.

Physiologists could study such processes and devise explanations for these compensations and investigate whether these explanations were correct. Wow! I had just finished a course in philosophy and read William James' *Varieties of Religious Experience*. Over one weekend, I felt a tremendous excitement and realized that I wanted to be a scientist—a physiologist. The professors in the physiology department were skeptical when I showed up wanting to be a physiology major.

The then department chair, Jessie King, said, "But you haven't had any college math, physics, or chemistry." I didn't tell her that I had not even finished high school math. But I persevered and went ahead, determined to do what I needed to do to become a physiologist.

I started making up the background science courses I lacked. The physiology department professors insisted that I take a position in a lab for the summer between my sophomore and junior years to make sure I really liked what I was doing. I applied for a summer job with Professor Curt Richter, a well known physiological psychologist, at Johns Hopkins Hospital. He hired several Goucher undergrads that summer; the other girls worked on experiments with the rats. He assigned me to a project measuring sweating in human beings as a way of assessing dermatome distribution.

Dermatomes are areas of the skin innervated by specific spinal nerves. A rise in body temperature causes a reflex sweating over skin dermatome areas and this cools the body (another reflex). If a nerve leading to a dermatome is cut, that specific skin surface area does not sweat. Before drugs that control high blood pressure were available, many hypertensive patients had spinal nerve branches cut to treat the condition because these branches contain nerve fibers that regulate blood pressure in addition to sweating.

The patients were brought to my lab on the top floor of the psychiatry building, and I tested their skin areas for sweating to assess the accuracy of the surgery. I also saw patients with "mysterious" diseases of unknown etiology, such as hardening of the skin or scleroderma. While the work was challenging, I did not like working with sick people and I hated Richter for his put-downs of black patients. He would come into the lab after I was finished with the tests to check the results.

I would say, "Dr. Richter, this is Mrs. Smith."

He would look over at the hospital record and say "Well, Myra, how are you today?"

I recognized, as a quasi-Southerner, that this was not friendly behavior, but an act of putting patients in their place, and I hated him for it. He also refused to spend any time answering my questions about the science behind what I was doing and sent me to the library to look it up myself. This was not a totally bad idea in the long run, but I needed a start at least. Also, I guess I needed someone to show some interest in my need to learn. My teachers at Goucher were always eager to help with questions.

Fortunately, I met Harry Patton in the library, then a postdoctoral fellow in the physiology department at Hopkins, later chair of physiology at Oregon. He saw me looking through some books with a puzzled expression and asked what I was looking for.

"I am trying to find out more about the sympathetic nervous system," I told him.

He directed me to appropriate books and encouraged me to learn more by guiding my reading and answering my questions. He was the first of a series of marvelous mentors for me.

At some point during the subsequent fall quarter after I had returned for my junior year in college, Dr. Richter called and asked me to come back at Christmastime to help pull together all of the data which I had gathered. I agreed after he reluctantly agreed to pay me per hour what I would have made at the post office.

◐•◑

During my sophomore year at Goucher, I began to suffer from overt depression. I began having difficulty studying. Before this, I had studied at home in the evenings in the basement of our house, alone so I could concentrate. However, I found myself feeling anxious when alone, and so I studied in our living room with the rest of the family while they were reading and listening to the radio.

During my junior year, I saw Dr. Grace Baker, a psychiatrist at Goucher, about my depression and guilt over my lesbianism. She urged me to get away from Baltimore the following summer, which I believe was very good advice. I looked for an opportunity to work elsewhere in a lab, and Gairdner Bostwick Moment, Chair of Biology, suggested that I apply for the summer student program at the Jackson Laboratory in Bar Harbor, Maine.

Thus, in the summer of 1947, I went to Bar Harbor as a summer student. This was a hardship for my parents, since I would not be making money, but instead had to pay to transport myself to Maine. I also needed tuition for the program and my parents generously agreed to provide the tuition for my summer and pay for a train ticket to Bar Harbor.

◐•◑

My God, was the Jackson Lab was a positive experience! It influenced the rest of my life as a scientist. I worked with Meredith Runner, a developmental biologist. He described the project he wished me to work on: the infertile yellow mouse. He wanted me to determine whether the failure of their embryos to implant in the uterus was due to a failure within the fertilized eggs or within the uterine lining. He proposed a strategy for testing the uterine lining hypothesis that entailed getting mice "pseudo-pregnant" and then using an electrical current to stimulate the uterus to respond with a deciduoma.

A deciduoma is a model for the genuine placenta, which forms from uterine and embryonic tissue after implantation. Pseudopregancy in the rodent occurs when the cervix is stimulated by coitus with a male whose vas deferens tubes have been tied (as in vasectomy in the male human). It occurs in female rodents because a reflex from the cervix through the spinal cord to the pituitary gland releases the hormone prolactin, which then preserves progesterone secretion by the corpus luteum in the ovary.

The female becomes "pseudopregnant" rather than pregnant, of course, because no sperm were released and no embryos are produced. The progesterone from the ovary prepares the uterus for the expected embryos, which, by burrowing into the uterine lining, elicit a placental response. I was to elicit the deciduoma, or false placenta, and quantitate the threshold for a positive response in control and "yellow" mice.

I remember going back to our dining hall and asking the other summer students what a deciduoma was! They directed me to the appropriate books and I immediately researched the topic.

So I planned the experiment, went back to Meredith with my protocol, and carried out the research. This is the way I always ran my own lab during later years—starting a student with a little background, a reference or two, and asking for a protocol. This then becomes a good starting point for a discussion of controls, timing, doses, and rationale.

I found no difference in my ability to get deciduomas between the infertile yellow mouse and control mouse, which indicated that the uteri of the two strains of mice were not significantly different. So I discovered that that hypothesis was incorrect. However, I did observe a real difference between the threshold nearer the cervix than near ovary; the one nearer the cervix was much easier to elicit.

The mouse uterus, as in many mammals, is divided into two horns, and each fertilized egg implants on the side near the ovary, from which the egg was ovulated. The mouse ovulates a multiple number of eggs, from seven to fifteen. This was not only my first lesson in negating a hypothesis but also in the value of serendipity.

Years later, as a faculty member at the University of Illinois, I suggested to an undergraduate medical student that he repeat this experiment in the pseudopregnant rat for his Master's thesis. He showed that the two ends of the uterus did not differ in their ability to form deciduomas in the rat, revealing an interesting species difference.

The conundrum of lethality in the homozygous yellow (referring to the fur color) mouse has continued to interest embryologists and biologists in general. Later work (Johnson and Granholm, 1978) revealed that the early embryo develops to the multicellular blastocyst stage, but then the embryo cells fail to push their way across the enveloping membrane to implant in the uterus, suggesting that the uterine environment per se is not at fault.

Actually this was a confirmation of my negative findings in 1947, which were never published. While the heterozygous yellow mouse, with just one yellow gene, implants into the uterus and eventually is born, it is obese, having two to three times the body weight of the ordinary mouse. With the current concern about increasing obesity of our population, this mouse has become an interesting model for studying causes of obesity.

The ability to follow a biological/clinical problem year after year as knowledge and methodology change is what makes it so exciting to be a scientist. Knowledge accrues, answers come, new questions arise, new methodologies are invented, questions can be revisited at a new level. What an exciting career I found myself having.

かゝ

My summer in Maine was not all work, work, work, although I certainly was busy. I hiked all over Mt. Desert Island with the other students. Early one morning, a group of us climbed Mt. Cadillac to see the sunrise, the earliest in the United States, and I rode my bike everywhere. My mother had not allowed me buy blue jeans before I left Baltimore (she thought they were not proper for ladies), so one of the male students took me to a Sears store and bought me my first pair.

We students lived in tents behind the lab and we had a very active social life. We had clambakes on the beach and swam together in the ocean and the lakes. Among nine men and nine women, I, of course, spotted the one other lesbian in the group—Barbara.

We circled around each other for a week or two, and then finally decided to climb one of the mountains together one evening. We wound up making love, on a wet stone surface, and then climbed down in the dark. The next morning, I discovered that my rear end was blue from my new jeans. Tired of the mountain climbs, we finally rode our bikes over to the other side of the island and spent one night in a Bed and Breakfast Inn in a real bed. She was working in a lab at one of the national laboratories at the time and we corresponded for the next year. Barbara was very bright, but painfully shy; she was a first rate biologist, with whom I later lived for several years in Chicago during graduate school.

When the summer ended, I went back to Goucher for my senior year, now hooked on science for life. In June of 1948, I graduated from college with a major in Physiology, as editor in chief of the *Goucher Weekly*, and with enough courses in English to satisfy—or close to it—a major in that subject. In addition, I received honors for a paper I wrote on my previous summer's experience.

❧❦

I went back to Bar Harbor, this time as a paid research assistant, where I again worked with Meredith. The preceding fall, just after my summer there ended, a forest fire had devastated the Jackson lab. It not only destroyed the tents and most of the lab building, but also killed many of the precious genetically inbred mice, like the yellow mouse, which were, therefore, being saved for breeding rather than being used for experiments.

Meredith asked me to find out about the control of timing of the postpartum ovulation so that he could time insemination and fertilization more closely for his developmental studies. I used a standard non-inbred strain of mice for this experiment.

The background to the experiment he suggested was that, within twenty-four hours after the delivery of a litter, the female mouse releases a new crop of eggs and mates. If a male is present, the female becomes pregnant again. (This is a marvelous mechanism for reproducing in a small vulnerable species in the wild, which keeps them pregnant during the brief annual breeding season).

Meredith had shown that the timing of this post-partum ovulation depended on the *time of day* of the delivery. The time interval between giving birth and ovulation varied systematically throughout the twenty-four hour day. The time intervals decreased from eighteen hours, when parturition occurred at 11 p.m., to twelve–thirteen hours when parturition occurred at 7 p.m. This is an example of a circadian or twenty-four hour biological rhythm in timing of hormone release.

Meredith set me to the task of determining whether the circadian variation in this interval depended on a variable time of pituitary release of Luteinizing Hormone (LH) after birth or a differential latency of the ovary to an invariant time of LH release. LH is the pituitary hormone that causes ovulation in all mammals, including human beings (see Chapter Five, figure 5.1).

At the time I was working with Runner (1948), it was not possible to measure LH in the blood because no methods sensitive enough had been developed yet, even for use in human beings. That was not possible until 1968! He suggested that I remove the pituitary gland at different times after delivery, and look for the *latest* time when this would block ovulation. If the delay in ovulation lay in the time of pituitary gland release, I should be able to remove the gland later after delivery in the mice that had a longer interval between parturition and ovulation. This would indicate that the latency between LH secretion and ovulation was the same in all mice, and that the delay in ovulation was in the timing of the release of the LH from the pituitary.

So I started learning to take out pituitary glands from mice without killing them, while I was also checking the cages of the pregnant females every four hours to see when delivery occurred.

As part of my stipend from the lab, I also had to work in the student dining room—I set the tables at 6 a.m. for breakfast before checking the mice, and cleared tables after dinner.

A long time passed that summer before I was able to do the surgery without killing a mouse—when I became adept at it, I started the experiment. Since I was anesthetizing the mice for the surgery with Nembutal (a barbiturate), I also ran some controls, sham surgeries (surgery but leaving the pituitary in), and with anesthesia alone.

I checked for ovulation by examining the oviducts under a microscope; when ovulation occurs you can actually see the eggs floating in fluid within the swollen oviduct. To our dismay, anesthesia itself blocked ovulation!

Those were the days when the relation between the adrenal cortex gland and stress were first being elucidated; an endocrinologist visiting the lab suggested to me that the mice were being *stressed* by the anesthesia and that was what was blocking the pituitary from secreting the ovulating hormone.

The problem remained and was not answered until two years later by two endocrinologists at Duke (John Everett and Charles H. Sawyer), who showed in 1950, in the rat, that pentobarbital (Nembutol) blocked the brain from releasing its hormone (Gonadotropin Releasing Hormone or GnRH), which was responsible for making the pituitary secrete the ovulating hormone LH.

Incidentally, this was a good lesson for me in the vagaries of doing research and the absolute necessity for doing adequate controls. Furthermore, the observations that anesthesia affected ovulation in rodents brought in the idea of the central nervous system controlling reproduction in animals. This eventually led to the discovery of GnRH, secreted by brain cells, into a portal system directly into the pituitary gland. Eventually, scientists discovered that a number of reproductive and other diseases in human beings, which had been assumed to be pituitary in origin, were actually due to a failure of neurons to secrete the factors necessary to maintain pituitary function.

≈≫≈

At the end of that second summer, Meredith asked me if I would stay an extra week after the other students left, for which he paid me, to finish up some data summaries. He had been such a good mentor and teacher for me, I said yes. I stayed on by myself, as the other students returned home, continuing to work in the lab as the autumn leaves started turning. I saw my first Northern Lights, a treat I have occasionally had at my house in Wisconsin.

I called home and suggested that my sister Pearl, who was thirteen at the time, meet me in New York City for several days, since I needed to change trains there on my way south to Baltimore. She had never been to the city before, and Mom agreed and put her on the train from Baltimore. I met her train, and we "did" New York. We saw the Bowery, Bronx Zoo, and the Statue of Liberty, ate in an Automat and her first French restaurant, and saw Ethel Merman in *Annie Get Your Gun*. Neither of us has forgotten that trip. We had been friends before as well as sisters, but that trip solidified our relationship, and we have taken many trips together since.

$\approx$

By the time I finished my undergraduate education at Goucher, I had had a remarkable set of experiences in science, working with patients at Johns Hopkins and with mice at the Jackson Lab. I had learned how to collect data and summarize it, how to do surgery on mice, how to find eggs in an oviduct, how to inject a mouse without getting bitten (usually), how to search for original journal articles in the scientific literature, and how to read and comprehend a scientific paper.

I hope that Meredith was as pleased with my enthusiasm for learning science as I have been by the dozens of undergraduates I have had in my lab at Northwestern.

I started graduate school in September 1948, at Northwestern University Medical School, in the Department of Physiology. Although I had applied and been accepted with financial support to four physiology departments (Northwestern, Yale, Rochester, and Columbia), I wanted to travel as far as I could from my mother, because she continued to talk with me about my lifestyle; so I opted for Chicago.

I knew that I could not remain near home and be myself. I had decided, because of my work at Bar Harbor, that I was interested in hormones and endocrinology, and so I became a student with Allen Lein, whose field was thyroid endocrinology.

Study Questions

(1) Offered the opportunity to attend an accelerated middle school for high achieving students, Neena decided not to attend in favor of attending her neighborhood school. She asks, "what moved this eleven-year-old kid to make this rather heavy decision on her own?" She then gives her reasons.
   - Discuss whether a child of this age should have been allowed to make this decision independent of her parents.
   - Discuss your reasons upon which you base your conclusions.

(2) Neena mentions that she found it notable that despite her father being a great salesman, none of his children went into sales careers.
   - Discuss whether you find that odd.

- Discuss how the work ethic of immigrant parents influenced their children other than giving them specific career paths to follow.
- Compare and contrast that sort of background with today's child rearing and family culture with regard to career choice.

(3) Neena writes, "when I was about twelve . . . . I began to have fantasies about becoming intimate with girls at the same time that my mother was encouraging me to take care of my appearance and to 'dress up' to attract boys."

- Discuss whether you believe Neena's fantasies were "normal" for a girl of that age.
- Discuss your view of Neena's mother encouraging her to dress in a way that would attract boys.
- As you reply, address the influence of factors such as the era (late 1930s), family religious orientation, socioeconomic status, and family culture and history.
- Consider whether the mother's "encouragement" may have been a subtle clue that she already recognized lesbian tendencies in Neena, of which Neena was not aware.

(4) Neena writes, "I had not been a tomboy, whatever that is. I had not played boys' sports; I wasn't brave about getting into mischief, and I never played with boys' toys."

- Discuss what these statements evince about Neena's current view of what a "typical" lesbian must be like.
- Compare and contrast it with your views of lesbianism and the relationship of being a "tomboy" with being lesbian.

(5) Neena writes that during her sophomore year at college, she began to suffer depression, and that during her junior year, she saw a psychiatrist "about my depression and guilt over my lesbianism."

- Discuss whether as stated, you think Neena saw her depression caused by her guilt.
- Discuss other plausible assessments of these two concurrent experiences (guilt and depression).

Four

GRADUATE SCHOOL IN CHICAGO

I am now occasionally horrified to think how very little I ever knew or cared about Medicine as the art of healing. The only part of my professional course which really and deeply interested me was Physiology, which is the mechanical engineering of living machines . . . . the working out the wonderful unity of plan in the thousands and thousands of diverse living constructions. . .

Thomas Huxley
Collected Essays

Northwestern University had awarded me a four-year graduate fellowship at $1200 per year. In 1948, that was enough to live in cheap housing, with cheap meals, and no entertainment frills. In terms of the relative consumer price index, that was equivalent to about $28,000 in 2005 dollars. I was also promised a teaching assistantship in the physiology lab for nurses, which would add a few hundred dollars to my salary and give me some valuable teaching experience.

So I said goodbye to my family and boarded an overnight train on the B&O railroad to travel from Baltimore to Chicago, which was 700 miles west. The train stopped first in Washington, going south along a route described in a favorite book by Thomas Wolfe, *Look Homeward Angel*. Then it went through the back woods to Harper's Ferry and headed northwest toward the Midwest. I sat awake with excitement all through the night. I knew that this was the beginning of a new life for me, although I certainly never would have believed that I was going to remain in the Chicago area for the next sixty odd years!

I was already missing my family and friends, but I felt relieved to escape my mother's daily scrutiny about my social life. I guess I was also a little scared; I felt "on my own" and wondered whether I could make it.

My first cousin Bernard Shulman, a son of my mother's brother Harry, was in a psychiatry residency program in Chicago at the time. I had called him and he met my train. I was tired from a sleepless night but beside myself with anticipation. He bought me lunch and took me to the YWCA in Chicago's near north side, close to Northwestern University's Chicago campus, where he had booked me a room for temporary housing until I found a more permanent living space.

๛

The next day, I walked from the YWCA to the medical school campus near Lake Michigan. The basic science departments were in the Ward Building; I took the elevator to the fifth floor and walked into the Physiology department office. I had met the Chair, John Gray, in Atlantic City, at a meeting of the Federation of Societies for Experimental Biology (FASEB). Phoebe Crittendon, Chair of Physiology at Goucher, introduced us. Gray greeted me with a smile and, in turn, introduced me to the endocrinologist in the department, Allen Lein. He specialized in the hormones of the thyroid gland, which became the focus of my graduate work. I liked Allen right away and discovered that I was his first doctoral student. He was about 5'9", a nice looking guy who had a warm sweet smile.

I learned that Allen had just been discharged from the Air Force, where he and other physiologists had been studying the physiology of the body's adaptation to the low oxygen content of air at high altitudes, a problem which sometimes affected our Air Force crews. That was familiar; after all, one of the aspects of physiology which brought me to the field was my fascination with the search for understanding of the physiologic pathway regulating adaptation to a low atmospheric oxygen level.

Allen showed me a desk within his office, which became mine, and then he separated out some lab space I could use. "Call me Allen," he said. "Where are you living?"

I told him about the YWCA. He suggested that the housing office could recommend a boarding house or apartment if I wanted. A boarding house seemed like a good solution to the meal and room problem, although I discovered when I met other grad students that they all ate lunch together in the lunch room. I could even keep a loaf of bread, some cheese, and salami in the lab fridge

Allen said, "One of the graduate students is talking about her research at lunch, why not come hear her?"

"Okay," I said.

I sat there mute during the hour and did not understand a single thing the student said! It threw me into a panic. By the end of the first quarter, however, I realized that I knew what everyone in the department was talking about, at least at some level. Later, every time a new graduate or undergraduate student in my own lab heard their first research presentation during our weekly lab meetings, I always told that story, acknowledging how overwhelmed someone new must feel.

❧❦

Being near the lake every day made me feel at home right away; much of the time when an east wind blows, the waves remind me of the Atlantic Ocean, an important part of my childhood.

Within a week, I found a room in a boarding house on the near north side of Chicago in the generally wealthy neighborhood just off Michigan Ave and north of Oak Street. Only a mile from the campus, it was an easy walk. Only a mile from the campus, it was an easy walk. It was run by a German woman who saw me, as a "student," as adding *caché* to her group of secretaries and file clerks. In a thick German accent she welcomed me and always introduced me to newcomers as "Neena Schwartz, our scholar." She had a piano and let me practice in the parlor. We got breakfast and dinner at the boarding house, but I made my lunch at school, gratefully, since the boarding house always smelled of cabbage.

As soon as I took my first walk around Oak and Rush Streets, close to the boarding house, it became obvious to me that I had landed in a gay area of Chicago. I did not personally know any gays in the city and was not sure how to meet anybody, so I decided to go for a beer to a bar on nearby Division Street. I took no identification with me, since in those days, the cops could, and did, invade gay bars at will and take everybody to the nearest station and book them. This was years before Stonewall in the Village in New York City.

When I tell that to young lesbians, they have a hard time believing that one could be arrested just for sitting in a bar.

I did not want my name in the newspapers the next morning. But nothing happened to me—in fact, I was so shy that I never even talked to anybody in the bar! I would just covertly watch other women and not make eye contact. I knew that if I approached a woman to talk, if she were attached to a tough "butch," I could get beaten up just because I would be suspected of having designs on her. I was lonely but not anxious for trouble.

It took a year or so before I finally met some lesbians through Alicia, who came to get a Master's degree at the University of Chicago. We were no longer involved sexually, but were still close friends. She introduced me to a group of women from the South Side of Chicago with whom I started socializing. Among them were a couple of women who had played baseball on one of the female teams formed during World War II. They were a welcome relief from the others, like me, who were going to graduate school and were relatively closeted and restrained.

Barbie, the woman with whom I had the affair while a student during my first summer at Bar Harbor, applied to graduate school at Northwestern after a year and joined me. At that point, I left the boarding house and the two of us moved into a tiny apartment in a slum building near the El on Wells Street. This was my first experience living with someone other than my family.

To save the twenty-five cent streetcar fare, I walked to school along Chicago Avenue from Wells to the lakeside campus. After we began living in the apartment, we started cooking most of our suppers at the lab, sharing dinners with fellow grad students Jack and Gerrie Emerson. We never "came out" in the department. During the 1950s, I assume it would not have been a good idea. But probably everyone figured it out.

My walk to school passed by lots of small shops and restaurants I could not afford. At the intersection with Clark Street, drug dealers and prostitutes were always hanging out. I was fascinated by them but moved quickly past, too scared to catch anyone's eye.

కర్ఆ

At the time I was doing this walk, the late Stuart Brent had a small book store called The Seven Stairs in a basement on Rush Street. I would sometimes stop there on the way home to talk with Stuart. He recognized how impoverished I was and sometimes fed me from a salami he had hanging up in the store. I saved up a few dollars from my stipend after three months and spent hours looking over his stock, trying to figure out how best to invest my dollars. He suggested Thomas Mann's *Stories for Three Decades*; I bought it, savoring owning a real book, not just something in physiology or neuroanatomy. Stuart later moved to a bigger space on Michigan Avenue and had a very successful business as a bookseller. Although he is no longer living, the bookstore is still in business in Chicago.

కర్ఆ

The building in which Barbie and I lived was a real slum. It consisted of one- or two-room apartments with community bathrooms on each floor. We had a tiny dinette and a bedroom/sitting room. A scraggly looking couple with a new baby lived on our floor. The child always looked dirty to us, and the couple drank and argued a lot. One day, we heard sirens and some police came in. The baby had died and it appeared that the cause was neglect or worse. We decided to move out of the building to an apartment further north in Chicago, near Broadway and Belmont, where it was further from work for both of us, but the neighborhood was better. We rode the Broadway streetcar south to the lab six or seven days a week.

కర్ఆ

The research project Allen suggested for my Master's degree was to develop a more sensitive measurement technique for iodine in the blood stream as an indicator for blood levels of thyroid hormone, which contains iodine as a necessary component. It was important to do this not just for enhancing lab research, but because Allen hoped that it would provide a more sensitive indicator of disease in patients with too much or too little thyroid hormone.

At the time I was a graduate student, patients with suspected thyroid dysfunction had their basal metabolic rate (BMR) measured. "Basal" referred to the conditions of the measurement of the oxygen usage, the test subject had to be at rest (not moving muscles), at a room temperature not cool enough to cause shivering (which used extra oxygen), and twelve hours post a meal (assimilation of proteins raises oxygen consumption).

Thyroxin increases the amount of oxygen a mammal uses, but measuring oxygen consumption was a cumbersome, expensive, and insensitive method of assessing thyroxin in the bloodstream. My first paper, with Allen as senior author, was published in 1951, based on my Master's thesis. We had successfully refined a chemical method, which was used to provide accurate assessments of thyroid function clinically for some years to come.

కావ్య

I asked Allen if I could work on something "more physiological" for my doctorate. He had done previous work measuring metabolic rate by measuring the consumption of oxygen in rats.

An excess of thyroxin in rats, as in human beings, causes an increase in basal metabolic rate, as demonstrated by an increase in oxygen consumption by the whole animal or even by cells removed from the animal. Allen raised the question with me of why an animal is "sick" just because its BMR is high. In fact, *both* hypothyroid and hyperthyroid patients are ill. Did metabolic rate mean anything as a central, crucial phenomenon?

Allen suggested that I measure some energy-requiring function in both hypothyroid and hyperthyroid animals to investigate the relation between the function and oxygen consumption. In other words, did thyroid hormone change the *efficiency* (amount of work per energy used) of biological work?

We decided to measure muscle contraction, which was relatively easy to quantify; it is the most obvious "work" produced by an animal when it moved. Simultaneously, I would measure the extra oxygen the animal was using for muscular contraction. I would anesthetize the rats to keep them from moving about spontaneously during the procedure.

We built and tested a homemade electronic nerve stimulator and a homemade oxygen consumption apparatus for use with the rats, and I proceeded to make some rats hyperthyroid by injecting them with excess thyroid hormone and some rats hypothyroid by giving them an inhibitor of thyroxin synthesis in their drinking water. I then tested, in some control rats, the frequency of muscle stimulation that would give a smooth muscle contraction and a clear increase in oxygen consumption during stimulation of the anesthetized rat. I was ready to start my doctoral dissertation!

On the day I ran my first experimental rats in the new apparatus, Jack Emerson, the graduate student with whom I shared lab space, was trying to anesthetize a cat. The cat broke loose and began streaking around the room. At the same time, I was anesthetizing my first rat, a control.

"Watch it," Jack yelled.

Seeing the cat loose, I grabbed the rat just before the cat jumped up on my lab bench. The cat knocked the stimulator onto the floor. Jack was running after the cat and I was scared to let the rat go, figuring we would then have Jack chasing the cat, the cat chasing the rat, and even more chaos.

The cat ducked behind a radiator, refusing to come out. Jack couldn't reach far enough behind the radiator to prod the cat to emerge. In the meantime, I picked up the stimulator and checked all the electrical connections.

"Whew, I said, "everything's okay."

Unfortunately, I did not check the dials on the stimulator. I went ahead with the anesthesia on my control rat and did not realize anything was wrong until I looked at the contraction this control was exerting. What I saw was that, instead of a smooth contraction from the muscle, I was seeing a wavy contraction, no "fusion" of individual contractions was occurring.

I then realized what had happened to the electric stimulator: the frequency of the stimulus to the muscle had been lowered by the knock to the ground. I made a quick decision to use the same (wrong) frequency for the hypothyroid and hyperthyroid rats I was also testing that day. I went ahead with the day's experiment, and discovered, because I was using the "wrong" frequency, that the hyperthyroid rats were less efficient than controls, but only because they were even less able than controls to sustain a steady fused contraction at a low frequency.

Thus I accidentally explained a clinical phenomenon of muscle contraction that had been used to assess thyroid disease for some years; slow muscle reflexes in hypothyroid patients or overly rapid reflexes in hyperthyroids.

That error proved to provide me with the most significant finding in my dissertation. It was serendipitous, the way a lot of science is. Allen and I published the study in the *American Journal of Physiology*, the official journal of the American Physiological Society, and this time I was the senior, first author. I continued to probe the relationship between the thyroid hormone and nerve muscle function for some years before switching definitively to reproductive endocrinology.

What about the cat behind the radiator? We couldn't lure him out with food or water. Finally, Jack poured some formaldehyde behind the radiator figuring the cat would come out to avoid the foul smelling fluid. He didn't, but there was a large night school class lecture going on across the hall and the smell spread from our lab, and the class finally had to be evacuated.

The cat came out the next morning, but the department was not very pleased with Jack or me.

∽∾

Before personal computers or even scientific calculators became ubiquitous, slide rules were the emblem of the scientist; I carried a circular seven inch slide rule from class to class to lab. On the elevator one day while I was going up to the lab, a male physician got on the elevator with me.

He stared at the slide rule and asked: "What's a little girl like you doing with that great big slide rule?"

I said nothing, but I have thought many times since of what I might have said! The incident, while I have remembered it for more than fifty years, did not make me crumble with self-doubt; I just thought he was a stupid jerk. Would it have been devastating if I had not had as much self-confidence as I did? It might have.

∽∾

The Department of Physiology was quite interested in theoretical modeling. Gray was a major modeler of the respiratory system. He and Fred Grodins also worked on models of the cardiovascular system. Modeling is an important way of using data obtained from experiments or clinical situations to make guesses about how a physiological system is regulated and controlled.

For example, we can observe on ourselves that when we exercise our breathing (respiration) increases in frequency and depth. Experiments have shown that respiration is increased because the oxygen in the major blood vessels drops because it is being used faster by muscles (as in the measurements I was making in the rat). This drop is detected by oxygen receptors in the blood vessels (just as it is at altitude), which send neural signals to the brain centers which regulate the nerves to the respiratory muscles. Cells, within the center, cause an increase in the contractions of those muscles. This results in deeper and more frequent breathing.

Well, in addition to a drop in the amount of oxygen, increased blood carbon dioxide and blood acidity affect other receptors which are also connected to the brain and change respiration. By making a theoretical model of the system, one can factor in all of these influences (oxygen used in cell work, and oxygen, carbon dioxide, and acid concentration in the blood) and make predictions of how the system will work under a variety of conditions and then test the model's ability to predict results in the real (actual) animal world. I know this modeling atmosphere was strongly influential on my subsequent work in endocrinology.

Of course, it was reading about these processes when I was in college that had hooked me to become a physiologist. I began to be more interested in the regulation of thyroid hormone secretion than in the mechanism of its actions on muscle and other tissue. Later in my career, I switched to examining the regulation of reproductive cycles.

ॐ∞

The department at Northwestern was intellectually tough, which was good for my intellectual growth. We were challenged continually by the faculty, and this felt familiar to me because my family had always been blunt and open about their beliefs.

The oral questionings to which we were subjected for our qualifying and dissertation exams were attended by every faculty member in the department, and all felt they had to ask some questions.

These exams took place in John Gray's office, which was regarded as an inner sanctum by the graduate students. One student clutched a plant in the office during his exam and became so excited he pulled the plant out of the pot during a particularly rigorous set of questions.

I remember also one of our Chinese graduate students who became so disturbed by the questions he received that he came out of Gray's office while the faculty debated his fate. He looked very glum and said, "I am going for a walk," and he left the building.

The faculty emerged from the room thirty minutes later to congratulate him for passing his oral exam, but he was nowhere to be found. All of us students fanned out looking for him, and I discovered him walking along the lake, contemplating suicide if he had failed because of loss of face.

The downside to the department, which took me some time to appreciate, was that the faculty felt so superior to others that they did not bother encouraging their students to go to professional meetings to hear other people's science. Neither did they invite other scientists to the department to present their work.

So my first presented paper was at an American Physiological Society meeting in Rochester, New York, in 1954, where I met Stan Glasser. But I did not meet any of the senior physiologists in my field, since not one of the faculty members from Northwestern was there to introduce me.

This is frequently the case for women in graduate school, even in more enlightened departments now. But this was not a gender issue at all; my department simply did not value the annual professional meetings as mechanisms to exchange information and mentor graduates.

ॐ∞

My graduate advisor Allen was always willing to argue with me, and this really made a difference in what I learned as a neophyte researcher. He made me defend my ideas, but he never made me feel dumb or foolish, even when I was wrong. It was such a contrast to my undergraduate research experience with Richter at Johns Hopkins.

Allen and I remained friends after he moved to the University of California, San Diego (UCSD) as Assistant Dean in the medical school. He was also a faculty member in reproductive medicine there and helped train medical residents in research. In addition, he initiated a training program for MD/PhD students at UCSD.

When Allen was about to retire from the University in 1983, thirty years after I received my PhD, I received a phone call from Dr. Sam Yen, Chair of OB/Gyn, asking me to come out to San Diego as a surprise for Allen's retirement party. I planned a few remarks and had this strange feeling that I was going to be asked to burst out of a large cake, shouting "Surprise."

Allen was indeed surprised, and we were both tearful. In 2003, I received an Email announcing his death in Texas, where his family lived. The Email ended with: "Allen was among the best of men—an excellent teacher, an unparalleled mentor, and a loyal friend. We will miss him dearly." Yes, I still do.

అఌఌ

While I was in graduate school, I took the basic physiology, neuroanatomy, biochemistry, and pharmacology courses with the sophomore medical students. At that time, no separate courses at the medical school were exclusively for graduate students—we were expected to attend the lectures with medical students and take the same exams. I used these lectures as a model for my own teaching of physiology throughout the rest of my career. I liked the way the material was organized; it made sense to me, and I found it made sense to my students.

అఌఌ

I also did a lot of teaching while I was a graduate student, for which I was paid extra, beyond the basic university fellowship. At first, I taught the nursing students in their physiology lab, assisting Ardelle Lane, who ran the quarter course. When Ardelle graduated, I took over the lectures, which paid a lot better than lab assisting. It was hard work but a wonderful experience. Not many graduate students get to run a whole course themselves. As I ended each day's lecture, I would announce the topic for the next lecture.

One day I said "I will lecture on sex on Tuesday."

One of the girls came up to me and asked, "Are you lecturing on social sex or scientific sex?"

I answered flippantly, "What's the difference?"—knowing full well what she meant. I would not be that flippant today. In fact, more recently, I have used that anecdote in class to illustrate the way we separate our thinking about the *biology* of sex from its place in society, or give biology so much credence that we sometimes think "biology is destiny."

As an advanced graduate student, I was also able to earn extra money teaching physiology at the Baptist Missionary Training School in North Chicago. At my interview for the position, the president of the school asked me

to emphasize reproduction, since many of the girls "come from very funda-
mentalist backgrounds and are unprepared for what they will encounter when
they go to another country."

I taught in the evening after supper at home and I enjoyed the experience—the girls were so different from the young women I encountered
teaching in nursing school, who were doing practice nursing on the floor at
Northwestern's hospital. These future missionaries were quite unsophisticated
and unworldly for the most part.

Apparently, many of these sheltered teenagers did not even know where
babies came from! Some told me that their families did not permit dancing or
card playing. When I gave them their first exam, I handed out the test and left
the room for awhile, assuming the same honor system we had at Goucher. The
next time I showed up for class, the president called me aside as I came in.

"I admire your faith," he said, "but some of the students came to me after your class and asked me to tell you that some students cheated."

At the ripe old age of twenty-five, I was surprised and disappointed by
this. Morality comes in many forms.

❧

After four years of graduate school, I was exhausted, but I had collected all the
data and I needed to start writing my dissertation. Barbie's parents had both died
within the year and she had inherited some money. She bought a car and we
piled some clothes into the trunk, threw my data into a brief case, and took off
for California for a month. I said "I'll work on my dissertation during the trip."

I never opened the briefcase. We saw a number of national parks and
hiked in the Rockies. When we returned, my four-year fellowship had terminated and I had no money to live on while writing my dissertation. The department made me a teaching assistant in the medical school physiology lab,
which enabled me to go on eating and paying half of the rent, and I finished
my dissertation in the late fall of 1952.

❧

What do I think of the training I received as a graduate student, looking back
from the vantage point of fifty years? It could hardly have been better. My
advisor Allen and all of the faculty in the department were supportive while
being intellectually demanding. They did not regard their task as just trans-
mitting facts. Their teaching was always directed toward understanding how
physiological knowledge is obtained and validated.

At the end of my Master's exam, I went through a "qualifying exam" to
certify my readiness for starting doctoral studies. In most departments, this
exam assesses students' competence on the fundamental facts of their field.
However, our qualifying exam consisted of being presented with a reprint of

an article describing a recent discovery in a subfield of physiology other than the one you were pursuing and being asked to review the literature, which led up to the discovery. You then had to write an annotated history of the field, including some suggestions for further research.

It was a tough assignment but tremendously educational. I was presented with an article demonstrating the presence of a neural center in the hind part of the brain that regulated vomiting. I totally immersed myself in this assignment for several weeks of twelve-hour work days. When I finished typing up my paper for submission to the faculty, I desperately subtitled it "Emesis, My Nemesis." But it was a valuable learning experience.

వా~అ

I was already looking for a job. Bob Scow, a thyroid/muscle/bone investigator at the National Institutes of Health, had heard me give a paper on my dissertation at a national meeting and offered me the opportunity to do a postdoctoral fellowship in his lab in Bethesda, Maryland. (There! That's another reason why it's valuable for students to attend professional meetings!)

I admired Bob and his work a lot, but was reluctant to get that close to Baltimore. Still, I applied to the National Institute of Health for a fellowship to work with Bob, and was awarded it, one of the first NIH postdoctoral fellowships ever awarded.

Phoebe Crittendon also called from Goucher. She offered me a position in their physiology department. Well, that was the only job offer I had, but since I had never met a Jewish faculty member there as a student, I asked, "You know I am Jewish?" "Yes," she said," but I talked to a few people and they thought you are okay."

So much for that offer!

I certainly did not want to walk into that kind of covert/overt anti-Semitism if I could help it. But just as I was thinking I had to move to Bethesda to take the NIH fellowship, Allen Lein received a phone call from a friend of his in the physiology department at the University of Illinois College of Medicine saying they needed a physiologist.

I interviewed for the position and was awarded an instructorship (non-tenure track) to start in January 1953.

&ne&

Barbara and I lived together until I finished grad school and I started my first job. Ours was a troubled relationship; she was very dependent and I was very impatient and wrapped up in my dissertation work. She finished her PhD a year later than I and took her first academic position several states away.

By that time, we were living on the north side of Chicago and I needed bus fare to get to work on the near west side where the University of Illinois Medical School campus was. As I started to teach in my new position, I began to run out of the money I had saved. The state of Illinois took two months to give me my first paycheck!

Embarrassed, I called my parents. I asked Dad to telegraph me a couple of hundred dollars to live on temporarily.

"I'll pay you back" I said.

"Don't worry," he said, "I can't think of a better investment."

Study Questions

(1) On her first day in graduate school, Neena was overwhelmed by not understanding a word of the presentation by another student. She recalls understanding what everyone else did by the end of the first quarter.
   - Discuss the personality traits and effort that was required to make this advancement in such a short time.
   - Relate the traits and efforts you mention in reply to the previous question to specific experiences Neena had during her youth prior to that time that contributed to her success.

(2) Based on Neena's recollections of her early graduate studies, discuss what we can learn from serendipity and error.
   - Discuss whether serendipity and error, or how we respond to them, makes the difference.

Five

ENDOCRINOLOGY 101

The doctor who sits at the bedside of a rat
Asks real questions, as befits
The place, like where did that potassium go, not what
Do you think of Willie Mays or the weather?
So rat and doctor may converse together.

Josephine Miles
"The Doctor Who Sits at the Bedside of a Rat"

Since the Enlightenment, however, wonder has become a disreputable
passion in workaday science, redolent of the popular, the amateurish,
and the childish. Scientists now reserve expressions of wonder for their
personal memoirs, not their professional publications.

Katharine Park and Lorraine Daston
Wonders and the Order of Nature

Before going on to describe my research and academic career, I wanted to provide the reader with a short "course" in endocrinology, which I still, after all these years, think is wonderful.

Let's face it—the public, the media, and I love hormones. They do such wonderful things. For example, the sex hormones are responsible at puberty for turning on bodily sexual phenotype. A new born baby not secreting thyroid hormone from its own thyroid will never show normal brain differentiation because crucial connections between neurons in the brain require the presence of this hormone to be completed. The mother's thyroid hormones take care of the baby's brain growth while the baby is still in the uterus, but after birth, the baby's thyroid must secrete its own hormones. Unless treated before six months of age with thyroid hormone, this child will grow up severely damaged, what one used to call a "cretin," with irreversible low intelligence and severe skeletal and muscular growth impairment.

We no longer see cretins in our country, where even the least experienced physician recognizes the early signs of lack of thyroid hormone in an infant. But when I went to China in 1983 with a group of endocrinologists, we saw cretins in the pediatric ward in a hospital in Beijing. They had grown up in rural areas where they were not diagnosed as hypothyroid until it was too late. This was a poignant experience for me, reminding me of my long ago dissertation work on thyroid hormone function.

The study of the secretions of the endocrine glands began in a formal sense late during the late nineteenth and early twentieth century. At that time, the concept of a hormone evolved. Scientists theorized that some cells or organs in the body influenced other cells distant from them, not by direct connections such as nerves, but by releasing a substance, called a hormone, into the blood stream, whence it would travel to a distant organ and influence cells in these distant sites.

But the *practice* of endocrinology, began much earlier. Remember the technique of castration of domestic animals to foster docility and to increase muscle fat and tenderness, the castration of men to provide eunuchs for harems, or the castration of boys to maintain soprano voices for church choruses. Human beings were carrying out this surgery without knowing why it worked. Well, how did the transition occur between what must have been the accidental finding of the relation between the lack of the testes and decreased sex drive or high pitched voices and the understanding that the testes manufactured and secreted a substance responsible for the masculine phenotype?

The concept of a hormone can be traced to experiments during 1902, when the William Bayliss and Ernest Starling asked how it is possible that swallowing a meal, resulting in the food entering the stomach and the initial part of the small intestine, could cause the pancreas, an organ some distance away, to secrete enzymes into the intestine? These enzymes are necessary to break down proteins into amino acids, which are small enough to be absorbed into the blood stream.

Two possibilities occurred to Bayliss and Starling: (1) nerve fibers could carry the information from the stomach or intestine to the pancreas, or (2) maybe a substance existed, which was carried in the blood from intestine to pancreas acting as a signal to increase secretion. They demonstrated that a substance they named "secretin" was formed in the inner lining of the duodenum in response to stomach acid reaching the small intestine after a meal. This hormone secretin could influence pancreatic secretion of enzymes by means of a humoral rather than a neural mechanism (secretin traveled in the bloodstream to the pancreas from the duodenum).

In 1905, Starling introduced the generic term *hormone* (from the Greek- "I excite") to describe such blood-borne messengers. Thus, by the beginning of the twentieth century, the blood was recognized as a carrier of hormonal signals in addition to being a transporter of nutrients to all cells and waste substances to the intestines, lungs, or kidneys to be excreted.

An interesting clinical association with regard to the ovaries was also made in the late nineteenth century, which has had therapeutic ramifications that are still being explored. A Scottish surgeon, George Beatson, noted that in sheep, milk production by the breast seemed to be associated with morphological changes in the ovaries. This suspected link induced him to remove the ovaries from a woman with advanced breast cancer, after which she lived for nearly four years. Subsequently, the role of circulating estrogens in breast cancer was demonstrated, leading to the present use of an estrogen antagonist, tamoxifen, in women with estrogen dependent breast cancer.

Unfortunately, the field was somewhat tarnished from the beginning by claims such as those from a French physician, Charles Brown-Sequard, that implanting testes from a monkey or other species could restore sexual prowess to aging men, such as himself. He announced this at a meeting of the Society of Biology in Paris in 1889, creating an international furor. Not to be outdone, a female physician in Paris, Dr. Augusta Brown, spoke to the same group about her own experiment giving a dozen old women juice filtered from guinea pig ovaries, which she claimed showed "good effect in cases of hysteria, uterine afflictions, and debility due to age." In the light of these claims, it is a surprise that the field of endocrinology did not die still born during the nineteenth century.

ॐॐ

The classic technique of identifying an organ as an endocrine gland is to take the suspected organ out and then to observe what happens to the animal. The rules enunciated by Robert Koch for proving that bacteria could cause disease, for which he won the Nobel Prize in 1905, are called Koch's postulates; these were early adapted to endocrinology:

> To prove an organ is an endocrine gland: (1) remove the organ from the animal; (2) describe the *biologic effects* of the operation; (3) inject an extract of the putative gland; (4) if the injection reverses the defects seen in (2), then the organ is a gland; (5) isolate, purify, and identify chemically the active hormone(s).

For example, if you remove the anterior pituitary gland, which lies just below the brain, or the testes, an animal is unable to reproduce. Or, if you remove the pancreas, an animal dies from lack of insulin; there is too much sugar in the blood and not enough in cells, leading to inadequate metabolic energy, diabetes, in other words.

The crucial experiment to confirm that the symptoms of organ removal are due to the absence of a hormone is to inject an extract of the gland. If this reverses the effect of removing the organ, then you have identified an endocrine gland. Indeed, pituitary extracts can reactivate the gonads, and pancreatic extract can cause sugar to move from the bloodstream into cells.

This sequence of experimental proofs grabbed me when I learned about it in college and while doing research at Bar Harbor; this is part of what seduced me into becoming an endocrinologist. Imagine the thrill of discovering a hormone no one else has suspected of existing! I was lucky enough to have this happen to me later in my career.

❧❧

As endocrinology expanded during the twentieth century, it divided into a number of specialized sub-areas, mostly related to concepts common to every hormone or gland. Some scientists became specifically interested in the subcellular processes, by which a given hormone, like thyroid hormone or estrogen, was synthesized and secreted by the gland. For example, it was already known in the nineteenth century that lack of iodine in the soil in the American Midwest and in the Swiss Alps could lead to an enlarged thyroid gland or goiter and other signs of too little thyroid hormone. This occurred because thyroxin, the principal thyroid hormone, contains iodine as an essential ingredient.

Thus, the steps by which the atom iodine was incorporated into the hormone molecule, thyroxin, became one major study focus. This is why Allen Lein and I were trying to measure iodine in the bloodstream as a test for circulating thyroxine when I was a master's student in his lab.

Other endocrinologists began studying the input signals to glands, asking, "How can the rate of secretion of a particular hormone be regulated?" For example: how does the pancreas know when to secrete insulin? This turned out to be that the insulin secreting cells of the pancreas actually measure the blood glucose level, and a rise in glucose causes insulin secretion from these cells to increase. How does the ovary know when to release an egg?

In 1930, it was shown that the ovaries and testes of animals shrank and stopped producing eggs or sperm if the anterior pituitary gland was removed, which showed that the pituitary in some way sustained function and size of gonads. Pituitary extracts injected into animals from which the pituitary was removed could restore normal gonadal growth and function, including ovulation.

Thus the pituitary gonadotropic hormones Luteinizing Hormone (LH) and Follicle Stimulating Hormone (FSH) were predicted and then discovered. As an undergraduate at Bar Harbor, I was trying to block postpartum ovulation in Meredith Runner's mice by blocking the secretion of pituitary LH by removing the pituitary gland before it released LH.

Still other endocrinologists began to study how hormones worked on target cells. How could LH, a molecule too large to cross the outer membrane of an ovarian follicle cell, cause that cell to secrete estrogen, as well as eventually cause rupture of the follicle to release the enclosed ovum resulting in ovulation? Research eventually revealed that protein molecules on the surface of ovarian cells, called receptors, specifically recognize LH at the cell surface, bind the LH to the cell surface, and then transmit an intermediary chemical signal to the cell nucleus, causing it to alter cell function and synthesize and secrete estrogen. Cells in the testes also contain LH receptors and secrete testosterone when these cells are stimulated by LH molecules.

Another subfield evolved that cut across some of the above questions, neuroendocrinology, which deals with the relationships among glands, hormones, and the nervous system. This field eventually captured my interest because it brought the external environment into the equation and led to questions about the relation between hormones and behavior. My growing interest in these issues was, in fact, part of what induced me to work on clinical studies with a team of psychologists and psychiatrists at Michael Reese Hospital from 1957 to 1961.

❧

The quintessential experiment in endocrinology is what my late dear friend, Manny Bogdanove of Indiana University called the "stop entry" experiment: first take out the source of a hormone—the gland—and then see what happens. At first, organs were regarded as "black boxes," which one could not enter; you could inject a hormone into an animal—say estrogen—see what the pituitary output of LH was, and make inferences about the "transducer" function of the pituitary gland.

But initially it was not possible to enter the box (pituitary cell) itself—at least physiologists started out thinking that way. This input-output approach led me and many other endocrinologists and physiologists to start to develop computer models of various body systems. As I once said in print, it was heuristic if nothing else.

Gradually, isolating organs and cells in vitro became possible. We could then study the output of these segregated mini-systems under strictly controlled input conditions. Of course, as cell biology continued to develop, studying subfractions of organs and cells became possible, opening the black box to microanalysis.

When I was doing research and teaching in the Physiology Department at the University of Illinois during 1965, a recently recruited young cell biologist chided me for working on whole animals. He was the first faculty member we had hired who worked exclusively on cells.

Henry was young and arrogant about working at the cellular level instead of the whole animal level (somewhat as I now find some of my present molecular biology colleagues are). He had apparently shown this same disdain for physiology of whole animals to others of my colleagues. Our cardiovascular physiologist was in the department library one day when Henry walked in.

Henry said, "Bill, I have often wondered why when I come into this room I sometimes have to flick the light switch up, to turn on the lights, but at other times I have to flick it down."

Bill laughed and said, "Henry, if you weren't a cell biologist, you would have noticed that there are two light switches in the room."

❧❦

These days, I frequently feel as Bill did about the stampede toward total reductionism in endocrinology. I hope that as physiological genomics
progresses, we will be able to metaphorically insert genes and their protein
products back into the whole organism. As a physiologist, I was trained to
believe that one needed eventually to study a whole organism to understand
it—*in vivo veritas*—but no doubt, even I moved on to cell and organ culture
eventually, and gained enormously from it.

❧❦

Changing methodologies continuously alter the face of endocrinology, as they
do other life sciences. When I started working on the regulation of the gonadotropic hormones of the pituitary gland in 1960, it was not possible to measure directly the very small amounts of the pituitary gonad-stimulating
hormones LH and FSH carried in the bloodstream and acting as signals to the
gonads. In fact, the field was still not sure that there were *two* gonadotropins
released from the pituitary gland rather than just one.

The standard way to measure the amount of a hormone, before one
could measure it by immunological or chemical means, was to do a "bioassay." A bioassay measured the amount of a hormone in a given volume of
biological fluid (like a small volume of blood) by injecting a standard amount
of that fluid into a test animal or applying it to isolated target cells and seeing
how much of a biological effect occurred. From this, one worked backward to
calculate how much hormone must have been injected.

A familiar bioassay was the rabbit pregnancy test. To see whether a
woman was pregnant, one could take a sample of her urine and inject a given
volume of it into a rabbit. After twenty-four hours, the rabbit was killed and
the ovary examined for signs of ovulation. If the gonadotropic hormone
(which resembles LH from the pituitary) produced by the cells of her placenta
was high in the donor's urine, the rabbit would ovulate and the pregnancy test
was considered positive.

Bioassays are necessary steps in developing more precise and sensitive
measurement techniques, but they are usually very insensitive and have a
wide degree of error. When I was up in Bar Harbor the second summer, I had
to look at *ovulation* in the mice after they had given birth, rather than just
examining LH levels in their blood for the time of secretion of LH.

In our first experiments at the University of Illinois, after I became a faculty member there and began studying the estrous cycle, it was still not possible to measure LH in the blood; we had to measure the larger amount of
stored LH in the pituitary gland itself. To do this in my first experiments undertaken during the early 1960s, we needed to collect four pituitaries from
rats in the same cycle stage and at the same time of day, and then homogenize

the glands. The homogenate was injected into five different bioassay animals at two different doses. The bioassay recipients were immature rats that had been pretreated with FSH from pregnant mare's serum (to stimulate ovarian follicles) and chorionic gonadotropin to make the rats ovulate (just as pregnancy urine made the rabbits ovulate in the pregnancy test).

After ovulation, follicles change into corpora lutea. Ascorbic acid accumulated within the corpora lutea of the bioassay rats and disappeared following an injection of LH. The degree of reduction of ascorbic acid was proportional to the amount of LH in the donor pituitaries, thus providing the bioassay for LH.

The whole procedure, in addition to being insensitive and expensive, was time-consuming and cumbersome. Even so, we were able to demonstrate that pituitary LH *content* dropped on only one day of the cycle- proestrus— thus showing that *release* occurred on only one day of four. This primitive experiment with primitive methodology launched my lab into the reproductive science business!

ॐ

The newer method of measuring hormone concentrations—radioimmunoassay (RIA)—is 10,000 times more sensitive than the bioassay and revolutionized endocrinology. Rosalyn Yalow, an American endocrinologist, received the Nobel Prize in 1977 for her work in inventing the radioimmunoassay. She was the first female president of the Endocrine Society.

The RIA method depends on making an antibody to the hormone one wishes to measure, and developing a way to put a radioactive "tracer" on to a small amount of the pure hormone. The "cold" hormone (standard known amount without tracer) competes with the "hot" (labeled) hormone for the antibody, and then one can separate hormone combined with antibody from free hormone.

The amount of tracer on the hormone remaining free is inversely proportional to the amount of standard or unknown, and it is very easy to measure the radioactivity at very low levels.

With RIA, it became possible to measure hormone levels in blood from minute to minute, even in rats, because a very small sample was adequate. The technique not only changed endocrinological research but also made it possible to measure blood hormones in human and veterinary patients with very small amounts of blood withdrawal.

A newer technique based on the same antigen-antibody type of reaction has now come into favor because it does not require the use of radioactivity. It is called an Enzyme Linked Immunoabsorbent Assay (ELIZA), wherein a *color* reaction is used instead of radioactivity to give the variable measured. With it, a pregnancy test can now be done with urine in a test tube (instead of injecting into a rabbit), where the placental gonadotropin in the urine is com-

peting with a standard gonadotropin for an antibody, and a color reaction develops as the indicator in proportion to hormone levels.

჻

Assay methods were not the only methodology that changed, of course. Cell
biology developed, as did molecular biology, permitting questions to be asked
and answered, which were inconceivable when I entered the field. It is the
powerfulness of tools such as these that has made life sciences develop to
such a high degree.

Incidentally, this also makes it possible to measure *progress* in science.
For example, a major concept in endocrinology that has evolved during my
professional lifetime was the identification of hormone receptors. Scientists
had predicted them: how else could hormones traveling in the bloodstream,
which reaches *every* cell in the body, find their appropriate target cells?

As I mentioned above, discussing LH and the ovary, receptors proved to
be specific proteins in the target cells for hormones; they recognize and bind
the specific hormone and then trigger an action within the target cell in proportion to the amount of bound hormone. Receptors for large protein hormones
like growth hormone or LH are on the surface of their target cells, but receptors for the smaller hormones, like the steroids and thyroxin, which can get
through cell membranes, are inside the target cells in the cytoplasm or nucleus.

The receptor concept and discovery of their chemical identity enabled a
quantum leap in our understanding of the mechanisms, by which hormones
change cell morphology and function. This has had crucial clinical implications. The whole area of "designer drugs," which will bind to some tissue
receptors but not others, a hot field now in estrogen replacement therapy,
grew out of this field. If one can design an artificial estrogen-like molecule,
which binds to estrogen receptors in the bone and blood vessels, but not in
breast or uterine tissue, then one could use estrogen hormone replacement
therapy to prevent osteoporosis or possibly stroke without risking breast or
uterine cancer. Such designer drugs (SERMs–specific estradiol receptor molecules) are being tested now.

჻

As I have said, endocrinology started with "stop entry" experiments, removing the secreting gland to probe the effects of loss of hormone action. It is
now possible instead of surgery to use chemicals that serve as specific antagonists to a given hormone to reduce its binding to receptors in animals and
human beings or to give an antiserum to a given hormone. These are widely
used as experimental and clinical tools, and we have capitalized on them in
our own research, having used antisera to LH and FSH to block ovarian ef-

fects, and blockers of estrogen and progesterone receptors to prevent these steroid effects.

These antagonists to hormone receptors are important medical tools. For example, an anti-estrogen, tamoxifen, is used to fight breast tumor metastatic disease in patients whose cancer cells are shown to have estrogen receptors. We also know that an antagonist to Gonadotropin Releasing Hormone (GnRH), the molecule from the brain which stimulates the pituitary to secrete LH and FSH, has been found to be effective in combating prostate cancer and uterine endometriosis by decreasing gonadal hormone secretion.

The newest experimental variant on these inhibitory or blockade techniques is the "knockout" mouse—where genetic engineering permits scientists to prevent a specific gene from working, with the result being that mice are born missing the ability to synthesize a specific hormone or its receptor. By studying these mice, one can determine, either by working backwards or by "knocking in" the missing gene, what the missing gene and the protein it codes for can do.

∽◦∾

Yet another concept that has been significant in endocrinology, and which really grabbed me from the beginning, is the close regulation of hormone levels, resulting in the hour-to-hour regulation of what the French physiologist, Claude Bernard, labeled *"le milieu interne,"* the internal environment of the body. For example, the level of thyroid hormone in the blood remains remarkably constant from hour-to-hour or day-to-day normally. We now know that this occurs *not* because no thyroid hormone is destroyed or excreted after it is secreted, but because the cells in the pituitary responsible for secreting Thyroid Stimulating Hormone (TSH) sense the level of thyroid gland hormone level in the blood.

When thyroid hormone levels drop, as for example when the external temperature is lowered, TSH levels rise. This stimulates the thyroid gland to make more thyroxin, which helps maintain body temperature. This compensation occurs because of the negative feedback mentioned above, wherein thyroxin levels control thyroxin secretion. This resembles the principle of operation of temperature regulation in a home; temperature sensors can compare room temperature with the thermostat setting and regulate furnace operation (or air conditioning) to match.

The steps in recognizing the signal cascade involved in negative feedback can be traced historically. While the recognition of infertility following ovary or testis removal occurred hundreds of years ago, we did not know until the 1930s that removal of the pituitary gland would result in ovarian and testicular morphological regression and lead to cessation of secretion of the steroids. Since removal of the pituitary gland also caused body growth to stop and caused regression of gonadal, thyroid, and adrenal function, the pituitary gland was initially dubbed the "conductor of the endocrine orchestra."

Carl Moore and Dorothy Price, working at the University of Chicago during the 1940s, showed that injection of ovarian extracts caused the pituitary to become smaller, paving the way for the understanding of negative feedback. Finally, the increasing number of examples of environmental influences such as the light:dark ratio and temperature, which could also regulate the pituitary via its connections to the brain, led to the present concept of joint regulation of the pituitary by feedback from the target organs such as the ovary and by signals from the environment acting via the brain. This interacting environment–brain-pituitary-gonadal relationship–has been the focus of my research.

ॐॐ

How do we study whether this type of regulation operates in controlling the reproductive cycle?

The observation that removal of the gonads stops all manifestations of reproduction led scientists to attempt, and then succeed, in identifying and purifying the steroid sex hormones, estradiol and testosterone. Removal of the anterior pituitary gland by itself accomplished the same end as gonadal removal and led to gonadal morphological regression, which suggested another link. Finally, it was shown that when the gonads were removed, the pituitary actually increased secretion of LH and FSH. This increase could be inhibited by injection of natural or artificially synthesized steroids.

This is the experimental basis of the action of oral contraceptives, which block pituitary secretion of LH. These experiments gradually led to the concept that the negative feedback by gonadal hormones provided the clue to the pituitary regarding how much LH and FSH should be secreted. Yet another link was added when it was shown that if the pituitary were disconnected from the brain, it stopped secreting LH and FSH. There proved to be another hormone, Gonadotropin Releasing Hormone (GnRH), from the brain, which regulated gonadotropin secretion from the pituitary gland.

Figure 5.1 illustrates the cascade of signals linking the environment to the anterior pituitary gland and the pituitary gland to the rest of the body. I have found these diagrams quite useful in teaching endocrinology, as well as in designing and interpreting experiments.

My interest in these models stems directly from my graduate student days. The ratio of light to dark (day length or photoperiod), temperature, stressful signals like predators, or food supply can each serve as signals to the brain via the sensory receptors in the body. Groups of nerve cells in the bottom part of the brain (the hypothalamus) synthesize and secrete peptide factors into the set of blood vessels called the "portal system," which flows directly to the pituitary, bathing pituitary cells with signals regulating pituitary secretions. Corticotropin Releasing Factor (CRF), secreted when an animal or human being detects danger in the environment, stimulates the corticotropic cells in the pituitary to secret Adrenocorticotropic Hormone (ACTH), which in turn stimulates the adrenal cortex to release cortisol, the stress hormone. Likewise, thyrotropin releasing factor (TRF) stimulates the release of thyroid stimulating hormone (TSH) from pituitary cells, which in turn causes synthesis and secretion of thyroxin from the thyroid.

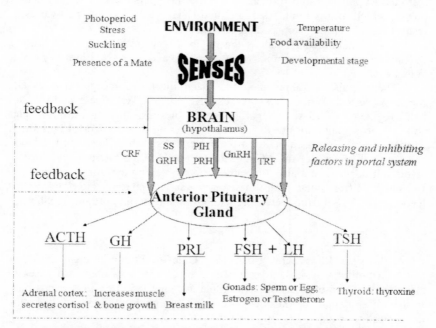

Figure 5.1. Cascade of signals linking the environment to the anterior pituitary gland and the pituitary gland to the rest of the body. (See Appendix A for details.)

The pituitary secretion of prolactin, necessary for synthesis of milk by breast tissue, is regulated by an inhibiting factor or Prolactin Inhibiting Hormone (PIH) and a releasing factor or Prolactin Releasing Hormone (PRH) from the hypothalamus.

The "lactation reflex" is instructive in looking at the complex signal cascade. When a mammalian infant or pup suckles, touch receptors in the nipple send a neural signal via the spinal cord to the brain in a pathway, which ends in the hypothalamus. In the absence of suckling, dopamine (prolactin inhibiting factor) prevents prolactin release; suckling inhibits dopamine secretion; thus prolactin release occurs and milk synthesis takes place.

Muscle and bone growth require release of growth hormone from the pituitary gland; its release is the net result of an inhibiting (SS-somatostatin) and a stimulating factor or hormone (GRH) from the hypothalamus. Gonadotropin-releasing hormone (GnRH) from the hypothalamus stimulates LH and FSH release from the pituitary.

In prepubertal mammals, including human beings, GnRH secretion is very low, as are LH and FSH, and the gonads are immature and not secreting steroids. At puberty, some process in the brain triggers the secretion of GnRH pulses, which results in pulses of LH and FSH, which turn on the ovaries or testes to start secreting sex-specific steroids.

In seasonal breeders such as sheep, GnRH release is present only during the breeding season (autumn in sheep); thus LH and FSH secretion only occur at that time.

The truly glorious thing about the system illustrated in Figure 1 is its self-regulatory aspect. While stress causes CRF and ACTH release and cortisol helps regulate against such negative aspects of stress such as cardiovascular collapse, it is important not to just keep secreting these powerful hormones. Cortisol itself serves as a brake to the system. As cortisol levels in the blood rise, cortisol suppresses the ACTH-secreting cells in the pituitary and cortisol levels fall back. Essentially, the same kind of braking system works to keep LH and FSH from continuing to rise (estrogen, testosterone, and progesterone feedback) and TSH from increasing without limit (thyroid hormone feedback).

⁖⁖

I love the story Lewis Braverman, then Chief of Endocrinology, Diabetes, and Nutrition at Boston University Medical Center, tells about the cases of "hamburger thyrotoxicosis" in Minnesota during 1985. This mysterious public health epidemic turned out to be solved using an understanding of the principles in the diagram in Figure 1.

A number of residents of the tri-state area of Minnesota, South Dakota, and Iowa developed a serious hyperthyroid condition, suggesting that their thyroids were secreting too much thyroid hormone. But they showed no goiters, which would be expected to accompany overactive thyroids. A group of Boston thyroidologists went west, convinced that the local doctors didn't know how to palpate goiters. But they found that, indeed, the patients did not have enlarged thyroid glands.

A sensitive clinical test for hypersecretion of the thyroid is to give radioactive iodine in a small quantity and then place a Geiger counter over the neck and count the uptake of iodine, which is elevated in the hyperthyroidism due to high TSH levels. Well, these patients had low uptake! Given this information and understanding the feedback relationship among TSH, TRF, and thyroxin, they guessed that somehow thyroid hormone was coming from outside the thyroid, since the iodine uptake test showed that TSH levels were low, and the thyroid wasn't incorporating iodine into hormone.

The public health officers went from house to afflicted house and looked at everything in the freezers and refrigerators. Their common finding was ground beef that had come from a local abattoir. It turned out that the workers who collected muscle for the ground beef had begun adding the strap muscle from the neck to the collection vats, and with it came the thyroid gland! Examined microscopically, the meat proved to contain thyroid cells, which contained large amounts of hormone. Score one for making and utilizing feedback diagrams.

కావ

A major interest of mine as an endocrinologist has been what makes reproductive hormones cycle, instead of being regulated to a steady level like the thyroid hormones.

Cycle lengths vary in mammals from four days between ovulations in rats and mice, to about twenty-eight days between ovulations in monkeys and human beings, and to a year between ovulations in sheep, cattle, and horses. Other mammals do not ovulate at all unless the cervix is stimulated in the act of coitus; these copulation-induced ovulators include the domestic cat, the rabbit, and the camel.

For every mammal, the release of pulses of a GnRH-like molecule is responsible for causing release of LH and FSH from the pituitary. Pulses of LH and FSH reach the ovary, bind to receptors in the granulosa cells surrounding the ovum (the follicle), and cause the cells to secrete estrogen and to divide, making the follicle grow. Some progesterone may also be secreted. The estrogen reaches the pituitary and hypothalamus.

In the cycling mammals, like the rodents and the primates, the rising estrogen levels trigger the release of a large amount of GnRH, which causes a major surge of LH release from the pituitary. The steroid hormones estrogen and progesterone also act on brain centers, which induce mating behavior in the female mammal.

The preovulatory LH surge causes the follicle(s) to rupture, releasing the egg into the oviduct; estrogen secretion is terminated and progesterone secretion increases. If mating and fertilization do not occur, the lowered estrogen levels permit GnRH pulses to increase, releasing estrogen from another follicle, which begins to grow and the cycle starts over again. Seasonal breeders like domestic cattle show very low GnRH release throughout most of the year. In the autumn, when the ratio of light to dark decreases, GnRH pulses increase. This stimulates the pituitary to release LH and FSH, which causes follicles to grow and release steroids. Mating behavior occurs, as well as ovulation.

In coitus-induced ovulators, GnRH pulses cause follicular steroid secretion when the light:dark ratio increases, as in the spring. The steroid by itself cannot lead to the large GnRH surge. The steroids induce mating behavior, and when coitus occurs, a reflex from the cervix to the hypothalamus takes place causing the GnRH surge to cause an LH surge from the pituitary, which causes ovulation.

I find these differences in timing of ovulation fascinating adaptations to the different environments in which mammals live. Of course, I first met them in Runner's lab in Maine, where I learned that rodents such as mice, rats, and hamsters, in addition to ovulating at four-day intervals, also ovulate within twenty-four hours of birth.

ớ∼ଙ

Even though I am not a physician, I have been involved, as are many basic scientists, with advisory committees that deal with human endocrinology. This includes work on psychosomatic issues of stress and adrenal hormones, examination of the possible role of oral contraceptives in breast cancer, and the etiology of polycystic ovary disease. Working with real world situations involving human beings has been sobering to me. In addition, I have had a dachshund with hypothyroidism, a Siamese cat with diabetes, and a Westie with hypoparathyroidism, putting me into the position of helping diagnose my house pets.

ớ∼ଙ

In January 2001, the editors of *Endocrinology* asked me to write an introduction to the July 2001 issue, reviewing the translation of reproductive endocrinology to reproductive health in the twentieth century.

I focused on five discoveries: (1) The development of oral contraceptives, based on discovery of the negative feedback of ovarian steroid hormones on the pituitary gonadotropins; (2) The invention of the radioimmunoassay by Rosalyn Sussman Yalow and Solomon Berson, which permitted close tracking of the hormones in the blood; (3) The demonstration of close control of the brain over the pituitary gland, which demonstrated that our minds are as much in control of our hormones as our hormones are in control of our minds; (4) The research on hormone receptors, which has permitted use of methopristone (RU486) as a safe, non-invasive abortifacient, tamoxifen as an antiestrogen in some cases of breast cancer, and GnRH antagonists, used in prostate cancer; and (5) Discovery of endocrine disruptors, which are environmental contaminants resulting from pesticides, which can act as estrogens on animals and human beings.

These have probably been responsible for feminization of male animals in the wild (like alligators in Florida) and have been blamed for possibly declining sperm counts in human beings.

As we enter the twenty-first century, endocrinology has shifted drastically from what it was when I entered the field in mid-twentieth century. It has become much more cellular and molecular, the result of increasingly sophisticated technology.

Another major shift, which is becoming increasingly important, is the realization that the cells in the classic organs called glands, which were shown to secrete the blood-borne hormones, are not the only cells in the body which secrete substances into the bloodstream to act on cells at a distance. The kidney is known to secrete erythropoietin, which stimulates red blood cell synthesis; fat cells secrete leptin, key in informing the brain of the amount of fat stored in the body; and the liver secretes insulin-like growth factor, crucial in enabling growth hormone to act. This is only a partial list of circulating substances that endocrinologists will be studying during the present century. I am envious of them.

Reproductive endocrinology has played an important role in human and veterinary medicine, as well as in the meat and dairy industries. It is particularly controversial because of its subject matter and, like all of the other sciences, exists within a social background.

Sex and reproduction are particularly meaningful to individuals; paternity, religious taboos, and societal ideas about appropriate behavior all are hot-button issues. Contraception is acceptable to some religions but not to others. Abortion "rights" depend on timing of abortion vis-à-vis the age of the fetus and on the societal milieu.

It is no coincidence that women in Japan were not given access to oral contraceptives by the legislature until Sildenafil (Viagra) was imported, at which point the women rose up and demanded the pill. Some religions permit in vitro fertilization, while others do not.

Surrogate mothering, in which a woman carries a fetus for another couple regardless of whether she has provided the egg, pleases some people when the surrogate is the sister of the eventual mother, but not when the surrogate is simply earning money.

PMS (premenstrual syndrome) has been cited as a permissible excuse for murder in some areas and for not electing women to responsible positions in government, while many scientists doubt its existence. The use of hormone replacement therapy with estrogen and progesterone, to alleviate symptoms of menopause, such as hot flashes and osteoporosis, has aroused protests from some women's groups against the pharmaceutical industry and fostered the growth of the unregulated supplement industry.

෯෧

When I taught my freshman seminar called "Menstrual Cycle: Fact and Fiction" at Northwestern, I required students to write a series of essays on topics that changed from year to year. The course was essentially an introduction to human reproduction, which covered the basic endocrinology of reproduction and some of the social factors behind taboos. We also discussed contraception and sexual diseases. One essay topic, however, remained the same from year to year. We talked about the often inaccurate media perspective on issues of sex and reproduction. Each student had to bring in a relevant story from a newspaper or news magazine and critique the accuracy of the story and its interpretations. Students never had a problem finding appropriate (or rather inappropriate) stories, or understanding the fallacies and the sound bites.

෯෧

Where is the field going that I have worked in for so many years? A lot of work is concentrating on the input to the GnRH neuron itself. What are the signals and pathways in the brain that link these neurons to stress, body fat, and light-dark environment?

Work on pituitary gonadotrope cells focuses on the ways in which the GnRH signal frequency acts on mRNA for the subunits of LH and FSH proteins. The role of transcription factors (local intracellular proteins) that help regulate LH and FSH synthesis in response to steroids and GnRH are being studied. Pituitary cells synthesize and secrete activin, and this local activin is a major factor in FSH synthesis and secretion. What regulates activin and how does it interact with GnRH and steroids?

The role of environmental light-dark signals on reproduction and many other physiologic functions has also moved to another level. Several genes have been identified which alter the ability of the biological clock in mammals to synchronize with the environment and have broad effects on the organism. My colleague, Joe Takahashi, has cloned a gene "clock" which regulates the periodicity of many 24-hour functions in the mouse. A mutation in this gene changes the timing of release of the preovulatory release of LH as well as changing the timing of release of other hormones.

A major direction reproductive endocrinology has taken is the unraveling of the relationship between a hormone, its cell receptor, and cell function. There turn out to be at least two, if not more, types of estrogen and progesterone receptors.

The receptors for the steroids and LH and FSH have been cloned and sequenced. These findings have not only advanced our fundamental knowledge of the reproductive cycle but have led to new treatments for breast and prostate cancer, and of course, they have led to a whole new industry: the infertility treatment field.

Reproduction is in the news nowadays, for better or for worse, with multiple pregnancies, RU486 abortions, stem cell harvesting, cloning, and surrogate mothering—all the centers of controversy. It seems more important than ever for women to be part of the scientific community since so frequently the fruits or burdens of new science fall on them.

❧

Thoughtless application of endocrinology and its related fields can have dire consequences. At the root of the current stem cell controversy lie a number of paradoxes, with which society as a whole, not just scientists, must wrestle.

Stem cells from discarded embryos might be used to make a pancreas transplant for a child dying from diabetes, an application with which I agree. Or, growth hormones can be administered to a somewhat short young boy with normal growth hormones levels, risking the effects of overdose because his parents recognize that our society prefers taller men, an application with which I disagree.

Athletes of all ages bulk up their muscles with illegally obtained steroid hormone or growth hormone despite the known danger of sterility with the former treatment or diabetes with the latter treatment.

Cloning has been touted for some human beings (of the wealthier sort) in case of possible eventual organ failure (the spare parts solution). (For a particularly poignant description of a world in which this kind of cloning is permissible, see Kazuo Ishiguro's novel, *Never Let Me Go*.)

I learned nothing in endocrinology classes to prepare me to determine the ethical and moral solutions to these issues. In 1998, I was asked by the senior class at Northwestern to give the graduation address at convocation. I did and titled it, "Trust Me, I'm a Scientist." In it I urged them, as they went through their lives, to think for themselves about issues, even scientific ones, and to run like hell whenever they queried a scientist about the effects of a new experiment who replied, "Trust me, I'm a scientist."

Study Questions

(1) Neena writes, "I learned nothing in endocrinology classes to prepare me to determine the ethical and moral solutions to these issues."
  - Discuss what you believe she meant by this statement and whether you think she believes it to be completely true.

(2) As you go through the rest of this book, reflect on whether this chapter made a difference in your understanding of the science Neena did in her laboratory.
  - Or, if you skipped this chapter, discuss why.

Neena at microscope, Northwestern University, 1975.

Allen Lein, UCSD, 1983.

Neena weighing rat, 1971.

Six

DEFINING MY SCIENCE
AND EXPANDING MY LIFE

But you may say, we asked you to speak about women and fiction - what has that to do with a room of one's own?. . . All I could do was offer you an opinion upon one minor point- a woman must have money and a room of her own if she is to write fiction . . .

Virginia Woolf
"A Room of One's Own"

I started my position as an instructor in the Department of Physiology at the University of Illinois in January 1953. Unbelievable now, I was hired because the only woman in the department had become pregnant and the department Chair, George Wakerlin, felt it "inappropriate for a woman in an advanced stage of pregnancy to lecture to medical students." This was my first taste of the problems women face in academia.

That attitude was fairly typical of the times, but Wakerlin was particularly concerned about appearances. So, she went on leave and I took her place. (After the baby came, she took a different job.)

When I talked to Wakerlin, a prominent researcher in the field of hypertension, at my initial interview, he said he was hiring me into a non-tenure track position but would move me to an assistant professorship if I "performed well."

Hiring women in non-tenure track positions was characteristic of the times. Sad to say, it frequently happens still in the twenty-first century. As I think back on it now, from the vantage point of a former department chair and former dean, it seems appropriate that I was hired into a non-tenure track position; I had no track record on my own at that point. But unfortunately, it still happens to women even after a postdoctoral fellowship and a number of independent publications.

At my first faculty meeting, Wakerlin actually said, "Dr. Schwartz, will you pour the tea?" I was the only women in the room, of course! I did it, but I suggested that the task be rotated in the future. He never asked again.

❧❧

I liked my colleagues on the faculty of the University of Illinois, who, except for the Chair, were congenial, helpful, and friendly and were on a first-name basis with each other. Wakerlin never addressed any of us by our first names. I was always "Dr. Schwartz." He assigned me to teach nerve-muscle physiology to the medical students, and I taught an entire quarter course of physiology on my own to the pharmacy students. In addition, I taught in the labs for both classes of students. This was a heavy teaching load for a faculty member of a medical school basic science department, where it was expected, of course, that one would also carry out an independent, funded research program; but I managed.

The students seemed to like my teaching and that was going well. In fact, several years later, I won a Golden Apple award for teaching from the medical students. I wrote my first research grant to NIH to continue the thyroid-nerve-muscle studies I had started in graduate school, and it was funded immediately. With that, I began putting together my very first lab.

ح‍م‍ص

After a year, I met with my chairperson and asked when I would be promoted to the rank of assistant professor, putting me on the tenure track. Since my teaching was going well and my research was funded, this should have happened without my having to request it. He hemmed and hawed and said he would consider it soon. His equivocation worried me, as well it should have.

But then tragedy struck in the Department. Al Schiller, a senior associate professor, who taught and did research in cardiovascular physiology, died suddenly while on a driving trip to California with his family to attend a professional meeting. The department needed someone to teach this aspect of physiology to the medical students during the next quarter. Wakerlin called me into his office, and after clearing his throat in his pompous way, asked if I could do this additional teaching. I hesitated. This is not my field, so the amount of additional preparation for my lectures would be enormous.

After a pause I replied, "Yes, if I am promoted to an assistant professorship"—and so I was. Was my assertiveness foolhardy? I guess it could have been, but it worked. I worked diligently to construct a new set of lectures while getting my lab going.

ح‍م‍ص

As a physiologist, as for most natural scientists not doing fieldwork, my laboratory was the crucial space at the university that I "owned," the center of my work. As long as a woman is working in someone else's space, she is not regarded by others as a truly independent scientist. This is a problem for many women in science who are not seen as independent. People assume that if you are in someone else's lab, you are being guided to do the lab director's work, even when this is not true.

When I had worked with Meredith Runner as an undergraduate at Bar Harbor, or with Allen Lein as a predoctoral student at Northwestern University Medical School, I understood that the lab was *not* mine. I carved out a comfortable niche, with instruments I could sequester, reagents I weighed out, or solutions I made up which were mine, but the lab per se was *not mine*.

I remember one day as a Master's student in 1949. I was standing in Allen's lab at the photometer about to measure a small amount of iodine using our very sensitive chemical reaction. The lab was old, and the ceilings were encrusted with accumulated dirt. As I stood at the photometer ready to go, a janitor entered with a ladder and said he needed to change a light bulb directly above where the photometer was. I asked if he could wait until I was finished; he asked me what I made in a year. I told him that I was making about $2,000; then he told me what he made (a good union wage). He said, "It is obvious who is more important to the university." With that said, he proceeded to change the light bulb. The accumulated dirt on the light fixture came raining down, ruining my experiment for that day.

•

I was excited and somewhat fearful when I allowed myself at Illinois to realize, "This space is mine! I have to order equipment, tables, balances, and surgical instruments, recruit graduate students and technicians, and raise money, but I can put the furniture, equipment, and glassware wherever I want!" The process was like furnishing a new apartment from scratch. I can still remember feeling exhilarated when I looked over my own lab space within the Department of Physiology. By that time, I had picked up many of the rituals of laboratory life at Bar Harbor and during my four and a half years as a graduate student at Northwestern, and I was ready to practice them on my own.

The space was small, but I knew what I needed to do to get going. It felt as though my life were starting at last. So I ordered the equipment needed to continue my thyroid/muscle experiments, and I was on my way.

NIH had awarded me enough money to buy a manufactured muscle stimulator instead of a homemade one like the one Allen and I had constructed at Northwestern, and an oscilloscope for observing the contractions, as well as money for rats and necessary supplies such as hormones and syringes. I began learning how to keep a budget and how to order supplies for a lab of my own.

•

Where do the people come from who work in your lab? One hires technicians with money from grants that come from outside the university. Once a scientist is more senior and has published widely, graduate students sometimes come to the university to work especially with you, having read your work or having been recommended by undergraduate advisors.

Other graduate students have come to University of Illinois or to North-western to join a particular graduate department program and have then become interested in our work and joined the lab.

But as a new faculty member at the medical school with no local track record, I started with some freshman medical students who wanted to work toward Master's degrees simultaneously while getting their medical degrees to gain research experience. Two of them who had liked my lectures started doing muscle experiments in my lab. They brought in a small radio, which they played while working. Although they kept the volume low, Wakerlin entered my lab one day when I was not around and told them it was "unprofessional" to listen to music while working; he directed them to shut it off.

When I came into the lab the next day, I discovered that they had plugged the output of the radio into a lab oscilloscope so they could "watch" the music on the small screen! I loved their rebelliousness and have always encouraged this kind of independence in my students. It is so much fun. For the rest of my career, I always played small radios and tape decks in my office and in the lab.

∾∾

To the non-scientist, a lab is a place for noisy Geiger counters, bubbling flasks, microscopes, and lab-coated silent scientists working in isolation. "A lonely career," some perceive it, which is a reason many women cite for not going into science. However, to see it as lonely is a mistaken impression. Countless interactions occur among lab personnel, some of which inevitably take place within the lab space, but others take place outside of it.

Intense interactions can take place in the lab over interpretations of what data mean and what should be the next experiment. Lab participants also talk a lot about movies they have seen, vacations, boyfriends and girlfriends, ambitions, and politics. Every lab I have ever seen or run has had a coffee pot or teapot readily available, and someone always makes sure hot water is available. We celebrate every birthday with cake and wine, and when someone defends a dissertation, we have a champagne party to which we also invite significant others.

∾∾

All of my first students started off working on the thyroid-muscle problem. I loved having young, eager students in the lab; they listened, asked questions, talked, and kept me hopping. We published several papers and my independent career was launched. I began the habit then of inviting my lab personnel to my house for meals and talk once a year or more. But at that time, I did not expect that eventually my lab would grow to the size it eventually became. In fact, I don't remember ever worrying about whether I would be successful as a scientist. I just did the work and the teaching and enjoyed it all. Certainly I never saw myself as an administrator in the future.

ঌৄৎ

A major problem gays experience in the work place, if they are not "out," which hardly anyone was in those days, is how to talk about your partner, as in, "So and so and I went to see a movie last night," or, "So and so and I are going to Cape Cod on a camping trip."

When a same sex partner is at home, called a "roommate," the lab is coming over for a potluck dinner and wants to see your apartment, and your place has only one bedroom with a large double bed, what do you say? I assume everyone figured it out, but hiding in this way takes a toll. I always felt afraid that my students would see me as a cardboard figure, with no personal life. Of course, as I stayed in my "closet," that is exactly what I showed them.

ঌৄৎ

While I was teaching and doing research at Illinois during those early years, I began to learn about the responsibilities and pleasures of mentoring graduate students and other trainees in the laboratory. One day, a doctoral candidate who had recently joined the lab from Hunter College in New York City, came into my office, shut the door, and began crying.

Student health services had notified her that she had a positive Kahn test, which could be indicative of a venereal disease. She came from a sheltered religious family and said that when she had told the young doctor that she had never had intercourse, he had smirked and said, "Really?"

I was outraged. I found out that a false positive test could result from immunization shots she had been given shortly before the Kahn test. That was what had happened. I called the head of health services and said I wanted this person fired. I told the story, and he was, indeed, fired. Unfortunately, the student was so traumatized that she dropped out of graduate school and went back to New York.

This incident early in my career as an advisor taught me how important being accessible to students in the lab about personal issues is as well as to mentor research problems. Over my long career, I have had students talk with me about personal contraception, crazy (literally) boyfriends, parents who urged them to quit graduate school, concern about symptoms of a possible sexually transmitted disease, and a prospective divorce. *In loco parentis.*

ঌৄৎ

Our research on the thyroid and nerve-muscle function was advancing, but I kept thinking about the research I had done on the pituitary-ovarian axis at the Jackson lab, where I inadvertently blocked ovulation by using Nembutal (pentobarbital) in the postpartum mice.

By the time I began seriously looking at the reproductive cycle instead of the thyroid during the late 1950s, John W. Everett of Duke and Charles H. Sawyer of UCLA had already published their classic studies showing that pentobarbital, an anesthetic which acts on the brain, could block ovulation in the cyclic rat.

Using the albino rat as a model species for research in female reproductive cycles began in 1921, when Joseph Long and Herbert Evans, at the University of California, published a monograph describing their observations on the events of the rat estrous cycle. They examined reproductive organ morphology, they weighed tissues and they looked at rat mating behavior. Utilizing what would be regarded as primitive technology today, examining vaginal cell samples microscopically every day, their remarkable work revealed a recurring four- or five-day cycle of events in the ovary, culminating in ovulation. They showed that it was possible to follow this timing by non-invasive external examination of the vagina without harming the animal in any way. The cervical or "Pap" smear, done on women to check for abnormal cell cytology possibly indicative of cervical cancer, and the use of cervical mucosa consistency to aid in the rhythm method of birth control are modern-day derivatives of this simple but ingenious technology.

Actually Long and Evans called the cycle "four and a half" days in length, and it was not until the discovery of the contribution of circadian, or 24-hour period timing, that we appreciated that ovulation per se took place either every four days or every five days in the rat.

Everett and Sawyer showed that under an alternating light-dark lighting schedule (lights on from 5 a.m. to 7 p.m.) for housing the rats, ovulation occurred a few hours after midnight on the evening between the days of proestrus and estrus. Freshly ovulated eggs are found in the oviducts on the next morning, called estrus.

Since the rat estrous cycle is the area in which I did most of my work subsequently, I want my reader to understand what I was doing. So bear with me while I expand on this topic. The specific experimental observations made by Everett and Sawyer were as follows: if they injected pentobarbital before 1 p.m. of the day of proestrus, the ovulation expected by the following morning was blocked. But if they delayed pentobarbital injection until 3 p.m., ovulation occurred normally by the following morning! Since the anesthetic was acting on the brain, this suggested that the brain was somehow stimulating the pituitary gland to release its ovulating hormone, LH, between 1 and 3 p.m.; anesthesia acting after that time could not prevent ovulation, since the LH had already been released.

It was already known that the latency between release of the LH surge into the blood and the ovarian ovulation response is about ten to twelve hours in both rodents and humans. Everett and Sawyer also saw that the blockade of ovulation that occurred with the earlier injection lasted a full twnety-four hours, even though the anesthesia only lasted two hours! What they had demonstrated was that a daily time-of-day signal from the brain was essential for the LH release from the pituitary gland.

These data clarified why my experiment at Bar Harbor as an undergraduate had not worked: the pentobarbital we were using as an anesthetic for pituitary surgery blocked LH release and ovulation by itself in the postpartum mouse! I was really excited by this demonstration of a "time keeping" biological device, by which one could predict precisely the time of day when a hormone was released from the pituitary gland, and I decided to focus on this LH release. This was a momentous decision, which guided my career in science for the next fifty years.

As I thought about it, I realized that Everett and Sawyer's blockade data could be interpreted in two different ways: (1) A time-of-day signal existed that originated in the nervous system *every day*, and LH was released every day, with ovulation taking place only on the one day out of four or five when the ovary contained mature follicles capable of responding with ovulation. (2)

On the other hand, while there was a time-of-day signal every day, as shown by the effects of PB blockade, LH release itself might *only* be occurring on the day of proestrus because *another* signal was necessary in addition, perhaps estrogen from the ovary, being secreted by the growing follicles. Hypothesis 1 said that the environment and brain were in total control, while Hypothesis 2 said that feedback from the ovary also played a major role in timing the four-day cycle.

It was obvious to us that we needed a more direct method than ovulation for measuring LH.

Luckily, a bioassay for LH, using the measurement of ascorbic acid in the primed immature rat ovary, had recently been developed by Al Parlow. The method was not sensitive enough for measuring LH in the blood, so we measured pituitary content of LH before 1 p.m. and after 3 p.m. every day during a normal cycle. We were hoping that when LH was secreted from the gland at proestrus, the content within it would at least temporarily fall. Indeed it did!

Pituitary content of LH dropped between the morning and the afternoon only on the day of proestrus! So we had shown that something in addition to time of day was operating to release the LH. The study that demonstrated this was published in the journal *Endocrinology* in 1962.

Delphine Bartosik, a medical student at the University of Chicago, worked with me on this study. She went on to become a gynecologist and a faculty member at Women's Medical College in Philadelphia, and I became a reproductive physiologist.

෧ඁ෧

On the personal front, Barbara had left Chicago for her new job, and I was living alone. I moved from the north side of Chicago to a new university apartment house right on the campus of the University of Illinois Medical School, on the southwest side of Chicago, near Cook County Hospital.

One of the male graduate students in the department, Bill, was an Army veteran about five years older than I. He began hanging around my lab when he wasn't working in his advisor's lab.

Mother called me once a week to see what was going on, and she always asked, "Are you dating?" Well, yes, but I was dating women I met at friends' houses. Mindful of my mother's weekly telephone questioning about my personal life, I began dating Bill, which pleased her no end. Although of course, this was an ethical faux pas, since faculty and students should not date. We did sleep together, and we managed to keep it away from the other faculty members (I think!), although some of the other doctoral students guessed. But after a while, we began detaching gradually from each other by mutual consent. I had enjoyed the sex, and the dating, but never felt the same "WOW" I felt with women. It was clearer than ever to me that I was lesbian, even though I still felt some anguish and guilt.

෧ඁ෧

As my salary increased, slowly, to be sure, I began to see a psychiatrist to talk about my guilt. Was it possible to change my sexual orientation? It wasn't, obviously. Interestingly, I also began seeing a dentist at the same time to repair my teeth, which had suffered from years of a bad diet as a student. The dentistry worked better than the psychiatry, although I began feeling a little less guilty about myself.

In August 1953, I drove home to Baltimore to attend my brother's wedding. On the day of Leon's wedding, the family received a phone call from Dad's brother Norton.

He said, "We think Mother has had a stroke."

As they were waiting for the doctor, I told Dad that I would go over to my uncle's to assess the situation. We learned that grandmother had suffered a minor stroke. I talked to the doctor, who assured me that it seemed under control. I called home and reassured Dad that he could stay for the ceremony. I said I would stay with Grandmother if nobody else were available.

My Uncle Norton said to me, "Why are you here? I didn't know you were interested in the family."

"Why do you think that?" I asked.

"Because you moved away from Baltimore."

Of course, two of his sons were also in Chicago, one a resident in medicine and the other a rabbi. His expectation was that a woman should stay home and take care of . . . what? Her parents? Her siblings? Fortunately, my own parents never said that to me, but his beliefs were typical of the times.

ॐॐ

On another of my annual trips back to Baltimore to visit my family, I attended a party thrown by a former lesbian buddy. There I met Jan, an elementary schoolteacher. She was somewhat gamin looking—cute as hell, with a warm personality. We liked each other right away. I had to go back to Chicago two days later but we went out for dinner and a drive on both those days. I returned to Chicago and we began a long-distance relationship, writing to each other and talking on the phone.

I bought a secondhand Rambler and drove east the next summer. I picked Jan up in Baltimore, and the two of us visited Cape Cod for two weeks, really enjoying each other's company. We relaxed around the beaches and slept together in various bed-and-breakfast places, always within the sound of the ocean.

My first visit to Provincetown, a local gay resort, was an eye-opener, revealing how closeted I had been. I had never been surrounded by so many overt homosexuals before, and I loved walking the streets with Jan, holding hands surrounded by so many people like us. After two weeks at the Cape, we drove back to Baltimore so I could drop her off at home before I headed back to the Midwest.

Jan decided she wanted to get away from Baltimore and her family, so she applied for a teaching position in Chicago. She landed one at a private school on the north side, so I moved to a larger second floor apartment in Chicago's Old Town. We lived there together for a number of years, first while she taught sixth grade, and then when she began working for a Master of Education degree at the University of Chicago.

Jan and I were doing well as a couple, working separately and living together. By that time, we had accumulated many like-minded friends, and began socializing with other lesbians and straights.

After a few years, we spent a great month traveling and camping around the west, visiting Mesa Verde and Yellowstone. One summer, we camped in New England on our way north to visit Bar Harbor and were nearly drowned when a major rain storm left over from a tropical storm in the Caribbean flooded the camp ground. Luckily, we had camped on the side of a hill. But the water began rising up the hill where our tent was, and we had to struggle to take the tent down and fold up the sopping wet tent and all our gear and get it back into the trunk. We were frightened listening to the radio that day and hearing about the people who had been drowned while camping.

When we arrived on Mt Desert Island, and I saw the Jackson Lab again, rebuilt from the fire in 1947 and now much larger, I found I had tears in my eyes. Jan and I camped in Acadia National Park, bathing in the ice cold lake, enjoying each other's company in an almost deserted campground.

I discovered that a meeting was scheduled at the lab, which I attended. The question being debated was whether the summer lab experience was worthwhile, since most students' experiments wound up just as indeterminate as the two I had done with Meredith Runner.

I spoke up at this point and said that had not mattered; it was the most exhilarating time of my life and permanently imprinted me with the joys of doing science. Other former students who were visiting said much the same. In 2006, the Jackson Lab was in its fifty-second year of the college summer school program, still going strong.

ॐ

Back in Chicago, a new faculty member had joined the Department of Psychiatry at the University of Illinois, with a joint appointment in the Physiology department: Ralph Gerard. Ralph was a major international figure in neurophysiology, and he brought with him a large group of less senior colleagues. I began attending their exhilarating seminars, which dealt with nerve conduction, neuron conditioning, and brain-behavior issues.

By that time, my interest in the pituitary gland and its relation to the nervous system was growing, and I found talking with Gerard's group much more exciting than talking with my own colleagues in physiology. It was becoming obvious that my research interests were refocusing on communication issues in the body. The endocrine and nervous systems were beginning to blend together with the discovery of how the part of the brain nearest the pituitary gland, the hypothalamus, was regulating the pituitary gland by means of the small peptide molecules, called the releasing factors (as shown above Chapter Five, Figure 1).

Ralph asked me to come to his office one day and suggested I switch my tenure line to the Department of Psychiatry from Physiology, but I was reluctant to do so despite being increasingly bothered by the stiffness and formality of my chairperson and the pall this cast on all of the younger department faculty members. (Strangely, many years later, when Ralph was gone, I did become a member of the Psychiatry department, heading up a laboratory of neuroendocrinology.)

ॐ

Several of us junior faculty in physiology had invented a "Wakerlin" unit of pomposity. One unit was equal to one hundredth of Wakerlin's pomposity level, the equivalent of the average boring male English club member.

A particularly vivid memory that stands out was the afternoon Wakerlin came to visit a teaching lab with medical students to see how things were going. One of the other assistant professors, Roger, was sitting atop of one of the lab benches surrounded by ten eager sophomores. He was answering questions about an experiment they had just completed. Wakerlin called Roger aside and told him not to sit on a lab bench while talking with students since doing so was not dignified.

&~<

In September 1957, Roy Grinker, the well known researcher and Director of the Psychosomatic and Psychiatric Institute (PPI) at Michael Reese Hospital on Chicago's south side, contacted Ralph Gerard saying he needed a physiologist interested in neurobiology and endocrinology to run the research laboratories at PPI. Ralph recommended me. Dr Grinker, who wanted someone to work with his team of research physicians on a project studying the relationship between clinical depression and adrenal cortical secretion (blood cortisol levels), interviewed me. He promised me a good raise, replacement of the equipment I had at Illinois, and a salary for a technician for my research, as well as funding to hire someone to supervise measurements for the clinical research program.

This opportunity to increase the size of my personal basic research program and to participate in clinical research was too tempting to turn down. I also liked and respected Grinker; he had a good sense of humor, was not pompous, and was doing good work, I thought, on psychosomatic illnesses.

I accepted the position. I retained my assistant professor rank at Illinois as a courtesy appointment. By that time (September 1957), I was teaching a graduate course in endocrinology, which I continued to do without pay while I was at PPI. I was willing to do this because I wanted to continue contact with graduate students, something difficult to do at the hospital.

Doing research in a hospital setting was very different from an academic setting, even in a medical school, and it was a very interesting opportunity to hone my skills in the application of physiology to medicine. The research team consisted of psychiatrists (some of whom were residents in training), psychologists, a biochemist, a statistician, sociologists, and me, the only card-carrying endocrinologist. But I quickly met the other endocrinologists, basic and clinical, working elsewhere at the hospital, many of whom were a good deal more experienced than I was. We met together informally in a weekly "Endocrine Club," which gave me my first glimpse of how much it can mean to be able to talk easily and frequently to others in a similar field. At each meeting, one of us presented a talk on data or on plans for the next experiment. Our exchanges were lively, challenging, and fun, and I learned so much from them.

Participating in the human experiments was interesting. These utilized a control group comprised of volunteers and another group of depressed patients hospitalized not at PPI but at a public psychiatric facility. The studies consisted of raising the anxiety level of the patients (by the use of stressful films or implied threats of electric shocks from an EEG machine), and then measuring the blood levels of the adrenal stress hormones. Although I do not believe these patients were harmed, this kind of experiment would not be possible today because of, fortunately, more stringent human experimentation laws and clear human "informed consent" requirements.

҈

While I was moving ahead in my own and the group's research, Jan discovered a lump in her breast and went to our gynecologist. I went with her. He recommended surgery. On New Year's Eve 1959, she went into surgery, and a diagnosis of cancer was confirmed. While she was still in the operating room, they performed a mastectomy. I sat alone in her room waiting for her surgeon to let me know what had happened and then beside her bed all night after calling one of her sisters in Baltimore.

It was snowing outside, and as I stood at the window watching the world grow white, I felt lonelier than I had ever felt before in my life. I knew that this catastrophic event would change our lives. But at least Jan's surgeon was willing to talk with me. One of the problems homosexual couples have is that physicians refuse to talk about their patients with someone who is not a "relative."

Jan was an athlete, a champion tennis player, and she immediately began doing physical therapy. Remarkably, she returned to teaching only a few weeks later. Tragically, however, exactly a year later, she discovered a lump in her other breast, and on New Year's Eve, she was again in surgery. This time, a sister of Jan's came to be there for the surgery, but in a very real way, I was lonelier than the year before because this time, I wasn't the one the physicians consulted at all.

The following year was hard for both of us. For Jan, there was the threat of the cancer recurring, although no metastases had been found in her lymph nodes on either occasion. Being with me, with my own anxiety about her health, made putting it to one side difficult for Jan. Her method for dealing with the "incidents," as she called them was to move ahead with some degree of denial about of how much losing her breasts meant to her.

As for me, I found it hard to put the nightmarish years aside and resume our old lives together. My depression mounted, as did my anxiety. Having a survivor's support group to talk with would have helped, but as far as I know, no such groups existed at that time.

Finally, we decided to live apart; we found two apartments in the neighborhood across the street from each other. With this degree of separation, but closeness still, we both began to reconstruct our lives.

Through some mutual friends, Jan met a woman physician who lived in the Boston area. Jan left Chicago to enroll in the doctoral program in education at Harvard. She obtained an EdD and taught psychology at the University of Baltimore for a number of years. We stayed in touch for many years after this.

In retrospect, I believe Jan's family must have carried one of the BRAC genes, which we later learned can result in ovarian and breast cancer. One of her sisters developed ovarian cancer later, and another sister also suffered from breast cancer.

৵৽৹

Eventually I became involved with Rue Bucher, who was, at that time a so-ciologist working at PPI. In addition to our group investigating psychosomat-ic interrelationships at PPI, another research group of sociologists, which was interacting with psychiatrists, was studying mental health professionals and settings. Rue was one of the sociologists working on the project while com-pleting a doctoral dissertation at the University of Chicago. We met in the course of working in the same building and soon recognized that we were both lesbian.

Rue and I were each living alone at the time, I on the north side of Chi-cago, and she in an apartment building near Michael Reese Hospital on the south side of Chicago. During an office Christmas party, we finally began talking with each other (those office Christmas parties!), and she invited me to a party on New Year's Eve. I said yes, and we went together, liked each other, and began dating. We fell in love.

In 1961, Rue and I found an apartment on the near north side of Chica-go, and launched a relationship that lasted for nearly twenty years. Our perso-nalities were very different; I am fairly outgoing and can be very boisterous, while Rue tended to be a bit shy and quiet in most social situations. She was great to talk with, as she was thoughtful, insightful, and had a quiet sense of the absurdity in life. We were a good match.

Rue's basic research interest concerned how trainees in the health fields developed into professionals. I had never thought about this as a focus for research, but it seemed to be a fascinating and important topic.

I knew I did not want to be a graduate advisor like my boss at Johns Hopkins, Curt Richter, but wanted to be like Meredith and Allen, my advisors at Bar Harbor and Northwestern University.

Talking with Rue about her studies on psychiatry residents and bioche-mistry graduate students was delightful; I found it very valuable for me per-sonally. At the same time, she learned from me about how biologists formulate their scientific problems and how we learn our science, which helped her in interpreting some of her own data. I have always been grateful for what I learned from her and my other colleagues at PPI about social/professional relationships. It has made a tremendous difference to me as I have taken on broader challenges in administration.

കൈ

While I was still working at Michael Reese Hospital, the first International Congress of Endocrinology took place in Copenhagen during July 1960. My lab had just started adapting the "ovarian ascorbic acid depletion" bioassay for LH to measure the hormone in the pituitary gland during the rat estrous cycle. We had the results I described previously showing that the pituitary content of LH dropped after the morning of the day of proestrus before ovulation took place. This was the first application of this bioassay method to a biological problem, and it was significant because it indicated that the bioassay was sensitive enough to be useful during the cycle. I sent in an abstract of the study for presentation at the congress and it was accepted.

I was excited about the meeting in Copenhagen, and since I had never been to Europe, I also wanted to see London and Paris while I was there. Rue couldn't come with me because she was writing her doctoral dissertation. So I went off on the big adventure myself, staying in hotels I found in London and Paris in the book *Europe on Five Dollars a Day*.

London was an Anglophilic pilgrimage for me. I found the city delightful—just what I had expected. As we flew over London to land at Gatwick, I could see the city spread beneath me. I had to see and do everything, from Madame Tussaud's to the Tower of London, from Trafalger Square to the Thames. I took a boat trip down to Hampton Court Palace and spent a delicious day walking the grounds and going through the maze. I visited the Tate and the British Museum. I bought cheap seats at the theaters and saw plays nearly every night. I wallowed in its familiar unfamiliarity, walked the streets of Soho, looking at the gay bars from the outside, took a train to Bath and Jane Austen and to Oxford and Dorothy Sayers and walked a day with Mrs. Dalloway in St. James Park.

I was lonely and didn't talk with many people, but that didn't seem to matter. I reveled in the experience, and then I flew to Paris. I missed Rue and my lab, but I did write to her about everything and received two letters from her at the American Express office, telling me about her time in Door County, Wisconsin, where she had rented a cabin to do her writing.

കൈ

Paris on my own was a city of culture and wickedness, of the *Well of Loneliness*, Natalie Barney, and Notre Dame. I put aside thoughts of Copenhagen—my straight world, which, in 1960, was totally separate from the me I was seeking in Paris.

Staying in a cheap hotel on the Left Bank, I began my search for the Paris I hoped to find. I had coffee at *Les Deux Magots*, found the house where Gertrude Stein and Alice Toklas held their salons, and walked up to Montmartre to see the cathedral, the city of Paris, and, of course, Pigalle.

In Chicago, I had gone to gay bars and bought a glass of beer and watched, too scared or shy to approach anyone. But my god, Paris was the mother lode, the center of gayness. Hadn't I read all about it? So I wandered, looking openly at famous buildings and covertly at other women.

I signed up for a bus tour to Chartres. The American Express bus was full of American women, and I was disdainful of these chattering females. At lunch, five of us were seated together. We talked about where we were from (Peoria; Athens, Georgia; Denver; Chicago; and Columbus, Ohio) and where we were going. I mentioned that I had just come from London.

"Good," Athens said, "my husband told me to go to London, but I don't know what to do there. Can you tell me what I should see?"

"Nothing," I said snobbishly, "there is nothing to see there."

We climbed back on the bus and headed toward Paris.

I had noticed another woman who had kept to herself during the trip; about fifty, dressed in an upscale wool suit, wrapped with a fox fur, and wearing a smart hat. When we emerged from the bus on the Right Bank I found her waiting for me.

"Hello," she said in a drawling Australian accent, "would you like to have dinner with me Saturday night?"

"Yes," I said "yes."

She asked where I was staying and then said she would come over in a taxi to pick me up. Could I suggest a Left Bank restaurant? I did and then I left to walk back to my hotel, feeling both apprehensive and high. I was living at last! During the next few days, I continued to see the sights, with Saturday night always in the back of my mind.

❧❧

Coming out of the Louvre one afternoon, I sat on the encircling stone wall, resting my feet. What did I look like as I sat or walked around Paris dressed in a short sleeve blouse, a cotton skirt, and a knapsack with my camera, a guide book, an umbrella and a novel? My hair was medium length, I wore glasses, and I was clearly an American academic in my thirties.

A woman in her 50s came out of the museum and sat down near me, sighing heavily. I glanced at her and saw that she was obviously another American academic, dressed the same way I was. Yes, she taught Medieval History at a college in a western state and her name was Agnes. We talked for a while and when I told her I was about to visit the Cluny Museum; she told me she would come with me as a guide since this was her academic area. She was indeed a wonderful guide. We decided to have dinner together, and gradually, as she talked about her home and work, it became obvious that she was living with another academic, a female professor of English. Well, this was Paris wasn't it? We spent the next day together, visiting Sainte Chappelle, and toward the end of the day, we decided to share dinner again. I was getting unkempt and wanting to wash my hair. She had a private shower, which I did not, so she invited me over to take a shower.

I was not absolutely sure what else that invitation entailed. But that was all there was to it. I brought some clean clothes over to her hotel and took my welcome shower.

We went to dinner that night and attended the Bastille Day parade the next day. As we stood waiting in the crowd, my cheap camera broke; I missed the chance to capture Le Grande Charles marching in front.

This was the beginning of a warm, platonic friendship, which lasted a long, long time. Agnes and I saw each other during subsequent summers in Paris, Oxford, and in Evanston, with her partner and Rue.

বচ্ব

Saturday night, my Australian acquaintance came for me at my cheap hotel, and we walked around to Boul Mich to eat outside at a sidewalk café. She ordered a bottle of wine and talked about what she was doing in Paris alone. Her husband was a sheep farmer in Queensland, and each winter she left the ranch to summer in Europe. She bought Parisian clothes and visited art museums. I suspect she also had lesbian affairs.

As we sat there, she picked up my hand from the table where I was fidgeting with a cigarette and said, "What long fingers you Americans have." She then invited me to go with her to Pigalle to a "nice little bar" for some dancing. My stomach lurched. All of my veneer of sophistication and worldliness fell away. I was too frightened to accept her offer. So much for my spirit of adventure. I stood up and told her I was leaving Paris the next morning for Copenhagen, and that I needed to pack. She looked at me quizzically. I hailed a cab for her. She went back to her hotel and I walked back to mine, where I was already packed for my next day trip.

বচ্ব

So I flew to Copenhagen, abandoning my private life, giving my paper, and hearing many others. It was a successful meeting for a young scientist; my paper went well, I met many eminent scientists, and heard plenty of good science. In a way, this meeting launched me. Getting ahead in academia is measured by advancing through the ranks, increasing salaries, and moving into committees that actually do important things at a university. This is the same in science and in non-science areas. Most important, however, is becoming recognized for one's research outside the university. This depends mostly on doing excellent research, but networking matters as well. Sometimes being in the right place at the right time makes a difference too.

Before I had left Chicago for London, Elizabeth, a woman with whom I worked at the time at Michael Reese, had told me that her Aunt Lizzie was the wife of Gregory Pincus, the father of the birth control pill. Elizabeth knew that Lizzie Pincus was going to be in London at the same time as I, before she headed off to Copenhagen to meet her husband at the same meeting I would also be attending. Elizabeth's sister lived in London; she wrote to her about me. The family entertained me in London, and I had the opportunity to meet Mrs. Pincus. When we shared a cab coming back from dinner with her niece, I told her that I was going to Copenhagen for the meeting.

"Oh," she said, "how nice. Pinky and I are giving a party. Please come."

I knew "Pinky" was president of the congress, and told myself I should not go, because she was just being nice to a young, insignificant scientist. But as I walked into the meeting in Copenhagen, Pincus himself approached me at the meeting and invited me! Needless to say, I went to the party and for the first time, I met the international "power" elite in endocrinology.

As I look back on this, I realize, of course, that I should never have considered *not* going to the party, since these serendipitous meetings and invitations lead to success and are crucial for women in science who need to learn how to take advantage of them. Ironically, seven years after that meeting, Pincus died, and I was asked to give the first lecture at the Laurentian Hormone Conference honoring him.

❧❦

After that visit to Europe and the meeting, I steadily moved along in my career, continuing to live my life split into two component parts. I have been back to Paris many times since 1960, but no one has ever again lifted my hand to admire my "long American fingers."

Study Questions

(1) Neena was hired as instructor in the Department of Physiology at the University of Illinois because her predecessor became pregnant. She states this was her first taste of the problems women face in academia.
- Discuss ways in which woman (in this instance, for example) cause their own problems in academia and the work world.
- Discuss which, if any, complaints are valid.

(2) In this chapter, Neena says that she stayed in the closet through most of her life. She also says that she regularly invited students for dinner at her apartment, where they easily saw that she had a roommate and only one double bed. She says, "I assume everyone figured it out, but hiding in this way takes a toll."
- Discuss whether you see any contradiction between what Neena said and what she did regarding "coming out."

- Discuss whether a formal "announcement" is necessary to the "coming out" process. Give your reasons.
- Discuss whether pleasing Neena's mother justified breaking the ethical rule prohibiting intimate relationships between faculty and students. Give your reasons.

(3) Neena states, "One of the problems homosexual couples have is that physicians refuse to talk about their patients with someone who is not a "relative."

- Discuss whether and how current times are different from the time described in this chapter in this regard.
- Regardless of physicians personal ethics, what provisions in the law allow us to name non-relatives as approved to receive private medical information?

Seven

CONFRONTATIONS AND RECOGNITIONS

As a scientist I try to work towards certainties. As a human being I seem to be moving away from them

Jeannette Winterson
Gut Symmetries

In 1961, Arnold Wolf, the new head of physiology at the Illinois Medical School, called to ask if I would consider returning to the department with an associate professorship and tenure. Wakerlin had retired, and Arnold, a renal physiologist, had become Chair; he had a couple of positions to fill. Other faculty members in the department had recommended that he try to get me to come back.

Several reasons contributed to my decision to leave Michael Reese Hospital and PPI. I had continued to feel haunted by the scenes of Jan's surgeries, which I was unable to escape in that setting. I felt that my career really belonged within a university medical school setting rather than in a hospital setting. I missed teaching the undergraduate health professional students, even though I had continued teaching the graduate course in endocrinology at Illinois. Finally, I wanted more access to graduate students for my lab than I had as an outsider to a university. I hoped that the atmosphere would be more congenial than it had been four years before, when I had left to join the interdisciplinary research team at Michael Reese.

❧

My lab and office, of course, were bigger than the one I had before. I began attracting a number of PhD students immediately and we became deeply involved in dissecting the events of the rat estrous cycle. The nine years I spent subsequently in the physiology department encompassed a whole series of events, which were important in my life, and some of which were important for other women.

My research in reproductive endocrinology began to be recognized outside the university in some very meaningful ways; I was being asked to speak at international conferences, and I became a member of the editorial board of two journals. I had my first experience in university administration, which proved valuable later on.

In 1971, a number of female scientists banded and bonded together to establish the Association for Women in Science, which has become a major player at the federal and university levels in promoting equality and increased opportunities for female scientists. I was involved in this effort from the beginning and still find mentoring my most satisfying activity. Since getting and keeping women in science proved to be a battle I continued to fight through the years, I will not go into detail on those efforts here, but will instead devote the next chapter to the onset of my involvement with it. The impetus for my involvement was not so much that I was not doing well, since I did have an independent lab of my own, but my recognition that many other women were not so fortunate. The sense of fairness I acquired from my parents drove me into this battle.

Arnold appointed me to the job of running the Department of Physiology graduate program. This meant working with faculty to establish the curriculum, reviewing applications and interviewing applicants, monitoring their progress into qualifying status and toward the thesis or dissertation, and generally "being there" for them. I loved doing this.

I continued to teach my graduate level course in endocrinology, which involved reading the original literature in a broad variety of topics and critiquing experiments in the original, published literature. By this time, I was lecturing to the freshmen medical students in endocrinology and metabolism, my very own field. I also started doing some coordinated teaching with a clinical colleague, Bob Ryan, a medical endocrinologist.

Bob and I constructed some joint teaching sessions based on diseases of endocrinology. He presented the clinical features, and I presented the basic physiology. I would describe how a gland works, say the thyroid, talking about how the hormone was synthesized in the gland and how it was regulated by the pituitary and hypothalamus. Bob would present a clinical case to them, perhaps a woman who was losing weight, feeling quite agitated, arguing with her husband about opening the bedroom windows. She wanted more windows open, and he wanted them closed because he was cold. Bob asked the students what might be wrong and what tests to administer to diagnose her.

The students loved it, calling out possible diagnoses. After they concluded that the patient was producing too much thyroid hormone, Bob and I would discuss whether her thyroid or her pituitary/brain axis was at fault; this would get the students calling out which clinical test to use. We kidded each other a lot about our relative expertise, and the students loved it. It is a great way to teach and learn endocrinology.

Even though I never team taught again, I have always discussed the clinical aspects of whatever I was teaching, even to undergraduates in college. Some basic scientists think it is selling out to discuss this kind of material with students to pique their interest; but students have never accused me of being irrelevant. What is wrong with having students enjoy a lecture?

❧❧

Our research was focusing more and more on the rat estrous cycle, expanding the studies initiated at Illinois earlier and continued at Michael Reese Hospital. Having a bioassay for LH, we continued probing for the signals that told the hypothalamus to release GnRH, because the ovary, now ready with ripe follicles secreting estrogen, was able to ovulate in response to a surge of LH in the blood. We showed that an anti-estrogen compound injected into a female rat on the day *before* proestrus did, in fact, block LH release the next day and ovulation the night following.

The estrogen receptor blocking drug we used resembled tamoxifen, which later began to be used clinically in breast cancer patients who had tumors which contained estrogen receptors, indicating that they are dependent on estrogen to grow. Then we went on to show that removing the ovary itself late on the day before proestrus prevented the large LH release, but waiting until the morning of proestrus was too late, and the LH surge took place. These data showed clearly that estrogen from the ovary was a necessary signal to permit the time- of day signal in the brain to stimulate GnRH release to the pituitary gland to cause LH release. (We had to do these roundabout experiments because at this time, it was still not possible to measure estrogen directly in the blood.)

Finally, we were able to show that if we injected pentobarbital into a female rat on the day of proestrus before 1 p.m., not only did it block ovulation, as Everett and Sawyer had shown, but it also blocked the drop in pituitary LH content (that we had previously demonstrated) and the rise in serum LH on that day!

As new methods of measurement (particularly the very sensitive radioimmunoassays for LH and FSH, estrogen and progesterone) became available, my lab and other labs began mapping the pituitary and ovarian hormones in the bloodstream during the entire four-day cycle.

By this time, I began to realize that I had a tiger by the tail and the work was coming along nicely. At about this time, I gave a seminar in the physiology department at Illinois; I spoke about the work on LH I have just described. In the middle of talking about one of the slides, I stopped for nearly a minute. Although Joan Hoffmann, who happened to have been my first PhD student, asked me why I had stopped, I didn't tell her.

Truth be told, I had listened to my own description and been suddenly overcome with the recognition of how good the work was and how I had done something important. It scared and exhilarated me at the same time.

Why was I scared? Somehow, I suppose that I had never believed that I would ever do important science. Unfortunately, this is not atypical of women. It is a little like poking your head up out of a crowd; people can then take potshots at you. It's much safer to blend in. Well, I was starting not to blend in, in earnest!

৯৮৩

After a medical student (Dave Calderelli, working on his Master's degree) and I showed that pentobarbital blocked the rise in serum LH on proestrus, I decided to send a short paper on this to a journal that promised rapid publication, since by that time I had become savvy enough to realize how groundbreaking this work was.

We sent the article to the *Proceedings of the Society for Biology and Medicine*, expecting to hear from them within a couple of weeks, but several months passed. I was puzzled by the delay in the decision from the journal but I was too naïve to call the editor directly to inquire.

At about that time, I was invited to present a talk at a symposium, which was being held at Colorado State. Also on the program was a well known neuroendocrinologist from Michigan State, Joe Meites. I had not met Joe previously, although I knew his work on prolactin and reproduction very well.

While at dinner one evening, he turned to me and said, "I was a reviewer on that really nice paper on LH you sent in."

"I haven't heard back from the editor," I said.

"Oh," he said.

Later in the evening as we walked back to the hotel, he told me that the other reviewer of the paper was probably holding it up because he was working in the same area as I. My heart sank.

"What should I do?" I asked.

Joe told me to call the editor and tell him what was probably going on and insist that the paper be published in the next issue. I did that when I returned to Chicago. The editor apologized, and our paper appeared immediately (in 1965), but it was too late to beat out the other reviewer's paper, which was also published that month in a different journal!

This was a disheartening occurrence for me; it had never occurred to me that anyone would do a thing like that! What naiveté. Becoming aware of the game was important for my future, but this experience was disillusioning to a young and ambitious young scientist.

৯৮৩

Let me review the timing of some of the pituitary and ovarian events I have been talking about. At the beginning of the cycle of four days, estrogen levels rise in the blood, a result of secretion from the maximum-sized group of ovarian follicles, which had grown under the influence of FSH from the pituitary. Rising levels of estrogen cause the receptors for GnRH to increase in number in the pituitary cells that contain LH and FSH (as we demonstrated in a paper some years later). The combination of estrogen from the ovary follicles and the daily neural signal in the brain causes an abrupt large release of GnRH from the specific neurons in the brain, which causes a surge of LH to be secreted by the pituitary. This causes the ripe follicles to ovulate and to switch from secreting estrogen to increasing progesterone secretion.

As we also demonstrated many years later, the secretion of another ovarian hormone (inhibin) also drops after the LH surge, leading to a prolonged rise of FSH, which causes the beginning growth of the next group of small follicles destined to ovulate four days later.

If a male is housed with the female, estrogen plus progesterone acting on the female brain causes her to exhibit mating behavior after midnight, permitting the male to inseminate her. This coordinated sequence of events is beautifully orchestrated by the interaction of the light-dark cycle, the brain, the pituitary, and the ovary.

These events we uncovered in the rat, which led to a recurring four- or five-day cycle, resemble the hormonal changes that occur during the human menstrual cycle during the first fourteen days, when the rising estrogen in the blood triggers a large GnRH release, which leads to the release of the preovulatory surge of LH from the pituitary. However, no evidence has been found in human beings or monkeys that shows that a time-of-day hypothalamic signal participates as it does in the rodent. The second half of the primate menstrual cycle occurs after ovulation when the follicle turns into a corpus luteum secreting progesterone. This does not occur in rodents unless mating occurs, which triggers the release of another hormone from the pituitary, prolactin, which causes the corpus luteum to secrete progesterone, leading to pregnancy or pseudopregnancy.

Before the second international endocrine meeting in London in 1964, some of the program leaders advertised a "Stop Press" session for new important material to be presented in ten-minute oral sessions. I submitted a description of the work on the rat cycle I have just described, but did not hear from the chair, Sheldon Segal. I went to London anyway, and I carried slides with me just in case. When I arrived at the meeting Shelley came up to me and asked if I had anything to present.

"Well" I said, "I have *fifteen* minutes worth of work prepared."

I was learning! Segal gave me the entire fifteen minutes, during which I talked about our data. This was a pivotal occasion for me because two influential endocrinologists, Roy Greep and Edward Astwood from Harvard, were in the audience. I had never met them before, although I had received a number of astringent, but cogent, comments on manuscripts I had submitted to *Endocrinology* from Greep, who was editor in chief at that time. After my talk, they both came up to congratulate me on the "wonderful" paper I had just presented. Three years later, they invited me to the Laurentian Hormone Conference to present the first Pincus Memorial Lecture. Thus, I came full circle in seven years, as I had met Gregory Pincus in Copenhagen in 1960 and was invited to present a memorial lecture honoring this "father of the birth control pill" in 1967.

&ni&

Rue had also come to London in 1964 to attend a Psychiatry meeting where she presented a paper. I had so much more fun doing London with her than I had on my own seven years earlier.

After our meetings, we took a train up to Edinburgh for a music festival. The highlight was hearing the Janacek symphony "Sinfonietta," which neither of us had heard before.

Rue was a very fine musician; she played piano very well, and she taught me to listen to classical music, particularly of the twentieth century. Then we rented a car and drove across the Highlands, staying in small inns, eating freshly caught salmon, hiking across Ben Nevis, and ending up in Glasgow. Even though we were driving on the left side of the road, no untoward incidents occurred, although a couple of near misses with cattle occurred in the Highlands. From Glasgow, she took a flight to Zurich to spend a few days with her father's relatives—her aunts, uncles and cousins—while I flew to Amsterdam to meet my former graduate student, Joan Hoffmann.

&ni&

Joan had completed her dissertation defense, and since she was interested in the role of light:dark ratios on reproduction, had applied for and won a National Science Foundation postdoctoral fellowship in the laboratory of Jacques Benoit in Paris. Benoit was a major international researcher on the effects of lighting conditions on hormonal cycles. Joan's family had presented her with a ticket on a cruise ship to Bremerhaven. From there, she drove a rented car to Amsterdam, where we met.

We drove across Holland and Belgium to France and then down to Paris, visiting canals and museums and World War I and II battlefields. Joan was not very much younger than I, and it was very nice being able to become a friend, not just a mentor, to one of my students. In Paris, she went off to her new lab and I met Rue, who had flown in from Zurich, and Agnes, the medievalist friend I had made in Paris some years before. Paris was much more fun this time with Rue, Agnes, and Joan. No Australians, however.

&ni&

As my lab grew, I took on graduate students interested in striking off in new directions, which was great. Joan Hoffmann had studied the suppression of ovulation by progesterone and examined the progesterone drop that occurs at the end of pregnancy, and which permits the post-partum LH secretion and ovulation that occurs in rats and mice.

Audrey Bingel showed that the mouse, like the rat, exhibited a 24-hour cyclicity in LH release throughout the estrous cycle, and then she examined the periodicity of LH release in the postpartum mouse. She did indeed demonstrate a periodicity of LH release susceptible to pentobarbital suppression, explaining why the pentobarbital anesthesia had blocked ovulation when I studied it in mice in Runner's lab as a summer student in Bar Harbor in 1948.

Another graduate student, Lynn Nequin, demonstrated that the adrenal cortex itself secreted enough progesterone on the afternoon of proestrus to precipitate mating behavior, even without the ovarian progesterone secretion.

Irene Lawton was interested in the effect of the light-dark cycle per se on the pituitary-ovarian axis. By this time, we knew that if the rats were kept in constant light conditions, they ceased releasing an LH surge and went into a constant estrogen-secreting mode from follicle cysts.

These experiments demonstrated how important the circadian aspect of LH release was in the rat. If, on the other hand, rats were kept in constant darkness, they continued to show estrous cycles, but the timing of LH secretion and mating behavior was no longer linked to the external environment.

All of these studies were published and contributed significantly to the understanding of the relative contributions of the ovary, pituitary, and brain to maintaining a cycle All of these young women went on to do postdoctoral fellowships or teaching or research positions in colleges or universities. (Many years later, a paper by Irene and me in the *American Journal of Physiology* was picked as a classic paper used for teaching undergraduates.)

As you can see, the lab was very active and exciting. My graduate students were very hard-working and pushed me to the limit. Jim McClintock, another graduate student, studied Follicle Stimulating Hormone (FSH) instead of LH, setting up a bioassay for this hormone and following the gonadotropin throughout the rat cycle. After Jim left our lab, he did a postdoctoral fellowship with Jack Everett at Duke. Sadly, Jim developed Hodgkin's disease while on his fellowship; he died just before the new treatments for this disease were discovered.

ॐᡃ᠊ᠣ᠋

At about this time during the late 1960s, the lab began a series of collaborations with scientists working at other universities, which considerably broadened our perspectives and methodologies. A professor of anatomy at Madison, Margaret Orsini, contacted me about doing LH measurements in the golden hamster, another four-day cycling rodent. We collaborated on a number of papers, with Margaret's lab doing the animal work and my lab doing the bioassays.

Margaret was great fun to work with—astringent, funny, and irreverent. I enjoyed my trips to Madison with the balances for weighing tissues in the back seat of my car and the days spent in her lab weighing hamster pituitaries and ovaries. Her husband Gian, in Comparative Italian Literature, had been a member of the resistance in Italy during World War II. His stories of acting as a courier in Rome (this short, rotund scholarly looking man with a brief-case) were amusing but frightening, his courage unmistakable.

At about the same time, I also began collaborating with a physi-cian/scientist at Case-Western Reserve, Irv Rothchild. He was interested in the corpus luteum and progesterone, the luteal phases of reproductive cycles. He started me looking at LH secretion during preudopregnancy and pregnancy in the rat and then the mouse.

A third collaboration that developed about this time was with Charles Ely, of Columbia University College of Physicians and Surgeons. I men-tioned earlier that we had started using an anti-estrogen compound to probe the contribution of estrogen to the estrous cycle. Charles had made antisera to LH and FSH, which could block the effects of these gonadotropins on ovarian and testicular functions. Together, he and I began experiments probing the effect of blocking these hormones on ovarian secretion and morphology.

❧❦

Life seemed good. Rue and I did a lot of camping around the Midwest; both sets of parents came to Chicago, at different times, and we enjoyed entertain-ing them. My mother, by this time, had stopped nagging me about my life style, which was a relief. Rue's parents seemed to be satisfied with the way we were living.

Rue and I were living on the near north side of Chicago, in a large apartment with a fireplace and a backyard, in which we planted flowers and vegetables. We acquired Song, the first of three dachshunds we eventually had, a black cat, Lucy, and a piano. I started taking lessons for the third time in my life. Rue had obtained her PhD by that time and had an academic posi-tion in the Psychiatry department at the University of Illinois Medical School. With an NIH grant, she began writing the book that became *Becoming Pro-fessional.* We were thoroughly domesticated.

However, I began not feeling well. My eyes were bothering me, and I felt exhausted much of the time. I made an appointment with my ophthalmol-ogist, Harvey Berlin. Harvey kept looking at my retina, using one instrument after another. I started worrying, since my vision has always been a problem. Not only had I been wearing glasses for nearsightedness since I was eight years old, but I also had a left eye that drifted to the side when I became tired after reading.

My mother had been concerned that I would be cross-eyed as an adult, just as she worried I would be too tall when I shot up to 5'6" at the age of twelve. She was quite concerned with physical appearance, and you can bet I knew it.

Our family ophthalmologist, when I was ten, had put me into thick lenses, which I hated. He also recommended surgery to "take a tuck in an ocular muscle." I protested so much at that suggestion that my mother took me to the Wilmer Clinic at Johns Hopkins for a consultation, where Dr. Walsh, who was head of the Department at that time, tossed my glasses away (literally!), said I did not need surgery, and told me that I would outgrow the muscle weakness. He was right.

కింe

But here I was, almost forty, with an obviously concerned eye doctor. He finished the examination and said, "I think you should see your internist. You have some floaters, which sometimes indicate systemic disease."

My internist saw me right away, and took my EKG. When he called me into his office, I knew something was wrong.

"Have you had any chest pain recently?"

"Yes," I said, adding, "but I wasn't worried because women don't get heart attacks."

"Don't drive home," he said. "I think you may have had a mild heart attack. I have called Michael Reese Hospital, and they have a room for you starting tomorrow."

I immediately called Rue at her office, and she told me to take a cab to our apartment where she would meet me. She arranged for a friend to pick up my car from the Loop parking garage. That night, we talked for a long time about our relationship, carefully skirting around our fears about my health. We talked about how we had met and our early days of living together. I kept remembering, or thought I was remembering, the statistics on the probability of a second and fatal heart attack. (No one panics more than a physiologist, confronted by a medical emergency, who thinks she knows the course of a disease from her teaching of basic physiology.)

Finally, I said, "I need to sleep, and I'd rather sleep alone."

"I'll sit here by the bed," she said. "I don't want to sleep just now."

We both knew that I was afraid I might have a second attack that night, and I didn't want her to wake up with me dead next to her.

Rue drove me to Michael Reese Hospital the next day, and I was hospitalized on the cardiovascular unit. The tests all seemed to indicate that I had had a mild heart attack. I went on anti-coagulant Coumadin treatment to lower the risk of blood clotting, rested for a couple of weeks, stopped smoking, and started losing weight. I also did a lot of thinking about the two weeks that had preceded the chest pain and eye symptoms.

I had driven by myself 800 miles east from Chicago to see my family in Baltimore, where my sister's husband had become ill. I had not been told that he was ill before my trip, and I was upset about it.

Still upset and tired, I drove from Chicago to Atlantic City to attend the physiology meetings, staying up late to talk and drink with colleagues. I also delivered a paper and then drove back west through Cleveland to visit my collaborator/pal Irv Rothschild and his wife Ellen. As usual, we talked for hours. Then I drove non-stop back to Chicago. As soon as I returned to my office on the University of Illinois Medical School campus after the trip east the graduate students in our department had come bursting in to see me.

"Do you know what that crazy guy Wolf has done now? He's restricted the hours we can use the department library."

"Why?" I asked.

"Who knows?" they replied.

I spent a few minutes calming them down, but then I stormed into his office and told him he was a jerk.

As I lay on my hospital bed, a group of our graduate students knocked on the door timidly, and shuffled in carrying a huge bouquet of flowers.

"We were worried that we gave you a heart attack."

I denied this, of course, but as I thought about those grueling two weeks, I decided to talk with my doctor about them.

ଚ୶ଚ

My doctor laughed and then gave me a tip for the future: "If you're tired, don't allow yourself to get angry. If you have to get angry at something, don't do it when you are tired." This is good advice I have tried to remember during the last thirty-five years, though I have not always done so successfully. He also put me on a stringent diet and suggested that I stop smoking.

"What's left?" I asked.

He smiled, "Sex and alcohol."

Several months after I returned to work, my internist called me and said the cardiovascular department at the hospital wondered whether I would participate in a clinical trial of a new drug.

"They don't believe you had a heart attack," he said, "and will give you free treatment with a drug for blocking arrhythmia."

I found out which drug they were testing. I had actually used this new adrenaline antagonist on rats several years before to look at the effects of adrenaline on symptoms of excess thyroid hormone.

"Okay, I'll do it."

So I grabbed a lot of books to read and checked into Michael Reese Hospital again as a patient. The resident took my history, including asking if I was still menstruating. "Sure," I said. So they started the drug and took frequent EKGs.

As a physiologist, I was able to read the records, so I would just casually glance over while the machine was running. It was obvious to me that no changes in the abnormal pattern were occurring. I didn't say anything.

After a week, the resident came back with a worried look and asked "Are you sure you are still menstruating?"

Since I had been resting, I allowed myself to get angry. "No wonder your statistics on women and heart disease are skewed. You don't want to list me as a heart attack because you already don't *believe* that premenopausal women have heart attacks."

Later I talked with my gynecologist about this.

"Nonsense," he said, "I have seen a number of patients who have had heart attacks. The internists just don't usually treat women."

ॐ๛

I have thought about this chain of events a lot since I started writing this memoir. I knew physiology and endocrinology, so I was not buffaloed by the resident into thinking that I didn't know about my own menstrual cycle.

Now that cardiovascular studies have been carried out on several cohorts of women, we know that premenopausal women may indeed have heart problems. In fact, statistics confirm that more women die of cardiovascular related diseases than breast cancer. The American Heart Association studies in 2001 showed that estrogen replacement therapy in women with previous heart problems will not yield cardiovascular benefits from estrogen. A few things have changed in women's health since 1965! Further, the most recent studies indicate that estrogen plus progesterone may not prevent heart attacks at all.

ॐ๛

During the summer of 1966, Rue and I vacationed, as we had been doing for several years, in a rental cabin on Ellison Bay, off Green Bay, in Door County, Wisconsin. I was still on coumadin, so we had to drive down to a small hospital thirty-five miles south several times during the two-week stay, to have my clotting time checked. One day, we were lying in the sun with Song, on the dock of the cabin, looking back at the shoreline. We talked about what had happened, musing on the vagaries of life, the evanescence of careers, and the wholeness we felt in these woods, near this water.

Looking at the wooded shore line of the bay Rue said "Wouldn't it be nice to own part of this?"

"Yes," I agreed.

Carpe diem! The idea sounded great, and we discovered that the family that owned a large piece of the shore to the west of our rental cabin planned to sell off a parcel. Could we afford it? Well, a local bank was willing to give us a mortgage, which was somewhat unusual to obtain for two women in those days. We bought 100 feet of wooded land, which went back about 700 feet to the county road.

We acquired a contractor and built a house on our land. That house, dock and woods have been a central part of my life ever since. In fact, a couple of years later, we bought another hundred feet, to protect our privacy on the first hundred. As one of my friends put it, "You have about two and one half acres of trees, swamp, and shoreline to temporarily nurture and take care of." It has been my lifesaver, my haven, and my joy.

The far-off dream I had as a kid of being in a cabin in the woods had come true. Surrounded by the north woods, with a view of the bay, this house became my shelter and retreat.

Rue and I called our place "*At Beigh*," a triple pun. (1) It was on Ellison *Bay*, (2) our spelling it "Beigh" satisfied a reverse snobbery brought on by some of the weird silly spellings we saw on homes around there, and (3) we felt "*At Bay*" many times when we were there, particularly when the dean began picking at me when I chaired the Biological Sciences department at Northwestern University years later.

At first, we had no phone, but the dean insisted I install a phone so he could reach me whenever he "needed" me. Two years after we built the house, a friend who stayed there made us a wooden sign that still stands just before the turn-around to the house. On one side, she whittled a dove and "Shalom," and on the other side she carved a dachshund and *Gruezi*, Swisser Deutch for Greetings.

When Rue and I contemplated building our house in Wisconsin, we discussed the venture with both sets of parents. Her parents and mine encouraged us to do it, interestingly; her father loaned her money for a down payment, and my dad told me, "You will never lose money on land." Both sets of parents asked what we needed for the house when we started building it, and they contributed sets of flatware and dishes.

Almost like getting married, right? Rue's parents visited us twice in Door County, and after her mother Grace died, her father Fred spent a whole month up there with us. My folks visited once, soon after the house was completed. When they arrived, Mother presented us with a copper tea samovar, which she and her family had brought from Russia in 1921. She had gotten the copper finish refurbished and believed it would bring luck to the new house.

I admit I was moved. Maybe it was not approval but acceptance, after all these years. Unfortunately, my mother's subsequent stroke prevented her from ever making the trip again. But the samovar still sits in its place of honor to the left of the fireplace.

ॐ∽◌

During this time, a significant encounter occurred between me and my siblings, with whom I had never discussed my sexuality. My sister and her husband, along with their two daughters, had moved from Baltimore to southern Maryland, where she taught learning disabled kids in public school and he was a civilian lawyer for the Navy at the Patuxent Naval Air Base.

On my way to a meeting on the east coast in 1971, I decided to visit them. Pearl and her daughters Nancy and Susan picked me up at the Washington National Airport, and we drove south to their new home. Bernie was away from home for naval training. I came determined to tell my sister that I was lesbian. She and I had always been friends, and I finally could not bear that this had gone unspoken.

I said "there is something I need to tell you."

She said okay and went into the kitchen to fix dinner. All weekend, I worried about the actual telling and tried to corner her a couple of times, but she seemed to avoid me. I felt really down and depressed, figuring she had never asked and didn't want to hear me tell.

Finally, as I was helping her strip the sheets from the bed I had used for the last few days, I said, "I have to tell you something." She sank down onto the bed and braced herself, visibly. "I am a lesbian," I blurted out.

"Thank goodness," she said. "I thought you were going to tell me you were sick."

Several days later after I had returned to Chicago, my brother called me and said she had called him.

He said "I'm glad you told us because it makes it so much easier to be close to you."

After years isolated from my siblings, the change was wonderful.

ॐ•ॐ

From September 1968 to August 1970, I served as Assistant Dean of Faculty Affairs at the Illinois College of Medicine, a half-time position and my first taste of administration aside from administering my lab and grants. Bill Grove, the Dean and a surgeon, felt he needed to improve his relationships with the basic scientists at U of I (he was right!) and was particularly interested in improving research on the campus. Bill and I had had some run-ins on school governance at faculty meetings, and I respected him highly for selecting me for the position despite our differences.

One of my jobs was to chair the committee that looked at internal grant requests from a sizable pot of money and to sign off on all external grant requests for money. I was also principal investigator on a couple of College of Medicine grants, such as a cardiovascular grant.

The job bored me almost immediately, but instead of leaving at the end of one year, I stayed for two, since Bill had a major heart attack and all the other assistant deans were new to the university. My boredom grew partly out of resentment that I was spending so much time helping scientists who were not very good repair simply awful grant requests for resubmission. But in other ways, I enjoyed being in the dean's office and helping to make some important decisions. I have always been grateful to Bill Grove for giving me my first real taste of administrative responsibility.

స్వ-్ఌ

In Mexico City in 1968, at the third International Endocrinology Congress meeting, I was invited to present a symposium paper summarizing the series of studies in which we dissected the sequence of the timing of ovarian and pituitary secretions by gland removal or antiserum to LH or estrogen receptor blocker. Rue came along to explore the city and we rented a car to take us to Guernavaca for a holiday after the meeting.

The Ballet Folklorico was performing in the stadium south of Mexico City, and the endocrinologists were bussed down for the dance. As the dancing was going on, I felt a sudden tremor and looked around. Rue, who had conducted interviews for the National Opinion Research Council during and after the Bakersfield, California, earthquakes, immediately recognized what was happening. She yelled, "Sit down!" to the endocrinologists surrounding us as people began to panic and run for the entrances.

We filed out quietly, and when we returned to our hotel found that it had sustained major damage and the plumbing was not working. This was really unfortunate, because two days before at the opening ceremonies, a number of us had picked up a gastrointestinal problem from a salad.

The next day one of my colleagues was presenting a paper, and he started by saying, "I am not sure which end of my GI tract is going to give this talk."

One of my graduate students confessed to me, when we returned to Illinois, her fantasy that the earthquake would wipe out the international community of endocrinologists, thereby allowing all graduate students in endocrinology to immediately obtain positions in universities.

స్వ-్ఌ

While my lab was working on understanding the rat estrous cycle and its causative sequence of events, the obvious question to me was, "What makes it keep going?" The same question has been asked of the human menstrual cycle. A number of endocrinologists began trying to provide computer "models" of their own systems (the ACTH-adrenal cortex; the TSH-thyroid) attempting to explain control of systems by means of theoretical models.

Influenced by my experiences as a graduate student in the department at Northwestern, which was interested in looking at regulation in the cardiovascular and respiratory systems and analyzing them, I began to work with a computer whiz, Paul Waltz, on a model for the rat cycle, attempting to put together known data and seeing whether the model "cycled." We published several models, succeeding in modeling a simple four-day cycle. (The most complex of my published models accompanied my talk honoring Gregory Pincus at the Laurentian Hormone Conference in 1968.)

An annual meeting was held in January, in Hawaii or California, of endocrinologists who modeled the control of the adrenal cortex, the thyroid, or reproduction. Some of us had received money from NIH for the work. I had a three-year contract for the cycle modeling, in addition to a separate grant for my animal work.

The Hawaii meetings took place on the beach at Waikiki. One evening, at our meeting inside the hotel, we looked around the room and discovered that we were all losing funding for our modeling research work because our peers who were reviewing our grants for NIH had decided that not enough "real" data existed upon which to base models. Although I disagreed, I still quit formal modeling in my research, not wanting to lose my funding for my animal research.

However, I have always taught endocrinology and written didactic chapters using modeling concepts. Figure 1 in Chapter Five shows a diagram, which I think is very useful in examining the complex relationships between the brain, pituitary, and target endocrine glands.

&r~&

The last model of the cycle I presented at a public meeting was at the 1969 meeting of the Federation of American Societies for Experimental Biology. The invitation to do so came from the late Ernst Knobil, then Chair of Physiology at University of Pittsburgh Medical School.

What led to that invitation, my first at a major American meeting, was this: Ernie and I had become friends because we kept serving together on site visit teams for NIH, reviewing applications for training grants from various research teams across the country. His research was on reproduction in the rhesus monkey, and his lab was the first to demonstrate that LH values in the blood showed pulses at hourly intervals, an observation that proved true for all mammals and was the result of GnRH hourly pulses.

Ernie had been very skeptical about whether modeling was useful in endocrinology. I kept telling him how valuable it was as a thinking tool. He finally challenged me to come to Pittsburgh and give a seminar on modeling in his department. I went to Pitt, and on the morning before my seminar, I drew my current model on the blackboard of the seminar room. Then, that afternoon during the seminar, I walked the audience through the model, simultaneously showing on projected slides the experimental data behind each of the arrows on the board. During the discussion, Ernie got to his feet after others had asked their questions and began his questions, arguing about one of my claims.

I kept trying to see what he was saying, and he finally ran up to the board and pointed to one of the arrows saying "This is what I mean!"

I looked at him, he blushed and I said "I rest my case."

Shortly after this incident I was asked to present the model at Federation of American Societies for Experimental Biology (FASEB) in Atlantic City. That was a major triumph for me, and I am sure Ernie was behind that invitation.

But several months earlier, I had experienced some major bouts of uterine bleeding; my gynecologist said I had a very large fibroid tumor, which had to come out. I tried to delay the surgery because I was anxious to give that invited FASEB paper, but the medical consensus was not to wait.

Alex Tulsky was my gynecologist; he and I discussed what he should do. I said reluctantly that if he could not remove the fibroid and leave my uterus intact, he should go ahead and take it out.

Had I ever wanted children? I loved my nieces and nephews and enjoyed having them visit, but I had never yearned for children of my own. Nevertheless, I felt very sad about this, as it is never happy to close a door forever. But I knew the tumor was very large.

Then he said "What about the ovaries?"

I hesitated. No one in my family had had ovarian cancer, to my knowledge. (This was before the BRAC family of genes for breast and ovarian cancer was identified.) I decided to take the risk, and said "no," because I felt that my own pituitary/ovarian axis would do a better job of regulating my well-being than some kind of hormone replacement therapy.

So I had the surgery, and it turned out that the doctor had to remove my uterus. It was major surgery, but I really wanted to go to Atlantic City to give the paper. I did, only three weeks later; and the paper was a success. I returned home totally exhausted and had to go back to bed for several weeks more before I could return to work.

❧

Although I was successful as a faculty member at the University of Illinois Medical School—teaching well, bringing in grants, doing some administrative duties, serving on many committees—I still experienced some problems, though they were mostly stupid and unnecessary.

Would the same problems have also happened to men? I don't think so. I had discovered rather quickly on my return to the department after working at Michael Reese that Arnold Wolf did not have a well-developed sense of quality in research and was very autocratic. For example, it made no sense that he had limited the hours graduate students could use the department library, since the room was free and empty at other times.

On another occasion, several well known neuroendocrinologists were visiting the United States from South America to study physiology and anatomy departments. Arnold spent time alone with them and did not inform anyone else in the department of their visit. He probably had not even bothered to inquire about their research areas. They then visited our Anatomy department, where the department head Sam Reynolds, asked if they had also visited with me.

"No," they said, "we thought she was here on this campus, but the physiology chairman did not mention her."

Sam phoned me, and, of course, the visitors and I knew each other from having met at international meetings. I bounded up to Sam's office, and we greeted each other enthusiastically. I asked whether they could give a seminar; Professor Ladowsky agreed, since he had slides with him. I gathered my students and found a projector and an empty room in the department.

Midway through the seminar, Arnold burst into the room, said we had no business being there without his permission, and kicked us out! This was beyond embarrassment; my visitors and students were appalled. Arnold obviously never understood that the key to being a good chair is to enhance the visibility of your faculty, particularly the junior people.

It became obvious to me that Arnold was so worried about protecting and promoting himself that he was unable to foster the growth of his faculty. This annoyed the hell out of me; my career has been characterized by my inability to tolerate bosses who were not confident enough in themselves to let people they were responsible for go their own way.

Because of the neuroendocrinogist incident, and other needless humiliations, such as Wolf insisting that everyone's technicians sign time-sheets (when the techs were actually performing above and beyond their duties and were insulted by this requirement), I decided to try to switch departments or leave the institution.

Leaving was difficult for me because I did not want to leave the Chicago area due to my continuing relationship with Rue. We were beginning to think about buying a house together in the Chicago area, which we did in 1970, in Evanston, Illinois. Again, as in Door County, we had no problem getting a mortgage with survivor-take-all benefits. We did hire a lawyer and made out wills guaranteeing preservation of ownership for each other.

కళ

Mel Sabshin, then head of Psychiatry at the Medical School, heard from Rue about my wish to change departments. He offered me a professorship with tenure in his department and permitted me to recruit a small team of basic science faculty researchers. Mel was responding to our colleagueship at Michael Reese Hospital, where we had worked together on several clinical projects, and also to the "two-body" problem Rue and I had. Networking and contacts are frequently missing for women in academia and knowing Mel was a bit of luck for me! And we took advantage of it.

Thus, from September 1970 to December 1972, I was professor of neuroendocrinology in the Department of Psychiatry. I organized a multidisciplinary program on the relationship between the brain and reproduction. I recruited an experimental psychologist, Chuck Rodgers, and a biochemist, Bob Chatterton, and we worked together very well on some hormone/brain/cycle issues.

ॐ∾๑

By this time, I was a member of the Population Research Committee at National Institute of Child Health and Development (NICHD), which funds collaborative research projects in reproductive science such as multi-investigator program project grants. Recognizing that we had a fair amount of strength at U of I in reproductive research in Psychiatry and some other departments, I talked with an administrator at NICHD, who encouraged me to organize the group and apply for a program project grant.

We needed a clinical project to round out the potential program, but when I spoke to the head of the Department of Obstetrics and Gynecology, who was a researcher, he said he would not join in unless he could be the program director. NICHD said no. Our new Dean, Alex Schmidt, equivocated when I talked with him about it. He wanted to put the head of Obstetrics and Gynecology at the top.

I was outraged and frustrated by this all too typical medical school near-sightedness and cast about for another position. I left to go to Northwestern Medical School in the Physiology department, where I had received my PhD twenty years before. The offer for this position came to me because the Chair of Physiology at Northwestern, Oscar Hechter, was also trying to organize a collaborative grant in endocrinology. He had identified several projects and beleived that I could contribute not only another project but also some know-how regarding what NICHD was looking for. I accepted the position, seeing it as a way to return to a basic science department from a clinical one. But I was always very grateful to Mel Sabshin, who had made this transition possible for me.

ॐ∾๑

I continued going home to Baltimore at least twice a year and to Canada every August for the Laurentian Hormone Conference meeting in Mont Tremblant, Quebec. By that time, I had been appointed to the program committee of the conference, a real honor for me.

In 1972, Dad called to say Mother had suffered a major stroke, just before I was due to travel up to the Laurentian Hormone Conference. Instead, I flew to Baltimore. I had always felt besieged by Mother asking, "When are you going to change your lifestyle?" I had asked her not to discuss this any more and she eventually stopped focusing on it. But she remained unhappy with me, or more accurately I suppose, *for* me. When I went to the hospital to visit her after the stroke, she was not conscious. I sat in her room reading. Suddenly, I felt that someone was watching me. I looked up to find that her eyes were open.

"Why are you here instead of in Canada?" she asked.

"I thought it was more important to be here," I replied.

Then she closed her eyes. She lived for about twelve years after the stroke (until 1985) but we never had a real conversation again because she had so much difficulty speaking and was always so frustrated by the need to search for words. I have always felt sad that we were unable to talk meaningfully with each other during those long years after her stroke.

෴

As you can see, the years from 1961 to 1973 were tumultuous for me—a heart attack, a house in the woods, a hysterectomy, confrontations with Arnold Wolf, and then frustrations about permission to build a multidisciplinary research program at the University of Illinois. In spite of this, our science was going very well and I was being increasingly recognized outside my university. But another series of confrontations concerning universities was simultaneously taking place: the feminist movement to obtain equality for women in the workplace. I jumped in with both feet.

Study Questions

(1) At one point, Neena describes having "been suddenly overcome with the recognition of how good the work was and how [she] had done something important." Scared and exhilarated, she continued, "somehow, I suppose that I had never believed that I would ever do important science. Unfortunately, this is not atypical of women."

- Discuss this comment within the context of current culture. Do you believe that this assessment was ever true of women, and if so, does it remain true of women now?
- Do only women experience this sort of shock at the realization of being capable of great things? Discuss your reasoning.

(2) Neena says she has always felt sad that "we were unable to talk meaningfully with each other during those long years after [mother's] stroke."

- Discuss why we often feel regret at the loss of opportunity to have meaningful discussions with people after they become disabled or die when we were not eager to attempt similar discussions with the same persons while they were alive and well.

Five Recent Presidents of the Endocrine Society. L-R: Neena B. Schwartz (1982–1983), Sue Smith (1994–1995), Peggy Shupnik (2007–2008), Kate Horwitz (1998–1999), Maria New (1991–92). Photo Credit: Endocrine Society, © Chuck Giorno, 1998.

Eight

CATCHING UP WITH THE BOYS:
BECOMING MEMBERS OF THE CLUB

Just consider: it's the beginning of the twentieth century, and until a few years ago no woman had ever come out by herself and said things at all. There it was going on in the background, for all those thousands of years, this curious silent unrepresented life.

Virginia Woolf
The Voyage Out

In my younger days, when I was pained by the half-educated, loose and inaccurate ways women had, I used to say, "How much women need exact science." But since I have known some workers in science who are not always true to the teachings of nature, who have loved self more than science, I would say, "How much science needs women."

Maria Mitchell, Astronomer

During the early 1970s, I was making my mark as a scientist and trying to live a reasonably full personal life with a home in Evanston, two dogs and a cat, a house in Wisconsin, a partner, and a successful lab and tenure. What else could an academic want?

The feminist movement was growing and some small changes were taking place in the workplace as well, but the glass ceiling was still everywhere. Most universities had no female department chairs or top female administrators. It was tough for women to become journal editors or have highly visible spots on the conference programs of professional societies. Women were not hired into tenure track positions in many science departments.

I was still the only woman in the physiology department at Illinois. I began to feel angry about all of this. The division between success in the university and success in professional societies is arbitrary, since the issues are interrelated. Promotion in a research university depends on getting outside grants and on the recognition you garner in the outside world. This recognition depends on your ability to get published and on your visibility in professional societies and influential committees such as NIH study sections. Selection for editorial boards and study sections, in turn, depends on your visibility as a scientist. If you are impeded in crossing any of these barriers, you will be held back in all of them.

Women needed to become involved in the research grants peer review system and they needed to gain positions of influence in universities to influence hiring and tenure decisions. They also needed to gain influence in the professional societies that published research and recommended speakers for highly visible program slots and better positions on editorial boards.

However, how to break into this men's club was not immediately apparent. Since we were mostly academic scientists, a sit-in seemed undignified, a picket line useless, and a protest during a plenary session at a meeting would be counterproductive.

For a couple of years before 1971, Kontes, a lab glassware company, had sponsored a wine and cheese evening for women at the annual meeting of the Federation of American Societies for Experimental Biology (FASEB; the societies that met there were the basic medical sciences, physiology, biochemistry, immunology, pharmacology, and pathology). If you don't want people to get together and gripe about their lot in life, don't let them meet in a safe place with a lot of wine!

At the end of the evening in 1971, a group of twenty-seven of us remained after the wine bar closed, and we started talking about forming an "association of women in science." Naturally, I was interested; was there ever a challenge I turned down? I was tenured and had my own lab (partly because I was in a second tier university, the University of Illinois Medical School). But I could see all around me that not all women who were as talented as I or more so were doing as well. Too many were working in untenured research positions in others' labs.

Fueled by the wine, we gathered in one of our hotel rooms. Squeezed in beside the beds and dresser, we formed The Association of Women in Science (AWIS). Judy Pool, a hematologist at Stanford, and I agreed to be co-presidents. AWIS adopted as its mission statement, "To seek equality for women in the professions."

The current statement has been modified: "AWIS is dedicated to achieving equality and full participation for women in science, mathematics, engineering, and technology."

When I returned to the medical school campus at the University of Illinois, I wrote a letter to Bill Grove, Dean of Medicine, telling him what we had done, so that he wouldn't be blindsided when he found out.

ॐॐ

Federal funding in the United States is the major source of research support in the sciences. The NIH fund principally biomedical research, while the National Science Foundation funds across the natural sciences. These two government agencies have professional managers who are scientists that no longer work at the bench or in the field. These managers administer committees (study sections) made up of scientists from appropriate fields, who essentially assign scores to each project application.

Thus, these groups act as a quality funnel through which grants flow. Women must be represented on these review panels to ensure that the quality of research submitted by female investigators is fairly evaluated. This is not to say that women do a different science (a topic I will discuss later), but that personal factors inevitably enter into such decision making.

A group of us in AWIS obtained the membership lists of study sections at NIH to look for women members. *Quelle surprise*! Very few members were women! We also looked at the "breast cancer panels" that reviewed clinical research on that topic and found to our horror only a couple of women were included in these groups.

We contacted a law firm in Chicago and went to see a female partner with our data. She suggested seeking an injunction against NIH to keep them from putting new scientists on the study sections until they began to add women. So the first major venture of AWIS was to sue NIH! We also developed a list of women obviously capable of serving in this capacity.

Several of us from AWIS, the Biophysical Society, Women's Equality Action League, National Organization for Women, and the American Women's Medical Association went to Washington and met with Robert Q. Marston, head of NIH at that time. My brother Leon was one of Marston's associate directors (for administration) at that time, so before we went I called Leon to warn him what was coming.

He laughed, but wasn't a bit surprised, and said, "I will tell Bob Marston you are my sister."

Our group met Marston and a representative of then Secretary of Health, Education, and Welfare, Eliot Richardson, on 19 November 1971. Our designated spokeswoman was Dr. Julia Apter, an ophthalmologist researcher from Chicago. We pointed out the extremely limited representation of women on study sections and the advisory groups of NIH. We suggested that further appointments to such advisory groups be frozen until women had had the opportunity to suggest names for the open positions. The representatives of NIH and HEW agreed to provide our groups with a list of current vacancies (413 at that time).

By January, we had compiled a list of over one thousand women as nominees to fill these vacancies. We finally determined to turn over the list as part of the documentation accompanying a class action suit to be filed against Richardson of HEW and Marston, of NIH. The suit asked that the United States District Court for the District of Columbia declare unlawful the policies of these two, under which women had been virtually excluded from appointments to NIH public advisory groups.

The officers of AWIS signed as plaintiffs in the suit on behalf of the membership; other plaintiffs were the Association of Women in Psychology, the Caucus of Women Biophysicists, Sociologists for Women in Society, Association for Women in Mathematics, National Organization of Women, and the Women's Equity Action League. Our suit was eventually dropped, since many of the women on our lists began to be appointed as members of study sections and other peer review groups. Eventually, I was one of them.

ॐৎ

Since that time, AWIS has grown to more than 5,000 members, has an executive office in Washington and an executive director, publishes a monthly magazine, and holds annual meetings in conjunction with the American Association for the Advancement of Science. It has had a major influence in advancing the participation of women in science, and, importantly, it has a major presence in Washington.

At the time of that first decision to go after NIH to increase the numbers of women on study sections, not one of us in AWIS had ever been on a study section, although our grants were being judged by them. Secretly, I wondered whether women were in fact being disadvantaged by not having women on these groups. I had a chance to find out in the late 1980s, when I was appointed to the endocrinology study section.

As I sat in the day-long sessions, it became increasingly obvious to me that female applicants were disadvantaged, particularly junior ones. As the mostly male reviewers read their critiques aloud to the rest of the section members, they would say about a woman applicant things such as, "Who was responsible for the ideas in this application?" or "She was a student of so and so's," or "Will she be able to master this new technology?" For young male applicants, they would say, "An up and coming young man" or, "He really knows how to go for the jugular."

One day during a coffee break, the four women on the twenty-member committee met serendipitously in the women's restroom; we talked about these comments. We discovered that, unbeknownst to each other, based on the comments we heard being made, we were all increasing the women's scores a bit to compensate for the obvious discrimination to which males subjected these applicants.

ॐৎ

Julia Apter, who had been our spokesperson at the initial Washington meeting, was an ophthalmologist and biophysicist who did research at one of the Chicago Hospitals. She and I were both interested in modeling biological systems. We spent considerable time talking about the gender-bias issue. We were both invited to a conference in California on modeling of biological systems, and one evening, while there, we talked together for a long time about how we were perceived as women in the "man's world" of science. I remember how upset she was that evening over a slight she had felt at the afternoon's session. She seemed jealous of my apparent acceptance by this group of biological modelers, and we did not meet much after that.

But not too long after, I heard that Julia had literally been locked out of her office and lab by the hospital administration because of an argument she had had with the chairperson of the department. She was not always the easiest person to get along with, but she was brilliant and very supportive of other women. I am convinced no man would have been treated the way she was by his home institution.

ॐॐ

The first National Conference on Women and science took place at the New York Academy of Sciences in 1970. In the opening remarks, the organizer of the conference Ruth Kundsin said:

> In the context here, however, a successful woman in the sciences is a woman able to function in her chosen profession with some measure of recognition. . . . We are particularly interested in women who are married and have children because we feel a complex personal life involving marriage and motherhood are circumstances both of which have made the pursuit of a meaningful career increasingly more difficult.

Having recently reread the conference proceedings, I am still appalled by this statement. Having led a complex personal life myself, albeit without a conventional marriage or children, I resented the statement all over again. It reminds me of the events that occurred at early National Organization of Women (NOW) meetings where lesbian women were shunned. I believe that some female scientists were afraid that they might be tarred with the lesbian brush if they were too outspoken about problems of women scientists.
Other quotes from the conference include the following:

> We're grateful to Women's Liberation for working to solve lots of sticky problems that remain, and most of us try to help when we can. But we feel that the querulous members of the movement have failed to recognize one basic fact about women: provided that they are willing and able to work hard, with self-discipline, they can do anything they really want to.

> Basically, the successful woman professional must acknowledge the mutual dependency of women, a point most women do not recognize.

> [Assuming] a young woman is determined to combine a career with marriage and motherhood, and that she is also determined to achieve at the highest level.

Three recommendations followed this last statement: seek an under-populated field, forego false pride, learn to put every moment of your time to good use.

While we recognize that women's liberation is a problem for some, we also hope it is a solution.

Right now the feminist pressure is so great that unless such arrangements for professional part-time work are made, employers will be unable to recruit enough women to meet the requirements of new anti-discrimination legislation; if they insist on full-time women they will have to reach down to the bottom of the barrel." The speaker then goes on to define currently successful women as "single women or single-minded superwomen.

Other women at the conference, however, were talking differently. Julia Apter spoke up:

I will agree that they [the thirteen married women scientists asked to speak about their careers] are very unusual women, . . . but I hope we won't go away thinking that they are the only ones. . . . there are 20,000 women listed in *American Men and Women of Science* and I personally know 1,250, . . . and any one of them is just as wonderful.

We've come a long way, baby—or have we? I am not always so sure.

⦊▪⦛

Lawrence Summers, then president of Harvard University, created a furor with his remarks in January 2005 suggesting that women may not have the same innate abilities as men in math and science. I was interviewed twice by the media about his comments, and many organizations and individual women have issued statements protesting the comments. The media, always eager to keep a story going, persist in identifying the protests as "political correctness" instead of as pointing out the lack of evidence for Summers' claim and its irrelevancy for explaining the dearth of women in math, chemistry, and physics departments.

While AWIS was getting underway, we began looking at our other professional societies. As a scientist, I belong to the American Association for the Advancement of Science (AAAS); as a physiologist I belong to the American Physiological Society (APS); as an endocrinologist I belong to the Endocrine Society (ES); and as a reproductive endocrinologist, I belong to the Society for the Study of Reproduction (SSR). As I look on each of these societies, I see different goals and different roles women have played in each. In fact, I myself have played different roles in each.

Professional societies such as APS, ES, and SSR serve several functions. They provide a venue for practitioners to get together, mingle, and discuss new findings. They sponsor journals for publication, they do some policing of practice, and they exert political influence in raising money for their respective fields.

The annual meetings of the societies are for idea exchange, job hunting, and faculty hiring. Except in the cases of female-dominated fields such as nursing or art therapy, the societies have been traditionally male-dominated. The officers have been male, invited keynote speakers have been mostly male, journal editors and reviewers have been male, chairs of meeting sessions and committees have been male. Since the annual meetings are the place for junior scientists to become visible (and frequently for finding jobs), women were and remain disadvantaged.

As feminism began to influence politics and the world outside of science, it also began to shake up the old boy's network of scientists. During the 1960s and 1970s, women in many professions started forming their own professional organizations. In general, these groups had four purposes (as I pointed out in a talk to the American Women's Medical Association (AMWA) in 1973: (1) to work for the achievement of equal opportunities and rights in reaching their professional goals; (2) to promote, recognize, and act on women's perspectives in the professional fields; (3) to train women in the administrative and political aspects of their professions; and (4) to promote consciousness raising among women in a particular group. The underlying strategy first was to form a club of our own (AWIS) and then use that to get into the "big-boy's" clubs.

„…›

In 1971, I was elected Vice President of the Endocrine Society. I do not remember asking what the duties were at the time (that shows how naive I was!), but I came to understand that the Vice President was usually chair of the scientific program for the coming year. At the annual meeting that year, I suddenly realized two things: that the next year's meeting (to be held in Washington, DC, in 1972) was an international one, so I would *not* automatically be chair of the program planning committee and that the program committee for the International Meeting was getting together just after the current meeting ended to plan the next year's program, and I was not even on the planning committee!

Angrily, I approached Bill Daughaday, then President of the Endocrine Society, and told him that I wanted to be sent to the program meeting and that I would not appear at the ES annual banquet as vice president unless he agreed to send me. He did; and I went to the planning meeting and added my thoughts to the program composition. But I remained angry at myself for being so naïve and for permitting myself to be elected to an empty position.

ॐॐ

The crucial event that led to the formation of Women in Endocrinology (WE) was a talk Janet W. McArthur gave in 1974 to the business meeting of the ES, as chair of an *ad hoc* committee on the status of women in the ES. Janet did pioneering research in women's endocrinology and was the first woman physician to become a Full Professor at Harvard Medical School. The committee presented a series of data documenting the (non)participation of women.

Members of the Endocrine Society are elected to the society only after being nominated by a current member. At that time, only about 8 percent of the ES membership was female. The number of women contributing to articles in *Endocrinology* and *Journal of Clinical Endocrinology & Metabolism* was at least equal to that figure or exceeded it, suggesting they were contributing to the science in proportion to their membership numbers. From 1955 to 1973, the years McArthur analyzed, women comprised about the same low percentage of journal editorial board members, but *no women* occupied senior managerial positions.

To me, the really discouraging information lay in the lack of representation of women in the administrative structure of the society, since this is where leadership can be exerted and changes can be made. Only one woman on the ES council (of nine); none were on either the nominating or finance committees, or on the awards or long-range planning committees. No women had been elected to the presidency or to the position of secretary-treasurer. Only four women had served as vice president, including myself.

I was so angry about this state of affairs that, in 1975, I decided it was time to form a women's caucus for the ES. Nettie Karpin was executive secretary at the time and covertly sent me a list of members, from which we picked out the women's names.

Julie Hotchkiss at the University of Texas and several other senior female endocrinologists came together, and Women in Endocrinology (WE) was launched. We moved immediately to begin supporting women to run for the parent society council by establishing our own internal nominating committee. The members of WE, which expanded rapidly, voted as a block for the most part.

WE publishes a newsletter and sponsors an annual banquet, which has become an official part of the ES social events at the meeting. WE also has an Internet Website and has accumulated money from outside sources to present a mentoring award each year and for travel awards for female trainees in labs of Endocrine Society members to come to the meeting. At the annual banquet, a speaker presents an address relevant to some social aspect of endocrinology and each year, the nominating committee submits nominations to the incoming president of the Endocrine Society for the parent society's committee memberships. Finally, WE helps young endocrinologists become members of ES, and acts as career mentors.

In 1990, members of the Steering Committee of WE also wrote a letter, which was published in the society journal *Endocrinology*, supporting the right to abortion. They also wrote protesting the firing of Dr. Jocelyn Elders (pediatric endocrinologist) as Surgeon General by President Clinton over her public comments about masturbation, which she recommended as an alternative to unprotected sex.

Many more committees have been formed in the Endocrine Society since Janet McArthur reported in 1974. Women are now much more likely than before to be chairing committees and serving on important committees such as the nominating, annual meeting (program), and publication committees. Women now constitute 37 percent of society members. Women are beginning to appear with greater frequency in the lists of those winning society awards. There are now four society journals.

In 2006, *Endocrinology* had a male editor, and of eight associate editors, three were women. Of 179 reviewers on the editorial board, forty-nine are women, about 27 percent. *Endocrine Reviews* had two women at the associate editor level, and six of the thirty-three members of the editorial board are women. *Molecular Endocrinology* has a male editor and two of six associate editors are women. There are fifty-five members on the editorial board, of whom twelve are women (22 percent). The *Journal of Clinical Endocrinology and Metabolism* has a male editor-in-chief, as do all the journals currently; three of ten editors are women, and of the 164 members of the editorial board, thirth-seven (23 percent) are women.

The June 1999 issue of all the ES journals focused on women's health and hormones, which would have been unheard of in earlier years. Clearly, the Endocrine Society has changed from what Janet McArthur described in 1974. A good part of the change is due to the continuous low level pressure exerted by WE for nominations to board positions and committee assignments. Also, block voting by the members of WE makes a difference in elections.

As a whole, one can say that the society has moved with the times, partly because of pressure,. But its progress stems at least in part from the inherent fairness of the male members of our profession.

Before 1978, no women had ever been elected president of the Endocrine Society; that year, Rosalyn Yalow became President. During the years since my presidency in 1982, there have been seven more women elected to the office.

In addition to increasing the central role of women in the core of decision making, the Endocrine Society has also expanded its outreach to minority endocrinologists, including a program of sending endocrinologists to interact with students at minority institutions.

I have made several trips to speak about endocrinology at colleges with a high enrollment of minority students, and I enjoyed the experience. In 2002, 2 percent and 25 percent of the speakers and chairs at the annual society meeting were minorities and women respectively; in 2004 those percentages rose to 10 percent and 40 percent.

৯৵৶

Why do I think women being able to move into positions of influence in the Endocrine Society is important? Those who assert that "biology is destiny" as the excuse for keeping women out of a position frequently call upon hormone changes during the menstrual cycle or differences between male and female brains, or sex differences in nurturing behavior as justifications.

I remember Dr. Estelle Ramey's article in *McCall's* in 1971 on the statement by President Kennedy's Surgeon General Luther Terry to the press regarding whether a woman could ever serve as president of the United States. He said that women's "raging hormonal imbalances" would render them unfit. He then went on to ask, "What would have happened at the Bay of Pigs if a woman had been president?"

Estelle pointed out that we were *defeated* at the Bay of Pigs and that Kennedy, who suffered from Addison's disease (low cortisol secretion), was *on steroids* at the time! Estelle was a member of the endocrinology group which I had joined when I was working at Michael Reese Hospital. She was always confident and outspoken, and was an important role model for me.

Women should be major players in research and interpretation of endocrinology not just because interpretations like "raging hormonal imbalances" are scientifically meaningless and such claims should be challenged, but also because female health issues, including hormonal ones, have not been a focus of research in the past by the male-dominated research and clinical community and it is crucial that they become so.

৯৵৶

Do not think that all women in the Endocrine Society have joined Women in Endocrinology, nor are all women supportive.

Rosalyn Yalow, a Nobel Laureate, was nominated by WE to the presidency of the Endocrine Society and won, primarily because of the support she received from the women. She thus became the first female president of the society. However, she began her presidential address in 1979 by saying:

> I believe my ascending to the presidency of the Endocrine Society is the final step in the general recognition that women have come of age in our Society and now participate with full equality in all its functions. I think it is unfortunate that the women's caucus of the society has chosen to remain a special interest group rather than changing its name and function so as to serve a developmental role for our entire membership.

Fortunately WE continued and, indeed, it has made a real difference to the society's women *and* men.

ঔ৽৽৾

Society for the Study of Reproduction. Newer societies without a well-developed "old boy" network are more ready to admit women. The Society for the Study of Reproduction, which formed in 1967, is an excellent example. Not only have women been participants in the central administration of the society from the outset, as board members and officers, but the society has also encouraged graduate students to participate in council affairs and program planning.

As of 2006, eight women have been presidents. From the beginning, one quarter of the directors of the society have been women. Not surprisingly, the age at which society members assume elected office is younger than it is in many societies.

To my knowledge, there has not been any move toward starting a women's caucus in SSR. A feature of the meetings, held on university campuses, is a luncheon at which trainees can sit at a table with a regular member to discuss whatever. In 2000, at the meeting in Madison, Wisconsin, all of the past presidents of the organization were mentors at these lunch tables. Women have been an integral part of the society from the beginning, although they have probably not yet won their fair share of awards.

ঔ৽৽৾

American Physiological Society. My first professional society was the American Physiological Society, but I gradually moved away and into the Endocrine Society as I started to identify myself more as an endocrinologist than as a physiologist. The papers I heard at the ES meetings were more relevant to my work. The APS always seemed like an old boy's club when I served on their committees. The last straw for me came when I was asked to serve on the long-range planning committee because, "we need a woman."

Well, what should I do? Become a lone female member of that club and burrow from within, or make a "statement" about their treatment of women? I turned down the opportunity to serve on yet another committee as the only woman and opted out of participation in the society, although I have remained a member. In marked contrast with the ES and SSR, in over 100 years, still only three women have been elected president!

ঔ৽৽৾

Honorary Societies. Two major honorary societies in our country recognize outstanding achievement among scientists. Since current members nominate for membership, it is not surprising that women scientists are vastly underrepresented. The American Academy of Arts and Sciences is the more eclectic, including both the humanities and the social and natural sciences. The inclusion of women in various sub-disciplines reflects the distribution of women in these sub-categories, but under represents them.

The National Academy of Sciences is highly exclusive; only recently have women become members. Elga Wasserman's *The Door in the Dream*, which reported interviews of female members of NAS about their careers, is an interesting read. Many of those interviewed are not in academic positions but at research institutes and some are married to academy members. A number of the married women said they could not have had such major research programs along with having children and doing teaching, making the environment of research institutes more desirable for them than universities.

Occasionally, critics point to the low number of women (far below the number of women participating in the sciences) in the NAS. In 2006, an international interacademy council on women in science, appointed to suggest how to remove barriers to women and girls entering science, suggested that the national academies themselves must "first put their own houses in order."

As I look at the three discipline-based societies I belong to—American Physiology Society, Endocrine Society, and Society for the Study of Reproduction—I can see clear differences among them in the ways in which women have been welcomed and permitted to gain central positions. The APS has had a vanishingly small number of women in central leadership positions, I think because of the domination of medical school departments of physiology in the society, few of which have female chairs. This society began in the nineteenth century and has not yet shaken off the mantle of male dominance. It does try though, I must admit. It has a committee on women and a committee to appoint an annual female lecturer for a major lecture sponsored by Federation of American Societies for Experimental Biology. The APS participates in selecting the lecturer: I represented the ES on this committee for a number of years.

In contrast to APS, the Endocrine Society, formed in 1915, has made clear strides in welcoming women into its central leadership roles, partly in response to WE. While physicians, particularly from Ivy League medical schools, dominated the society in the beginning, the increasing numbers of prominent endocrinologists, basic and clinical, from midwest and pacific coast schools changed this elitist picture. In addition, endocrinology has been an attractive field for women in basic science and is an important aspect of clinical practice in pediatrics, obstetrics and gynecology, and internal medicine, specialties which have particularly attracted female physicians.

The Society for the Study of Reproduction, formed in 1967, has been open to female participation from the outset. In a way, its base has been the land grant universities, with their veterinary schools and departments of animal husbandry focused on reproduction in large domestic animals. But participation from basic biological scientists like me has contributed science from rodents; primate center scientists come to present data on monkeys and lemurs; and zoo researchers talk about reproduction in endangered species. This makes for a lively, informal, very egalitarian meeting.

Having women participating centrally in professional societies has enhanced women's opportunities to influence the public role of societies and the direction of research emphasis, in addition to enhancing professional opportunities for women. But it has done something else as well: it has enlivened the science and the scientists.

In 1992, the trainees in the Society for the Study of Reproduction decided to have a talk on women in the society. Colleen Jo Nolan, then the trainee representative, asked me to talk for fifteen minutes on the "emergence of women scientists as members and officers of SSR and your role as first woman president." She also said, "it would give the women in the audience some insight as to the changes that have occurred within our society in regard to the roles and acceptance of women."

Well, it was straightforward to start the talk with a list of women who had served on the board and as officers. So I made a table of that information for a slide. But I wanted to do something more than just talk about each of the women's careers. I really wanted to produce a three dimensional representation of the women for our trainees and our colleagues to see. So I wrote to each of the women who had held office (except to Cornelia Channing, my initial collaborator on the inhibin studies, who had died of breast cancer in 1985), asking each:

> Could you send me a picture, either of you as a child, in your lab, or doing something spectacular? I am trying to do two things: show the role women have played in our organization and also inject some humor and life into the proceedings.

The result of my request was fantastic. I was inundated with pictures. It was hard to choose which ones to show. As I told the audience before I presented the slides, I was trying to illustrate "where some of us came from before we became reproductive biologists, where others of us are right now, and what we are doing when we are not being reproductive biologists—to show us in three dimensions."

Nancy Alexander sent me a picture of herself palpating an elephant and attempting to reach its cervix.

Janice Bahr, who was the president-elect at the time, is a Professor in Animal Science at the University of Illinois, Urbana. Her research is focused on ovarian function in chickens, pigs, and other species, including bears! Her picture showed her at eight years old holding two rabbits. She also described the family around her in the picture and described herself thus:

Third daughter. I doubled as my father's son and my mother's daughter on a dairy farm; cleaned house each week, learned to cook and sew; and had the responsibility to get the brown Swiss cows milked.

My former collaborator on the inhibin discovery was *Cornelia (Nina) Channing,* a director from 1978–1980. She was the first woman to win the SSR Research Award (in 1978) for her work on peptide factors in the ovary. At the time of her death from breast cancer in 1985, she was Professor of Physiology at the University of Maryland. She and I had gone to India to attend a conference on gonadotropins. I showed a picture of Nina, Bob Ryan, and me in front of the Taj Mahal.

Joanne Fortune was president of SSR in 1994–1995 and is a Professor at Cornell. Her research is on the biochemistry and physiology of ovarian function in cows. Her picture was taken with her brother, grandmother, aunt, and uncle. In it, Joanne was carrying an Easter basket.

Anne Hirshfield was a director and treasurer of SSR. Her research is on the development of ovarian follicles. She is now an associate vice-president at George Washington University Medical School. The picture she sent was of her playing the guitar and "imitating Joan Baez." As she put it, "I was sweet sixteen, in high school, and part of the sixties generation."

Mary Hunzicker-Dunn was president of SSR in 2003–2004. She was a Professor at Northwestern's Medical School. We have been friends and colleagues for over thirty years. Mary sent me a photo of herself drinking beer in the bleachers during a Cub's game at Wrigley Field, which is something I've had the privilege of doing with Mary's lab members several times. The last time, I almost caught a Sammy Sosa homer. Mary has now moved to Washington State University, where she is a distinguished Professor—a major loss for Northwestern University.

Marie-Claire Orgebin-Crist was a director of SSR. She is now Professor Emerita at Vanderbilt University medical school. She sent a photograph of herself hiking in the Alps, saying "where I am when I am not at the SSR meeting in July."

Margaret Orsini served SSR as director in 1972–1974. Margaret and I published the first papers examining LH secretion in the golden hamster. When I was in Madison on sabbatical in 1990, we spent a number of evenings eating dinner together and watching movies on the VCR. She sent me a very somber picture of herself deep in thought. I also showed a second picture of her on a motorbike. Margaret died recently in Madison, Wisconsin.

Anita Payne was president in 1990–1991. Anita has retired from the University of Michigan but is still doing research at Stanford University, where she is near her grandchildren. Her research continues to focus on aspects of testosterone biosynthesis in the testes. Anita sent me a picture of a clipping from a San Francisco newspaper, which appeared early in her career. She was identified as a "glamorous housewife," and the photo had appeared under the headline "Two Bay Housewives Win Cancer Award." This "housewife" won the Carl Hartman Award for research in 1998 and the SSR Distinguished Service Award in 2004.

Judith Ramaley was treasurer 1982–1985. Her research was focused on the hormonal and environmental factors inducing puberty in rats. At the time of my talk, she had just become president of Portland State University in Oregon. She sent me a picture taken at an informal presidential reception. She had been cooking something over a brazier, and the tablecloth had caught fire. "President Ramaley setting the world on fire."

JoAnne Richards served as a director in 1981–1983; won the SSR Research Award in 1989 for her work on the intracellular signal pathways in the follicle cells of the ovary. She is a Professor at Baylor College University Medical School. She sent pictures of herself as a student at Oberlin College twirling on their new ice-skating rink as a freshman.

I was president of SSR from 1977–1978. I showed a slide of myself in a bathing suit, barbequing a chicken while crouching over a Weber grill at my house in Door County, Wisconsin.

Susan Smith was a director of SSR: she is the director of the Oregon Regional Primate Center. Susan is a neuroendocrinologist who has focused on the regulation of prolactin secretion during lactation. In 1994–1995, she was president of the Endocrine Society. She sent a picture of herself at the twenty-mile mark during the Pittsburgh marathon where her finish time was "3hours, 36minutes, 38 seconds."

Phyllis Wise was an SSR director in 1991–1994, while a Professor of Physiology at Maryland. She is currently provost at the University of Washington. Her research is on aging of the hypothalamic-pituitary-ovarian systems. She sent a picture of her young daughter Erica, who was smiling for the picture, her two front teeth missing.

I still marvel at what this group of women working in the field of reproductive biology has done with their careers and their lives. That the Society for the Study of Reproduction was wise enough to choose them as officers is a tribute to the membership. SSR has had a public affairs committee for many years, and has been very influential in Washington, lobbying for reproductive research. Trainees have been an important part of the central governance of the society almost since its beginning. It is still a pleasure to attend the annual meeting, particularly the one in 2006 in Omaha, Nebraska.

As I look back over my career and my life, I believe the work I have done in helping other women and me to have meaningful careers in science, rather than playing "handmaiden" roles, is my major contribution. For so many reasons, as Maria Mitchell said, "how much science needs women."

Study Questions

(1) Discuss "the boys club" concept in terms of today's culture.
- Does it still exist? If yes, give examples.
- Discuss whether we should and how we can influence it.

(2) Discuss Neena's claim to be victim of the boys club in terms of the actual evidence of her professional career.
- Does the evidence appear to support her claims?
- Consider and discuss to what extent the barriers were broken due to Neena and her colleagues' groundbreaking advocacy.

Nine

INSIDE THE IVORY TOWER

I have known the inexorable sadness of pencils,
Neat in their boxes, dolor of pad and paper-weight,
All the misery of manila folders and mucilage . . . .
And I have seen dust from the walls of institutions,
Finer than flour, alive, more danger than silica,
Sift, almost visible, through long afternoons of tedium . . . .

Theodore Roethke
"Dolor"

From January 1973 through August 1974, I was a Professor in the Department of Physiology at Northwestern's Medical School. *Déjà vu,* all over again! The department's faculty had turned over almost completely in the twenty years since my graduate student days, which was good; it meant that my colleagues did not have to shed any previous images of me that might have lingered.

It was hard to remember the young me, what my dreams were, whether I had ever thought I would return, full circle, to this department. Luckily, all three of my technicians came with me from the University of Illinois Medical School to the Northwestern campus on Lake Michigan, and some graduate students also, so our lab was up and running almost immediately.

Then something surprising happened; at least it was surprising to me. During the eighteen months I spent back in the department, I was interviewed for a number of chair positions in physiology departments at other medical schools from coast to coast.

At that time, to my knowledge, no women were chairing physiology departments. A few biology departments were being chaired by women, but medical schools were slower to take the plunge.

This suggests to me that by the early 1970s, some deans had begun to recognize that hiring women as chairs could be a good thing. The offer I took most seriously was the Chair of Physiology at University of Iowa in Iowa City. The department had a reasonably good reputation, and I knew some of the endocrinologists in other departments at the university.

However, I worried about being a lesbian in a relatively small town like Iowa City. As Dean John W. Eckstein drove me around Iowa City showing me some possible houses for sale, he pointed out a number of other houses and said, "Professor So and So lives there," or "Dr. John Doe and his family are in that place." Not at all like Chicago!

Of course, Rue and I were living in Evanston by then, also a small university town, but being near a big city like Chicago tremendously expanded our possibilities for a varied social life. I knew I could not go without her, and she obviously would need a job if she went.

With my heart in my mouth, I talked with the Dean about whether they could offer a position to Rue and gave him a copy of her CV.

In fact, Eckstein was interested in having a medical sociologist on the faculty and rather quickly found a position for Rue, but she was very reluctant to move to such a small town. As she said, "Every bone in my sociologist body tells me it would be a mistake."

My chief technician Bill Talley, an African American, was flown in to Iowa City by the Dean. Bill was also reluctant to go there, since by the end of one afternoon, everybody in Iowa City seemed to know him!

What clinched my decision not to take the job came when the Dean told me proudly that the Chicago Symphony Orchestra came to town for two concerts a year. Rue and I heard the CSO thirty times every year, and neither of us was willing to give that up.

෨෬

While I was still mulling over this offer, Oscar Hechter, Chair of the Physiology Department at Northwestern, fired the best young faculty researcher in our department for "contradicting him in front of a graduate student!" This was Lutz Birnbaumer, who was an untenured assistant professor at the time, and who subsequently went elsewhere, on to a marvelous research career on intraovarian signal pathways. This immediately brought back memories of the University of Illinois and the Physiology Department there, ringing a warning bell in my mind. I knew it was just a matter of time before *I* contradicted Oscar in front of a graduate student! Of course, he would not be able to fire me, since I was tenured, but I knew I could not live with a chairperson unwilling to tolerate disagreement.

Furthermore, Lutz was crucial to the multi-research grant application the chair was intending to send to NICHD, and it was clear to me that without him, we would not have enough projects to put on the application. I went to talk with the Dean, Jim Eckenhof, behind Oscar's back. I was reluctant to do this, but I could see how destructive the situation was. Jim did not disagree with my assessment but felt he could not act on it. I knew I needed to make a move.

When Hanna Holborn Gray, Dean of the College of Arts and Science at the Evanston campus of Northwestern, offered me the Chair of Biological Sciences and an endowed professorship, just days before she left to become provost at Yale, I snapped at it.

I had been identified as a prospect for the chair by a search committee at the Evanston campus; apparently she and they felt I was a good bet. This solved my problems with the medical school and the dilemma Rue and I had about leaving our comfortably social city of Chicago as well.

෨෩

So in September 1974, I became the William Deering Professor of Biological Sciences and Chair of the Department of Biological Sciences in Evanston. I welcomed the opportunity to get away from medical schools with their autocratic department heads. I also welcomed the chance to join a broader biology community, to have contact with undergraduates, and to become a member of a real university community. Medical schools are a world apart from the rest of the academic scene because of their necessary affiliation with hospitals and their major service obligations.

But something else was happening to me during this time of changing opportunities. In 1973 and 1974, while I was looking at these various chairs, something began happening to my *amour propre*. I began to experience serious bouts of depression and started seeing a psychiatrist again regularly. I also started on a regimen of anti-depressants. It seemed an odd return to the time when I had been depressed early in college.

What I began to realize was that the depressions were partly associated with the onset of autumn: Seasonal Affective Disorder (SAD). But then in 1974, my father sent me a clipping from the *Baltimore Sun*. It was the obituary of Alicia, my first lover. I wept as I read it, and I could still remember and feel the overwhelming emotion between us, the discovery of passion, closeness, and togetherness with each other. She was only forty-six years old.

I called Alicia's younger sister, who practiced clinical endocrinology in New Jersey, to ask what had happened. Alicia had developed a sudden headache and collapsed; her husband called an ambulance. An aneurysm had ruptured in her brain. She was unconscious for a day, and her brain swelled, but she became conscious while her sister was sitting in her room.

"What is it?" she asked.

"You've had an aneurysm and they are about to operate."

"No, I don't want it," said and she closed her eyes and died.

I still think about Alicia when I return to Baltimore and drive along twisting, hilly Green Spring Avenue north of the city, as this was our favorite drive together, especially in autumn, when the colors were a mixture of reds and yellows. I remember how guilty I felt about the relationship but how compelled I felt to continue it. I will always cherish and love her, our relationship taught me who I was and am.

How much did Alicia's death have to do with my depression? I don't know. During the years from 1974 to 1996, I kept a "Depression Diary" on loose-leaf paper, and would write in it regardless of where I went. I started with occasional entries, but as my personal and professional lives seemed to be dissolving around me, entries became more frequent. It was a place to express joys and anxieties about lovers, family, and colleagues as well as work. I have now gone back to read it to help me recapture my feelings during the years I am recording here.

As I started as Chair in Evanston, I dwelled on the "chance not to be incompetent, and have some power, and use it well." But I also complained, "research is different than it used to be. The team is so damned big the only things I do are light fires under people and rewrite papers." Ah yes, but you can't go home again.

෴

Several members of my new department had split off the year before I was recruited to form a separate Department of Biochemistry, Molecular Biology, and Cell Biology (BMBCB) with some members of the chemistry department. The week my appointment was announced, BMBCB happened to have a party and their chair laughed about the "new woman chair" of the old department; he said, "BMBCB will have the Hogan Building (where both departments were located) away from Biology by the end of the year." He was wrong, but I became aware of antagonism from some members of that department and lots of bitterness about the split from many of the senior members of my own department. The atmosphere was contentious and contributed to my depression.

෴

After I became Chair, two female graduate students, one in Biology and one in Chemistry, came up to me at a welcoming party and asked, "Do people laugh when you give a paper?"

I answered flippantly "only when I make a joke," but then went on to talk with them in detail. They had had no female professors in graduate school and had received no mentoring whatsoever. They really believed that women presenting papers at a scientific meeting would be objects of ridicule. They both dropped out of graduate school before finishing, which did not surprise me. They seemed so different than I was after I had finished graduate school in 1953.

I had a lot of confidence in my abilities as a teacher and researcher, as I had lectured to nursing students and run labs as a teaching assistant with medical students. I certainly recognized the importance of presenting papers at national meetings and began doing so. This has become a major requirement of being a trainee in my lab; all of my own graduate students and post-docs (and even undergraduates) have learned to present papers.

Of course, my own students know that no one laughs at me when I present a paper. But the incident alerted me to the need for more visible women in the sciences on the Evanston campus. At the time that I became

chair, no tenured female faculty members at all were on the faculty in physics, chemistry, or mathematics, and only a few of us were scattered throughout the two biological sciences departments.

❧

The next four years were hard work. The department sorely needed to be rebuilt and reanimated. Several of the die-hard senior faculty assumed that
since all of my previous experience was in a medical school environment, I
would make members of the department, particularly any I recruited, work on
my research. That thought had never occurred to me, although I *was* interested in recruiting a couple of faculty members who might be interested in collaborating with me on research.

The department had weekly faculty meetings, which were stressful due to
the rancor some members felt toward me and others in the department. But I
thought it was necessary to face the problems and try to deal with them.

I asked Sid Simpson, one of the mid-career associate professors, to serve
as part-time Associate Chair; he did and this helped a lot. (Nowadays, no one
would consider taking the chair of a big science department without having a
full-time assistant chair at the PhD level to serve as an office manager and
head up the teaching scheduling.)

Hanna Gray had told me that the undergraduate teaching in the department was a problem. After attending a few of the lectures, I saw why. Some
of the lecturers were flat in their teaching and so pedantic. One of the professors, a senior member of the department, missed a number of lectures, which
I discovered when students came to complain. I met with him about it and
became immediately convinced that he was ill, so I arranged for him to take
early retirement and appointed someone else to pick up the teaching.

Students also complained about the teaching labs. I attended a couple,
and they were right again. The labs were being run in a slip-shod manner by
faculty who had not revised them for years. All of the equipment was antique,
old fashioned and hardly state of the art.

I obtained some funds from the college and hired a full-time lab director, John Bjerke, who changed the whole aspect of lab exercises and the atmosphere within the lab itself. I took over the teaching of physiology in the
core curriculum for sophomores myself.

We started recruiting up-and-coming young assistant professors and the
votes in our faculty meetings began turning my way.

❧

My career was also progressing well. At that time, I was a member of the
National Institute of Child Health and Development (NICHD) Board of
Scientific Counselors, which has the role of overseeing the internal research

at that particular NIH institute in Bethesda. I was also president elect of the Society for the Study of Reproduction, the first woman in that position. At Northwestern, I was a member of the Task Force on Life Sciences, a group organized by then Dean of the Graduate School, Clarence VerSteeg. The plan developed by that task force became the blueprint for progress in life sciences at Northwestern for the next twenty years.

My research and visibility flourished. The research was well funded; I was giving many symposium papers, and I had presented the inaugural Gregory Pincus Memorial Lecture at the Laurentian Hormone Conference.

Life at last seemed rosier than at Illinois. But my depression diary grew in length.

೫०९

Shortly after I became Chair, several female graduate students and a junior faculty member, Connie Campbell, asked me to meet with them one evening a month to "talk about problems of women in science." I refused at first, saying I was "chair of everyone in the department not just the women." But they persisted, and I joined them. It proved as valuable for me as it was for them when the senior faculty of the department was harassing me. I gained as much from ventilating and discussing as the others in the group did.

This opportunity to talk about feelings and check them out with others is critical when one is in a hostile environment. Otherwise, one blames oneself, asking always "What did I do wrong?" Not one of the students in the group dropped out of graduate school, and many went on to clear success as scientists and administrators.

One of the participants, Meriamne Whatley, now an Associate Dean at the University of Wisconsin, mentioned the importance of this group for her in her self-description in Sue Vilhauer Rosser's book on teaching feminist science. Another, Joan Herbers, became a Chair at Boulder. She has just been elected to an office in AWIS. She is currently Dean of Biological Sciences at Ohio State.

೫०९

Connie Campbell had been a postdoctoral fellow in my lab while I was in the psychiatry department at Illinois. She had been in the Peace Corps before attending graduate school at the University of Illinois. Connie had a PhD in psychology and had come to my lab at Illinois to study interrelationships between hormones and behavior.

When I became Chair at Northwestern in 1974, I had her give a seminar and the department hired her as an assistant professor. She and I continued to collaborate on some studies while she began developing a strong behavioral program in her own lab. Her teaching was excellent and she also received a research grant from NIH. She started an undergraduate honors program in the biological sciences and had lots of enthusiastic students doing research in our labs and writing papers for honors. Her tenure decision came up in 1980.

People on the tenure and promotions committee were afraid that Connie was just working on *my* research, in other words, that I had hired her just to expand my own research program. While it was true that I had felt the department needed a behaviorally oriented scientist, it seemed clear from her CV that she was doing her own work. She received tenure, to our relief.

Sadly, a year later, Connie developed colon cancer, which was misdiagnosed by physicians at the HMO responsible for her care. Even after she was clearly flagging physically, she insisted on coming into the lab every day and working with her graduate students. Finally, she was unable to continue, and she died in 1981. Her friends, colleagues, and family set up the Constance Campbell Memorial Fund at Northwestern. It is used for prizes for the six trainees who present the three best posters and the three best oral presentations at the annual mini-symposium sponsored by the Center for Reproductive Science at Northwestern.

❧

Not long after I started chairing the department at Northwestern, I went to see the vice president for Research, Dave Mintzer. I had met Dave when I was being recruited for the medical school position, so I knew him already. In fact, he had provided money for equipment for my recruitment to the med school, which he needed to purchase again when I moved to Evanston from the lakeside in Chicago.

"Dave, I think with a little start-up money I can put together a strong interdisciplinary program in reproductive science at Northwestern. I want to start by bringing faculty and students from both campuses together."

I suggested that we form a program for reproductive research. I proposed that my first order of business would be to attract relevant faculty already at Northwestern to become members. Dave liked the idea and gave me some money to hold informal research meetings on both campuses. Some faculty members indicated interest immediately. Dave said he would make us an official center, rather than a program, if we could start bringing in research funds from outside the university to support a research program of a multidisciplinary nature. Naturally, I accepted the challenge.

This proposal was really a reworking of the interdisciplinary group plan that I had tried to initiate at the University of Illinois which was blocked by their Chair of Ob/Gyn. In contrast, at Northwestern, the Chair of Ob/Gyn at the Medical School, Jack Sciarra, was very supportive, and many members of his department, including him, signed on to the program. A number of collaborative research projects started among various faculty in both the college and the medical school and eventually led to a highly successful center.

෯෧

Why was I so persistent in trying to initiate a multidisciplinary program in reproductive science? I believe that such an approach—bringing together physicians, endocrinologists, physiologists, psychologists, biochemists— permits the use of state-of-the-art methodology quickly and efficiently and brings different approaches to bear on shared problems.

I mentioned earlier how my collaboration with Charles Ely at Columbia enabled me to obtain antiserum reagents which would block gonadotropin action. My collaboration with Margaret Orsini, at the University of Wisconsin, permitted us to do a series of studies comparing control of the rat estrous cycle with the hamster cycle. It had not occurred to me before Irv Rothchild at Case-Western contacted me about studying LH regulation in the luteal phase of the rat cycle to use this experimental model to compare LH synthesis and secretion when progesterone levels were high, as occurs in human beings during the second half of every menstrual cycle.

How valuable these collaborations had been! Why not try to bring together scientists in-house to talk together, plan experiments, and interpret data? Thus, a number of research collaborations started taking place slowly among members of the program, even before we began applying for outside collaborative grants.

෯෧

My own laboratory experiments on the hormone inhibin were launched during this time too. We fell (or backed) into the inhibin story. During the rat cycle, and that of many other mammals, including human beings, estrogen stimulates the release of GnRH from the brain, which then triggers the preovulatory pituitary secretion of both LH and FSH. But after the initial or primary LH/FSH surge which causes ovulation, there is a *continuing rise* in serum FSH in the rat and some other species, while serum LH falls.

We could think of a rationale for this; in a short four-day cycle like that of the rat, hamster, or mouse, it is necessary to prepare another group of follicles ready to grow in case the current cycle does not result in pregnancy. FSH is the pituitary hormone that causes follicles to grow. We hypothesized that this was the *adaptive significance* of this secondary rise of FSH, but what was the cause?

Perhaps the LH surge was inhibiting something coming from the ovary, which might have been inhibiting FSH. This was reminiscent of a similar search for a hormone from the testes during the early 1920s. It had been proposed back then that a hormone from the testis existed that suppresses FSH, but not LH, but many years of work in a number of labs had not isolated this so-called "inhibin."

❧

I have described in a Remembrance written on request in 1991 for the journal *Endocrinology*, how Nina Channing, from the University of Maryland, and I started looking for inhibin in ovarian follicular fluid. I titled the remembrance, "Why I was told Not to Work on Inhibin and What I Did about It." Some friends had told me, when I started to work in this field, "You are going to ruin your reputation if you continue." People still did not believe inhibin was a real hormone.

Channing had been visiting the slaughterhouse in Baltimore to retrieve fluid from pig ovarian follicles, testing its ability to inhibit meiosis in ovulating oocytes, which it did. She hoped eventually to purify this factor and test it as a possible contraceptive. The onset of meiosis (reduction in chromosomes in the egg to half in preparation for fertilization) of the ova in the ripe follicles is triggered by the LH surge, just as the secondary surge of FSH is. This prompted me to look for inhibin in these ripe follicles. I called Nina and told her I would like to see if the fluid could lower FSH.

She agreed, froze some fluid, and shipped it to Evanston. I decided to inject it into proestrous females late in the afternoon after the LH surge had taken place and then collect blood samples at 4 a.m. to see if we had blocked the expected secondary FSH surge.

After thawing the fluid Nina sent, I injected a small amount into a number of rats I expected were ovulating that night and actually collected the blood myself at 4 a.m. (I kept my students out of the project at first, because I thought if it proved unsuccessful, they should not be tainted by it.)

As a control, I injected other rats in the same cycle stage with a saline solution. I gave the samples to Brigitte Mann, my technician, who ran the FSH radioimmunoassays for me. I was leaving for Hamburg to attend the international endocrine meetings the day after Brigitte finished the assays, and I asked her to phone me at home with the results before I caught the plane. I was going to see Channing at the Hamburg meeting and wanted to tell her what we had found.

Brigitte did not have the code which could distinguish which rats had received the follicular fluid and which had received the control injection. When she called, she said, "Well, there are some very low FSH values and some high ones." She read off the sample numbers and data to me, and with the code, I saw instantly that the ovarian fluid had severely lowered the blood levels of FSH. We had found an inhibin!

Nina was ecstatic, and we decided to present the data at the physiology meetings the following spring.

After I returned from Hamburg, my lab set up a bioassay for inhibin in follicular fluid using the acutely ovariectomized female rat, in which serum FSH rises within a few hours. We were able to block that rise in a dose-dependent manner by injecting porcine follicular fluid. We had identified inhibin in females!

Subsequently we showed that it was a protein over 10,000 Molecular Weight. Nina and I went on to study the physiology of inhibin in the female and male rat using a radioimmunoassay developed by Wylie Vale's group at the Salk Institute for blood inhibin.

A highly productive interdisciplinary collaboration also ensued between my lab and that of Kelly Mayo, a newly recruited molecular biologist in the BMBCB department, who had a molecular probe for the ovarian inhibin mRNA. This probe was able to detect messenger RNA for inhibin within granulosa cells of the ovary where it was being transcribed. These are the cells that surround each oocyte and are deemed "nurse cells" for the oocyte.

Kelly and I, along with grad student, Teresa Woodruff, and postdoctoral fellow, Jo Beth D'Agostino, went on to demonstrate and publish a number of important aspects of inhibin and FSH regulation during the normal estrous cycle and after a series of relevant experimental manipulations.

JoBeth is now an associate professor at Loyola University, in the Department of Biology, and Teresa is now a professor in the Department of Ob/Gyn at Northwestern, after working in industry for a number of years and then in our Department of Neurobiology and Physiology.

These FSH/inhibin experiments were critical to the field of ovarian/pituitary regulation not only because they explained some missing normal physiology but also because they provided a rich source of inhibin: follicular fluid. Follicular fluid proved to be such a potent source that biochemists and molecular biologists were able to purify inhibin and identify its structure in the late 1980s.

Inhibin has now been measured in human blood in males and females. It is a useful marker for some types of ovarian cancer and in differential diagnosis of infertility in males. Inhibin is a member of a whole family of proteins, the "Transforming Growth Factor beta" family, which is widely involved in many phylogenetic classes of animals and in many functions in developing vertebrates, as well as in bone synthesis.

The discovery of this widespread family of molecules was initiated by our simple physiological experiments designed to discover how FSH was regulated. Nina and I tried to name our hormone "folliculostatin," but the original name "inhibin" was too firmly entrenched, and that name stuck.

ॐ

After inhibin, my research career really took off. Lots of invitations for symposia, congresses, and chapters for books followed the beginning of our inhibin research. One of the most interesting meetings took place during 1973 in Bangalore, India. It was a conference on the gonadotropins, sponsored by the Rockefeller Foundation Population Council.

Before the conference, Rue and I both had to go to Milan, me to give a seminar at the Luciano Martini lab and she to launch a new international sociology journal. We left Milan after being wined, dined, and talked at for several days and then drove north toward Switzerland, where we were meeting her parents in Zurich for a family reunion.

Driving through Switzerland with Rue was a lot of fun. We enjoyed the inns and the flowers and the lakes. I discovered suddenly that I needed a visa for India, and so we had to delay going to Zurich and first drove to Geneva, where an Indian embassy was located.

From Geneva. Rue wanted to drive straight across the mountains to Zurich. My reading of our maps was that the mountain passes were closed by then. She was so proud of being Swiss, and she insisted that the passes all had to be still open. But as we drove up to the first pass we saw the sign: "*Ferme*, *Geschlossen*, Closed."

We backtracked then and took the car-train to Zurich. I was leaving for Bombay from Zurich a few days later, and Rue and her parents drove me to the airport for my Air India flight. Her mother, Grace Bucher, made me promise that I would visit them in Seattle, where they had retired. We set a date for that trip, and I took off for India. Unfortunately, a few weeks before the date I had agreed to go to Seattle, Grace died unexpectedly, and Rue and I went out for the memorial service instead.

কব

The trip to India was both exotic and chilling. The temples and other buildings and the food and the music were exotic and never to be forgotten. But the poverty and the beggars were depressing and ever present.

The meeting itself took place in Bangalore. When I arrived in that city, the streets were being swept clean by people, on their hands and knees, because Indira Gandhi was visiting the next day.

I knew most of the other speakers at the meeting, and Nina Channing and I were sharing a room. When the time came for my talk, I handed the projectionist my numbered slides. He was quite elderly and wearing thick glasses. He dropped the slide box and the slides scattered.

I said, "They are numbered," and he put them back into the machine. To my horror, I discovered after I started my talk that he was showing them in completely random order, which was quite a challenge to me as a speaker. I discovered later from my hosts that he was legally blind but had to be employed by the institute for a "political reason."

কব

In spite of the slide snafu, the meeting was fun. As we ate lunch in the courtyard, roving monkeys came down from the trees and grabbed at our food. I wanted to buy some records of Indian music, so one of the local graduate students drove with me, in a pedicab, to a local music shop. We were, of course, chased by beggars.

Our group also traveled together to Agra to see the Taj Mahal. My brother had asked me to take a photo of the palace with the fountains in front. As kids, he and I had both read Richard Halliburton's tales of traveling to see the Seven Wonders of the World, and had told about visiting Agra and hiding during the day on the grounds of the Taj Mahal on a night of the full moon and bathing that night in these fountains.

I stood in front of the fountain, which was not spouting, with Nina Channing and Bob Ryan, with whom I had taught at Illinois. The water in the channel was peppered with coke bottles and beer cans, paper candy wrappers, and discarded cigarettes. I dutifully took some pictures and sent them to Leon when I returned to Chicago. He called after he received them and said he was thoroughly disillusioned.

☙❧

When I returned to Evanston, the lab and department were continuing to do well in its recruitment of faculty and acquisition of external grants. The teaching of biology to the undergraduates had improved and the department had become less contentious. But I was still somewhat depressed.

As I look back at my diary, I see statements like, "losing my cutting edge," and, "we are doing too many things: adrenal vs. ovary as a source of estrogen, stress on FSH levels, brain lesion effects on mating behavior, constant light on the estrous cycle, puberty and stress . . . ." From a later vantage point, it seems clear that this was depression talking, since the work all turned out to be important, connected, and publishable.

☙❧

In the midst of the extensive research work, department chairing, and traveling to meetings, two disasters shook me. First, Rue and I began having problems in our relationship. At that time, she was a tenured associate professor in the University of Illinois Psychiatry Department. Her research was well funded by National Institute of Mental Health, and she was writing her second book. Both of us were beginning to wander a bit in our affections, thinking we were satisfied with an "open" relationship.

I became involved sporadically with someone in a different city whom I saw at professional meetings; Rue unfortunately became involved with someone who was a colleague of mine and whom I could not avoid seeing daily at the university.

I was devastated by this, and I believe Rue was too. We still loved each other, but we were clearly no longer in love—an old, and hackneyed story—

we did not know how to deal with it. We began talking about splitting up, which was painful for both of us, but it began gradually to seem the only thing to do. We had lived together for sixteen years, but somehow we were no longer meeting each other's needs. While having young children may save some marriages, having two dogs and a cat were insufficient.

❧

Toward the end of 1977, I went to Israel for a meeting, by myself. I knew I was taking a risk leaving Rue and Evanston at this crucial stage in her budding relationship, but I had accepted the invitation to speak the year before and had already planned a vacation week in Greece after Israel.

While sunbathing in Tel Aviv, walking in Delphi at night, swimming in the Aegean, and exploring the Greek islands by boat, I came to terms to some extent with the break-up.

When I returned from Greece, Rue and I finalized a decision to split. I rented a house for a year, and she stayed in our house while we decided how to divide our belongings. I took the black and tan dachshund Joey and our cat Snooky, and she took Gretchen, our standard schnauzer. After a year, she bought a house in downtown Chicago, and I bought out her half of our house in Evanston. Neither one of us could bear to give up *At Beigh*, in Wisconsin, so we held on to it but began going up separately, with other lovers.

❧

The second disaster struck in 1978. After Dean Gray left, a new Dean had been appointed for the College of Arts and Sciences. He was a somewhat Teutonic philosopher from Vassar, Rudolph Weingartner. How he did at Vassar, with its feminist culture, I cannot imagine, but he clearly had trouble at Northwestern with women who did not instantly buckle down to his authority.

As far as I remember, Weingartner did not appoint a single woman to a chair while he was Dean. He asked me to install a phone at *At Beigh* in Wisconsin so he could reach me whenever he "needed" to. He did not seem to be able to use his own judgment about our department when issues about us came up. He began criticizing the department. As I noted in my diary in late 1975, he and I met and he told me that we were "not improving our teaching program" (the students had complained about two part-time lecturers), and that we were "incapable of hiring good people." Of the three people he cited, one left to become a research director at a pharmaceutical company, and the other two achieved tenure later at Northwestern.

One was Connie Campbell, who I have already mentioned and who became tenured. The other is Fred Turek, who later chaired the department for twelve years and is currently Director of a prosperous Center for Circadian Rhythms at the university. Rudy's basis for downgrading these people I suspect came from the then Chair of the Department of Biochemistry, Molecular Biology, and Cell Biology (BMBCB), the man who had said he would take our building away from us. The Dean also suggested I get an advisory committee for the department and said, "You should make decisions without consulting the department." (Shades of medical schools, precisely what I did not want to do.)

In late 1977, Rudy called me to his office on a Friday afternoon, with then Assistant Dean Steve Bates in the room. This was a few months after Rue and I had broken up, which had already left me feeling alone and insecure. He put on his sternest face and asked me to sit down. Steve couldn't look at me.

Rudy said, "I am firing you from the chairmanship."

I asked, "Why?"

He coughed and replied, "You are not there enough."

The irony of Rudy's statement was overwhelming. When I look at most of the male chairs at that time or at present, they are out of town far more frequently for NIH or other professional or consulting business than I was, or ever have been.

He continued, "You should not be doing so many things like being on an NIH committee."

The ridiculousness of that needs no comment. How much did the members of BMBCB influence Rudy in firing me? They probably objected to my hiring endocrinologists and neurobiology types, and most of them had no feeling for questions about regulatory systems. They were only interested in individual cells or parts of cells.

కడఆ

With that, I plunged into an even greater depression. That evening, I sat alone in my rented house and wept. The next morning I had to go into the university to attend a committee meeting of a group of local highly respected scientists and physicians, which was putting together a master plan to enhance the life sciences across the university, under the aegis of the Graduate School Dean, Clarence VerSteeg. I must have looked awful, because after the meeting, Clarence asked me what had happened. He was aghast that I had been fired and called Rudy that afternoon, who told him, "Neena said things about me to my wife Fanya."

At the time, I belonged to an interdisciplinary group of faculty women and wives of faculty ("Portia") that met once a month to discuss their research. (A group that still meets, by the way, with a turnover of participants, but still going strong!) I certainly never had said anything about him to Fanya, who was a member of that group. So Weingartner lied to Clarence, I suppose because he was unable to defend the firing on the basis of incompetence on my part.

I discussed the firing with my attorney, Carol Bellows, a Northwestern alumna who was, at that time, trying to settle some property issues between Rue and me. Carol called the provost, Ray Mack, about my firing. Ray was very supportive of me in my attempts to retain not the chair, but my position as a major researcher and faculty member.

Ray made sure I had secretarial help and salary rises during his tenure at the university. In September 1978, I became just the Deering Professor. At the time I was fired, I was the only woman chair in the College. I am happy to say that, under other deans, in 2000, there were ten women chairing departments among twenty-five departments in the college.)

కొ~ఈ

Rudy firing me and getting away with it is poignantly indicative of the situation in which women found themselves then and even now at times. I know that I was extremely busy outside the university, giving talks and serving on committees. In fact, I was preparing to serve the Society for the Study of Reproduction as its first female president. This is exactly the kind of successful biologist a dean should want as Chair of Biological Sciences.
Of course, I was depressed by my personal life, but my own lab was thriving and the department overall was improving.

Why did I not sue the university? Looking at the careers of other women who had brought suits against universities, I became convinced that whether the suit was won or lost, their careers were ruined. I decided not to do it, especially since the provost kept his promises.

కొ~ఈ

The firing had a mixed effect on my career. On the positive side, it left me with more time for research and for organizing the group of reproductive biologists at the university. But something negative must have spread to the outside world, because before that time, I had been getting inquiries all along about chairs of biology or physiology departments or deanships from all across the country. After that time, these abruptly stopped.

The firing probably saddled me with a reputation for being a "difficult" woman. (Heaven forbid that it gave Rudy a reputation as a "difficult" dean.)

Within the university, however, I continued to be asked to serve on central committees. Perhaps this is not surprising, since there were still so few senior faculty women around!

Study Questions

(1) Discuss the advantages and disadvantages of collaborative research among scientists.

(2) Discuss the values implied by Neena's focus on having a lab of her own as opposed to being content to do her research at any lab that welcomed her.

Ten

BEGINNING AGAIN

Now it costs to say
I will survive . . .
I will lift the leaden
coffin lid of the surface
and thrust my face/into the air.
I will feel the sun's
rough tongue on my face,
Then I'll start swimming
towards the coast that must somewhere
blur the horizon
With wheeling birds.

Marge Piercy
"What It Costs"

As I look back to the late 1970s, I ask myself how I survived the loss of my partner and the Chair of Biological Sciences at Northwestern at the same time, since both were so much a part of what I wanted in life. I wrote a lot in my diary, which may have helped, and going back to read it is still painful. It is also boring; I keep wanting to shake the diary at me and say, "Get moving, do something, see somebody."

Well, I was seeing a psychiatrist and getting a lot of research done, with my students and technicians. I was also teaching well in the undergraduate and graduate courses. But it did not seem to be enough to shake me loose from a deep feeling of despair.

Weingartner appointed Larry Gilbert to chair our department. Larry was a senior professor, an insect endocrinologist, who was still bitter about the split-up of the Department of Biological Sciences five years before, when the biochemists and molecular biologists had formed a new department. He did not stay at Northwestern University long before going to the University of North Carolina as Chair of Biology.

The department began electing rotating chairs among the senior professors, and the acrimony within the department continued to fade away with an influx of new faculty.

∂∽∾

A group of faculty within the Department of Biological Sciences, who were physiologists and neurobiologists, began to be impatient with some of the other faculty in Biological Sciences and petitioned the dean to let us break away to form a separate department of neurobiology and physiology. He agreed reluctantly.

Since 1981, we have achieved a stable, excellent department that teaches well, carries out vigorous research programs, and contains splendid colleagues. We have recruited a cadre of wonderful young investigators, including three young female scientists who are doing particularly well as teachers, mentors, and researchers.

∂∽∾

I busied myself doing many things, trying to fight off the depression I was feeling about living alone, the anger I felt toward the dean, and the anguish over the break-up with Rue. She and I had divided up our furniture. Our books had always been separate, but the record collection was inextricably meshed. We also divided up our tickets to the Chicago Symphony, she taking two tickets for fifteen concerts, with me getting the other fifteen pair. We scheduled separate weeks *At Beigh.*

I continued to be active outside the university and was invited to join the National Research Council Committee on the Education and Employment of Women in Science and Engineering. Lilli Hornig was Chair at the time, and it was really exciting to be working with this group of women scientists.

The report we turned out was the first such analysis published by NAS. Its conclusions about the status of women in sciences were glum. I continued to be depressed, but I note from my diary that I was dating three different women at this time!

I finished my term as president of SSR, having enjoyed the task very much. I was asked to run for the council in the Endocrine Society and won a seat. At my first council meeting I discovered to my horror that the same issues over which we had argued during my years on the board of SSR were still being argued at the older society

∂∽∾

As I noted in the diary, on my fifty-third birthday, I heard *Tristan und Isolde* at the Lyric Opera, "for a rapturous five hours." Two days later, I wrote that a "window" seemed to have opened in my mind, a lessening of depression. I saw my life as a continuum:

papers always waiting to be written, journals always waiting to be read, and I can just work as many hours as I enjoy and keep chopping away in a steady state. And also simultaneously enjoy reading, being with friends, loving.

⊱⋅⊰

In 1978, I heard about several lesbians in Chicago who were trying to organize an area social group for lesbians. I went to the meeting; about twenty women attended. We talked about the kind of group we might like. The women who had organized the meeting wanted to restrict the membership to "professional" women and have an admissions committee to determine eligibility. Well, I had enough of that in the university and didn't need a committee to tell me with whom to socialize.

A small subset of the group met again and started the Saturday Night Potluck Group, which meets on the second Saturday of each month. It has no membership restrictions, and has been meeting for thirty years by now. The size of the group has varied over the years between twenty-five and thirty-five people, and remains my favorite Saturday evening event.

We meet at a different house or apartment each month; the food is great, and the conversation sparkling. We decided in the beginning not to discuss politics, which was a lucky decision. Although most in the group are Democrats, a few Republicans have sneaked in.

We have always been just a social group, with no joint causes or goals other than having a good time together. The group has had lawyers, nurses, physicians, teachers, librarians, business people, academics, and therapists from time to time. A lot of networking takes place—I met my attorney, because she is in the group, and my current partner Claire and I share theater tickets and symphony tickets with another couple in the group. I also became a science board member of an encyclopedia because one of the editors was in the potluck group.

We have seen some relationships solidify and others break up, but it has never been boring. The group has aged, of course, and has experienced several deaths since its inception, but still attracts new, younger members. Being in on the formation of the group was a lucky break for me.

⊱⋅⊰

At the same time, I plunged myself even deeper into research. The lab was getting bigger with more technicians, research associates, post docs, graduate students, and undergraduates. Several of my trainees began a new focus on the relation of the adrenal cortex and stress to reproduction. The clinical studies on which I had collaborated years before at Michael Reese Hospital on depression and cortisol regulation continued to pique my interest, and I had done a couple of small studies at that time on the independence of LH and ACTH release from the pituitary.

In a way, every endocrinologist working with living animals studies some aspect of stress, purposely or inadvertently, since every experimental procedure may be interpreted by a subject as stressful, and thus elicits stimulation of the hypothalamic/pituitary/adrenal cortex system, resulting in increased secretion of cortisol.

The field of studying stress per se had started in 1915, when Walter Cannon began to study the subject of stress in his definition of the "fight or flight" syndrome, wherein stress elicited secretion of adrenalin and noradrenalin from the adrenal medulla gland. This prepares the animal to flee or stand and fight.

Years later, Hans Selye, a French-Canadian endocrinologist, described a broader stress syndrome, which involved the adrenal cortex gland and the pituitary. In a manner similar to the control system in the gonads, a peptide hormone from the pituitary called Adrenocorticotropic Hormone (ACTH) controls the adrenal cortex gland, which secretes a steroid, cortisol, in the human. Also, like the axis controlling reproduction, a hypothalamic peptide factor regulating ACTH, called Corticotropin Releasing Factor (CRF) has been identified. Selye suggested that the reason reproduction was compromised during stress was because of a "competition" at the level of the pituitary between secretion of the gonadotropins and ACTH.

❧

We decided to investigate how stress and ACTH release could interfere with reproduction. We asked: "Is the competition at the level of the hypothalamus or at the pituitary level?" At the time Selye made the suggestion that the competition was at the pituitary level, the role of the hypothalamus in controlling the pituitary had not yet been elucidated.

It turns out that the GnRH-LH-gonadal steroid system is dampened by stress at least partly because adrenal corticoid hormones can lower LH secretion acting directly at the pituitary gland level, as demonstrated elegantly by Sonia (Sunny) Ringstrom in my lab.

Sunny had a Master's degree when she entered the lab while teaching at Loyola University in Chicago. She applied for admission to the graduate program of our department at Northwestern; some faculty members asked whether "She is too old to admit," etc., etc.

I pointed out quietly that ageism is illegal, and Sunny was admitted and finished her PhD in two years. As she advanced on the academic ladder at Loyola, ending as Professor and Chair of the Natural History Department, she continued to work on the adrenal/reproduction issue in collaboration with my lab, and we coauthored a number of important papers over the years.

Several other graduate students and postdocs in the lab also worked on this problem, studying both male and female rats. One of their most interesting findings was that LH secretion was *inhibited* by steroids from the adrenal cortex, while these steroids *stimulated* pituitary FSH synthesis. This seemed paradoxical, since GnRH is known to stimulate the synthesis and secretion of both LH and FSH from the gonadotrope cell. But, with our ongoing work on inhibin, the lab was, of course, continuously interested in how one hypothalamic-releasing hormone (GnRH) and essentially one kind of gonadotrope cell in the pituitary could secrete different ratios of LH and FSH at different times. Since we had shown that glucocorticoids have different effects on LH and FSH synthesis and secretion, this immediately linked the adrenal research to the FSH-inhibin issue.

Also, a postdoctoral student in the lab, Diane Suter, now retired from a position as an associate professor at Loyola University, came up with a very persuasive argument as to why it was adaptive for cortisol to suppress LH while maintaining FSH.

During stressful periods in the wild, reproduction must stop temporarily to keep staying alive as the first priority. During this initial time, LH secretion drops as GnRH secretion from the brain lessens, and thus steroid secretion from the gonads drops, and animals will not be stimulated to mate. This is obviously useful in keeping them alive, since seeking a mate and mating can leave one more vulnerable to predators. By keeping on synthesizing FSH, however, as a result of the increased stress-related cortisol levels, the pituitary maintains stores of this hormone. When the emergency ends, GnRH stimulation can start FSH secretion up immediately and prime the ovaries (or the testes) to start growing follicles again (or increase spermatogenesis).

☙❧

As I described in the previous chapter, we had started the program for reproductive science in 1974 and had already hired a number of faculty members interested in doing collaborative research. In our search for outside multidisciplinary grants, it seemed simplest to apply first to NIH for a training grant for graduate students and postdoctoral fellows, as these grants were available from NICHD.

By that time, both of our departmental recruits, Fred Turek and Connie Campbell, had received research grants from NICHD, Fred working on light-dark effects on gonadotropins in the hamster, and Connie working on lighting conditions on sexual behavior and reproduction in hamsters and rats.

I thought having some faculty preceptors from the Medical School would be helpful, and I was eager to start up some clinical/basic science collaborations. I quickly identified Gwen Childs, who was in anatomy, working on the morphology of the pituitary, and Mary Hunzicker–Dunn, in biochemistry, who worked on the ovary. They also had their own research funding from NICHD.

With my work on FSH and LH regulation, this seemed to be a good combination of training grant preceptors. But I worried that I was the only one with advanced experience, the others being untenured and junior.

Erv Goldberg, a senior member of our Biological Sciences Department spoke of himself as a "developmental biologist," not a reproductive biologist, because he did research on sperm development within the testes. But the work had clear-cut contraceptive possibilities, which he was exploring. I persuaded Erv to join in on the application and he did, to my relief, and we were awarded the training grant in 1978.

I served as director of the training grant for about five years; Fred Turek then took over for a few years. Jon Levine, a later recruit to our department, then ran it for a number of years, but has recently turned it over to an even newer member of the department, Teresa Woodruff. Turning over the grant to successive directors is a good way for junior faculty to learn to run somewhat complicated grant programs—each of these colleagues has been very success-ful at "grantsmanship," a necessary asset these days.

The grant is now in its twenty-seventh year. Six of its preceptors are from the Evanston campus and four from the medical school. More multidis-ciplinary grants have followed, but I believe winning and retaining that first multi-investigator grant was the foundation of Northwestern's strength in reproductive science.

কৈ

In 1979, I proposed that the program for reproductive research sponsor an annual minisymposium. I suggested that we bring in a major outside speaker and have the trainees set up the program. We would start with coffee and sweet rolls, have some papers given by trainees, then have a poster session and lunch, then more papers by trainees, and then wind up with a talk by the outside speaker, followed by a wine and cheese reception.

That is what we did, with some funds contributed by the vice-president for research and some from the university president.

The minisymposium has successfully brought in participating trainees, not only from our labs, but also from every major midwestern university. Our trainees, including the undergraduates in our labs, have gained a great deal of experience and confidence from this annual event.

During 2004, we had a special program to celebrate the twenty-fifth an-niversary of the grant and the minisymposium. We invited several former trainees, now successful researchers and administrators elsewhere, to join us on that occasion, and each of them described for our current trainees the work they were doing in their present positions. This was such a hit we have now incorporated it as a permanent annual feature of the event.

Meanwhile, my lab attracted more graduate students and post-docs, and our research areas of study were expanding. A popular field of study in endocrinology (and seemingly in everything else) is measurement and causality of male-female differences. Why does the male rat or male human not show a cycle in reproduction?

In the rat, mouse, and hamster, we have known the answer for about forty years: testosterone is secreted normally in the male pups immediately after birth. This steroid wipes out those neurons in the brain that are responsible for estrogen triggering the preovulatory LH surge. Conversely, if male hormones are injected into female rats before the first five days postnatally, they will never show estrous cycles as adults because this destroys these neurons.

In addition, mating behavior is set in a male-like direction by the identical testosterone secretion, which erases the LH preovulatory response, whether the infant male secretes the testosterone normally, or the hormone is injected into a female pup less than five days old. So, the genetically male rodent, whose testes are removed on day one of life, does not exhibit normal male mating behavior in response to a receptive female. Unlike the normal male, he *will* show an LH surge if treated with estrogen as an adult. The opposite syndrome is seen in the testosterone treated female.

During the 1940s and 1950s, these observations on rodents elicited much excitement among people trying to "explain" homosexuality in human beings. They proposed that homosexuality is the result of inappropriate steroid hormones acting on the brain while the fetus is in the uterus. Untreated adult human males will not release an LH surge in response to estrogen, just as male rodents do not. However, men who are on prolonged estrogen treatment, the preliminary to a sex change operation, will show the LH surge, unlike similarly treated male rats (Gooren).

So human males, unlike rat males, do not have the "Estrogen causes an LH surge unless blanked out early by testosterone" hard-wired in their brains. Gooren's study demonstrates that this attribute is not organized prenatally in human males. In the light of its importance, I will return to the hormone/homosexuality theme in a later chapter.

In my lab, while some trainees were working on the stress problem, and others on the inhibin story, a few of my students became interested specifically in sex differences in the regulation of gonadotropin secretion. An observation that many pursued showed that the pituitary-brain axis of adult male rats responds very quickly to removal of testicular negative feedback on LH.

Within six hours or so after castration, LH secretion increases dramatically, and serum LH is significantly higher. However, after ovariectomy, LH in the female rat does not show escape from estrogen negative feedback on LH for five or so days!

We felt that this sex difference was very important, because it seemed to be part of the explanation of why females cycled and males did not. We have done many experiments probing the difference; several doctoral dissertations have resulted for graduate students, as well as a couple of postdoc projects.

ঌ৽৶

The methods we have followed in these studies provide an instructive insight into how endocrinologists go about their studies sequentially. When one is looking for a mechanism, as for what causes the sex difference in rapidity of the LH response, one first needs to discover in which organ in the body the critical mechanism lies.

We first asked if the sex difference lay at the pituitary level, that is, is there a difference in the LH secretory response to GnRH in vitro in pituitaries taken from males and females after removal of negative feedback from the gonads? This allows us to look at the pituitary in isolation from the brain or other influences.

This work was done using an organ perifusion system called the Acusyst. This system contains a number of tiny chambers into which one can put small organs or pieces of organs. The chambers containing pituitary pieces were kept at rat body temperature and provided with oxygen. Computer-regulated pumps pumped a fluid containing necessary metabolic substances and a balance of ions past the fragments.

When we wished to stimulate the pituitary cells we added pulses of GnRH in amounts we deemed similar to what happened in the animal itself. The fluid coming out of the vessels was then collected, and we were able to measure LH and FSH concentrations in that fluid, which was collected every ten minutes for assay.

We removed pituitaries from male and female rats at varying days after removal of the gonads and tested the ability of various doses of GnRH to elicit LH secretion from the isolated pituitaries in the Acusyst. The answer to our question was no: the LH secretory response to GnRH of the isolated pituitaries from gonadectomized males and females was the same. So the sex difference did not lie at the level of the pituitary gland but presumably at brain level.

We then started experiments in which we removed the hypothalamus from treated rats. Isolated pieces of the hypothalamus placed in the chambers continued to secrete GnRH, the hormonal signal from the brain which causes LH secretion from the pituitary. These pulses of GnRH showed lower amplitude from female hypothalami after ovariectomy than from male brains after castration, indicating that the neural cell fragments from female rat brains were secreting less GnRH than fragments from male brains.

In the next set of experiments, we measured GnRH pulses secreted in unanesthetized, freely moving rats, confirming this sex difference we had seen with the isolated hypothalamus. The technology we used to measure GnRH secretion in living rats was invented by my colleague Jon Levine.

A tiny catheter is inserted into the portal veins carrying blood to the pituitary from the hypothalamus, and samples can be withdrawn and GnRH pulses measured by a radioimmunoassay. Using this technique, we showed that the inhibition of GnRH in ovariectomized females was the result of increased secretion of an endogenous inhibitor compound acting on GnRH secreting cells in the female brain after estrogen withdrawal. Thus, we had pushed the question of sex differences in LH secretion after gonad removal back to the synapses connecting to the neurons secreting GnRH.

Since I retired before we could take the next steps to trace how testosterone and estradiol accomplish their different effects, I am hoping others will take up the search. However, we believe that we clarified the adaptive significance of the sex difference in the female rat.

The brevity of the ovulatory cycle in the rat means that after the LH surge, which causes ovulation and a drop in estrogen secretion by the follicles, LH must remain low in order for the next cycle to be launched if fertilization does not occur. So a delay is built in between the drop in estrogen during the cycle and the LH increase. Ovariectomy simulates this drop in estrogen, and the system responds in a delayed response. In the human, by contrast, the longer length of the cycle before the next ovulation occurs (28 days) permits estrogen to fall and rise again before follicle growth for the next cycle takes place.

❧

I found myself traveling to Mexico City and Madrid to discuss the adrenal-reproduction work and to Aquila, Bellagio, and Genoa in Italy to discuss the inhibin/FSH regulation studies. Unlike many of my male colleagues, who travel to and from meetings quickly, wasting no time on sightseeing, I took advantage of every trip to take a short vacation, do sightseeing, and hear music. I am pleased to say that I have heard opera in London, Paris, Milan, Florence, Savonlinna, and Venice.

The opera in Venice stands out as a favorite; the opera house is sinking into the canal. The night I was there, they were performing Rigoletto, wherein Gilda, who is pursued by the lascivious Duke, was played by a particularly obese soprano. She is stabbed by murderers hired by her father, whose intention was for them to murder the Don, Giovanni. Gilda was hidden in a sack, which was supposed to be carried away by her father, the clown; but the soprano was so heavy, he could not lift the sack and could barely drag it a short distance. The audience began throwing tomatoes onto the stage and yelling. I loved it all.

❧✦❧

In a way, these trips to other countries resembled my time *At Beigh*, where I frequently would work and then reward myself with a bird walk or a swim. But each year, I was still recording being depressed, even while in the Everglades and the Florida Keys for bird watching with a lover, where we saw seventy-five species of birds.

By the middle of January, as the days were noticeably longer, I began to emerge from depression. It was interesting to be reading Virginia Woolf's diary at the same time, and see her recording alternating entries of darkness and then accomplishments.

❧✦❧

Late in 1980, I was called by a member of the nominating committee of the Endocrine Society to ask if I would run for president. I agreed and became the second woman to serve as president. My presidency ran from 1982–1983.

When I was president, the president was expected to give an erudite but amusing after-dinner talk at the end of the meeting banquet when the awards were presented. My having to make that speech haunted me the whole year.

As the time for the meeting in San Antonio approached, two further issues arose. The executive secretary called to say that she could not get permission to serve alcoholic drinks at the banquet. That really scared me, because the thought of giving a talk to a bunch of sober endocrinologists was more daunting than giving a science paper!

The other issue was that I needed to wear a long dress at the banquet, and I did not own one. I desperately went shopping in Chicago's Loop but found nothing I wanted to wear. Two weekends before I had to leave for San Antonio, I spent some time with friends in a small town to the west of Chicago—there, in a small shopping mall, I found a full length muumuu that was flattering and appropriate.

Only one week ahead of the meeting, we finally obtained permission to serve alcohol at the banquet and I was saved. Incidentally, how many of the male presidents of the society have worried about what to wear at the annual banquet? None, I bet.

I gave a talk entitled "Endocrinology as Paradigm, Endocrinology as Authority." I spoke of the danger of endocrinologists making "authoritative" statements about issues without understanding how the public and media grab hold and run without examining the caveats. I talked about how the public looks to us scientists for their information and how careful we should be not to let our *interpretations* of data get mixed up with our observations.

I still think the speech says something important today. For example, I discussed a paper that had appeared in the journal *Science*, which had examined differences in performance between girls and boys in the seventh and eighth grades on the math SAT tests from 1972 through 1979. The boys did better each year. The authors concluded, "not all of the sex differences could be accounted for by socialization."

The article created a furor. I then went on to say:

> a careful perusal of the data reveals an alternate interpretation: All students, boys and girls, showed a clear drop in SAT scores between 1973 and 1979. In fact, the girls in 1973 showed higher scores than the boys in 1979! Can any test which shows such a decline over time be a measure of mathematical ability per se?

Well, SAT scores are still declining and Lawrence Summers is still talking about women's poor math ability.

᪣᪣

During the summer of 1980, my mother, who, since her stroke, had continued living with Dad in their apartment, developed a kidney infection and wound up in the hospital. The surgeons decided to remove the kidney. This left her in a precarious health position, and it was decided that she should be moved to a constant care facility.

Although Dad stayed in the apartment, he visited mother every day at the facility until she died five years later. He usually wheeled her down to the cafeteria for lunch, where they would eat together. I visited them as often as I could.

᪣᪣

The years 1981 and 1982 were filled with triumphs and downers. My grant funding increased and Goucher College awarded me an Honorary Doctor of Science degree. My Endocrine Society presidency went well and I went to many meetings.

I spent time in Wisconsin with Joey and Snooky, walking the woods and lying in the sun. In Baltimore, I visited Mom at Levindale. I was never sure she knew who I was, but we sat together and listened to some old Russian/Yiddish songs; I watched her moving and laughing with the tunes. Both of us had tears in our eyes. But as autumn rolled around, I wrote in my diary an "Ode to Depression (of the endogenous kind)":

> An error of the synapses
> Macabre dance of receptor and transmitter
> locked together in a devilish coupling
> which drives me to hunch here trembling
> Under attack from the enemy forces
> walking in my shoes.

❧❦

In 1982, I received a phone call at home from Rue. She said, "I seem to have throat cancer and need to go to the Mayo Clinic for surgery. Can you take care of Gretchen for me?"

I went to pick up the schnauzer, and talked with Rue. The surgeons were probably going to take out her larynx, and I was shaken by this news. After she returned from Mayo and her surgery, she took the dog back. We talked together, and I found that the anger I had felt against her since our separation had vanished.

That winter, we began to use our symphony tickets to go to concerts together again. She continued to teach in the Department of Sociology at the U of I, but with great difficulty. In the summer of 1984, Rue and I decided to spend a week together at *At Beigh*. We walked and talked and sailed Ellison Bay and Green Bay on Ariel II. The sailing frightened me, since if she had fallen into the water with her throat open from the surgery, saving her would have been next to impossible. I never expressed my fears; maybe she was halfway hoping for something like that. Clearly the cancer was spreading.

❧❦

Early in 1985, my Dad called to say that mother had had a second stroke, which left her in a coma. Pearl, Leon, and I met Dad in the hospital in Baltimore and talked with her doctor. She had little hope of recovery after all these years. Dad was unable to make a decision, but the three of us told the doctor not to use a respirator if she stopped breathing. Mother died a week later—Rue wrote Dad a letter about the times she had met Mom.

In May of 1985, Rue was hospitalized for the last time in Evanston Hospital, two blocks from my home. I visited her every day, along with her other friends. My sister's two daughters were graduating that June, Nancy with an MBA from Maryland, Susan with a BA from Goucher. I had already arranged a trip to London and Paris for the three of us after their graduation. Rue died the week before I was to leave.

I chose a poem by May Sarton for someone else to read at Rue's memorial service, which was packed with her friends and colleagues:

I was halfway to silence
when I heard your voice…
Shall I take you with me?
All the way to land's end
Is there a choice?

❧❧

After Rue's service, I flew to Baltimore to pick up my nieces. We went on to London and Paris. It was their first European trip, and we had a wonderful time going to the theater, the Thames, Bath, Cambridge in England, the Seine, St. Chapelle, and the Louvre in Paris.

But I spent some time by myself visiting St. Paul's in London and Notre Dame in Paris, lighting candles in a defiant, atheistic way, and thinking about what I had so recently lost: my mother and Rue, within a few months of each other—the two women who had been the most influential in my life.

Mother had, it is true, made me feel guilty about being lesbian, but she had taught me to love books, and learning, and to stand up for my principles in the face of opposition. Most importantly, she had confidence in my abilities to accomplish what I wanted in life.

Rue had shared many adventures with me, including the adventure of buying a house in the woods. I had learned so much from her about music, and sociology, and we had traveled together in Mexico, England, Scotland, and Switzerland, laughing and loving all the time.

The loss was irreparable.

Study Questions

(1) Neena writes, "I busied myself doing many things, trying to fight off the depression I was feeling about living alone, the anger I felt toward the dean, and the anguish over the break-up with Rue." Only five lines later, she writes about how exciting it was to be invited to join the National Academy of Science committee on the education and employment of women in science and engineering.
- Discuss the whether you see these two paragraphs immediately juxtaposed as emotionally relevant, and if so, in what way.
- Does Neena apparently battle emotional disturbance with intellectual activity or does this passage evince a significant detachment from personal emotions?
- Look for other specific passages in this and other chapters that support your view.

(2) Neena writes that her mother taught her "to stand up for my principles in the face of opposition."
- Discuss evidence you find in the book that shows how this value influenced how Neena related to the world.

Honorary Doctor of Science, Goucher College, 1982. L-R: Sister, Pearl Schwartz Imber; Dad; Neena; Niece, Susan Imber Smith.

Eleven

A LAB OF ONE'S OWN

I have been standing all my life in the
direct path of a battery of signals
the most accurately transmitted most
untranslateable language in the universe
I am a galactic cloud so deep so invo-
luted that a light wave could take 15
years to travel through me And has
taken I am an instrument in the shape
of a woman trying to translate pulsations
into images for the relief of the body
and the reconstruction of the mind.

Adrienne Rich
"Planetarium"

In spite of the turmoil at the university and in my private life and my intermittent depressions, my lab continued to produce successful trainees, talks, manuscripts, and good science. Somehow or other, this aspect of my life did not get messed up. I am sure that my depression and anger spilled over into the lab frequently, but luckily the rituals that governed duties and relationships in the lab kept things on an even keel, and, of course, I was surrounded by wonderful, talented people who kept the work moving forward.

I have gone back to my old "depression diary" and counted the number of entries I made per year over the years from 1973 to 1996. I plotted the number of entries against the number of papers published over the same time period. My findings show that the lab had no change in productivity during the entire time I was writing! The science just kept rollin' along. (Of course, quite possibly without my depression, the lab might have doubled its productivity and discovered three more hormones, but I doubt it.)

෯෯

I remember Rue standing around the lab waiting for me one afternoon early in our relationship, watching what people were doing.

"I feel as though I am doing a sociological field study" she said.

She was very interested, as a sociologist, in lab rituals. The rituals in my lab fell into four categories:

R and R included eating and talking at lunch or any old time, buying cake and champagne for each birthday, potluck suppers at my house, or at Ravinia Park with the Chicago Symphony Orchestra, and talking incessantly about the overall research trajectory of the lab.

General Lab Routines included everything routine and regulated, which ensures the proper tracking of data and maintenance of quality control. Everyone had to learn how to handle animals carefully, keep lab notebooks, keep data safe, and analyze data statistically. Everyone was responsible for keeping the lab clean. This was the rule; I wanted to make sure the technicians and work-study students did not always wind up with this "dirty" work.

Experiment-Specific Rituals are those tailored to each individual experiment. All of us were responsible for writing protocols for our own experiments and testing them orally in front of our whole group at weekly lab meetings. Everyone had to learn how to use equipment and methodology. Until a protocol was deemed satisfactory, a trainee could not start an experiment.

The fourth ritual was *External Affairs*. This includes the relationships between the lab and the outside world of collaborators, granting agencies, journals, equipment and supply vendors, and internal and external research regulators. Certainly, graduate students and postdocs need to learn about all of this as part of their training.

When we had a grant to write, everyone did some writing, even if I changed it before submission, and everyone read parts of the grant. However, in a very real way, everybody was responsible for everything, and everyone had the obligation to report problems. But the lab chief (me) is always ultimately responsible.

కాలలు

Bill Talley, who came to Chicago with a bachelor's from Morehouse College, worked with me at Illinois and Northwestern from the early 1960s until he retired in 1995. He was responsible for ordering supplies and animals and did all the histology on the ovaries and other tissues. He taught everyone how to do surgery and how to take care of their animals. He also served as overall lab supervisor. As each new student or fellow came into the lab Bill gave him or her a packet of introductory materials for orientation on lab rituals. Here is part of it:

The Way It Is in the Schwartz Lab

Welcome to Endocrines and all that jazz. Everyone has his way of doing things; so just to keep us all happy, I thought I would create this opus to explain how Dr. Schwartz likes things done.

Supplies: You will find attached two mimeographed sheets. To activate a protocol, you must first get approval from Dr. Schwartz. Then fill out these sheets, listing everything you can possibly need. It is important that you anticipate your needs, since we are many and supplies can dwindle rapidly. In general, you should allow at least three weeks for supplies to arrive. Animals can take up to a month. . . . Be specific: give the brand, quantity, and quality. Also, most companies have minimum order conditions. If I know soon enough, I can often combine several orders to total this dollar amount

Animals: Incoming animals are weighed and numbered with an ear punch. . . . Each shipment of animals is given a letter and a number code, e.g. AA1, AA2, AA3, etc. Record date of arrival, birth, and weight. The animals are allowed to light-adapt for 6–7 days (Light schedule: 0500—1900 hours lights on), and then they are ready for use. We always use Central Standard Time. It is well to be aware of possible disruptions of the light seal from outside sources. . . . Check the timer at least once per week.

Autopsy, Sample Procedure: It should be abundantly clear, from your discussions with Dr. Schwartz, what data are to be collected. But, in general, be sure to get the following:

Body weight, gonad weight, pituitary weight; date and time of every procedure, and appropriately aliquoted serum samples and pituitary. At autopsy, blood is collected by decapitation and centrifuged. Serum samples receive a pool number; the pituitary also is snap-frozen in a vial with same number label. Serum is aliquoted before frozen. When serial samples of blood are drawn, serum samples are aliquoted in a predetermined volume directly into an assay tube. Pituitary and serum samples are assigned a pool number by using the next unused numbers from serum pool book.

Miscellaneous: Data books never leave the lab and a copy of all raw data should be on file in your research notebook. Double entries must be used; each rat appears in an animal book and a serum book. The items needed for autopsy are located in the autopsy area . . . . When you finish an autopsy, please clean up. Wash and dry your instruments and put them away. Avoid leaving them on the sink, etc., where they can be lost or damaged. Put dead animals in a plastic bag and store them in the freezer provided in the animal care center. When you ask me to order rats, be realistic about your work-load. One hundred rats can eat up a lot of money in a few weeks. Cheers, Bill Talley

క్రా

To my readers who don't do science, lab rules may sound pedestrian and even stultifying. Do they squelch creativity? I don't believe so, they simply ensure that data can be traced and verified, and that samples stored in the freezer for later assay can be linked to animals, experiments, and investigators.

With eight undergraduates, five graduate students, and three postdocs each doing an experiment or two or three, plus two or three technicians, two undergraduate work-study students, and two research associates, the absolute necessity of regulations becomes obvious.

I was fortunate to have a second technician, Brigitte Mann, for most of my career, who initially did our bioassays or immunoassays, but eventually also handled most of the administrative issues. Without her and Bill, my research career would have been—well, I can't even imagine what it would have been like! Brigitte started to work with us while I was at the University of Illinois, early in my career; it was her first job after finishing college.

Bill Talley was afraid that Brigitte seemed, "too young and inexperienced and blonde," and he told me "she won't last long."

Brigitte moved to Northwestern with us. We have now been together thirty years; through her marriage, the birth of her son, and his acquisition of a PhD in history. Brigitte has now won a thirty-year service award from Northwestern. Her work (now in the lab of Jon Levine) is always reliable, creative, and committed.

క్రా

Lest it appear that with this devoted technical support and dedicated young trainees nothing ever went wrong, let me quote from a note I wrote to all of the graduate students, postdocs, and undergraduates in the lab in 1985:

Dear People:

I have been remarkably easy-going, for me, about the issue of your maintaining contact with me via notebooks. There is not a single one of you at the present time who is keeping me up to date on the status of your data . . . I cannot allow this situation to continue. It particularly impressed me during a meeting . . . last week with Roger Guillemin I was unable to pull out of my own files . . . data, which I wished to show him. [Roger was a visitor from the Salk Institute who had won the Nobel Prize for identifying GnRH]

There are several reasons why I need this information: First, if I want to talk about data to somebody else I need to have it ... Second, you forget that, while each of you is concerned with your own narrow field, I need to be... at least as close to the top... Third, if I have data in my possession I will occasionally look at it, think about it and maybe even come up with an idea. . . . Finally, to be absolutely frank, these notebooks... assure me that you will not leave Northwestern leaving me stranded without data... Even if you do write it up, there are many times when I need to look at the data in order to change the way you have written it or to reinterpret it later on in the light of further experiments. . . .

I am sure there are both good reasons and bad reasons why you have not provided me with this information. I suspect . . . each of you really wants to own your own experiments and not have to put up with my interpretations, comments, and negativity. However, I must not permit this to go on. If you have a notebook already, update it and give it to me. If you do not have a notebook, let me give you one. If you have any questions about what I want in the notebook, see me. Specific comments for each one of you from me appear below.

Neena

కావొ

A major burden of doing research as one's lab becomes larger is the responsibility for the personnel who are paid with so-called soft-money. This is salary money that comes from grants (governmental or from private foundations such as the American Cancer Society) and must be competed for at intervals of several years (five years generally).

The "softness" is in contrast to the guaranteed salaries received by tenured people in the professorial ranks. When a grant receives a score from the study section assembled by NIH or NSF that is not good enough for funding, everyone working in the lab, except for the tenured professor, is at risk for losing a job. As you can imagine, grant application time is stressful for everyone. As of 2007, funding for research in the biological and medical sciences is very poor, and a lot of excellent science is not getting funded.

కావొ

Running a lab is like running a business. You hire and manage personnel, buy and maintain equipment and supplies and, of course, decide with the lab collaborators the experiments to be done and how to do them. After the data are collected, analyzed, and interpreted, the director and others who have worked on the project write up the results for publication. The director divides up the menial labor, such as who cleans up instruments, who cleans up spills, and who determines research priorities when the director is not around. As in business, the director also sets the tone or atmosphere, determining whether it is a friendly, relaxed, cooperative lab or a competitive, rigid, and business-only lab group.

&~&

When I returned to the University of Illinois Medical School as a tenured associate professor from Michael Reese Hospital in 1961, I was provided a bigger and better lab. Then I moved to Northwestern at the medical center, and then up to Evanston. I was there in the Hogan Building from 1974 to 1997, with lots of space.

The Hogan building was new when I moved into it in 1974, and though the building was not ever a well designed space, I did a lot of work there, had lots of students and fellows in that space, and we did some great experiments.

After we received multidisciplinary program project and center grants from NIH, this lab grew and was used not just for my animal surgery and measurement work but also served as a core lab for doing hormone assays for many other investigators at Northwestern and some other universities.

The Hogan Building was designed with slits as windows by an architect who believed that scientists were so immersed in their work that they never looked outside. One of my undergraduates was so disturbed by not being able to see outside while we were conferring about his experiments that he came into the lab one morning carrying a tall, narrow mirror. "I can't stand not seeing the sky while we are talking" he said and mounted it against a window slit in my office. From then on, we could at least see whether it was snowing or raining while we talked.

Two years before I retired, I turned over this large lab to my colleague Jon Levine and moved into a smaller lab in a newer building. My office now has a view of Lake Michigan and the soccer field. This is a real pleasure for me.

&~&

My office was reserved as a sanctuary where I would write letters, do committee stuff, write manuscripts, and see students I was teaching in formal courses. The lab was for doing the hands-on work and for talking with the hands-on people.

Lots of conversations take place in a lab, particularly when you are sitting around waiting to take a sample in the middle of the night. Early in my experimental career, we did a number of 24-hour studies, and I stayed through the night with a student or two autopsying animals, collecting samples or injecting hormones. It was a good chance to talk about science, life, or politics, as there are no phones ringing and no undergraduates coming around.

Occasionally I would be in the lab by myself at night, and I always found it comforting to be in this quiet, warm place, surrounded by equipment and books I had "earned" by my work in science.

Once, late in my career, I volunteered to collect a blood sample at 4 a.m. for a graduate student who lived much further from the lab than I did. She had placed an indwelling catheter into the vein emptying into the heart of her treated rats. The presence of this catheter permitted the rat to wander around its cage normally while allowing the investigator to take timed samples of blood for hormone measurements.

Unfortunately, when I tried to take the sample, I found that with my new trifocals I could not see the end of the catheter tube for inserting a needle and syringe, and I missed her timed sample. It was very hard to admit my failure when she showed up the next morning.

ॐॐ

Where should the lab chief's office be? Until I moved to the Cook Building, two years before I retired, my office had always been *within* the general lab space. So going to my office was the same as going to my lab. As I walked in each morning, I would see what was happening without really focusing on it: who was at which instrument, or reading, or doing surgery or calculating data. I could track experiments automatically. After I took off my coat and picked up my messages, I would walk around with my cup of coffee or tea and say good morning to everyone, catching the flavor of the day.

After my move to the downsized but more elegant and modern lab in the new building, my office was separated from the lab. My co-workers would look up and ask what I wanted when I walked into my own lab!

In many newer buildings lab space is deliberately separated from the office, taking advantage of outside windows for offices and sequestering the labs into the middle of the building. I don't like this new arrangement, but then again I no longer have a lab of my own to worry about.

But the new arrangement reminded me of the time I attended a conference in Bangalore, India in 1973. After the conference, I went to Delhi, where I visited the Department of Biology at the university to give a seminar. Professor Prasad offered to show me the department and introduced me to the faculty. As we entered each lab, everyone stood up because the professor (Prasad, not I) had entered.

One student was doing surgery on a rat and stood up, jeopardizing the life of his subject. It was very difficult to make him sit down in our presence. This does not happen in our country, but I received a taste of it when I entered my lab during the last two years of its existence.

ॐॐ

A lab group is a team where the hierarchy is fluid and flexible. The physical intimacy of sharing space can be and is a bonding experience. The cast of characters of a typical midsize lab in a university includes the director, undergraduates, graduate students, and postdoctoral trainees, with perhaps a more senior research associate and technicians. Technicians work under relatively tight supervision; they generally do not establish the rationale or priorities for experiments. But they are invaluable, because the basic techniques of the lab are in their hands, quite literally, and they maintain quality control over the long haul.

Graduate students, on the other hand, are working for degrees (Masters or PhD), and they may strike off on an entirely new project or take a piece of a project currently being worked on and carve out a sub-area.

My policy with graduate students has always been to suggest several alternate directions for projects that fit somewhere within the overall work we are doing in the lab and then let them choose the specific area on which they wanted to concentrate. In many ways, graduate students are the most vulnerable group in the academic community. They are almost totally dependent on their advisors for resources and recommendations.

Among the pleasures of doing science at a good undergraduate school are the undergrads who wish to work in your lab, usually because they have taken a course with you. Undergrads came in two categories: the independent researchers and the work-study students. The latter are paid by the hour from NIH grants to provide technical assistance. The former are unpaid and are seeking a project on which they can write an honors thesis.

This is an opportunity I did not have when I was a student at Goucher, where faculty, if they did research, did it somewhere else. This is why I went to Johns Hopkins and the Jackson Lab in Bar Harbor during my undergraduate summers, and in fact, I received honors when I graduated from Goucher because I wrote that work up for the faculty.

The undergraduate students who do research do so for a variety of reasons, some to get recommendations for medical school, others to test out how it feels to do research (which was my purpose). But always they are enthusiastic, excited, and very helpful in getting the research done.

Finally, the postdoctoral fellow is a growing segment of research participants in the biomedical sciences. At this time, a life scientist must do a postdoctoral fellowship after graduate school to qualify for a tenure track assistant professorship in a research university.

Having postdoctoral students in a lab is quite different from having graduate students. Postdocs have already been shaped by their graduate experience, and they come specifically to your lab seeking a new technique or a new specialty, or sometimes just to gain a new point of view. I have had postdocs who came from psychology, anthropology, or ecology, who wanted to learn endocrinology, and others coming from endocrinology labs where whey worked on large farm animals or primates and so wanted to gain experience working with rodents.

An advantage of having people in the lab who are at various stages of their careers is that you have access to a wide range of mentoring skills; graduate students help mentor undergrads and postdocs help mentor graduate students. Not only can this cascade make it easier on the lab director, but it also gives everyone a chance to mentor and be mentored.

Nowadays, postdocs are having serious problems finding independent research and teaching positions. The postdoctoral fellowship has become a kind of "holding" position, which is great for lab bosses but often the end of the line for the postdoc.

Finally, one collaborates with colleagues with a different set of expertise, with different instruments in their own lab spaces. I have been fortunate to have a number of collaborators who have provided my lab with important reagents, ideas, and methodologies. I have already talked about some of those outside the university. My colleague at Northwestern, Kelly Mayo, has been a wonderful mentor for me on molecular biology while I was mentoring him on using the rat as a model for the estrous cycle.

&⋄⋄

Teaching students how to do research in the lab is, of course, quite different from the didactic techniques of teaching about a subject matter in the classroom. It really is an apprenticeship, and I always enjoyed the give and take with new trainees as they learned to ask the right questions, learned what a control is, and learned how to ensure their data is not biased.

Having a student, or anyone for that matter, fill out an experimental protocol with details about drug dosages, timing of treatment, and sample taking, as well as spelling out hypotheses and possible interpretations, is a marvelous way of teaching meaningful experimental design. Teaching basic skills such as how to do surgery, or how to anesthetize an animal, or how to run an instrument, is easier, of course, but just as much fun.

How do experiments flow into each other? How do different individuals within a lab decide to collaborate on a project or pick up a small offshoot of one project and run with it? This occurs as a result of various negotiations and ideas circulating within a lab. Let me take one slice of time, the mid-1980s, and try to reconstruct this situation in my own lab.

&⋄⋄

Channing and I had made the basic discovery that follicular fluid contained a substance that suppressed FSH secretion but not LH. Sunny Ringstrom was working on her doctoral dissertation; picking up the stress theme, she showed that removal of the adrenal blocked the elevated LH and FSH secretory response to castration. She was also trying to see what about removing the adrenal secretion was responsible.

Diane Suter, a postdoc who had worked on cow ovarian physiology as a graduate student, came to the lab "to learn rat endocrinology." She became interested in the stress issue and performed studies using isolated rat pituitaries to see whether cortisol would alter LH and FSH secretion differently when allowed to act directly on the pituitary cells themselves. She made the important discovery that the cortisol suppressed LH, but increased FSH synthesis, in both male and female pituitaries.

Another postdoc, Rosemary Grady, began her studies by injecting neonatal female rat pups with testosterone; she wanted to find out if their failure to cycle when they became adults was explainable at the pituitary level. She showed that, in fact, the pituitary did not have a normal response to GnRH.

Another postdoc, Ruth Moore, set up a collaboration with a colleague at Michigan (John Marshall) and demonstrated that the estradiol secreted by the ovary during the estrous cycle caused an increase in the number of GnRH receptors in the pituitary, explaining the increased sensitivity of the pituitary before the time of ovulation. This resulted in the lab's first paper in the prestigious journal *Science*.

Kay Jorgenson, a graduate student in Connie Campbell's lab at the time Connie fell ill, continued her studies on LH and FSH secretion in the golden hamster in my lab. Chris Charlesworth, a graduate student, obtained a potent antagonist to GnRH from colleagues at the Salk Institute in LaJolla and tested the effects of the antagonist on LH and FSH secretion, showing that LH in the blood dropped more than FSH.

An undergraduate, Karen Kartun, did an honors' thesis utilizing the same GnRH antagonist in male rats. Eve Hiatt, a graduate student, tested a new machine we had obtained—the Acusyst—which enabled us to put pieces of tissues such as the pituitary, ovary, or hypothalamus into chambers and run fluid through the chambers, collect the effluent, and measure secreted hormones. She spent a long time troubleshooting the machine and finally got it working. Her thesis was on the baseline secretion of LH and FSH in pituitaries from male vs. female rats.

Each one of these graduate students or postdocs had at least one undergraduate as a collaborator. But while these trainees were doing their own thing, every one of them became interested in inhibin! They began coming up with ideas for new experiments and new collaborations. Some of them helped set up an *in vivo* bioassay for inhibin in the ovariectomized rat. One of them received follicular fluid from cycling pigs from collaborators at the University of Illinois and assayed the inhibin content during the pig cycle.

The postdocs and students also collaborated in writing some reviews on inhibin. It should be clear that all of these projects were tied together because they were related to reproduction, and they coalesced into three overarching issues: regulation of the estrous cycle, relation of stress and the adrenal cortex to reproduction and differences in pituitary/brain regulation in male and female rats.

These years were exciting, obviously productive of science and a lot of fun for all concerned. The graduate students and postdocs went on to productive teaching or research careers and most of the undergraduates went to medical school, many of them to practice endocrinology.

కళ్ళ

One question of general sociological interest has been whether female scientists run their laboratories differently from the way male scientists run theirs. I have not observed a difference in the life science labs I have been close to, where there seems to be a spirit of cooperation fostered by the lab chief and spreading to all personnel. Of course, I have heard horror stories about some labs, which I believe are true, but I have not personally seen this among my *close* life science colleagues.

But when *Science* magazine ran a questionnaire about this issue in 1994, respondents believed that a difference did, in fact, exist. Of course, more respondents who felt this way may have bothered to answer the questionnaire than those who did not, skewing the results. I might have guessed that women would run more democratic, cooperative, non-hierarchical labs, but I have no evidence for this. It would make an interesting study.

As scientists gain more people, space, and money, they stop actually doing much of the bench work themselves. Some feminists have argued that this is wrong, because it assumes that "routine" lab work should not be shared by everyone and establishes a hierarchy of social distinction. But I have already done every task in the lab, and the lab will profit more from my writing a grant or discussing research with a student than if I wash the dishes.

The negative aspects of an assumption of "social hierarchy" only occur if the lab director broadcasts the message that some tasks are less meaningful than others. Nothing is ever totally routine in a lab; dishwashing and keeping counters clean is important to the work and should be shared. But one does get away from the bench.

After a major snowstorm in the Evanston/ Chicago area some years ago, none of the technicians or more senior people could get to the lab because the El stopped running from Chicago and driving was not possible. I lived closest to the campus and used cross-country skis to get there. I phoned an undergraduate who lived on campus and was doing research with us and asked her to collect that day's vaginal samples from the rats in our colony, from which we deduced stage of the estrous cycle. I skied in and sat down at the microscope to read and record in the data book.

My student looked startled and said: "I didn't know that you know how to do that."

It had, in fact, been a long time since I had actually done a lot myself in the lab when I took a sabbatical in Jack Gorski's lab in 1990. The first thing I set out to do there was to make an agarose gel. This is a chemical reagent one uses in determining the size of a given isolated DNA fragment.

So I went into the balance room to weigh out a small amount of agarose. This was the first time I had used a microbalance since I had started wearing trifocals. In my own lab, someone else weighed chemicals. I discovered I was unable simultaneously to see the balance optical scale, the bottle containing the powder, and my hand with the scoop.

After twenty minutes of intense concentration, I heard a muffled sound. I looked up, and there were all of Jack's graduate students and fellows laughing and watching me.

ᡒᡆᢙ

This incident illustrates a serious paradox for lab scientists. They start their career working "at the bench," but as the lab grows, more and more time is spent supervising others, discussing experiments, and examining and interpreting data. More time must be spent on the entrepreneurial aspects of convincing NIH or NSF or private foundations to provide resources. The game is not only writing grants but giving seminars and talks at national or international meetings, writing review articles, and deciding to which journal a given article should be sent.

For the successful scientist, lab space generally gets bigger, personnel more numerous, and, of course, the budget has to expand to accommodate more supplies, salaries, and equipment. Methodology changes steadily and more papers must be published. All of this leads to increasing distance from the bench.

In the meantime, there are other responsibilities. Increasing seniority in an academic institution in any discipline leads to increased committee work. This is a particular burden on women, because still so few women are in senior ranks, and universities have had to become sensitive to including women on committees.

You are also expected to serve outside of the university on funding agency peer review committees and on boards of professional societies. All of this is interesting and necessary, but it takes away from research time.

However, women in science fought for these responsibilities because the recognition they bring makes it easier to get grants, promotions, and job offers. It also means that women can exert influence on professional society affairs. These responsibilities can be seen as either a stiff price to pay for an independent research career or a necessary evil in terms of securing parity for female scientists.

ᡒᡆᢙ

Running a good lab means running one where you know you can trust the results, where you do not have frequent turnover of personnel, and where you can demand quality while permitting mistakes. People from senior associates to undergrads must understand why the work is important; but one also needs to understand that everyone has an occasional personal crisis.

Over the years, we weathered a number of crises (in addition to mine): the death of parents, the threatened suicide of a lover, a divorce and two weddings. We did it together and survived together, having fun.

Above all, it is crucial for everyone in a lab to be able to admit they have made a mistake. While we always discussed an experimental protocol thoroughly before ordering animals and reagents, it is important not to spend too much time discussing how it "should" turn out. If you knew that, you wouldn't need to do the experiment at all! Moreover, you run the risk of someone trying to please you by making it turn out the way she or he thought you wanted it to.

In fact, a major nightmare in a large lab is losing your grasp on the quality control of the methodology or, at an extreme, harboring someone who is cheating on data. We all know some horror stories, and some of them hit the media.

As far as I know, only once have I had a student try to cheat by producing data without doing an experiment. She was doing an experiment that involved her having to visit the rat room for observations two times a day. My other graduate students began to believe she was not actually making the observations, since they never encountered her in the rat room. Without saying anything to me, they set up 24-hour surveillance, and when she did not show up during that time span, they informed me. The student admitted to me that she was fabricating the data. She was also drinking heavily, which (to my shame) I had not recognized. She promptly left the lab.

કે∾ક

Once a week, all lab personnel attend a lab meeting. These meetings are the most important learning experiences for everyone, including the lab director. Our lab meetings generally went like this: someone with new data or a new protocol would do a show-and-tell, with everyone else asking questions and making comments.

I know my undergrads and new gradutate students felt frightened and insecure with the process at first, but they would all gradually participate more and more.

After the show-and-tell session on our own work, one student generally discussed a published article from another lab, which had been distributed to everyone. Many labs, including ours, use the weekly meetings to share food as well as science and to exchange other news, gossip, and anecdotes.

One Dilbert cartoon illustrates this well: the boss, Dilbert, and others are sitting around a conference table. The boss says, "Let's go around the table and give an update on each of our projects."

Dilbert replies, "My project is a pathetic series of poorly planned, near-random acts. My life is a tragedy of emotional desperation."

The boss says, "It's more or less customary to say things are going fine."
Dilbert replied, "I think I need a hug."

The result of these weekly meetings is that everyone knows what everyone is doing and why, and everyone has been given practice at getting up and speaking in front of a group (and gotten a hug).

৵৵৶

I cannot emphasize how valuable the training in speaking is for everyone. We made sure that anyone of us who was presenting a poster or paper at a meeting or giving a job seminar had several practice sessions. This experience is important for everyone, but I believe it is absolutely crucial for women.

Young women need to learn to present their results and their conclusions in a positive, forceful manner. One of the greatest compliments I have ever been given came at a professional meeting during presentations at an oral session in which ten-minute research presentations were presented. One of the women in my lab had presented a paper and another member of the audience told me "I can always recognize a Schwartz student, they speak clearly and confidently."

৵৵৶

The relationship between graduate students and their preceptors is different in the lab and field sciences than in the humanities. We live together in the workplace and it takes continuous cooperation and give and take to make it work. In addition to our lab meetings at the university, my lab met frequently for potlucks at my house. We have a Schwartz lab recipe book that a postdoc (Kerry Knox) and graduate student (Joanne McAndrews) put together.

The cover has a picture of a rat (what else?) on it, and the great recipes in it are international in scope—Indian, Russian (my mother's cabbage borscht), Italian, and Swedish—reflecting the ethnic origins of my lab group. The introduction to the compendium says:

We always tell people there are two main ideas of interest in the Schwartz lab: (1) the differential regulation of FSH and LH; (2) sex differences in gonadotropin secretion. However, as we all know, there is a third interest in the lab: FOOD."

৵৵৶

A lab can be a very intimate setting and it is important to set boundaries on the intimacy, of course. Trainees need to be able to talk about problems, and frequently these are personal problems. Unfortunately, the physical closeness within a lab may lead to sexual encounters. In light of the power hierarchy between lab chief and trainees, this is dangerous for trainees and totally out of bounds for faculty.

৯৯৯

The coin of the realm in science is the papers one publishes in well regarded journals. More and more frequently, at least in the sciences, these papers are multi-authored. My colleagues in the humanities do not understand why my name is on a grad student's or a postdoc's papers. This is an outgrowth of the expense of doing science these days. The lab director has raised all the money and provided the space and context in which the research is done. Including the director's imprimatur on the research that comes out of the lab has become standard practice.

Until postdocs have been out on their own for several papers, it is not always easy to judge what they are capable of doing independently. We always negotiated among ourselves in the lab, or with an outside collaborator, which names should go on the paper and in what order. We also always made sure everyone named actually had read and contributed to the final article.

Some of the more egregious scandals about publications in life science have happened because not every author listed has read and approved the entire final manuscript. Unlike our colleagues in the humanities and the social sciences, the output of scientists is principally original manuscripts in peer reviewed journals.

Chapters in books are not uncommon, but entire books per se are rare products. It has been said that "Old physiologists never die, they just write books," and I have to laugh as I write this one.

৯৯৯

For most scientists, science is fun, but applying for grants is not. In some other countries, once a scientist has achieved a certain degree of fame, fortune follows and continues, but in the United States, you have to continue applying for money regardless how important and well recognized your work is.

Our country's budget is negotiated every year by Congress and the executive branch, and for those scientists dependent on National Institutes of Health or the National Science Foundation or Department of Defense or Department of Energy funds, what the next year will bring is never certain. What will the agency budget be, what will the cut-off score for funding be, how will the study section view the work proposed, how will it fit into this year's priorities at the funding agency? One's anxiety level and career progress are too closely tied to the vagaries of crucial funding.

These days, tenure in a research university for young scientists depends on getting external funding, and that is why we in universities frequently use the actions of NIH or NSF committees to help decide whether an assistant professor becomes an associate professor with lifetime tenure. This almost forces new investigators to pick relatively safe projects.

The outside grant and the papers published from the university are necessary for tenure, bearing the same necessity as "the first book" for the scholar in the humanities and social science. With tight federal funding, this puts an extra burden on young scientists. I certainly had it easier to get tenure when I did than it is nowadays.

Do I agree with how tough achieving tenure has become? In a research university, no choice exists, as it is expensive to hire even a junior scientist. Setting up a lab costs megabucks! A scientist who cannot get funded simply cannot accomplish independent research.

᷐᷈

So how did I keep a lab that grew and kept running for fifty years? The lab really almost ran itself. It started running in a particular way when it was small and retained the same underlying ideology of cooperation, nurturing, personal responsibility, and organization while it expanded.

With some really creative young scientists working on their careers and several experienced technicians who knew what they were doing, my science continued and expanded for nearly a half century.

Now, I no longer have a lab of my own. What a strange place to be.

Study Questions

(1) Discuss the publishing requirements that underlie achieving tenure.
  - Compare and contrast the pressure to publishe with the need to have excellent teaching available at research universities.

(2) Neena closes this chapter by saying, "the lab really almost ran itself. It started running in a particular way when it was small and retained the same underlying ideology of cooperation, nurturing, personal responsibility, and organization while it expanded."
  - Discuss the possibility that this statement could be true.
  - Postulate specific factors that would require daily attention to keep a lab as described in this book running successfully for fifty years.
  - Discuss the values as a scientist and as a person the author evinces by this statement.

Twelve

PAY-OFFS

To say O God Almighty!
To come back! To complete the curve to come back
Singing with procedure back through the last dark
Of the moon, past the dim ritual
Random stones of oblivion, and through the blinding edge
Of moonlight into the sun
And behold
The blue planet steeped in its dream
Of reality, its calculated vision shaking with
The only love . . .

James L. Dickey
"Apollo"

The ten years that followed the events I described in Chapter Ten, from the mid-1980s to the mid-1990s, were much better ones for me than the preceding ten years, professionally and personally. The decade began with a bang when I won the Williams Award for Service to the Endocrine Society in 1985. At that time, the award consisted of a very large, man-sized, black cloth chair with an inscribed plaque mounted on the back. The chair is on a pedestal that rotates. When I sit in it, my feet cannot touch the floor.

My students called the chair "The Throne." It sits in my study, and my cat loves to curl up in it and sleep. Despite feeling like Alice in Wonderland whenever I sat in that chair, I was grateful for the recognition. Service awards are not specifically for research accomplishments but for activity in the organization. I had served on several committees and as a reviewer on the journal *Endocrinology,* and I generally contributed to the society.

I continue to go to the annual meetings of the society and was Chair of the Awards Committee of the Endocrine Society in 2003–2004. I recently agreed to chair the history committee. One's career perhaps can be summarized in terms of one's trajectory within a professional society: membership committee 1972, council 1974, president 1982, nominating committee 1997, awards 2004, history 2005.

The meeting when I won the Williams Award happened to be in my hometown of Baltimore, about a mile from the hospital where I was born. My sister Pearl and her daughter Susan came to the ceremony and brought my Dad. I acknowledged in my acceptance speech that he and my mother had always supported education for women and had always been very supportive of me. I mentioned that he was in the audience and asked him to stand. Not only did he stand, but he waved and smiled to everyone. It brought down the house and brought tears to my eyes.

I won two other awards during those ten years: in 1987, I received the Northwestern University Alumnae Award (winning over actress Ann-Margret, I heard); and in 1992, I won the Hartman Award from SSR. This is a research award, and I was very proud to have been nominated. Then in 1992, I was admitted to the American Academy of Arts and Science.

I was finally invited to serve on a NIH study section from 1985 to 1989—fourteen years after the AWIS suit against NIH! This was not on the reproductive biology section but on the endocrinology study section, where I reviewed the pineal, adrenal, and thyroid grants.

The inhibin research and our adrenal/stress/reproduction work were attracting a lot of attention. I found myself giving talks at several universities.

My personal life was also looking up. In 1986, I gave a sixtieth birthday party with two other friends in our lesbian potluck group who also reached sixty that year. My sister and brother came with their spouses, as well as a number of my good friends from other cities and locally. We had speeches, an open bar, and dancing. My brother made sure he danced with all of my friends, being one of the few men present. We held the party at a Chicago restaurant. By that time, I was dating a younger woman from Evanston, who was a lot of fun; tall, good looking, and very bright and funny, just exactly what I needed. We had met at the potluck group and also at Northwestern, where she was a faculty member in one of the other schools.

Then, I was invited to Madrid to attend the International Steroids Conference to present a talk on our adrenal steroid work. My lover and I arranged to meet in Madrid, where we enjoyed flamenco, tapas, and art, interrupted only by my giving two papers at the meeting. Then we drove south, or rather she drove and I sat beside her lazily watched the scenery. She spoke Spanish and Portuguese and did all the phoning for hotels and ordering in restaurants. I loved being pampered.

We visited synagogues and the Alhambra, and we enjoyed staying in a parador in Toledo and eating and drinking in outdoor cafes. The beach was great in Costa del Sol, and then the Algarve in Portugal was fragrant with squid and large anchovies cooking on grills. I decided that this was the way to travel Europe.

My return was marred by having to make a decision about Joey, the black and tan dachshund Rue and I had bought in Flint, Michigan, years before. Now he had a cancer, which was spreading. He began to have serious difficulty walking. I finally relented and took him to our vet. I held him on my lap while he died. A few months later, I acquired my Westie, Fingal.

❧

Our group of reproductive biologists on the Evanston and Chicago campuses began getting together during the mid-1980s to make plans to submit a program project grant application to NICHD. These are large interdisciplinary grants consisting of a minimum of three research projects that crosslink in purpose and personnel. I was attempting to apply for this kind of grant at the University of Illinois before I left to go to the department of physiology at Northwestern's medical school, where we were also going to put one together until we lost a crucial project.

This time, I met no local opposition, only support. We put together a proposal with five projects that included seven faculty members. The overall theme we chose was FSH. The projects covered work on inhibin and pituitary/brain interactions, FSH action on the ovary, and FSH and seasonal reproductive quiescence in hamsters. We requested money for research and for administration of the grant, and for relevant seminars and travel to meetings.

Each of us applicants had already had NIH research grants awarded for our individual labs and a strong publication track record. We got the five-year grant! This was the signal locally that our program for reproductive research could become a center. In 1987, I became director of the Center for Reproductive Science at Northwestern, while also directing the program project grant.

Having an officially designated center made a tremendous difference in the visibility of reproductive research at Northwestern, on both the Chicago Medical School campus and on the Evanston campus. It made recruiting to the university easier; a number of clinical and basic science faculty have subsequently joined the university and the center.

The program project grant was renewed for five years in 1993, 1998, and in 2003. In 1998, Mary Hunzicker-Dunn took over as Program Director. Kelly Mayo is now the Program Director. We also applied for a P30 type ("center") grant, which was funded in 1991, and which was designed to provide core labs specializing in specific methodology such as radioimmunoassay for measuring hormones in blood or *in situ* hybridization for detection of mRNA within the gonads, brain, or pituitary. The NICHD has now stopped giving these grants, substituting U54 grants, which are broader. Teresa Woodruff and others on our faculty subsequently received a U54 grant titled "Center for Reproductive Research at Northwestern University," which focuses on the ovary.

Our Center for Reproductive Science was formally reviewed by the Northwestern University Program Review Committee in 2000 and received high marks. Our training grant, which was the first multi-investigator grant we received in 1978, has just been renewed for the sixth five-year period.

ॐ

In 1987, I was invited to present at a symposium on inhibin in Tokyo, which was sponsored by Serono. I arrived a week in advance to visit Kyoto and other cities before traveling by bullet train to the conference, where everybody in the international community who was anybody regarding inhibin was invited.

ॐ

My research program had become even bigger. Our interest in the adrenal steroids led us to demonstrate that these steroids increased pituitary FSH synthesis and release. This occurred whether the adrenal steroids were administered to the intact animal or to pituitary cells cultured in vitro, either in static plates or in the dynamic Acusyst. We went on to show that progesterone from the ovary, as well as testosterone from the testes, did the same thing. I began to feel that it would be of interest to see whether these steroids acted directly on the gene for the FSH-beta subunit in the pituitary gland.

To do this, I needed access to the gene and some molecular biology techniques in my lab. It would have been easy to collaborate with a local molecular biologist, but I decided I needed to get away from Evanston.

I had never taken a sabbatical before, but here I was, living alone, with Fingal, and my Siamese cat Chaiya for company and we could travel.

I called Jack Gorski in the biochemistry department at Madison, Wisconsin, and asked if he would be willing to give me some space for a year. Jack was a friend of longstanding; he trained many young men and women who have become first-rate molecular biologists. It was his lab that did the seminal work on the estradiol receptors in the uterus and other target cells. He said yes, and Bill Chin, who was at Harvard at the time, sent me the gene for the FSH beta subunit. Northwestern gave me a full year sabbatical with pay. Madison was a lot closer to Door County than Evanston was, and this was another perk!

ॐ

However, while I was making arrangements for the sabbatical in 1989, I met a new member of our monthly lesbian potluck group who was interesting, artistic, lively, and attractive: Claire. She was an artist, psychologist, and art therapist who was directing an art therapy graduate program at the University of Illinois in Chicago when we met. She invited me to a party at her house in Chicago. I was really attracted to her, trying to figure out how to get closer. While I was at the party she told me that she had heard that I sometimes rented my Door County house.

"I would like to rent your house and go there," she said, "if I can find someone to go with."

I looked at her and said, "No, you can't rent it. You will go up for a week with me."

We drove up in early spring, with the bay still frozen and icicles dripping from the roof of the house. A great place to start a relationship: a fireplace, a tape deck, and cross-country skiing on the quiet state park trails. We began dating—going to the symphony, opera, and plays. Claire was and is a great one for "playing." As I recorded in my diary, she was (and still is) ready to play any old time, and she loves to travel.

When Claire learned that I was leaving the Chicago area at the beginning of 1990 for a sabbatical, she was disconcerted, to put it mildly. What worried her most was that in a university town like Madison, which has a strong lesbian community, I might meet somebody else. I was determined to go ahead on my sabbatical, but we agreed to see each other on weekends. I rented my Evanston house to someone taking a sabbatical in Evanston and moved some clothes, tapes, stereo equipment, files, and Fingal and Chaiya into an apartment I rented on the east side of Madison.

The animals and I came back every other Thursday to Chicago, and stayed in Claire's apartment for the weekend. I spent two days troubleshooting in my Evanston lab. On most alternate weekends, Claire drove to Madison with her two cats. What a traveling menagerie we had!

෨ඏ෨

Just two months before I went to Madison, I received notice that I needed to rewrite my NIH individual research grant for my Evanston lab. Claire and I had planned two weeks in Thailand over that Christmas holiday. My gut told me, "Don't go to Thailand. Stay and rewrite the grant so you can get to Madison on time." But Claire insisted that we go on our trip as planned.

In the end, we had a great time exploring the rivers, towns, and beaches of Thailand, and I rewrote my grant application when we got back, delaying my move to Madison by two weeks. I showed up in Madison on 15 January 2000. The year I spent there was wonderful.

When I walked into Jack's lab for my first working day, I unexpectedly experienced a great flood of relief.

"What's this about?" I asked myself.

Then I realized it was because I was not responsible, for the first time in many years, for anyone or anything in the lab except for myself!

෨ඏ෨

Many years had passed since I had actually carried out complete experiments myself, without a student or technician. I started reading molecular methodology in earnest and began watching people doing things in the lab. Everyone was very helpful; Jack assigned one of his graduate students as my mentor

(Kataro Kaneko, now at NIH), who kept watch over my technique. I enjoyed attending Jack's lab meetings, which made me feel right at home, as they all started with the speaker for the week bringing in doughnuts or sweet rolls and went on from there.

As a lab director in Chicago or Evanston, I had gotten out of the habit of cleaning up messes that weren't administrative. While I was on sabbatical, I was once careless about hooking a glass flask into a shaker, and it broke loose and shattered. I went down on my hands and knees to clean up. In the course of doing so, I found some mouse droppings in the bottom of the shaker. I pulled them out and asked one of the students and the technician how long these had been seen around, and they didn't even know what they were! Well, biochemists and molecular biologists may be able to do their research without encountering rodent droppings, but physiologists certainly cannot.

ॐॐ

I worked and played hard during the year of my sabbatical. The people in my lab in Evanston were not allowed to call me at Jack's lab because I did not have a phone in my space; I did not want his trainees to have to interrupt their work to answer calls for me. They had to call me before 8 a.m. or after 6 p.m. at my apartment or send me an Email. When I went back to Chicago every other week or so, they would line up in the lab with data to show, questions to ask, or manuscripts to be edited. Those who had been around before I left had few problems. A couple of grad students and a post-doc, however, who were new, needed more attention. In the end, the extra dose of independence did not seem to harm anyone, especially me.

Meanwhile, I fell in love with Madison. I had some old friends at the university, and I was happy to spend time with them again. Claire and I explored the area around Madison together when she was in town. We saw the eagles nesting along the Wisconsin River and explored the local parks and zoo, the caves at Blue Mound, and the area near Taliesin, where Frank Lloyd Wright's house and studio still stand. I did a lot of walking around campus and took Fingal on long expeditions to the many state parks on the weekends when I was alone.

ॐॐ

Jack and I agreed that during the sabbatical year he and I would not eat lunch together in his office, since I was in such close touch with his students and other lab personnel who were helping me carry out my project. It seemed a good idea to separate me the trainee from me the professor, so I asked the trainees and techs if it would be all right to share their lunchroom. I did, and I got involved in some terrific conversations. The students were marvelous in teaching me about molecular techniques. In turn, I taught them some physiology and wrote lots of letters of recommendation for many of them for several years after we all finished.

At the end of the year in Madison, I gave a catered party for everyone in the lab, with spouses, including Claire, to say thank you for all the help I received. The students brought me some "gifts," including a sheet containing seven different ways to make a DNA miniprep. (This is a simple technique for isolating DNA from cells to test whether the particular DNA one wants is present. As I was learning this basic method, I found that everyone I talked with had a different technique, which each swore by! This is what lay behind that gift).

Their major presentation was a board game based on Monopoly, which they called "SABBATICAL," including dice, markers, and cards with rewards and penalties. It must have taken them many hours to make it. On it, they made fun of my trips out of town and my molecular biology "expertise." It was great fun, and I cherish the game still.

They also presented me with a "degree" in Molecular Biology. The citation reads:

> In recognition of diligence and perseverance in the face of adversity, fluency in foreign jargon, steady hands while loading gels, demonstrated ability to detect non-existent bands and/or pellets, and repudiation of the adage "you can't teach old dogs new tricks."

During the party, I felt like Dorothy, the Scarecrow, Tin Man, and the Lion all rolled into one, receiving gifts from the Wizard of Oz.

I returned to Evanston at the end of 1990 utterly refreshed. I was eager to initiate experiments concerning the regulation of the FSH beta subunit DNA fragment I brought back with me.

৵৹৶

Sadly, Jack Gorski died in 2006, leaving behind a large number of students and fellows who mourn this wonderful, caring, and warm man who made brilliant discoveries in the field of estrogen receptors, leading to many clinical applications in the field of breast and uterine cancer.

৵৹৶

In 1991, Claire and I decided to buy a house together in Evanston, having grown tired of the frequent seventeen-mile drives between our homes in Evanston and Chicago. She continued to teach in downtown Chicago, driving south every Tuesday and Thursday for her classes.

The house we bought is "Prairie style," built in 1923, with the original woodwork still unpainted and the original stained glass window in the dining room. It has a great deck and backyard. Claire has an office/studio, full of masks on one wall, where she continues to see clients. I have a small office to supplement my office at the university, a mile away. The house proved to be wonderful for entertaining my lab folk, Claire's students, and our potluck parties.

࿔࿔

In 1991, Claire traveled with me to Italy to attend a conference in Modena on stress. We flew to Milano, spending a couple of days, then drove slowly to Modena, staying a night in Buseto on a pilgrimage of sorts to Verdi's home.

The conference was a lot of fun; I presented a paper on the effects of adrenal cortical steroids on the ratio of LH to FSH secreted by the pituitary.

On Thanksgiving Day, we left Modena by car on our way to Ravenna. We had picked up a bottle of wine, some balsamic vinegar, a hunk of Parmesan, and a loaf of bread before we left. We dined sitting in the warm sun on a hillside outside Bologna. We wound up in Venice, where we spent a few days avoiding the flooding Adriatic. We loved that trip to Italy so much that we went back in 2001. After Claire taught a summer course in Assisi, we drove around the northern lakes area, and then on into Switzerland.

࿔࿔

I enjoyed returning to teaching in Evanston. During my career, I have taught nursing, pharmacy, physical therapy, dental, and medical students, as well as undergraduates and graduate students. As a teacher in Northwestern's Biology Department, I taught physiology in the core biology year course for majors in addition to endocrinology, environmental physiology, and mammalian reproduction for advanced students.

But my two favorite courses, which I taught toward the end of my career at Northwestern, were a freshman seminar called "Menstrual Cycle: Fact and Fiction," and a course for nonmajors (a "science distribution" requirement) called "Human Reproduction." This was payback for the distribution course I took at Goucher on physiology that changed the course of my life.

The Human Reproduction course, which always closed out at 200 students, was a lot of fun to teach. I don't think the students were ever bored, and I had packed office hours concerning course issues along with more personal questions. My favorite comment in the latter category came from a young man who told me, "I am on the wrestling team. Coach says we should not have intercourse the night before a match because it saps the energy." I told him I was unaware of any evidence for this but that he perhaps should follow his coach's suggestion.

∽∾

Joanne McAndrews, a PhD candidate in my lab, began working with the DNA I brought back. Her dissertation examined the effects of testosterone and corticosterone on mRNA for FSH beta subunit in the pituitary, examining these steroid actions on FSH synthesis, rather than just secretion. She worked first on the pituitary gland in male rats, showing that testosterone and the adrenal corticoids enhanced synthesis of FSH in the pituitary, even when GnRH was prevented from acting, because a GnRH antagonist had been given to the rats. This showed that these steroids were acting directly on pituitary cells, not just via an action on the brain to alter GnRH secretion.

Both steroids also blocked LH secretion and synthesis at the same time, but testosterone was more effective at this than glucocorticoids. Joanne succeeded in getting the DNA I brought from Madison into some cell types (by a process known as transfection) and getting a synthetic glucocorticoid molecule (dexamethasone) to enhance gene transcription. Unfortunately, using pieces of the DNA which did *not* contain what we had been told was the promoter region for the FSH gene, we also obtained a response to the hormone. So, our system lacked specificity. We did not proceed beyond that point in the lab because Joanne graduated and went on to do a post-doctoral fellowship.

∽∾

Joanne's work increased our general interest in steroid effects on FSH synthesis and secretion to complement the inhibin work we had been doing. We began using methopristone (RU486) to study progesterone action during the rat estrous cycle.

RU486 is a member of a class of compounds called "hormone antagonists" since it blocks the progesterone molecule from binding to its receptor in its target cells (specifically the uterine cells), just as tamoxifen, the drug used for some breast cancer patients, prevents estrogen from binding to its receptor in breast tissue.

Since hormones cannot act on their target cells without binding to the cell protein molecules called receptors, RU486, which competes with progesterone for receptors, acts clinically as an early contragestive (or abortifacient). The drug causes loosening of the microscopic fetus from the uterus, since progesterone secreted by the maternal ovary or the placenta, is necessary to keep the uterus quiet to maintain pregnancy.

∽∾

In 1992, it was illegal to bring RU486 into this country for use in humans. My lab was not studying the abortifacient action of this drug (which would have been illegal since our research funds came from NIH for a different purpose) but was instead trying to map out the role of progesterone in regulating the pituitary gland during the rat estrous cycle.

Elizabeth Brackett, the local Chicago reporter for the PBS McNeal/Lehrer News Hour, tracked me down and said the show would like to do a short sequence of film on my thoughts about the controversy about testing RU486 on early pregnancy in the USA. I agreed, and she and a cameraman came over to the lab. They first did the requisite "scientist in the laboratory" shots. They had me put on a white lab coat, which I hardly ever wore, and photographed me looking over the shoulder of Joanne McAndrews.

Joanne was using a pipette for transferring samples to measure messenger RNA for LH and FSH from the pituitary glands of her rats. She had treated the rats with adrenal cortical hormone for her dissertation studies on the effects of stress on reproduction. The PBS camera man wanted me to appear to be instructing her in using the pipette (ironic, of course, since Joanne was much more skilled than I at this).

Then the PBS crew filmed me walking into my adjoining lab and talking with a post-doctoral fellow, Kerry Knox. They wanted her to inject a rat, under my "supervision," and she did, her hands shaking visibly. (Kerry was using RU486 to test whether progesterone was involved with inhibin's suppression of FSH secretion.) The crew then directed me to look at a slide under a microscope. Of course, this was for the mandatory "scientist peering into a microscope" shot! They were in a hurry, so they had me use a dissecting scope, the only one set up in the lab at that moment.

I protested that it was the wrong kind of scope for looking at slides. "Nobody will notice" they said. Then they filmed me talking about the importance of permitting RU486 to come into the country in the light of its safety as an early non-invasive contragestive and its possible use in treating breast cancer. The night after the show aired on PBS, I received a number of phone calls, some from admiring friends and relatives but most from fellow scientists, who said, jokingly, "Don't you know what kind of a microscope to use for slides?"

∂∞∞

In 2000, the FDA announced that RU486 would be approved as a contragestive, but the physicians using it had to be "registered" and their names made publicly available, which was another victory for the anti-choice lobby. Ultimately, the medical community protested loudly about this and the restriction was withdrawn.

RU486 blocked the effects of progesterone in enhancing FSH synthesis in the pituitary. We discovered that when it was injected into rats on the day of proestrus, it prevented the rise of serum FSH expected on estrus, even in the presence of a lowered inhibin level. This threw us for a loop, since, after all, it was our hypothesis that it was the drop in inhibin that caused the rise in FSH that led to our discovery of inhibin in ovarian follicular fluid.

The RU486 observations led us to launch further studies examining the changes in the levels of the progesterone receptor in various tissues, such as the uterus, pituitary, and brain during the rat estrous cycle. The observations also led us to examine possible interactions of steroids with the hormone activin.

Activin *stimulates* FSH synthesis and secretion, unlike inhibin, which inhibits these processes, but the two protein molecules are quite similar in structure. Activin was also first isolated from ovarian follicular fluid, just as inhibin was. It turns out that it is also synthesized in the pituitary gland, where it exerts a major local positive stimulus to FSH synthesis and secretion.

We subsequently showed that ovarian and adrenal steroids, as well as testosterone, act in an obligatory fashion through activin to stimulate FSH. Furthermore, our studies using RU486 as a progesterone receptor blocker during the estrous cycle turned up an unexpected dependence of FSH secretion on progesterone receptors in the pituitary gland, leading us to launch several studies, continuing to the present, on the role of these receptors in the pituitary and brain.

෯෯

The research projects I have been describing throughout this memoir evolved over a span of fifty years, with over a hundred graduate students, post-docs, undergraduate students, and technicians working on them. Generally, they flowed into one another. These studies resulted in over 200 articles and numerous chapters in peer reviewed professional journals and books.

The bottom line criterion we used to dictate whether to pursue a lead has always been—what will the experiment tell us about the animal?

Chasing a molecule by random DNA destruction has never been my style. Chasing the adaptive significance of a phenomenon is so much more interesting. The research was fun too.

During the last twenty years, as the number of personnel increased in the lab, we adopted a technique for following different experiments by designating a five-letter acronym for each. The trainees got to name their own experiments, resulting in some wonderful acronyms: "RIPPL" for measurements of inhibin during pregnancy; "BATMA" for corticosterone (originally called hormone B) or androgens on pituitary mRNA for LH and FSH; "PRABE" for the effect of estrogen on progesterone receptors A and B, etc.

෯෯

I continued to serve on panels outside the university, and was elected several times to the Northwestern College of Arts and Sciences Promotions and Tenure Committee. Three outside committees on which I served during this time also took me to Washington frequently and had broad societal and policy implications. The Institute of Medicine had a review panel on oral contraceptives and breast cancer and I was one of the few basic endocrinologists in the group. In 1991, the panel published a study that concluded, "There is little evidence that oral contraceptives had increased breast cancer significantly; the up-side was the reduction in ovarian cancer."

The National Research Council established a Committee on Biological Markers in Reproductive and Neurodevelopmental Toxicology to develop markers (indicators) of exposure, effect, and susceptibility to toxins in the environment that influence reproduction and development. The final study of the panel was published in 1989. I learned a lot from other members of the panel and have since served as a reviewer for the Environmental Protection Agency (EPA) on environmental estrogens.

Finally, the Office of Technology Panel of the United States House of Representatives established the Advisory Panel on Reproductive Hazards in the Workplace to examine factors in the workplace (chemicals, radiation, stress, infectious agents, metals, hormones) that may cause damage to reproductive capacity of workers and to advise on risk assessment, sex discrimination, worker's compensation, tort liability, and ethical considerations. The committee was varied and had a mix of reproductive and other biologists, representatives from industry, toxicologists, unions, Occupational Safety and Health Administration (OSHA), American Civil Liberties Union (ACLU), and law firms. These Washington committees that I was privileged to join have had a major impact on Congressional lawmaking. This kind of public service duty provides very important information to Congress as its members legislate regulations and budget.

But, sad to say, since 2004, we have seen many news stories on infringements by the George W. Bush administration on appointments to study sections and other federal advisory boards such as the ones I have just described. Some individuals slated for such appointments have been asked if they favor abortions, for example. This is very worrisome.

The peer review system in the United States has been crucial in ensuring research quality and access to funds. This is why the first target of AWIS was getting women on to NIH peer review panels. Now this procedure is at severe risk of encountering political and religious pressure from the radical religious right. To politicize scientific advice sets a dangerous precedent, and it is already damaging the strong life science we have had in the United States of America.

The ban on stem cell research with federal funds has also seriously set science back in the United States.

Occasionally, Congress has attempted to micromanage federal grants to NIH or NSF. In July 2003, two congressmen called five proposed studies a "waste of taxpayer funds." These studies concerned a variety of issues researchers wanted to investigate concerning Asian prostitutes, female sexual arousal, the sexual habits of older men, and of transgendered individuals.

Some right-wing groups (the "Traditional Value Coalition") exerted pressure to cut these grants. As *The Scientist* magazine commented in December 2003:

> The sexual mores farce, "No Sex Please, We're British," was a long running stage comedy in London's West End. "No Sex Research Please! We're American" also could become a farce, but of a different type: devoid of humor, fraught with danger.

❧❦

In 1994, I was asked to give three talks honoring three different physiologists. In London, Ontario, the talk was in honor of James Stephenson, whom I had not known. Downstate at the University of Illinois in Champaign, the talk was in honor of Andrew Nalbandov, an old friend.

Andy had invited me to give a symposium talk on LH and FSH differential effects on follicle growth and ovulation at the SSR meeting in 1973, in Athens, Georgia, the year he was president of SSR. (I remember the *trip* to the meeting better than the meeting itself, as it was a bumpy ride on a small plane between Atlanta and Athens, and the stewardess dropped a tray of drinks on me and my brief case where my slides and manuscript were stored. She was very apologetic and tried to wipe me off while I was trying to wipe off the materials in my briefcase.)

Andy had always been very supportive of women scientists and was the advisor/mentor for a number of us including Janice Bahr, president of SSR during 1993–1994; and Mary Hunzicker-Dunn, my colleague at NU and president of SSR during 2003–2004. I felt truly honored to give this talk.

The third talk was in Davis, California, honoring Irving Geschwind, an important comparative endocrinologist, who was cynical, tough, and a highly valued editor of the journal *Endocrinology*. I have a few searing letters from him commenting on articles I had submitted, but taking his advice always made for clearer, more trenchant presentations.

❧❦

In 1995, I made a trip into my past to honor my mother and grandfather when I went to Russia to meet the remnants of our family there. The year before that, my brother Leon and his wife Joan had visited Russia and had seen cousins in Kiev, Ukraine. Their enthusiasm and pictures had whetted my appetite. My cousin Bernie, who had met me at the train station in Chicago when I came to graduate school in 1948, came too, with his three grown children.

We had written ahead to indicate our time of arrival, and when we got to our hotel, Bernie, whose Yiddish is better than mine and who spoke a little Russian, called the home of one of our cousins. Within an hour, our first cousins Nina, Mischa, and Fima burst through the lobby door with Elena, their great-niece, and Mischa's sons, Peter and Boris. Peter and Boris had driven everyone over; they were carrying two bouquets of flowers for us. They drove us back to the apartment of Elena's mother Pearl, who was named, like my sister, for our grandmother Pearl, who had come to America. We went into the apartment to find more cousins and a table spread with wine, vodka, soda, salads, meats, breads, and desserts.

❧

When my mother emigrated to America with her parents, two of her sisters and two brothers, including Bernie's father, my Uncle Harry, came also. The family's two oldest sisters were already married and settled in homes with children, so they had stayed in the Ukraine. One sister, Nechuma, had two daughters. The other sister, Lisa, had four children: Nina, Fima, Mischa, and Lena, my first cousins, three of whom I met in Kiev.

For the first time, I learned what had happened to my Aunt Nechuma and her family. As the German army approached, the two families arranged to meet in the Ural Mountains, knowing that the Germans were killing Jews as they marched across Russia. Well, Nechuma's family did not get out in time, and they were all killed at Treblinka.

I sat listening to this story with my cousins and found myself weeping for the lost family and wishing my mother could have come with me to see her niece and nephews and their children. I looked around the table tearfully at the surviving generations who spoke Russian, English, Yiddish, and German as we tried to communicate with each other. We spent a week in Kiev, getting to know our family and visiting the one remaining synagogue and the monument to the Kiev citizens slaughtered by the other Nazis. We walked together in the parks, but mostly we ate, drank, and talked, talked, talked in our halting, multilingual interchange.

❧

Back in the United States, my life was about to change again. After Mother died in 1985, Dad had lived on for a while in their apartment, essentially isolated, except when Pearl drove in from southern Maryland or Leon or I came back to Baltimore. He was losing weight, not liking the meals from Meals on Wheels, and clearly getting depressed.

On one of my trips back to Baltimore, I spoke to a Jewish Federation social worker about him. She met him and suggested we move him to a senior citizen housing building in north Baltimore. He resisted, but his three children insisted; we arranged for the move over his protests. The social worker told me "Some people thrive, but others go under when their children move them like this. It is a chance you are taking."

We took the chance, and it turned out to be the right thing. He liked the building where he moved and became a translator for new residents who did not speak English well, since he could also speak Yiddish and some Russian. He became a favorite of the many widows in the building, who brought him cookies and cake.

One warm late summer evening in 1995, he was sitting outside talking with a gentleman with whom he had played basketball as a young man. He went up to his room and died that night while eating a bowl of cereal.

Two days later Leon, Pearl, and I sat remembering him and Mom, looking over the pictures and books he had in his apartment. He was a wonderful and supportive father and grandfather.

Leon's son Howard came to Baltimore to deliver a eulogy on the family's behalf, remembering his grandfather Paul taking him to feed the ducks in the park and always having a toy in his pocket for each grandchild.

Study Questions

(1) Discuss whether you view Neena's activities during her sabbatical as related in this chapter to be consistent with the concept of sabbatical as you understood it prior to reading this volume.

(2) Compare and contrast Neena's relationships within her family and those within her academic community, including those with her students and with her colleagues.
- Postulate reasons for similarities or differences that you identify.

Harriet Claire Wadeson and Neena, 1990.

Thirteen

WRAPPING UP

In my new robe
This morning
Someone else

Basho

No bars are set too close, no mesh too fine,
To keep me from the eagle and the lion,
Whom keepers feed that I may freely dine,
This goes to show that if you have the wit
To be small, common and live on shit.
Though the cage fret kings, you may make free with it . . .

Howard Nemerov
"The Sparrow in the Zoo"

After Rudy Weingartner fired me as Chair of Biological Sciences in 1978, he remained as dean until 1987, whereafter he moved to become provost at the University of Pittsburgh. During the years before his move, we maintained a distant but reasonably cordial relationship. We continued to interface some; we couldn't avoid it since I was an elected member of the college Promotions and Tenure Committee and was appointed a member of the college Committee on Committees.

After Weingartner left, when Larry Dumas, Chair of Biochemistry, became Dean, life suddenly became much happier for me and the other women at Northwestern University.

In the fall of 1995, Larry asked me to see him. We sat together in his wood-paneled dean's office; I had no inkling of what he was about to say.

"I have agreed to take the office of Provost at Northwestern," he told me.

I had heard some rumors from search committee members, so I was not too surprised. I knew he had interviewed in a number of other universities for a provost or president position.

"Congratulations," I said, and I meant it. Larry had been a good department chair of Biochemistry, and a good dean.

He smiled and said "Would you be willing to serve as Acting Dean while we are looking for a new dean?" he asked.

Given my history of being fired from the position of department chair by Weingartner, with all of his complaints about me, I was surprised by this request and said as much to Larry, who laughed about this "ancient history," as he called it. Larry told me that as he had informally talked with faculty members around the college, my name had emerged frequently, and that our University President, Henry Bienen, had agreed.

I then talked with Henry about what my deanship would involve. I did not want to be serving as a token in an empty position, as I had done as Vice President of the Endocrine Society so many years before. I had at least learned something from that fiasco. Both Henry and Larry assured me that I really would be serving as *the* dean, with the usual responsibilities and prerogatives.

Indeed I believe I did, doing the job of recruitment of faculty, appointing of chairs, and deciding on cases of promotion and tenure. None of my decisions was reversed by the provost or president. My brother Leon, who was by then Vice-Chancellor at University of California, Irvine, told me later that I should have been designated "Interim Dean" instead of "Acting," because I did, in fact, have the responsibilities. This had not occurred to me. I had never consulted Leon about the title, a clear example of failing to utilize an administrative mentor!

❧

The dean's office traditionally held a Christmas party each December for all of the staff and their significant others. Larry and his wife Sally invited Claire and me to join them at the party in 1995 after I had accepted the job. Larry gave a lovely speech, welcoming "Neena and Claire" to the office.

My God, what a way to be "outed" after so many years of pretending nobody knew! It was so meaningful that Larry did this, as it signaled from the beginning that I would be visible in a three-dimensional way. He explicitly introduced *both* of us to all the associate and assistant deans (whom *I* already knew), as well as the office secretarial, business, and computer staff.

That introduction of my partner and me was a first, and this was followed by many joint invitations for all formal and informal university occasions. This brought me, for the first time, at the age of seventy, to a true blending of my personal and professional lives. This has continued to the present since Claire is still always asked to university affairs, and she is always greeted warmly by all. It never fails to surprise me. Isn't it sad that it took so long?

❧

Before I could start my new job, I needed a new wardrobe. I bought three wool pants suits for everyday "deaning," and a new pair of shoes and a new topcoat. I was even coerced by Adair Waldenberg, an associate dean at the time, into occasionally wearing a skirt when I was scheduled to meet with "outside" people.

❧

My tenure as Acting Dean lasted from January 1996 until the end of June 1997. During the fall of 1995, Northwestern unexpectedly won the Big Ten championship in football. Even before I had *accepted* the offer of the deanship, I was asked if Claire and I wanted to go to the Rose Bowl game in Pasadena at the university expense! This was a real irony, as, while I was a graduate student in 1952, Northwestern's football team went to the Rose Bowl and I remembered lamenting to one of my professors in physiology that I could not afford to go.

He said "Don't worry—we will go back again lots of times and you will have your chance."

But that hadn't happened *even once* in the intervening years. I have been living within two blocks of our football stadium since 1970, and I've watched lots of games, most of which we have lost.

Claire and I did indeed go to Pasadena with the other Northwestern administrators and alumni, and I wangled two extra tickets for my brother and a friend of his. We lost the game to USC by a score of 41-32, but it was an "honorable" loss, and Leon rooted for us against UCI's enemy, USC. Some of my colleagues even hinted that I accepted the deanship to get a free trip to the Rose Bowl.

❧

Before taking on the deanship, I had made two travel commitments, which I kept. In October 1996, I went to Australia. Claire was teaching there on a sabbatical, and we met in Sydney. I arrived jet-lagged after the long flight from Los Angeles, only wanting to sleep. But in her usual enthusiastic, commanding way, Claire dragged me off to the park for a gay pride parade. I stumbled along after her for an hour. We were interviewed by Australian radio, and I finally was permitted to go back to the hotel.

After I had recovered, we explored Sydney, attended an opera, "*Falstaff*," in the wonderful waterfront building, explored the harbor on the ferries, and visited a colleague of hers in the Blue Mountains. While Claire was teaching, I went to Monash University in Melbourne to gave a talk on inhibin to a group of scientists who were friends of long standing and who had been involved in the inhibin story in the male from the beginning.

Claire then took a week off from teaching, and we visited the Great Barrier Reef, where we birded, hiked, and snorkeled. She stayed in Australia for a few more weeks, while I flew back to Chicago to resume my duties as dean.

❧❦

But my duties were again interrupted. I had made a commitment to attend the twenty-second Brazilian Endocrine & Metabolism Meeting in November 1996, in Salvador, Brazil, before I was even approached about the acting deanship. So I went ahead, giving a paper updating the inhibin story.

The meeting was great fun, and the Brazilians were wonderful hosts. The hotel was on the beach, and the music and dancing were spectacular. Since not many females attended the meeting, I found myself dancing, of course, with many of the male endocrinologists—a change of pace and orientation for me.

I liked Central and South America so much that I have visited Chile, Costa Rica, Argentina, Ecuador, Mexico, and Peru since retiring. I observed eighty-five new (for me) species of birds in Costa Rica, saw a seal give birth to a pup in the Galapagos, and walked the ruins of Macchu Picchu in Peru.

❧❦

I was concerned that my lab would fall completely to pieces during my stint as dean. I tried to keep it running by being there on Tuesday mornings and all day Thursday. I realized that if the dean job had gone on much longer, the lab would have had to go. The pressures of the deanship were all-encompassing. The responsibility for a faculty of over 300 people and a large budget weighed heavily on me. Being compulsive as a scientist *and* as a dean nearly overwhelmed me.

Fortunately, I did no formal classroom teaching during this time. But the position still took a toll on my health; before this, my blood pressure was appropriately low, but since taking the job, it has been persistently high, in spite of medication.

The job of acting dean was complex and challenging; I enjoyed almost every minute of it. It lasted a full year and a half, which began with my missing the first weekly Tuesday intra-office deans' meeting because Claire and I (and three cats and a dog) were trapped in a snowstorm driving back from *At Beigh*.

It was snowing so hard as we drove south on the interstate that we were forced to pull into a motel. Our stay was stressful since a "No Pets" policy was clearly stipulated on its front door. We were desperate and sneaked the animals under our coats into our room by a back door as it was too cold to leave them in the car overnight. Fortunately, they behaved in the room—no cat fights, no bathroom accidents, no barking. Well, only once: Fingal barked like the good watchdog she was when the maid knocked on our door in the morning. The TV set was on, and her bark blended in nicely with the news, so we escaped detection and a $200 penalty.

જ઼ જ઼

Lots of events took place in the college during my service in the Dean's office. Students staged a sit-in in one of the language departments about the treatment of research assistants, and another by the Asian-American students who wanted us to form a division of Asian-American scholarship.

An associate professor in one of the humanity departments was accused of sexual harassment by an undergraduate student, who had documented the occasions by Email to a friend in law school. What followed were lots of consultations with the university lawyers and a mediated resolution.

A number of faculty members came up for promotion or tenure, and I talked to a lot of people outside the university and inside it about the questionable cases. I promoted a number and did not promote some others. I hired a new secretary when Larry's secretary followed him to the provost's office. The person I hired was new to the workforce but had managed a large family, was very assertive, and really understood the issues. Cindy Nash has been promoted and is now working in the Office of Admissions.

My favorite times during the deanship were when I met candidates for faculty positions. I expected to be able to interview the science candidates easily, understanding their professional milieu. But I found that my interviews with the social scientists were informed by my long-term contact with Rue and her colleagues, and my interviews with candidates in the humanities were informed by my friendships and shared seminars with faculty in the Gender Studies, and Science and Human Culture Programs at the university.

Promotions and tenure decisions were a major worry of mine before I became dean because of the serious responsibility involved with both. But I had been elected to the Promotions and Tenure Committee of the college several times during my years in the college, and I had a lot of cross-college experience as a result. Also, I had been a member of a committee looking at tenure issues at the medical school while I chaired the Biological Science Department. It was customary for the college dean to attend the meetings of the Promotions and Tenure Committee to hear the arguments and to meet with department delegations when the committee had a preliminary test vote that was negative. Making the subsequent recommendations to the provost and president and providing my arguments was taxing, but I was comfortable with the procedure.

During my tenure as dean, I also had to appoint several department chairs. Before the present chair's previous appointment is over, the dean inquires what the department's wishes are: to reappoint the incumbent chair or make a new appointment, which was generally for three or four years. This is in marked contrast to the medical schools I worked in, where "heads" not "chairs" are appointed for indefinite terms by the dean, and generally department members are not consulted about these decisions. I have argued frequently with my medical school colleagues about this, and they maintain that longer, appointed terms give the department head more power to "build" the department. This is, of course, my objection to it, following my experiences with three department heads at two medical schools!

Development functions were my least enjoyable duties as dean. I met potential alumni donors in San Francisco, New York City, and Florida, as well as in Evanston and Chicago, with the college development staff. While I enjoyed meeting these alumni, and some have become friends, I never felt comfortable with the underlying reasons for the meeting. Plainly, I did not like asking for money.

One day in San Francisco, while I was walking across Union Square after one meeting, a pigeon hovered over me and let loose. The development person with me and I had to go back to the hotel for me to change. The event seemed to express my feelings about what I was doing.

Another function that was not much fun was chairing the quarterly faculty meetings. One of the associate deans kept me adhering to *Robert's Rules of Order*, so that I would not make any unfortunate errors.

Invariably, some faculty members were deliberately contentious and sometimes insulting to each other or to me. I remembered the adage that faculty arguments are so violent because there is so little at stake. I feel good about one of the changes that came out of the meetings; the rules were changed permitting lecturers (non-tenure track faculty) to vote on teaching issues. Since they do so much of the teaching to undergraduates, this seemed not only fair, but wise.

One of the tense times in the dean's office is the annual two-day spring quarter meeting with the Visiting Committee. This is a committee of successful and diverse alums, interested members of the local community, and potential donors, who come in to hear about the successes and problems of the college—a sort of "show and tell." The college staff was quite nervous about these meetings, but I enjoyed the two in which I participated. I made lots of friends on the committee, and when Goucher College asked me to serve on its Visiting Committee during 2000, I accepted with alacrity.

⇛⇝

The search committee seeking the new permanent dean asked me twice if I was interested in becoming dean, and I met all of the candidates they brought to the campus. But I was clearly too old for the job. It was obvious to me that I would not have had the necessary energy for initiating new endeavors. My rising blood pressure was a clear warning signal.

I have asked myself whether I would have enjoyed ending my career as a scientist and becoming a dean; perhaps I might have had I been younger. While I have enjoyed the administration I did at Illinois and Northwestern, in the deans' offices as well as the Center for Reproductive Science, I feel that a career of doing science research and writing and teaching has been more satisfying, That kind of career enjoys maximal flexibility. Administration is very much tied to meetings and deadlines. But as a scientist and teacher in a university, I have been able to travel, combining business with pleasure, and I could do my writing in Door County when I wished. As long as I held my classes, met my grant deadlines and continued to publish, I was on my own clock, not somebody else's.

Do scientists make good deans for a liberal arts college? I think yes, if they respect the work of non-scientists. I greatly enjoyed talking about non-science scholarship with the prospective candidates I interviewed.

But some were obviously bothered by my being a biologist, even though I made sure to have the appropriate associate dean (humanist or social scientist) with me during the interviews. Sometimes candidates would try to explain "criticism" in English or Germanic literature to me or tell me why sociologists might study the history of the abortion movement in the United States. I would try not to get insulted, while my associate dean colleague would be afraid to look at me. Yes, scientists can do it, and they at least have had experience at budgeting a program and interacting with a staff.

৵৽

The dean who followed me was Eric Sundquist, who did an excellent job, I believe. He was an English scholar; unfortunately, he returned to UCLA after only five years at Northwestern. But while he was here, he appointed a number of female department chairs.

Larry Dumas was a splendid provost for a number of years. Unfortunately he died in 2008. Our present Provost is Dan Linzer, a formerly active member of our reproductive biology center. The new Dean of the college is Sarah Mangelsdorf.

Anticipating retirement in January 1999, I stopped taking new graduate students and post-docs and began trying to get some closure on the research projects I still had running in the lab.

In addition to having graduate students, postdocs, and undergrads in the lab, I was lucky to have two research associates working with me then, Marta Szabo and Signe Kilen. They were women who had returned to science after raising families; they helped get my lab through my deanship and made a tremendous difference to my graduate and undergraduate students. They participated in tying up our progesterone receptor/RU486 studies and our continuing studies on the issue of glucocorticoid and other steroid hormones on the pituitary gland.

Marta has now retired to California, and Signe is becoming a molecular biologist in Teresa Woodruff's growing laboratory.

৯৵৺

After obtaining the surprising RU486 results, in which this antiprogesterone compound prevented a drop in inhibin from increasing FSH secretion from the pituitary, we became interested in the progesterone receptor. We measured mRNA for progesterone receptor in the uterus, pituitary, and several areas of the brain throughout the estrous cycle. The amount of "message" within a cell for a protein such as the progesterone receptor predicts the amount of progesterone receptor synthesized. We showed that this changed with the estrous cycle, depending on estrogen secretion. We demonstrated that activin, the homologue of inhibin, stimulated FSH synthesis and secretion in cultured pituitaries, whether or not estrogen was given simultaneously. But RU486 blocked FSH stimulation from activin only when estrogen was present. Thus, we confirmed in vitro what we had seen in vivo. From these data, we predicted that activin stimulation of FSH synthesis and secretion would not occur in the absence of progesterone receptors.

My colleague, Jon Levine, had a colony of mice in which the conventional progesterone receptors (intracellular) were "knocked out." So we tested pituitaries from these mice and found they were unresponsive to progesterone or RU486, as expected. But they did, in fact, increase FSH secretion in the presence of activin. From this we concluded that the effects of activin may depend on another form of progesterone receptor, a form recently identified in neural cell *membranes*.

We continued to publish the results from our final experiments throughout the end of the 1990s and into the new millennium. But during this time, I also wrote several chapters on reproduction and the estrous cycle for the *Encyclopedia of Reproduction* and the *Encyclopedia of Neuroscience*. (When I was on the Promotions and Tenure Committee, I was always bothered to see junior faculty writing encyclopedia articles, because I felt their time should be spent doing original scholarship. So here I was, confirming my early suspicions that this was something for superannuated scholars!) I have also written a couple of textbook chapters on the regulation of reproductive cycles.

৯৵৺

My "career" has now settled into the *éminence grise* phase. I have received a couple of awards for mentoring and given several talks on what a good mentor is or should be. The Endocrine Society presented me with the Distinguished Educator Award in 1998. I was elected to the executive board of the American Association for the Advancement of Science (AAAS) in 1998, serving until 2002, and I have finished a term on the AAAS committee on opportunities in science.

In the fall of 2000, I found that I had agreed to give three oral presentations at three different meetings. Not cutting edge research contributions, mind you, but representative of where my time goes these days.

The first was in Chicago; my colleague, Joel Michael, at Rush Medical School, was presenting a workshop sponsored by the American Physiological Society for teachers of undergraduate physiology. The workshop was entitled "Teaching Physiology: Updating Pedagogy and Content." Joel asked me to provide them with an update on a problem in reproductive physiology using a systems approach.

My talk was entitled "Sex Differences in Negative Feedback from the Gonads: Science and Soundbites." I talked about our studies on serum LH rising faster in male rats than in females after removal of the gonads. The "sound-bites" referred to the hype the media would provide if they were to run the story about any sex difference. I emphasized the ways in which the media sensationalized sex differences and frequently distorted the importance of the differences in influencing the relative roles men and women play in politics, child rearing, and intellectual pursuits. These teachers agreed with me that students must learn the crucial difference between scientific observations and interpretations.

The second presentation was at Northwestern, in a conference sponsored by our Gender Studies program: "Gender, Race, and Reproduction: Bodies, Ideas, Cultures." I was a discussant for two papers, one by Martha McClintock of the University of Chicago on "Mind and Biology: A Biopsychologist's Approach to Fertility and Disease," and the second, by Anne Fausto-Sterling of Brown, was "Beyond Nature/Nurture: A Systems Approach to the Body."

Martha discussed her studies on effects of male and female steroid derivatives that are released in perspiration on men and women, as *modulators* of human behavior rather than *determinants*.

Anne discussed the flimsiness of the evidence for resolving the nature/nurture dichotomy in defining differences between males and females and between heterosexuals and homosexuals.

Their talks were wonderful. Privately, I thought how convenient for me to feel so confirmed while writing this memoir, which reflects the same ideas and positions. Yes, life would be simpler if we could have definitive answers to the etiologies of these differences, but simplicity would not be nearly so much fun as complexity.

The third presentation was at a Women and Science conference in 2000 in St. Louis: "Writing the Past, Claiming the Future: Women and Gender in Science, Medicine, and Technology." I shared the platform of a plenary session with Margaret Rossiter, a prominent science historian, who wrote the classic studies on women in science in the United States.

Meeting Margaret Rossiter and Sally Kohlstedt, the science historian who invited me to the conference, has influenced my perspective on the histo-

ry of women in science, just as Rue Bucher helped me look at how people
become socialized into their professions.

Our session was titled, "Power and Expertise." A scientist (me), a physician (Wanda Ronner, Philadelphia), and an engineer (Jill Tietjen, University of
Colorado) were each paired with an historian. The session was designed "to
explore the dynamics between history and practice." Margaret talked about me
first from the point of view of a historian. Following her talk, I spoke of my
career in science from the point of view of a scientist "practitioner."

I think my readers will be interested in a quote from what the historian,
Rossiter, gleaned about me from her *traditional* historical sources:

> We live in interesting, even historic times, and some of the people that
> some of us "work on" are still alive. This is a bit unusual for those of us
> trained as historians, because history used to "end" about the time of
> World War II. This more modern and even current emphasis has certain
> disadvantages—there is as yet no obituary of the major figures by a
> close associate, there is probably no stash of archives and manuscripts
> (and if there is it is immense and unarranged and possibly restricted),
> and there is a certain sense of caution that they might take offense at
> what we say about them. . . .

> Over the last several years, I have come across Neena Schwartz about
> five times. One time was in the Dorothy Stimson Papers at Goucher
> College. So I made a mental note of this protégée chain extending into
> modern times.

(I had taken a wonderful course from Dorothy Stimson on the History of
Science, and written two papers for it, one on Vesalius and one on Galen, two
very early physiologists.)

> On another archival foray, this time into the John F. Fulton Papers at
> Yale University, I also came across Miss Neena Schwartz. She had ap-
> plied to Yale Graduate School in physiology in the fall of 1947, and
> Miss Stimson . . . had written a letter of recommendation.

> Then on another occasion, after I got permission from Sharon L. John-
> son to look at her papers at the Schlesinger Library at what used to be
> Radcliffe College. A biochemist, she had a major lawsuit against the
> University of Pittsburgh in the 1970s whose medical school had denied
> her tenure. Among her supporters was one Neena Schwartz . . .

(I had not known Sharon—she asked me to testify since I was Chair of Biology at Northwestern at the time and presumably could discuss criteria for te-

nure. I testified. As I recall, the judge dismissed her claim saying that a department had the right to freely choose its colleagues.)

> And then later on I was at the. . . New York Public Library up in Harlem going through the Jewel Plummer Cobb Papers and came across a clipping about the medical school at the University of Illinois in Chicago . . . Cobb had been there in the anatomy department in 1952–1954. I thought isn't this the same school and maybe department that Neena Schwartz was in for a while?

(I did know Jewel and all of the other women Margaret mentioned.)

> And then my own autobiography intrudes. Neena Schwartz was one of the people who invited me to Northwestern University in the 1980s . . . to be a Kreeger-Wolf visiting professor for a week.

> And then a decade or so later in December 1996, I was in a position to return the favor. I was on the Nominating Committee of the AAAS . . . . Also on the committee was one David Hull of Northwestern, who pushed for Neena Schwartz for Board member and Gould for president. So we combined forces "and got all three of our candidates ranked high enough to be asked to run. And they got elected . . ."

These glimpses of my life, visible to a historian, fascinated me. I can only imagine what a historian of the future might make of the present book as a primary source.

Study Questions

(1) Neena writes, "I can only imagine what a historian of the future might make of the present book as a primary source."

- Place yourself in the position of that future historian using this volume as a primary source. Derive from the evidence presented so far a list of values, personal and professional, that you would conclude are characteristic of Neena B. Schwartz.
- Thinking from the viewpoint of an historian concerned with objectivity and fact, are first person recollections good sources from which to determine history? Defend your position.

At Beigh, Ellison Bay, 2000.

Neena & Leon birding, Southern California, 1990.

Dock at Ellison Bay, 1975.

Fourteen

DON'T ASK, DON'T TELL

A thump, and a murmer of voices
(Oh why must they make such a din?)
As the door of the bedroom swung open
And two plainclothes policemen came in:
"Mr. Woilde, we'ave come for to take yew
Where felons and criminals dwell.
We must ask yew tew leave with us quoietly
For this is *the Cadogan Hotel."*

John Betjemen
"The Arrest of Oscar Wilde at the Cadogan Hotel"

As a woman in science, I always felt I had the right to be where I was and that I could go as far as my abilities and desires would carry me. I knew that some men felt either that I did not belong or that I couldn't become successful in my own right. I also suspected, at the time I started graduate school, that the expectations were that I could not go very far as an independent scientist and that I could certainly never hope to be an administrator in a research university.

But my parents had always encouraged me to achieve to the maximum, while acting with honesty, integrity, and concern for others. Goucher College taught me that women were unquestionably capable of being scientists.

The Jackson Lab had many senior women scientists doing important, independent science while I was there. The Department of Physiology at Northwestern respected all of their graduate students, challenging men and women alike to do their best. So, with respect to my science and my roles in academia, I was relatively confident.

☙❧

But as a lesbian, I could never shake off the messages that I had received throughout my teens that *it* was wrong, and so *I* was wrong. Not only did my mother not approve of who I was (my Dad and I never discussed it!), but also, neither did society.

While my feminist activism has at times seemed separate from my science, it, like my career, has been played out in the open. My lesbianism, however, has always been *hidden*, even when others acknowledged it. It seems to me to somewhat resemble espionage living this way, where one has a "cover" (my public life) and a hidden agent identity (my private life). In that life, one's "real" work is being a spy. One's cover is merely the apparent work.

To quote again from John Hollander's "Reflections on Espionage," "Cover and work must embrace without touching; too crude an intrusion of either into the other endangers the security of both." Keeping the overt and covert separate without touching was a stressful lifestyle.

During the time while I was growing up, well-publicized warnings abounded about the dangers of exposure as a homosexual.

Alan Turing, a renowned mathematician, advanced the theory of what came to be known as a "Turing Machine," which was, and is still, a model for understanding control and regulation. He worked with other mathematicians and cryptologists breaking German codes during World War II.

Turing was gay and frequently took his holidays where he could meet other gay men. After the war, he became a faculty member at Cambridge University in England. A man with whom he was involved sexually (of a "lower" social status) told someone else about Turing's home; subsequently, the third man robbed Turing of some minor items. Turing reported this to the police, naively telling them the whole story. He was charged with being a homosexual, which was against the law in England at that time.

A public trial ensued, and he was found guilty and given the choice of receiving estrogen injections or going to jail. He chose the estrogen, a treatment that undoubtedly reduced his sex drive by suppressing gonadotropic hormones, thereby suppressing endogenous testosterone secretion. Two years after the trial, he died of cyanide poisoning in his home, and was presumed to have committed suicide.

☙❧

I can still remember the McCarthy hearings in Congress, with McCarthy calling out how many "homosexuals and Communists" were in the State Department. The numbers seemed to change daily, but the message was clear to me and other homosexuals. Before my brother went to work at NASA, he needed security clearance, and I know that I and the entire family were checked out. I worried constantly that someone would give me away and ruin his chances at the job.

☙❧

Lillian Faderman, professor of English at Fresno State, California, has written about many of the women who made a difference in the United States in social movements involving abolition, suffrage, societal changes, and education. She describes women who were mostly "woman" identified, perhaps as lesbians, who lived and worked together during the nineteenth century and the early part of the twentieth century. This was before the Havelock Ellis/

Freudian definitions of "sexual inversion" associated with "illness" became household terms. She points out that from the 1920s on, until very recently, lesbians were condemned, regarded as sick and perverted, and needed to be kept away from young girls. This is just the time when I was coming of age.

Jill Conway in *True North* talks about her years as president of Smith College and the frequency with which trustees, alumnae, and others raised the "question" of lesbian teachers in women's colleges. What exactly was the "question," one might ask?

No wonder that I covered my lesbianism as best I could. Faderman's recent memoir, *Naked in the Promised Land*, is very open about her coming out; the book was particularly interesting to me because she grew up in poverty with an unwed mother, a home life in such contrast with my own. However, we ended up in the same place, both of us in academia. Her subject matter as an academic has focused on homosexuality in literature and in the lives of women in America.

Had I been completely open about my sexuality, could I have succeeded as a teacher and scientist in the academic workplace and in professional societies? I think not, but I don't know.

I admire the younger women whose autobiographies appear in the Ambrose volume on women in science, who state, proudly I believe, that they are lesbians. I am aware of other women in this same book, who did not come out; I understand their reluctance. A group of gay and lesbian anthropologists has described interesting interactions between their coming out and their research endeavors (Ellen Lewin and William L. Leap). For experimental biologists like myself, this would be analogous to studying sex behavior and hormone-brain interactions in animals or in human beings. I have chosen not to do so, but some others have done so, of course.

I have loved May Sarton's journals. However, Margot Peters' biography of her has troubled me. Sarton obviously had a lot of problems with her lesbian relationships; in fact, they were abusive, according to her biographer. After Sarton came out as a lesbian in her published journals, she lost some appointments she had teaching at small colleges.

Like Sarton, I have had more trouble in my personal intimate relationships than in my relationships with colleagues, students, or technicians. I remember getting angry with a lover who said, while we were on a camping trip, "Don't treat me like one of your technicians." I was taken aback: I never treated my technicians that way!

ঔৎড়

Being lesbian coextensive with being a scientist and an academic has had its positive and negative sides. I have never been responsible for the direct care of a child; I find this to be a positive, as I never wanted children of my own. I am, and always have been, great friends with my nieces and nephews; their

presence in my life is another huge positive. I have never had to move to follow a husband's job, although the issue of considering job locations for the
sake of personal relationships has come up in my life.

A major reason I have spent my professional life in Chicago, in fact, has
been my reluctance to shake up a satisfying relationship. But since I was already not conforming, in a very major way, to societal expectations, I never
felt that I had to conform to expectations about what field I should work in,
how I should teach classes, or how I should run a lab. Moreover, I did not
have to view myself as "second" to anyone, which is probably why it was so
easy to identify myself as a feminist.

Living as a lesbian in a large city like Chicago does not have to be a
lonely existence, and for me it has not been. My life has been filled with
many social events and lots of friends, but this social life has been virtually
completely disconnected from my workplace. As I think about it, I suppose
that that is true for many people of any orientation in any job. Aside from the
obligatory invitation to the spouse or significant other to the odd office party,
most people, I imagine, don't know their mate's professional social set.

ନ୍≈∕ଚ

Students come to professors wanting help and advice about many things. I
have been approached by students wanting to know how to tell their parents
they don't want to go to medical school or asking for advice about a suspected STD or how to end a pregnancy. But what happens when a student
makes a sexual overture to you? This has happened to me occasionally, but I
have never acted on it.

This does bring up an important question. Is it fair not to be open about
homosexuality as a fact of life with our gay students? I have only once been
approached by a student about being gay. This was a male student who
brought me some gay magazines after I discussed the so-called gay gene in
class. I took them, told him that I knew about them, and then I listened to him
talk about his medical school future. We did not talk about me or about homosexuality in any way.

ନ୍≈∕ଚ

The annual meetings of the Society for the Study of Reproduction are small
and fun, and they usually take place on a university campus. Meals during the
conference take place in the cafeteria with students and colleagues.

As I noted in the first chapter, I was once carrying a tray toward a table
when a young female scientist approached me and said quietly, "How have
you managed to become so successful and be a lesbian?"

I suggested to her that we not talk about this in the dining hall. Later, we
did talk. She had heard from a group of women she knew in her university

town that I was lesbian. I was not sure at first what her agenda was; would she blackmail me, was she confronting me, or flirting with me? As it turned out, she was asking because she was lesbian and a flirt. She was just starting her career, and her subsequent trajectory indicates that she has learned quite well how to manage her life as a lesbian with a successful career in reproductive biology.

❧

I never had an affair with someone in my lab. I never talked about my lesbianism with my lab people, although I assume they knew. Also, I was usually careful not to drink very much in their presence.

Once, at the Laurentian Hormone Conference in Canada, I was part of an evening social group and I drank more than I should have. I started to make advances to one of my post-docs. A second post-doc from my lab came over to me and quietly suggested that we go for a walk.

The proximity of preceptor and student/technician or postdoc in a lab setting can be sexually arousing and can easily lead to intimacy, as many students and faculty have learned. Some have said that graduate students are the most vulnerable people in an academic setting, as far as their preceptors are concerned. All of the power is in the hands of the lab boss, and a sexual relationship between student and preceptor is an unforgivable use of this power.

❧

The annual meetings in the Laurentian Mountains at Mont Tremblant resort were particularly prone to social interactions of various sorts. Perhaps not surprising—the scenery was beautiful, and the meeting was structured to leave lots of free time for hiking, sailing, conversation, and drinking. After the evening presentation and discussion, people continued conversations in the bar.

One evening, one of the junior endocrinologists bought me a drink, and started moving closer to me on the wooden bench. I had met her several times at meetings, while she was a post-doc with a friend of mine. I moved a little away from her body, which was pressing against mine, and wondered whether she was conscious of what she had done. After a couple of drinks, with two other endocrinologists at the table, I rose and announced that I was retiring for the evening. As I left the bar, she also said good night and followed me out.

As we walked along the dark path, she said, "I've been wondering what it would be like to go to bed with a woman."

I was feeling the beer by that time. The evening was cool and I could smell the pine needles. The Big Dipper was visible in the bright sky. "It feels good," I said—and it did.

৵৵

When I was Acting Dean, I was amazed to see how openly some of the people I recruited to the faculty discussed their gay partners, who often also needed a job at the university or elsewhere in the Chicago area. They did it with the same ease heterosexual recruits did. I remembered the one time I managed to do the same when the Dean of the University of Iowa Medical School tried very hard to recruit me as head of the Physiology Department in 1973.

৵৵

The downside to being lesbian, with regard to my professional life, is that my support network—my partner—was never formally recognized by the external world until I was in the dean's office at the end of my career.

I was fired by the dean as Chair of Biological Sciences at the same time that my long-term personal relationship with Rue was breaking up.

I have always felt that I was seen by the outside world as two dimensional. This was probably not as true as I thought, since many people knew that I was in lesbian relationships. But people did not talk with me about this. I do not know whether this was due to my terrible need to pretend that I was in the closet, or because my lifestyle made other people uncomfortable.

When things went wrong in my personal life, I could not look to my colleagues for support, and this was very hard. I was reminded of this when one of the men in my department went through two serious illnesses with two family members within a few years. The rest of us were quick to help run his lab or do some teaching for him. But years ago, when Jan had breast cancer surgery, I kept right on working and did my grieving alone at home.

৵৵

The suicide in 2006 of Denise Denton, provost at the University of California campus at Santa Cruz, chilled me to the bone. I met Denise when we were both at a meeting of the AAAS in Washington, and I guessed that she was a lesbian, but (of course) we did not talk with each other about it.

At that time, Denise was Dean of Engineering at the University of Washington. When she accepted the provost position in California, I became aware of a nasty campaign in a San Francisco newspaper about her because she had asked that a position be made available for her partner, who appeared to be quite professionally competent. This is, of course, a common and accepted occurrence when recruiting a new faculty member or administrator. She had also asked for repairs and additions to the residence provided and owned by the university. The vicious campaign continued, ending in her suicide. I do not know what other factors may have contributed, but I have no doubt that these personal attacks on her played a part. The perks provided for her by the University of California are absolutely standard for recruiting at the provost level, but as a woman who was lesbian, she proved to be a tempting target for the self-righteous right and their followers.

~~❧~~

Why have I engaged in feminist activism but not in gay rights activism in science? I felt guilty about being lesbian, and the world was often not a friendly place for me.

I am not sure that gays and lesbians are handicapped in our present academic environment if they "don't tell," but, of course, that isolates them—us.

It is no secret that when you are a woman in science, your Curriculum Vita says it all. But battles in Universities about spousal rights, medical insurance, and other rights such as fees and tuition have also been fought on campus. These have been generally won, as the world outside academe has changed. Northwestern University now has a partner's rights program in health insurance, course discounts, and other coverage. But to get them, you do have to "tell"—with frightening sequelae, perhaps, still.

Recently, I read Karla Jay's *Tales of the Lavender Menace* and Newton's *Margaret Mead Made Me Gay*, reminding me that during the 1960s and 1970s, I was not a radical feminist/lesbian. I was a closeted lesbian working in a predominantly male academic setting. I never fought the gay rights fight.

This movement has not been very visible among scientists, although many professional societies now have gay and lesbian caucuses. In the life science community, some homosexual scientists and others have studied or commented upon the issue of the etiology of homosexuality as a "problem" in biology. But because of writing this memoir, I have now joined the National Organization of Gay and Lesbian Scientists and Technical Professionals. I decided the time had come. I attended my first meeting of this organization at the 2003 meeting of the American Association for the Advancement of Science. Not many people were in the room, but it felt good to be there.

~~❧~~

In April 2006, my partner Claire and I drove south to Evanston from the house in Door County, along the roads of Wisconsin and northern Illinois, with Lake Michigan occasionally visible on our left, a familiar route I have driven for more than forty years.

The long weekend we had just spent had been momentous; I had had a knee replacement a year before and Claire had a hip replacement just several months earlier. Neither of us had been able to do much walking when we closed the house for the winter the previous December, and we had just walked the "Trail Tramper's Delight," which weaves through the woods of

Peninsula State Park between the Lighthouse and the boat ramp, a round trip of about three miles.

What a triumph! The drive back home is a long one—260 miles door to door—and we talked and listened to music as we drove. Chaiya, our nineteen-year-old Siamese, growled occasionally from her travel cage. By 5 p.m., when we reached our house in Evanston, I was exhausted, having done most of the driving, with occasional stops along Lake Michigan. It was good to be back.

ঙ৵ঙ

I picked up my Email and discovered that within an hour, a meeting would commence of students in the Rainbow Alliance on Northwestern's campus on "the genetic basis of homosexuality." The speakers were Lane Fenrich of the History Department, who is an expert in cultural history, Nicky Beisel in Sociology, whose research has focused on the abortion/antiabortion movements in the United States, and Bill Leonard, a biological anthropologist.

"Wait a minute," I thought, "there is no biologist on the program." While I respected all three of my colleagues very much, in fact had hired two of them when I served as Acting Dean of the College of Arts and Science in the mid 1990s, it seemed incomplete, to put it mildly, to discuss genetics without a biologist present.

I got back in the car without dinner or a change of clothes and raced over to the Psychology building, where the conference was taking place. I listened to what my three colleagues had to say and the questions students asked them. An implicit assumption appeared to be present in the room that indeed, a "genetic basis for homosexuality" exists, which, in my opinion, is far from settled. I asked for some time and discussed the .scientific data from a biological, rather than a cultural, viewpoint. The students wrote me a letter later thanking me for speaking up.

ঙ৵ঙ

In this chapter, I have been discussing my understanding of lesbianism from the perspective of a lesbian. But what is my view as a scientist, as a reproductive endocrinologist, on homosexuality?

What did I discuss with those students in the Rainbow Alliance? Does a "gay gene" exist that affects the brain and causes a person to develop into a gay man or a lesbian? Do gay males have less testosterone or more estrogen than heterosexual males? Do lesbians have too much testosterone? Does homosexuality develop because the uterine environment of the fetus had the wrong hormones?

A few years ago, *The New Yorker* magazine ran a cartoon depicting a nurse showing a newborn baby to the father; the caption under the picture read "It's a lesbian." I loved it!

A play on Broadway entitled *The Twilight of the Golds*, which was later made into a movie, posited that a gay gene could be detected *in utero*, leaving the fetus vulnerable to abortion after amniocentesis.

☿

As a woman and a scientist, I have frequently been horrified by assertions about the "math" gene, the "female" brain vs. the "male" brain, or the "genetic" basis of intelligence. The media lap up these stories, the public cannot get enough. The issues rapidly become political, leaving any kind of objective view behind.

If the relationship between homosexuality and biology is real, it must be very complex. "Biology" in this context has meant different things at different times to different people. One can mean many things by the word "biology," such as the sex hormone levels in the adult, the hormones or other factors during early brain development of a fetus *in utero* or early postnatally, or the genes for some factor affecting the brain or some other organ, which is responsible for our gender identity. These are the hypothetical "natural" or biological factors people mean when they are trying to bridge the nature/nurture dichotomy.

Nurture presumably means some familial, societal, or peer influence. Considerable interactions occur between nature and nurture. Since we are not sure what "nature" factors influence homosexuality, nor what "nurture" factors do either, the issue of which, if either, influences our sexual preference, is unanswerable at this point in time.

My personal opinion is that a "behavior" as complex and as variable as homosexuality cannot possibly be due to a single altered gene or even several genes alone. I know so many women who lived happy heterosexual lives for a number of years, before changing to a lesbian lifestyle. This seems so non-deterministic, in contrast to the genetic factors which cause such devastation in cystic fibrosis, or Tay Sachs disease, or Down's syndrome.

On the other hand, homosexuality as a lifestyle is so compelling to so many, including myself, that it seems unlikely to this biologist that it can be due wholly to "social factors" completely isolated from bodily functions.

☿

The general public was fascinated by the growth of endocrinology as a discipline during the first half of the twentieth century. The concept that an infinitesimal amount of a chemical circulating in the bloodstream could mean the difference between life and death, as is the case for insulin, or the difference between normal intelligence and cretinism, as in the case of thyroid hormone, was mind-boggling. After all, that was one of the aspects of the discipline that made me *become* an endocrinologist.

The endocrine/homosexuality hypothesis started during the first half of the twentieth century, when it was demonstrated that many of the overt phenotypic characters that we call "male" or "female" in animals and in people (genitalia, fat distribution, height) are the result of the secreted estrogen in the adult female and the testosterone secreted in the adult male.

For people to assume that homosexuality itself was due to the "wrong" hormones being present in the adult homosexual was, perhaps, a natural progression of thought.

To my knowledge, *no* definitive data exist that show this to be at all true. We have no evidence that gay men have lower or higher testosterone or lower or higher estrogen levels than heterosexual men. Similarly, no reliable data are available on sex hormone differences between lesbians and heterosexual women.

While castration, estrogen, or anti-androgens have been prescribed for homosexual men, under some conditions in some cultures (as for the unfortunate Turing), these treatments would be expected only to interfere with erections and with sex drive, and not to change sexual orientation or gender identity.

With the failure to demonstrate clear abnormalities in adult hormone levels in homosexuals, investigators then began to look for other explanations. In rodents, androgens during pre- and post-natal life permanently alter the brain in such a way that female rodent pups given such treatment do not ovulate as adults or show typical female sexual behavior. Conversely, male rodents deprived of this early androgen grow up with some female endocrinological and behavioral characteristics.

If the same thing is true for human beings, then maybe the uterine prenatal hormonal environment is what determines homosexuality. But people are not rodents. Rodents have been marvelous models for the way gonads work and for studying the interactions between the pituitary and the gonads, but they have not been good models for the study of complex psychosocial factors.

Furthermore, in rodents, the early androgens in neonatal males prevent forever the stimulating action of estradiol in eliciting a preovulatory surge of Luteinizing Hormone from the pituitary gland. This is not true in human beings or non-human primates. Adult men can be induced to release a surge of LH from the pituitary following estradiol treatment, under particular conditions, such as when they are being prepared for sex change surgery (Gooren).

જ∾ૐ

My colleague at Northwestern, J. Michael Bailey, and other psychologists have done numerous studies looking for a heritable component in sexual orientation. The usual way the studies are done is to advertise for gays in the gay media and then check for homosexuality in siblings or twins. In male twins, monozygotic (single egg) twins are more likely than dizygotic (two different eggs fertilized by two different sperm) twins to be concordant for homosexuality. That is, if one twin is gay, the probability rises that the other twin is gay in cases of twins who share all of the same genes.

But the degree of concordance is only about 50 percent at the highest. Data for females also ranges near 50 percent concordance, but the studies are less consistent.

Data on twins raised apart are scarce, but may support the above findings of some concordance. One problem with these studies, readily discussed by the authors, is the way in which the respondents were recruited: from homosexual magazines, which allows for the possibility of non-randomness in the population surveyed.

Is this a random sample? Of course not. Is there a "volunteer" bias? That is, are the men who volunteer for these studies different from homosexuals who do not volunteer? There may very well be.

Given the varying degrees of social stigma or of gay pride within specific populations, it is difficult to predict who is most likely to have participated in these studies. Finally, 50 percent concordance means that for 50 percent of the sampled population of single egg twins the two brothers *differ* in their sexual orientation, with one identifying as gay, the other as heterosexual. This is hardly a definitive genetic etiology.

Carrying this one step further, in 2001, Bailey published a paper (with Aaron S. Greenberg), in which he discussed the "ethical" aspects of parental selection of sexual orientation in their unborn children. He concluded, "allowing parents to select their children's sexual orientation would further parent's freedom to raise the sort of children they wish to raise . . . and is unlikely to cause significant harm." Shades of the Nuremburg trials. I was reminded of Linus Pauling's suggestion in the 1960s, that carriers of sickle cell disease be tattooed on the forehead for easy recognition.

In 1993, a study appeared in *Science* magazine by Dean Hamer and colleagues. They claimed that they had evidence for a gene on the X chromosome that was linked to homosexuality in males. They recruited seventy-six subjects through HIV clinics. There were also thirty-eight pairs of homosexual brothers and relatives recruited through homophile publications.

The Kinsey Scale was used to ascertain the degree of homosexuality. The scale asks questions like "Have you ever had sex with another male?" The *Science* study found a high number of homosexual brothers and maternal uncles or maternal cousins (aunt's sons) of their respondents who scored high on the scale, suggesting genetic inheritance through the X chromosome.

They did a gene linkage analysis on families with two homosexual brothers, typing for twenty-two markers on the X chromosome. They found a linkage between sexual orientation and the presence of an area in the X chromosome described as "distal Xq28," which contains several hundred genes. This was not so in seven pairs of subjects. The study concluded, "one subtype of male sexual orientation is genetically influenced." The media attention to this admittedly weak claim was overwhelming, demonstrating again how the public is attracted to stories about sex and genetics.

However, in 1999, a second study was published in *Science* by another group (George Rice) that received no media attention at all. This group of researchers recruited subjects by advertising in gay magazines for families in which there were two gay brothers. They had responses from fifty-two sibling pairs from forty-eight families. They measured linkages to four markers at the gene site Xq28 and found no significant linkage. They concluded that there is *not* an X-linked gene for male homosexuality. Unlike the Hamer study, they did not look for maternal transmission specifically.

If a "gay" gene exists, it cannot be deterministic in the sense that eye color is, because even those studies that point toward some genetic component indicate that the linkage is weak. The human genome may contain only about 30,000 genes, suggesting that much of differential individual development results from combinations of genes and interactions with the environment. Furthermore, in complex traits like behavior, discovery of underlying genetic contributions is very difficult, owing to interactions not only between genes and the environment but also the interactions among genes themselves.

Hamer has recently published another article in *Science*, entitled "Rethinking Behavior Genetics." He says that the failure of linkage studies in examining many behavioral disorders is due to "the assumption that the rich complexity of human thought and emotion can be reduced to a simple, linear relation between individual genes and behavior." He does not discuss homosexuality in this article, I assume, because he does not regard this behavior as a "disorder."

అ

For years, studies have been conducted to measure sex differences in human brain size and morphology. I must confess that I tend to avoid this literature, because with whatever good intentions a study starts, whatever is being measured, the data always seem to be interpreted as favoring the ruling, dominant group.

If a brain nucleus (which is a local accumulation of nerve cells) is larger in males than females, then "bigger is better." If it is smaller in men, then it favors "closer precision or finer thinking." Now a growing body of literature compares brains of gay males with "normal heterosexual" men and women. The studies measure the area of a given nucleus *whose function in the human is not understood* and then compare the size.

Inevitably, the authors claim that brains from dead gay men, usually dead from AIDS, resemble those of dead women more than they resemble brains of dead heterosexual men. The sexual orientation of the donors of the "heterosexual" brains is not known but only inferred to be heterosexual.

༄·ঙ

A new set of experiments has now surfaced from the labs of physiological psychologists examining other aspects of homosexual brain functions. Hearing acuity and response to pheromones are the most recent measures that appear to be different in homosexuals and heterosexuals. Are they the cause of homosexuality? Are they the result of years of homosexuality? Do they indicate differences in the brains of the subjects which are causative or differences which result from being raised differently? We simply do not know.

Jean Wilson, a former president of the Endocrine Society, and the author of a major textbook of clinical endocrinology, is an expert in hormonal effects on sexual differentiation. He has analyzed the role of androgens in male gender role behavior in a masterful review. He concentrated on gender role behavior in subjects demonstrating two genetically influenced enzyme abnormalities, where the sex chromosomes are unambiguous but the external genitalia are ambiguous. These are 17β-hydroxysteroid dehydrogenase 3 deficiency and 5α-reductase 2 deficiency.

The deficiencies in these enzymes make it impossible for the fetus to synthesize the androgenic steroid hormones responsible for external genitalia differentiation in a male direction. Jeffrey Eugenides' novel *Middlesex* is a marvelous exposition of the sequelae of such genetic alterations. In both types of cases, genetic (XY) males are born with female genitalia and have been assigned to the female gender at birth.

Many of these individuals remain female in their gender role; some eventually change their sexual orientation. Wilson says the following:

> other [than androgen] factors—social, psychological, biological—are of equal or greater importance in modulating human sexual behavior. Indeed, the sex of rearing may be more important than the endocrine milieu . . . it may not be a coincidence that many (although not all) of the instances of reversal of gender role behavior in these two disorders [to a male direction] have occurred in countries and/or ethnic groups in which men play a dominant role.

These intersex issues, where there may be a discrepancy between external genitalia at birth and presence of XX or XY sex chromosomes, are as complex as the homosexuality genetics/hormones/society interactions.

While some genetic males without male genitalia may successfully be raised as girls, as recommended by the late John Money, others may not be, as described in John Colopinto's recent bestseller, *As Nature Made Him*. That book describes the true case of a boy deprived of a penis by an accident in the hospital.

Money suggested the child be raised as a girl; the parents did this, but the "girl" refused to identify him/herself as a girl, insisting instead on identifying as a boy. Some years later, the man committed suicide, never having settled satisfactorily on his gender identity.

An article in the *New York Times Magazine* (24 September 2006) describes the dilemma of the "intersex" child, the parents, and the pediatrician. If homosexuality is a scientific and social conundrum in the face of normal hormones and normal genitalia as well as XX or XY sex chromosomes, one can imagine the problem of discrepancies of anatomy, hormones, receptors, and social upbringing in the "intersex" child and family.

҈

But the issues of determination of phenotypic sex, XY and XX chromosomes, gonadal hormones, and sexuality grow increasingly complex, as more and more species are studied, and new techniques are devised for probing questions in familiar species. Four recent examples of this complexity demonstrate how simplistic our notions of the determination of sex and sexuality may be at present.

The first example is work done on the spotted hyena, a mammal found living in groups or clans in Africa. The female hyena is more aggressive in general than the male. Her anatomy reveals a surprisingly prominent phallus, which resembles a penis superficially.

The social structure of the group is such that females are dominant. Young males are forced to leave the colony and "immigrant" males from other colonies move in. The females choose their mates and preferentially choose the alien males over the familiar ones.

The female phallus appears to be relatively independent of androgen action, while in the male hyena, male phenotype is typically dependent on androgen as in other mammals. It has been suggested that the benefit of the high level of female aggressiveness occurs because feeding in the colonies is highly competitive; females need the extra food since they become pregnant. Incidentally, hyena mothers also deliver their babies through her extended phallus, which makes for some problems, as can be imagined.

҈

The second example concerns the whiptailed lizard, which lives in the American Southwest. These lizards reproduce parthenogenetically (no male contribution) and their colonies consist mostly of clones of females.

David Crews has observed what appears to be "sexual" behavior between females, finding that the "courting" female has ovaries with fewer large preovulatory follicles than the courted female. It is not clear whether this behavior has an adaptive value in the wild.

The media labeled the story about these findings as "lesbian lizards." A few years back, some lesbians asked me whether becoming pregnant via parthenogenesis in human beings is possible. Not at this time, I told them. Since sexual reproduction induces variety into species, it may not be a good idea in the long run.

&‑∾

The third example is the recent work suggesting that sex chromosomes per se may alter neural cells, before the intervention of the sex hormones. Arthur Arnold has suggested that some XX cells and XY cells in the brain, and elsewhere, differentiate even before the onset of gonadal hormone secretion.

In the marsupial wallaby, differentiation of the scrotum and the mammary glands seems to be under the regulation of whether the cells contain one X (as in the male) or two X's, as in the female.

In the rat, cultures of brain cells harvested from the brain before sexually dimorphic blood levels of testosterone occur show differences between cells of XX or XY composition. Since it remains controversial whether or not some homosexuals have altered XX and XY sex chromosomes, this aspect of genetic composition may be irrelevant, but it may not be.

&‑∾

The *fourth* complexity of a different, but quite pragmatic, character is the issue of whether androgens should be administered to women who complain of diminished sexual libido. Many women obtain androgen either from prescriptions or via substances sold by compounding pharmacies in the belief that the androgens will improve libido after menopause, when production of the steroid from the ovaries and adrenals diminishes.

But the Endocrine Society has recently issued guidelines on the use of androgens, pointing out that androgen deficiency in women has not been documented, that the role of a possible androgen deficiency in sexual dysfunction has not been established, and that no safety data on long-term androgen use are available. This example points up the interaction of the marketplace, gonadal hormones, and sexuality, which leads human beings to reach out for hormones to solve any problem, or in some cases to reject hormones when their efficacy and safety are known, as in the case of the oral contraceptives.

&‑∾

The social paradox in homosexuality is this: if homosexuality is "chosen" (voluntary), then it can be considered an illegal activity or even a crime. If true, then it could, therefore, be "unchosen."

If homosexuality is biological, then it can't be helped, like cystic fibrosis. But scientists can abort the fetus or fix the gene.

The same issues have been raised over studies of violence: is it due to aberrant concentrations of brain neurotransmitters, to the wrong diet, to the neighborhood in which a child is raised, to bad parenting, to a permissive society? Can we cure it with a drug? Or is it a "social disease"?

Anne Fausto-Sterling has urged in her books that we stop viewing sex as a given from birth but look instead at how biology and nurture can interact in sexual development. She talks about describing sexual orientation as a continuum rather than a bifurcated path. This is a much more rational view of sex, in my opinion. Milton Diamond has urged this also, particularly with reference to intersexuality cases he has seen, where individuals wish to make choices for themselves.

❧❧

It is instructive to contrast the stance of feminists and gays with respect to theories of biological etiology. For members of both groups, the overt biological phenotypes are "normal," and both groups have supported changes in the laws, urging equal treatment.

Feminists have argued that women's biology, acknowledged to be *genetically* different at least with respect to sexual phenotype, is *not* definitive and that the differences do not impact on ability to do chosen work, run for political office, or do anything men can do.

In contrast, many gays have argued that our biology *is* different and determinative, that gayness is no more a "choice" than hair or skin color is. Clearly, this might make a difference in the view of some non-homosexuals. As Deborah Blum says in her book *Sex on the Brain*, "the same people who readily accept biology of homosexuality argue against biological theories of race and sex difference."

Natalie Angier has also said it well in *Woman: An Intimate Geography*:

Among the cardinal principles of the evo-psycho set is that men are innately more promiscuous than women are . . ., the hardcores love to raise the example of the differences between gay men and lesbians . . . just look at how gay men carry on...in the hard core rendering of inherent male-female discrepancies gay men are offered up as true men. . . . In other theoretical instances, gay men and lesbians are not considered real men or women, but the opposite: gay men are feminine men. . . . In brain studies that purport to find the origins of sexual orientation, gay men are said to have hypothalamic nuclei that are smaller than a straight man's and closer in size to a woman's . . . . And so gay men are sissy boys in some contexts and Stone Age men in others, while lesbians are battering rams one day and flower into the softest and most sexually divested of feminine gals the next day.

❧

As a scientist, I refused to study the issue, because whichever way the biological studies come out, the prevailing political culture will dictate the use to which the data are put. This is a hot button issue sociologically and politically. While studies can be designed to examine various aspects of homosexuality, interpretations inevitably will be constructed according to the biases of the interpreter. I feel despairing about this and only hope that having more women and gays in biology as well as more women and gays controlling the media will help lead to more rational interpretations of data.

At the time I am writing this in 2007, political and social conservatives are stepping up their campaign against gay marriage and are continuing their frenzied attacks on abortion and stem cell research, I watch with bated breath to see how they will solve the dilemma of prenatal diagnosis of homosexuality.

If homosexuality is "genetic" and can be diagnosed prenatally, will they support legalized abortion of a "homosexual" fetus? Will they then drop their opposition to legalized abortion of any fetuses? Stay tuned . . .

Study Questions

(1) In this chapter, late in the volume, Neena writes "my lesbianism, however, has always been *hidden*, even when it is acknowledged."
- Discuss what you think this apparently paradoxical statement means. Explain your reasoning.
- Can lesbianism remain hidden even when it is acknowledged?
- Can we attribute this apparent contradiction to oversight in writing or do you believe Neena was attempting to convey a deeper meaning? If the second, explain what you believe she meant.

(2) In discussing her being lesbian, Neena admits, "I have had more trouble in my personal intimate relationships than in my relationships with colleagues, students, or technicians."
- Consider to what extent you believe this fact relates to lesbianism vs. overall personality.
- Using evidence from the book, hypothesize what personality traits or personal experiences might contribute to this interpersonal trouble.
- After completing this volume, reconsider this question in light of Neena's discussion of her parents' way of relating presented in the final chapter.

Fifteen

WOULD SCIENCE BE DIFFERENT IF WOMEN PARTICIPATED EQUALLY?

The goal is not to create a feminist science, if that means (as it does for many critics) a special or separate science for women or feminists. Science is a human endeavor; it must serve us all, including women and feminists.

Londa Schiebinger
Has Feminism Changed Science?

To imagine a future with women integrated into science is to imagine a culture transformed. Such a society...would insist that science, the key to understanding the natural world in which we live, be accessible to everyone...ways of allowing the majority of citizens to set priorities and goals for research projects would have to exist.

Anne Fausto-Sterling
"Women and Science"

Without question, until the feminist movement occurred during the 1960s in the United States, few women held influential positions in the sciences; in fact, most of those working in research labs played "handmaiden" roles. But Londa Scheibinger makes the case that feminism has made a difference in science as it is now practiced, and not just because more women are practitioners.

Feminism has intersected with science in a number of ways. Female scientists, working for the most part in male-dominated fields, have struggled for opportunities, salaries, promotions, and resources just as women in non-science fields have. I described in Chapter Eight my involvement with the formation of such organizations as AWIS and WE, which were founded specifically to help level the playing field for woman scientists in academia and in professional organizations.

But many essays and books that deal specifically with the relationship between feminism and science postulate a priori that a number of aspects of science would be different if women participated equally in the endeavor, quite simply because of the social and cultural differences between the genders. I have classified these predicted differences into three categories: (1) women will do different science; (2) women will have a different "connecting" style; (3) women will use results differently.

While I share with the authors of feminism and science treatises a feeling that some of these things are (or will be) true, I am unaware of specific evidence for most of these assertions.

☙❧

Prediction: Women will do different science. What determines the questions a given science laboratory asks? First and foremost, the personal interest of the senior investigator, because the principal investigator on research grants controls the money to do the research. On the other hand, the processes involved with getting the money per se also play a role. To a great extent, investigators are forced into projects that interest a funding agency or industrial company or foundation.

But do women actually *do* different science? Well, women choose to go into biology and psychology much more frequently than into mathematics, physics, or chemistry, so in that sense they do "different" science. What causes this difference in choice of fields?

It could be due to the fields being inherently more or less attractive to women (I know of no specific evidence that this is true), women advancing less well in some fields than others (because of hiring/promotions prejudices), or the culture women find within a given field is distasteful, thus they are discouraged from entering or staying.

Men and women might be attracted to a field and enter it, that is, enter graduate programs that offer training in the field of interest. As they encounter the "culture" of the field and meet the practitioners, they might be positively influenced or negatively. The practitioners determine the culture of the field and the science involved in the field per se.

As women enter a field originally dominated by men (the situation in *all* sciences at the beginning of the twentieth century), they may encounter men who welcome them, men who show intense hostility, or some combination of the two. Fields relatively welcoming to women will draw increasing numbers, and these women presumably will start to change the culture, which probably makes the field increasingly hospitable. (A social positive feedback system!)

Let me point out an assumption I have just been making: different fields may have different cultures. Feminist thought posits that science (or anything else for that matter!) is not culture-free or value free. I fervently agree and have seen for myself how the entry of women into medicine focused attention on women's diseases.

On the other hand, in some fields, the culture may be less attractive for women, and the practitioners more resistant to permitting women access to funds, space, and colleagueship. This story is not lost on women who might have originally been attracted to the science. This could account for the slow entry of female scientists into these areas. The book on computer science and women by Jane Margolis and Allan Fisher, *Unlocking the Clubhouse*, demonstrates the cultural blocks to women in the usual computer science learning environment. But it also describes how these impediments can be overcome by trying to change the culture of the classroom and understanding that the women in computer science may have entered the field with *different computer applications* in mind than many of the male students.

But some feminist literature posits not just that women may enter different fields of science but that they will do "different" science within the same general field. For example, that female scientists will be less *reductionistic* in their research than their male counterparts.

Is this true? Certainly many women are highly successful molecular biologists, a field which is about as reductionistic as one can get in the life sciences. Their methodology is the same as that used by their male colleagues.

Do they apply their data to more holistic concerns, as a group, than their male colleagues do? I don't know.

We should recognize that reductionism is more valued by granting agencies and pharmaceutical companies than is systems research these days. With respect to granting agencies, reductionism can lead to "explanations" at a sub-cellular level for many phenomena, although frequently failing to explain how a whole body system works. As for the commercial companies, *molecules are more translatable than organ systems into patients and patents.*

It would be instructive to obtain data, within a given field, regarding whether women do different science, use different methodology, collecting different data, and so forth. To my knowledge, these kinds of studies have not been done, except possibly in primatology and anthropology.

With respect to human health research, women are now subjects in many studies, where before only men were studied, as in the early cardiovascular disease etiology projects, which led to the recommendation that older males take one baby aspirin per day to reduce heart attacks. Since women were not included in those studies until recently, they were not advised by their physicians to do the same.

Drug dosage studies are also a simple example of the sex difference inequality of studies: women generally weigh less than men, and since drug doses need to be adjusted to body mass, the "one dose fits all" (on the basis of studies only on male patients) of medicine in the past is now recognized as inadequate.

Perhaps the undisputed observation that women go into different science fields is a reflection of their fundamental desire to do research differently, since the way in which research is accomplished is different in different sciences and different sub-fields within a given science.

Other predictions about the different science women might do, if they had the opportunity, include such things as *formulate hypotheses differently, combine qualitative and quantitative methodology,* and *use more interactive methodology.* I suppose I could claim these attributes for my own work on the control of the rat estrous cycle. I have certainly been less reductionistic than *some* other endocrinologists.

We have used interactive methodology (RIA, bioassay, morphology, behavior, mRNA measurements). We collected some data other people had not bothered with, like organ weights, and, of course, chose to work on females as subjects, not just on easier-to-use males. Collecting vaginal cytology to follow the cycle is a seven-day per week job, but if the cycle is what you are interested in, that is what you need to do.

But my science itself has resembled that of other neuroendocrinologists, both male and female, I believe. It has roamed through several different fields, which perhaps is more feminine than a narrower and more focused research trajectory. My own science has tried to take a global view of the way the animal works. How does a reproductive cycle repeat itself? Why does an animal stop reproducing when it is stressed?

In general, these questions relate to the between-organ interactions within an animal and the animal's interaction with its external environment. This is why I have done modeling, worked with three species of rodents, and been interested in stress and photoperiod.

My science has not been narrow. But my close colleague, Jon Levine, has been equally diverse. His work with control male and female rats and mice, and mice lacking the intracellular progesterone receptor, has examined receptor distribution within the brain, pituitary hormone secretion, and maternal and paternal behavior toward pups.

⇛⇝

Prediction: Women will have a different connecting style. The feminist science literature predicts that women will "run their labs differently," "balance their lives better," and "collaborate more with other scientists." Certainly, having more women in professional societies, as members and as officers, has turned the societies toward such issues such as mentoring, which was never recognized in these societies previously as an obligation of senior scientists. In my university, mentoring of young faculty was not a concern until the Organization of Women Faculty was formed.

Have I run my own lab differently than many of my male colleagues? I don't think so. My departmental colleagues have pretty much the same informal, interactive style in their labs as I had. Jack Gorski's lab in Madison, where I spent my sabbatical in 1990, operated in the same way my lab ran, with weekly lab meetings and lots of discussions and interactions.

Do female scientists "balance their lives better"? In families with children where the wife is responsible for everything then, of course, somebody has to do childcare. Many of my female colleagues in the sciences are not married, or, if married, have no children.

What is a balanced life? I live with someone and do most of the cooking; she waters the plants and does the gardening except when I do. I attend twenty Chicago Symphony Orchestra concerts per year, eight Lyric operas, and as many musicals as I can find in the Chicago area. I see many plays with friends, play the alto recorder in a group (Evanston Sunday Players), and get to my house in Door County when I can. My colleagues do a lot of the same things. In fact, I see more scientist colleagues at the opera than colleagues in the humanities.

In September 2002, Kate Horwitz, professor at the University of Colorado Health Sciences Center and a former president of the Endocrine Society, presented a seminar on our campus titled "Two Progesterone Receptors for One Hormone: Implications in Breast Cancers." Her lab has done very important research at the molecular level on the possible role(s) of progesterone in breast cancer in women and has probed the relevance of these very basic observations on etiology and treatment of breast cancer. (Her research is very molecular in its methodology, but broad in its health implications.)

At the end of her seminar, Kate showed a picture of the personnel in her lab, pointing out each of the people she had cited in the course of the seminar; this is a frequent way of thanking lab personnel used by male and female scientists alike. However, she then went on to show a picture of a baby, her new grandchild. I have seen female scientists show pictures of this kind before, but I have never seen a male scientist use a slide like this.

I certainly connected with her on this event, which I assume was her intention. (Oops—a male speaker, Mark Roberson from Cornell, just last week as I write this paragraph, ended his highly molecular talk on the pathways by which GnRH influences gonadotropes in the pituitary with a photo of the people in his lab and another of his young son with a fishing rod on a pier.)

ॐॐ

Prediction: Women will use research results differently. Another set of predictions from the science feminist literature posits that women will "critique studies differently," "interpret data differently," and "apply scientific information differently." The Endocrine Society, in 2000, devoted the June issue of their four journals specifically to "women's health."

The Women in Endocrinology group has become a major force in the Endocrine Society, successfully nominating women for awards and offices. Even the American Physiological Society, which has still managed to have only three female presidents in over 100 years, has a committee on women, which does its best to mentor young women in the society. But we must recognize that much of the current attention paid to women in science among professional societies and universities is not just due to the women who have entered science per se, but to the attempts to increase all kinds of diversity and to the laws which govern federal funds going to universities.

The rhetoric and metaphors of reproductive and developmental biology have noticeably changed with increasing number of women in biology, as has self-consciousness about sexist language, so that investigators of the relationship between the egg and sperm can no longer with impunity talk about "passive" eggs and "active" sperm. Female scientists such as Ruth Hubbard, Sue Rosser, Anne Fausto-Sterling, and the late Ruth Bleier have written eloquently about the misanthropic interpretations of some male scientists. In addition, books written by journalists, such as Natalie Angier's *Woman* and Deborah Blum's *Sex on the Brain*, do a splendid job of reinterpreting some of the "science" previously misinterpreted. So taking charge of interpretations has made a real difference to biology.

The whole story of sexual morphology being simply "default" in the female mammalian embryo, with the *sry* gene on the Y chromosome exerting all of the control, is no longer accepted by developmental biologists, regardless what the media continue to state. The development of the testes is initiated by expression of the *sry* gene; the testes in the fetus begin to develop earlier in mammals than the ovary, which is clearly of adaptive significance, since the male embryo is developing in a potentially "hostile" maternal hormonal environment. But the normal development of the female genital tract requires the presence of *both* X-chromosomes, and other genetic factors must be present on other chromosomes for an ovary to develop. An individual missing one of the X chromosomes can survive; this "Turner's syndrome" baby has female external genitalia, since testosterone is not produced (this hormone masculinizes external genitalia in XY individuals), but no ovaries.

Sexist language and anthropomorphism in biology is self-perpetuating. When someone talks about a female bird during courtship as appearing to be "coy looking" I roll my eyes not just as a feminist, but also as a scientist.

An outrageous article in the *NY Times Magazine* (2 April 2000), written by a man taking testosterone injections, about the "power" of "testosterone biology," based on his subjective experiences from injections reminded me, as an endocrinologist, of the implants of "monkey glands" (testes) by Brown-Sequard during the nineteenth century. Anecdotal evidence from one user is not the stuff of which new discoveries are made. I think that it is the ability to *interpret data in science* that makes having women in the field so important.

Does interpretation make a difference? Isn't science about hard facts, with data being immutable? In a speech I gave as president of the Endocrine Society I focused on the responsibility we have as scientists to interpret our data fairly and carefully. I quoted from an article entitled "Female Moorhens Compete for Small, Fat Males":"Females initiated courtship more frequently than males. . . . In both years, unpaired males were in significantly poorer condition than paired males. . . . A female moorhen paired to a fat male might produce more offspring in a season." I ended the series of quotes suggesting what a sociobiology one could construct based on the moorhen!

My last graduate student, Susan Hood, demonstrated in her dissertation the probable mechanisms biologically responsible for the observation that, in the rat, blood LH rises more rapidly in the male following removal of the testes than it does in the female after removal of the ovaries. Susan proposed an adaptive significance for this sex difference that takes into account the cyclic nature of reproduction in the female in contrast to the male.

Please understand that there is no *better* or *worse* in this difference. But imagine how this sex difference might have been displayed in the news media: "Northwestern researchers show that reproduction in females is more dependent on hormones than in males," or "Estrogen not as effective as testosterone in regulating pituitary gland," or "Female cycles increase dependence on brain hormone."

Evelyn Keller has raised a troubling issue: "Is there a conflict between our commitment to feminism and our commitment to science?" I do not think this is true for me. But I work in a field with very strong implications for women's (and men's) health, where the personal is inevitably political. Personally, as a sometime insider in science, I do not doubt that science *can* be objective and rational, but there is no question in my mind that the way science is used frequently seems irrational and non-objective.

Is there a "feminist science"? I do not know of anything that can be so-labeled, agreeing with Helen Longino and Evelyn Keller. However, attracting more women into endocrinology has made a significant difference in legitimizing some kinds of studies on breast cancer, premenstrual syndrome, and osteoporosis, for example. If diversity is ever an argument for inclusiveness, and I think it is, then science must become more diverse in its practitioners.

Endocrinology now has many more women in the field since the formation of Women in Endocrinology in the early 1970s. Unfortunately, far too few African-American endocrinologists work in the field than there should be, especially in view of endocrinopathies that appear to be especially prevalent in this population, such as diabetes mellitus, elevated blood pressure, and preterm deliveries.

The Endocrine Society has a committee on minority affairs, which brings minority students to the annual meeting and also sends endocrinologists to traditionally black colleges to spend time talking with biology majors and giving some lectures.

I was pleased to go to Cheney College in Pennsylvania several years ago for conversation and lectures. The faculty wanted to hear .about environmental endocrine disruptors, and I learned a lot while preparing for it. More recently, I went to the University of Hawaii to talk with their group of native Hawaiian students about research opportunities in endocrinology. Hawaiian natives have a higher incidence of diabetes than people of Caucasian descent living on the islands, probably because of changing diets with the changing availability of fast foods and sugar.

To paraphrase Scheibinger, "Have women changed science?" Do women do different biology or endocrinology than men do? Marcia Linn, a psychologist at Berkeley specializing in educational psychology, told me that she believes that men and women are so culturally influenced differently that difference in their points of view in their science must exist.

Some things have changed—more studies are being done on diseases of women, more women are in science, and many interpretations have changed. I am not convinced, however, that the underlying *nature* of the scientific enterprise has been altered, for better or for worse.

Turning the science/feminism issue around, one might ask, are scientists ever feminists? Are the members of AWIS or WE feminists? I believe so, since they are concerned with conditions in the workplace, mentoring young women, and ensuring that women receive excellent health care. They not only wince but speak out loudly when they hear a sexist interpretation of data.

Do these women do "feminist science" or utilize "feminist theory"? I don't think so. Do women not go into physics because they can't do math, because they want to deal with soft, fuzzy living objects instead of hard, dead ones, because they don't want to help the defense establishment, or just because they don't feel welcome? I have a feeling the last reason is still important.

The Fausto-Sterling quote at the beginning of the chapter suggests that science should be more accessible to all citizens, not just women, than it presently is. With her, I believe that the problems scientists study should be more focused on the real needs of the people, not just on the priorities of commerce.

However, research is expensive, and the marketplace and the politicians drive the funding. Part of the solution to this is to provide a better education in science in our schools so that people are more aware of what science can and cannot do.

Unfortunately, as I write this, uninformed politicians are legislating against stem cell research in Congress, President Bush is protecting frozen eight-cell embryos doomed to be discarded eventually, and creationism is being favored over evolution in many school systems. Surely, admitting more women to the science laboratories and classrooms couldn't hurt!

But aside from the issue of whether women would change science, does a gender gap in women's participation still exist, or has this now been remedied? In an earlier chapter, I talked about the gap in the representation of women in the influential National Academies of Science, Medicine, and Engineering. Our government frequently calls upon these bodies for advice about medical, ethical, and other issues of importance to our citizens. The small number of women in the Academies means that women's voices are not heard in establishing policy. The situation is so one-sided that the academies themselves are now seeking to rectify the situation.

An interesting study appeared recently in the *New England Journal of Medicine* examining sex differences in authorship by academic research physicians of articles in six preeminent medical journals. The analysis revealed that while the overall percentage of senior authorship by women had increased from 1970 to 2004, the number of women authors of these important medical contributions still lags considerably behind that of male authors.

These data suggest that while the number of female medical students continues to increase, the percentage of female authors is leveling off. Understand that I am talking here about the *most* important journals of internal medicine, pediatrics, obstetrics and gynecology, and surgery.

When we consider that these articles represent the frontiers of medical knowledge, and are extremely influential in guiding medical practice, the new data on lagging authorship by women are discouraging at best and dangerous at worst.

Study Questions

(1) Critique the views Neena gives about women in science from your point of view.

- First frame your reply by stating within what context your view emanates; for example, are you a straight male banking executive with three kids and a wife considering the question

Undergraduate students do lunch during summer research, 1995. At left, Mr. Rafiqi, Neena's secretary for many years.

Eve Hiatt with Neena, 1985.

Neena showing technician how to program Acusyst, 1982.

North American Inhibin and Activin Congress; Evanstan, Ill., 1999. L-R: Terry Horton, Janice Urban, Neena, Kathy Ryan, Brenda Bohnsack, Lynn Nequin.

Sixteen

MENTORING: THE GIFT THAT GIVES

Who is a mentor? A person who coaches, advises, supports, and initiates a protégé into the adult professional world by teaching her the tricks of the trade.

Association for Women in Science
Mentoring Tips

The rewards of mentoring are so great that it is surprising that more people are not involved with it. For the mentor, the achievements of the person encouraged are akin to the victories of one's own child. Mentoring is a gift that gives.

Elizabeth (Betty) Vetter
Contribution in *A Hand Up*

Autumn is the most brilliant season in the Midwest. Too cold for swimming in the lake, but it does not have the chilling austerity that winter will bring. The foliage colors are brilliant, if only for two or three weeks, before the bright reds, warm oranges, and tart yellows fade.

Being alone in Evanston on the second of November in 2002, except for the cat who left the house to sit in the sun on the back porch, I walked across the golf course to the canal, to enjoy the cold air, sunshine, and the leaves floating on the water. The herons that fished along the shores were gone and so were the golfers; I stood on the bridge watching my shadow below on the floating island of yellow leaves.

That week I learned that I have won another mentor award—this time the Lifetime Mentor Award of the AAAS. But I am SAD—yes, Seasonal Affective Disorder again, which rolls around as the days shorten. I was not just downcast because of endogenous neurotransmitter inadequacy.

The previous night, I had spoken by phone with my brother Leon, who was terminally ill with prostate cancer. I saw him the previous month in California and brought him a very rough copy of what I had written so far of this memoir. He read it all while I was there and told me that he had learned so much about me that he had not known before, especially how insecure I was!

Before I left to return to Evanston, he said, "You have really made a contribution. I think you have captured what your science is about." I was unable to tell him about the award at that moment.

෴

During a coffee break at a recent Center for Reproductive Science annual minisymposium, Martha McClintock and I were talking about my attempts at writing these memoirs. She asked what I was going to say about mentoring. (Martha is a biopsychologist at the University of Chicago, who has made major contributions to the field of olfactory signals and their regulatory role in the reproductive cycle in rats and humans. She was in Evanston with two of her students who were presenting papers.)

"Can you say something in the book about why we mentor? What's in it for someone?" she asked.

She reminded me of what I had said when, many years before, she had asked if my lab could run hormone assays from blood collected from her experimental rats. I remembered that she had been reimbursing us for these measurements for many years, but I had forgotten the start of it. She said that she had asked me then if we could collaborate on her olfaction/pheromone/estrous cycle studies, with her lab doing the behavioral observations and my lab running hormone assays.

I had told her at that time that it would be a mistake for her to do that, since I was more advanced in my career and people might credit me for the work. So, we arranged for her to pay my lab per sample. This arrangement was advantageous to her since it permitted her not to have to set up the assays, and it made it cheaper for us, since the price per sample for both labs would drop. Of course it also permitted her to get the credit for her work.

Why did I do it? Well, why not?

The scientific questions Martha asked about pheromones were so clearly delineated by her previous work, not mine, that they represented no real contribution from me other than sheer methodology. I knew I was already spread fairly thin, and I didn't want to dilute our own work even more. Sure, I could have gotten my name on lots more research papers, but how many did I need?

෴

Most of the awards I have received have recognized teaching or mentoring skills involving undergraduate students, medical students, graduate students, or colleagues.

During 2002, I was on a panel on mentoring sponsored by the American Physiological Society at the Federation meetings in New Orleans. At a recent SSR meeting in Baltimore, I spoke on mentoring at a session sponsored by trainees. In 2007, I participated in a discussion locally with another emerita professor at Northwestern, Julia Weertman, for trainees in the life and engineering sciences about the satisfactions of a lifelong career, and mentoring is certainly part of that.

But I have had a hard time grasping that I am being *praised and re-warded* for mentoring, which seems to me to be a critical element of what being a researcher and teacher is about.

෪෪

While I have been able in general to be patient, nurturing, kind, and caring with my students and other trainees, I have not been nearly as successful with my intimate partners. Maybe this is why it has been difficult for me to address the issue of mentoring head on.

Of course, mentoring is the way to help students become self-reliant, careful, creative, ethical scientists! But why have I not brought to bear the same attributes in my other more intimate relationships?

My failure in this regard is embarrassing. Perhaps I feel responsible for trainees and less experienced colleagues, and usually I know more about the system than they do, so I feel good about helping them. But with a partner, I am on equal footing; I feel uncomfortable and certainly not "in charge."

෪෪

How much does my not having children of my own influence my need to mentor others? Is this substitute parenting?

I have certainly felt close to my nieces and nephews and now their kids. I am an oldest child, and I know I always felt somehow "responsible" for my younger brother and sister. When my sister was six, she came home and told me that she did not understand how to add. This surprised me, since she knew how to count. So we got down on the floor and took some blocks and put three in one place and three in another place.

She said, "There are three here, and three over there." I moved the blocks together and asked her how many there were. Her face brightened and she smiled.

"Oh," she said.

End of problem.

෪෪

Why didn't the issue of mentoring young colleagues come up in a formal way in professional associations before women began gaining entry? Apparently, the insiders did not feel they needed specifically to pay attention to mentoring. But as the feminist and legal pressures were brought to bear, it was apparent that "outsiders," now entering graduate school, needed help.

It is no accident that AWIS, WE, and other women's professional groups have focused on career mentoring from the very beginning of their

organizing. We were worried that the old boys might not provide these ups-
tart women the tools they needed to become successful.

෨෴

Mentoring is the process of helping others grow and become more competent
scientifically and politically in their chosen field. It is definitely a two-way
street. If communication lines are open, everybody benefits.

As I look back on my mentors, I can see how lucky I was. Harry Patton
guided me to sources of information I needed to read when I was an undergraduate working in Curt Richter's lab at Johns Hopkins.

Meredith Runner was my advisor for two summers at the Jackson Lab.
He briefly outlined what he wanted studied in the mice, gave me a reference
or two, and then had me work up protocols, which he reviewed and offered
comments. He was always willing to answer my questions about what we
were doing. He included me with some of his family outings, and I baby-sat
for them.

My advisor in graduate school, Allen Lein, encouraged me to work out
my own experiments. We argued endlessly about protocols and interpretations, always on an equal basis, or so it seemed to me.

Both at Bar Harbor and in Northwestern's physiology department all of
the faculty members were accessible, eager to provide advice or critiques. My
fellow students in graduate school were also encouraging and open about
their research.

Importantly, I never sensed any discrimination because I was a woman,
in either place, from faculty or from peers. (That only came later, when I was
a faculty member!)

෨෴

But I've heard lots of horror stories. Frequently, my students have told
me about how other advisors are treating their students. Graduate students
have complained to me that their advisors prevent communication within the
lab, do not introduce lab personnel to visiting scientists, do not write adequate
letters of recommendation, make trainees keep working on an unsuccessful
projects, or are more interested in their career than the student's.

The list is endless. The relationship between graduate students and their
preceptors is very different in the lab and field sciences than in the humanities. We live together in the workplace; and it requires continuous cooperation and give and take to make it work for everyone.

Mentoring trainees in the lab is a crucial step in producing good scientists. I would guess it really is the same for mentoring trainees in the social
sciences and humanities as well. But the physical closeness in a lab, or a field
project, enhances the opportunities for informal training. Of course, in the

sciences, senior lab members gets their names on research papers, even if they have not done a single measurement at the bench. Good mentoring, if nothing else, is a payback.

☙❧

The rules for mentoring trainees are straight-forward and quite simple. Help the mentee define research and career goals. Start small and don't assume an undergraduate or even a graduate student wants to have *your* career. What does a postdoc want to learn from you? Why does the undergraduate want research experience?

Nurture trainees and help them grow by guiding, but don't stifle independent thought. I always started new trainees by presenting them with several possible projects; this obviously captures interest. Then listen to them tell about a proposal once you have given them that start. Don't create trainees in your own image. Don't assume each trainee needs to choose your career; be open and supporting. If asked for advice about personal life decisions perform as a friend/parent/advisor. Be a good listener; that is usually all that is wanted.

Demand the best, but permit mistakes. Everyone can make mistakes, even you. If you yell and scream about a mistake, you may not be told about it the next time, which can be a disaster. Set a very high standard for yourself and others. You may want to come down from the heights later, but if you don't start high, you are bound to get low level performances. Teach trainees to cooperate with others. A cooperative lab is a joy; a toxic lab is not. You call the shots.

Make trainees design their own experimental protocols. This is tough at the beginning, but this is what they need to learn to do, and there is no point to training researchers who can't do this. Examine failed experiments carefully and be on the alert for serendipitous opportunities. You should do this anyway, because a well-designed, well-executed experiment should always teach you something. But it is also important for trainees not to feel they have failed simply because an experiment has failed.

Help dissect ideas in a public setting but in a non-threatening way. It is important for trainees to learn to defend their ideas. In a large lab it conserves time to talk about ideas with everyone present; and it is also good for each individual to be able to critique the work of others. This works as long as it stays friendly and fair. Train students to present their research in a public setting; always have a one sentence and a two minute and five minute description of their results ready.

It is important for trainees to learn to speak forcefully and with confidence. I had my students prepare three different length presentations, matching each to a situation they might encounter. Don't tell people more than they want to know. Of course, whether students will be presenting a poster or a ten-minute talk at a meeting, or a fifty-minute seminar on a job interview, practice with them enough times to make sure it goes smoothly. Everyone in the lab should try to anticipate the questions the audience might ask, and have everyone discuss good answers.

Introduce trainees to scientists in their field. A problem in my own graduate training was the attitude of the Physiology department that they were the best, so we did not have much contact with other physiologists outside the university. Maybe it was true, but trainees still need to meet people who visit the lab or who are encountered at a professional meeting.

Show them—don't just tell them—about scientific ethics. The Institute of Medicine and the National Research Council have made suggestions about how to maintain integrity in scientific research and one suggestion is a *course* in ethics. We have run a course on ethics at Northwestern, and I have supported and taught in it. But all the courses in the world will not elevate a students' ethical stance if they see advisors cheating on data, undercutting a colleague, or stealing an idea for an experiment from an article the advisor is reviewing for a journal.

If you succeed in accomplishing the above in your mentoring, postdocs will have learned to mentor graduate students and undergraduates, and graduate students and undergraduates will be mentoring each other. Never forget: this is a two way street—just think what you can learn from your trainees!

෨෴ඟ

Mentoring colleagues requires another, somewhat different set of rules.

Make sure your colleagues are recommended for talks, committees, and positions, and that women are recommended on merit equally with men. Making speeches at symposia and during professional meetings is crucial for professional advancement and promotion of research. Having women on program committees helps ensure that women are not overlooked.

Critique CV's for junior people to make sure they are appropriate and clear. Department chairs don't always advise junior faculty accurately on what a good CV should include. Offer to look at CV's for young men and women in your department.

Open for others the doors you have gone through. Do you want to be a queen bee? Surely you are good enough to handle competition from other women (and men)! The company with whom you mingle at meetings and so forth is better when you are surrounded by people you like, so include them!

Listen constructively when people need to ventilate. Everybody needs a hug sometime. Sometimes people just need to gripe. But if that is all someone does repeatedly, see if you can figure out whether the complainer is doing some things wrong. On the other hand, don't blame the victim.

Make sure junior people understand the rules of the game whether in academe, industry, or government. Sometimes these rules are not explicit. Help your mentee find out about explicit rules and to discover implicit rules as well. In research universities, regardless of how many people tell you that teaching is important, make sure that when tenure decision time comes, your mentee has written the expected number of articles and grants. Be willing to read their manuscripts and grant proposals for clarity and completeness. Remember how tough that first grant was for you to get or how devastating it was to have an article turned down. Even if you are not an expert in your mentee's subfield, an experienced researcher learns clues about how to say things and format presentations.

෴

Women in Endocrinology has recently gone on line with an "open mentoring" program, where potential mentors and mentees can describe themselves, their talents, and needs. The program arranges contacts via Email between appropriately matched individuals; these pairs can take it from there.

The Endocrine Society has undertaken the mentoring of another group of potential students—minority students. I have already mentioned sending endocrinologists to schools, like the University of Hawaii with its large native population and to the traditionally black colleges, to recruit potential graduate and medical students as well as to alert the students to endocrine diseases prevalent in such populations. Here the mentoring goes beyond the students to include the science faculty also.

The society also supports minority students to come to the annual meeting and provides mentors for them while they are there. They hold an evening dinner meeting where students and volunteer faculty can discuss endocrinology. The American Physiological Society also has a number of mentoring programs available, many of which are available on their web site.

෴

What about the unspoken traditions in one's field, the "acceptable" and the "non-acceptable" behaviors? I told above how I did not contact an editor when a reviewer took overly long to review a manuscript. I assumed that it was not correct to complain until Joe Meites suggested to me that I do it. He was right.

By contrast, Candace Pert has described how she contacted Mrs. Lasker of the Lasker Foundation when her postdoc advisor, Sol Snyder, received the Lasker Award for the demonstration of opiate receptors in the brain, the project she had accomplished in his lab. She pointed out to Mrs. Lasker that she had done the work. For major prizes such as this one, an award is frequently given for a *body* of work and goes to the lab director. Was this the case in this situation? It is difficult to say. Candace's "behavior" on this occasion was costly for her in terms of her career.

Is the practice of giving awards to the lab director fair? The issue of fairness is thorny, because usually a single important finding comes about because of a whole series of observations, which lead to a seminal observation. Sometimes, of course, the findings are serendipitous and need to have a prepared mind to recognize their importance and implications.

☙◦❧

Many sticky issues in academia are not clear-cut, where women and junior faculty are held hostage to senior tenured faculty members. For instance, senior faculty votes on tenure at departmental and school levels.

Recently, Nobel Laureate Susumu Tonegawa, a professor at MIT, was accused of sending an Email to a potential (woman) recruit for his department, discouraging her from coming to the department because he was uncomfortable with the competition her lab would provide to his research. As of this writing, the issue has not been resolved. If it is true that he did, in fact, discourage her, was this a case of *good* mentoring (keeping her from making the mistake of being in a position where a comparison with him could be harmful to her) or *bad* mentoring (keeping himself safe from comparison to a young, up and coming energetic junior faculty member?)

☙◦❧

My mentoring days are not over, and I find I keep asking myself why I get so much pleasure from doing it. Why does it feel so good?

At a dinner recently with Claire and another art therapist, I posed this question, being reminded of it because her colleague was thanking Claire for being her mentor. They both agreed that mentoring is an investment in the future, a way of broadening your impact and extending that impact into the future.

☙◦❧

After my brother's death, the University of California Irvine held a memorial service for him. I discovered that he had been regarded as an incredible mentor. Four of the current vice chancellors for business and administrative services in the University of California system had served under him, and all of them praised him for his careful nurturing of them. I wish I could still ask him why he did it.

Study Question

(1) Describe a positive mentoring relationship that you have experienced.
  - How has this shaped or reshaped your values and worth ethic?

Seventeen

THE NORTH WOODS: A SAFE HAVEN

I will arise and go now, for always night and day
I hear lake water lapping with low sounds by the shore;
While I stand on the roadway, or on the pavements gray,
I hear it in the deep heart's core.

William Butler Yeats
"The Lake Isle of Innisfree"

At Beigh, the house, dock, and woods in Door County, Wisconsin—have been a central part of my life ever since Rue and I acquired it in 1966. The far-off dream I had as a kid of being in a cabin in the woods came true on Ellison Bay, Door County. Surrounded by the north woods, with a view of the bay, this house became a shelter and retreat for both of us.

The rear 200 feet of the land near the county road is a swale, which is a swamp in which trees and other vegetation are permitted to fall. In the late 1990s, the Department of Natural Resources declared this part of the property "permanent wetlands," which pleases me. In the spring, as the snow cover melts, the swale is filled with peepers calling to each other in the dark. Muskrats, frogs, grouse, and unfortunately, mosquitoes have always inhabited the swale. Sometimes a woodcock or two shows up, and frequently we can hear the drumming of ruffed grouse during the mating season. Pileated woodpeckers and screech owls have occasionally wandered by, and a red fox and deer have been known to use our road to get down to the bay for water.

❧

My first real experience of being in the woods came in 1947, in Maine. When I received my notice of acceptance at Bar Harbor that first year, I had only a couple of days to pack. I took the train to New York, changed for a train to Bangor, and caught a bus to Bar Harbor. I had a trunk full of clothes and books, and a bicycle with me. My clothes were shorts, sweaters, dresses, bathing suit, and slacks.

I loved Bar Harbor and the Jackson Lab. I rode my bike all around Mt. Desert Island and hiked the mountains with the other summer students. We also swam in the ocean and the lakes. Years later, I went camping with Jan all through the Midwest and in the East too. Camping in the national park on Mt. Desert brought back my ecstatic student days: learning to do science, learning to hike a mountain, learning to live with my fellow students.

I also became a birder, which is a passion that remains with me. It's a great hobby since it satisfies my need to discover, to see beauty around me, and to walk in the woods lazily while keeping an organized list of what I saw and where I saw it. This became a great way to travel too; I have carried binoculars to all the meetings and seminars I've attended. I remember when I went to Connecticut to interview for the position of Chair of the Biology Division, I took a bird walk with some of the ecologists in the department. For at least twenty-five years, I shared my love of birding with my brother, who lived first in Washington D.C. and then in California.

In the more than forty years since the house on Ellison Bay was built, many things have happened there, but it is a life outside of time that seems separated from life in Evanston, from crazy chairmen, from compulsive deans, from granting agencies. Yet it is a place for genuine thinking and writing. My graduate students always said that when I returned after spending time there, they knew I would have new ideas for new experiments and new interpretations for old experiments. This was particularly true when Rue and I were becalmed for hours at the mouth of Ellison Bay, before we put a motor on Ariel II, and had to wait for the late afternoon breeze to take over or paddle back to the dock.

෨෧

The house in Door County is a great place for having visitors. When my nephew Howard was about fourteen, he contemplated becoming a biologist. He came to Chicago from Washington, where he then lived. He worked in the lab for a few days with a visiting graduate student who was studying voles in Wyoming and who wanted to learn the bioassays for LH and FSH in my lab. Howard worked with him as a technician; in turn, the guy showed him how to build a vole trap using a stick and a coffee can.

Then Howie, Rue, and I went up to Wisconsin, where Howie spent a week trying to trap a vole in between swimming and walking in the woods. He made a property map for us, which is still on the refrigerator, of some of the local footpaths, but he never saw a vole. However, Snooky, our first Siamese cat, killed several during that time, depositing them on the steps to the front of the house. Can this be why Howard wound up becoming a rabbi, then a Hebrew studies scholar, and lastly an executive in a software firm?

When my niece Susan was about the same age, she spent a week in Door County with Rue and me when she learned to sail. She also met several female friends of ours who were staying for a time, who all were lesbian. She told her mother when she returned home, "Aunt Neena has a lot of neat friends."

෬ංඥ

Ellison Bay has always been a place for closeness with our animals. All of our dogs have had their share of adventures up there. Our dachshund Sam fell into the freezing water when the dock was being built.

The dock was built by waiting until winter and driving a bulldozer across the frozen bay and digging out the bedrock and sand. These were then temporarily tossed onto the ice. Then a cedar L-shaped "bed" was pushed across the ice from the town dock and slid into the opening. The rocks and sand were then dumped back into the cedar crib. Then, when the weather warmed up, a wooden top was laid on as a deck.

We drove up to see the work in progress, walking down our snowy hill to the shore. Sam followed but did not notice that the ice on the shore abruptly vanished where it had been cut. He fell in and began paddling desperately. I jumped in after him without thinking. Fortunately, I felt the sand beneath me, scooped him up, and threw him onto the icy shore. Then I scrambled up with help from Rue and ran up the hill, throwing off my freezing clothes as I made my way to a warm bathtub.

෬ංඥ

Early on, we would fish from the dock, or take the rowboat out near the bluff to catch the brown trout, coho, or perch that occasionally came into Ellison Bay. One day, I was practicing casting with a rod and reel, using a worm as bait. The reel jammed, and the line, hook, and worm flew behind me and sunk through my jeans into my right calf muscle.

I was on the dock with just our black and tan dachshund Joey, who kept jumping up on me to try to get the worm, which was sticking out of my jeans. I shooed him away, cut the line, and climbed the hill, where Rue was typing an article. We got in the car and drove to the small hospital in Sturgeon Bay, thirty-five miles south. A nurse cleaned the surface of my leg and then put me in a room to wait for the resident on duty.

The resident walked into room, smiled, and said "Well, Professor Schwartz, did you catch anything else?" As it turned out, I had taught him physiology at the U of I some years before when he was a freshman. He took out the hook, cleaned the wound, and gave me a tetanus shot. I have frequently encountered other past students, but none so dramatically.

෬ංඥ

The books I typically read up at *At Beigh* are different from what I read in Evanston. This is particularly true of the John Buchan adventure stories and the Dorothy Sayers mysteries. I have reread many times a yellowed crumbling Penguin paperback copy of Buchan's *John McNab*. I also knew his *The*

Thirty-Nine Steps and remember talking about it with Terry Baker, of the Royal Infirmary Hospital in Edinburgh, when we met at an international endocrinology meeting sometime during the 1970s. He told me there was a sequel to *The Thirty-Nine Steps*, which he thought I ought to read, called *The Three Hostages*.

"I'll find a copy for you," he said. He sent me a copy he found at a bookstore in Edinburgh with a note. "Sorry this is rather a soiled copy, but it is in old stock. All the 'better' bookshops have sold out, and the book is no longer in print. Hope you enjoy it! Regards, Terry."

I cherish the copy and reread it about every three years or so.

Having a second house cuts down on going to other places for vacations but has the marvelous upside of familiarity and nostalgia. It's so nice to be able to accumulate books and have them waiting there. I have a paperback copy of each of Dorothy Sayers' books, lots of ghost stories, a shelf of nature books, and a shelf of poetry. Fortunately, we can listen to NPR from Madison for classical music, and a large tape collection and CD collection is growing at *At Beigh*.

⤔⤙

In September 1967, Rue and I established a nature journal that stayed up in Door County, which consists of spiral bound notebooks. I started the third volume in March 2003. The journal proved to be a record of animals and plants we saw or heard, people who visited, dogs and cats that came for the first time (and the last time), boats we bought and sailed, and the story of our dock building.

An overview of the journal in 2003, though, makes one thing very clear: the animal life has become less and less abundant. At the beginning, we saw towhees, rose-breasted grosbeaks, brown thrashers, and ruffed grouse, as well as pileated woodpeckers in trees right near the house, and blue and green herons and loons down on the shore—but no more. We used to hear a barred owl and a screech owl while walking dogs (and cats!) out to the county road for a last look at the stars before bedtime. We do still have cardinals, chickadees, nuthatches, and the smaller woodpeckers around, but the more exotic species no longer hang out where we can see them from our dining room window or from the porch.

Here are some of the recorded high spots, and some downers from over the years:

4/12/68— A full moon eclipse.

6/20/69–When we came up from the city, a robin had built a nest in the eaves in the back of the house, and there were fledglings in it being fed. [This nest was reused for many years by robins. We always worried about one of the fledglings falling out and being snapped up by one of the cats, but as far as we could tell, it never happened.] Christened the new rowboat "Mal de Mer."

7/4/69—One bare-breasted, bifocaled biped in kitchen near feeders [female]—in summer plumage. [I don't remember who this was!]

12/69—We watched the ice coalesce on Ellison Bay in late December and early January. And then in March 1970, we were here for the break up.

7/71—We bought a Day Sailor "Ariel," a 15 footer—small enough to be docked at our own dock.

7/14/73—[In this entry there are *five porcupine quills* scotch-taped to the page.] Gretchen had returned to the house from a foray into the woods, where she had obviously met up with, and probably attacked, a porcupine. We removed them from her muzzle with the help of a neighbor. At other times we recorded Gretchen coming back smelling of skunk. We always kept a supply of tomato juice and/or vanilla extract in the house to take care of unfortunate encounters.

9/15/73—Sam died today in Wilmette. [He died on the operating table at our vets in Wilmette, when he was being operated on for kidney cancer which had metastasized. He had been with us since we built the house.]

Sam was a brown and tan short haired dachshund. We had taken him to the vet's the day before for surgery and had to come up to Wisconsin for a meeting. The vet called us after he opened Sam up and discovered he was riddled with cancer.

"What should we do?" I asked, horrified that we were so far away. "If he were my dog," the vet said, "I would deepen the anesthesia."

The book continues:

He belongs in this book because he was with us when we bought this place, he was named while we sat on the dock at Shirley and Kitty's looking at our future land, and because he was part of the 'nature' at Ellison Bay. He hunted a red fox, and a muskrat, he walked through forest and through snow. He always wanted to be with us. He was on the dock and on the beach. He waited for us there when we sailed, and walked into

the water to try to retrieve things. And when we built our dock,
he fell into the freezing water and I rescued him."

With Sam, we had our standard Schnauzer Gretchen. After Sam died,
we had Joey, with Gretchen. Then Fingal was my beautiful Westie. Gretchen
was the most intrepid of all the dogs, but she never learned not to confront
skunks and porcupines.

12/26/73—Joey a black and tan smooth haired dachshund came up for
the first time. [We still had Gretchen, who was slowing up but
still intrepid.[

Another observation recorded from time to time in the books was the
water level of the Bay. It is interesting to glance back over the years—the
dock was under water or almost completely out of the water at five- or six-
year intervals.

6/27/75–7/6/75—This was a very eventful week. Drove up from Evanston with the two dogs in a non-air conditioned car. When we arrived, Joey was unconscious in the back seat. [As a
physiologist, it should have occurred to me that it was heat ex-
haustion and I should have tried a cool bath or an immersion into the lake; but I panicked.] The nearest vet was about ninety
miles south. We phoned and he agreed to see us. Back into the
car. I held Joey in my lap next to the driver, with windows
open. About halfway there, Joey suddenly sat up, shook his ears
vigorously, and began looking out the window with interest.
When we arrived, Joey climbed out of the car.

The vet, hearing our car door slam, came out, pointed to Joey,
and asked, "Is this the patient?"

The cool air on the drive down had cooled the dog off, and he
recovered fully. That is the way the week began.

Two male friends (a poet and a philosopher from Evanston) had
driven up to Door County to help sail our new boat (Ariel II, a
Rhodes 19), which had to be berthed at the Ellison Bay town
dock) up to Ellison Bay, from the marina in Sister Bay, five
miles south. We drove down to Sister Bay with a bottle of wine
and a picnic basket to get the boat after two days spent recover-
ing from our dachshund drama. The four of us boarded the boat
and began sailing north to home. We ate, drank, and sailed up
Green Bay on a beautiful sunny day, the cliffs of Door County on

our right. When we entered Ellison Bay, our poet—who had had most of the wine, decided we needed a bowsprit and he climbed up in front of the mast and dropped his shorts as we sailed grandly into the bay. We tossed him off the boat at that point.

5/1 to 9/76—I came up with only Joey and a grant to write. Still, I recorded a lot of animal sightings—two green herons perched in a tree in front of the house, two wood ducks in the swamp on the part of our property near the road, trillium in the front of the house, and peepers in the swamp at night. Two nests of robins had appeared below the front upstairs deck!

7/4/77—Glorious Northern Lights!! This has been an occasional treat up here. The first time I had ever seen them was in Bar Harbor in September 1948, where I was finishing off my summer's work before going to Chicago and graduate school.

7/27/78—Snooky, our Siamese cat, was the most adventurous huntress up here. I always felt apologetic about bringing our domesticated beasts up but they loved wandering off into the woods on their own and always returned. The dogs did not hunt to any extent as far as we knew, but cats do tend to bring their kill home to display. During this week, Snooky brought home one dead chipmunk, a fledgling oven bird, three house mice, one deer mouse, and one frog, which we saw her bringing up from our swamp.

Rue and I split during the fall of 1978, and the nature entries (now separate) were fewer. We were coming up at different times with different partners:

5/28-30/83—I came up by myself with Snooky and Joey, and recorded a record 62 bird species, including 14 different warblers!

9/28/84—Gretchen, the indomitable standard schnauzer, died in Chicago.

Over the next couple of months, three page-length obituaries for her appeared in the journal, written by three different mourners (Rue, her new lover, and me):

—It was almost too much to bear, coming up here without her.

—Morning sunshine memory: Gretchen turning in circles awaiting breakfast.

—I spent two wonderful weeks in August 1984 with Gretchen up here. She had trouble getting up and walking but she was still top dog.

5/26/85 [I recorded a single sentence]—Rue died in Evanston Hospital.

By this time, Rue and I had become friends again and had spent a week-end together sailing the previous summer, and had been going to the symphony together in Chicago.

(Date not recorded, circa 1995)—So many times up here have been clouded by difficulties with work, arguments with Arnold Wolf and then with Rudolph Weingartner. As I sit at the table looking out at the woods, I feel a wholeness which I never feel any-where else. Even when I have felt at bay because a chair or a dean was hounding me, this place gives solace. A pileated woodpecker just rested on a nearby tree. Today I walked in the woods with my companion and my dog, and saw a Northern harrier overhead and butterflies among the mid-August fields. And Ellison Bay is outside my window, blue in the late after-noon sun, the bluff across the bay green and inviting.

3/27/97—Drove up yesterday with Claire and without animals because the caretaker Bruce said there was too much snow to plow the driveway. The snow is beautiful, the bay is all white, although the Mink River bay area is open water. As I look back on my previous notation, I see my note about all the problems I have come up with and how they influenced my time here. And how nice to know I am up here without worrying about my chair, my grant, my dean.

That week the Hale-Bopp comet was visible. We went out at midnight onto the second floor porch and looked at the comet. There was a full moon that night, and as we stood on the porch we glanced down to the bird feeder where a red fox was nosing around.

So the books go, recording life and death, snow and water, skunks and raccoons, foxes and porcupines, or ice and mosquitoes.

On 2 October 1999, our Westie Fingal died in Evanston and we came up on 2 April 2000 to spread her ashes *At Beigh*. A poem appears in the journal at this point. *Fingal's Cave*, written by my partner Claire. Here is part of it:

The brown water bowl on the floor
is empty.
I think to fill it.

I save steak scraps for the dog.
Her presence pulses like a phantom limb
Cut off but still connected . . .
We walk the trail
We walk our dog.
What is left of her fits into a plastic Ziploc bag.
Birds flit through the birches
And we sprinkle pieces of her
At their bases below.
White on white—
She feels like chalk
And bits of bone . . .

ॐ∽ॐ

How many times have I driven up to the house on Ellison Bay from the Chicago area, through the flat corn fields of Illinois, past the dairy farms of
southern Wisconsin, along Lake Michigan on my right, through Milwaukee
with its church spires and breweries sprinkled heavily through the city, and
then through the small coastal towns of Lake Michigan: Manitowoc, Algoma,
and Sturgeon Bay? Already, the big city starts to drop away and I become
anxious to complete the journey. As we drive north from Sister Bay, we are
five miles from home and we see mostly cherry orchards, the blossoms pink
in the spring, trees bare of leaves in the fall, but other trees have bright
orange, yellow, or red leaves. The road undulates, following the contours of
the land, which is no longer flat, making me remember the hills of Maryland.

   As we approach Ellison Bay, we don't see the water at first, but pass the
remnants of the motel-like single story buildings where the Mexican migrant
workers used to live when they came to pick cherries for the canneries or ap-
ples for the cider press. The wooden buildings have been empty for years now.
Driving past the cherry trees we see the electric towers with lights blinking.

   We are coming closer now. If we are driving up in winter, we see the
whole sky, and Orion strides the sky to the east. If we are driving up during
the day in summer, we see the whole bay suddenly stretched out before us,
with the far bluffs green atop the blue water. We have reached the last hill
before our road. We plunge down the hill and if we continue without turning,
we are in the town of Ellison Bay, with its gas station, general store, and restaurants. We turn left midway down the hill in to Hillside Drive. "Dead End"
the sign says. Hillside Drive skirts the back of the houses down the next decline, with gravel driveways to the right where all the houses are perched on
the shore.

   Once, as we were driving this last segment at night, we saw a baby owl
on the road, and waited until it moved to the side. Then, after a few hundred
feet, we come to our driveway. We turn slowly to the right, into our own drive.

"Whose woods these are/I think I know . . ." They are ours.

When Gretchen was a passenger she would be so excited now that we had to let her out of the car to run ahead and get to the house before us, where she would turn and bark at us as we drove slowly into the turnabout.

In spring and early summer, the back part of the property nearest Hillside Drive is water logged from melting snow. Under the gravel road at one point is a short culvert that permits the water to flow from east to west downward toward the bay.

By late summer, the water has usually dried up, but the woods remain muddy. The woods of cedar and aspen still surround us until we see the house at the end of the road. As we park, we see the back of the house, the bay is visible only when we enter and walk into the living room.

❧

This is what it is like to come home to *At Beigh*. When we leave, we have no anticipation, only sadness. We pack the car for the trip to Evanston, 261 miles south. After the car is packed, and all the animals rounded up and put inside, I walk back to the house "To see that all the lights are out and . . ." But what I am really doing is saying goodbye.

I think: "Will I ever come back? Will you wait?"

Study Questions

(1) Discuss the role being outdoors in nature plays in Neena's life.
 - Does it represent a cherished value per se, or does it give her a place to contemplate other values?

(2) Discuss whether, in your estimation, you think being a biologist makes a difference in one's enjoyment of nature?

(3) Discuss the competing values you see evinced in the concluding thought of this chapter, "Will I ever come back? Will you wait?"

Eighteen

OUT OF THE LAB

I wish these lines could end in an orchard where
we stopped and loved each other with generous
strength, sweating like they do at harvest,
gasping with joy at the peak, in sunlight.

They end at sunset, back in a room where I've
Talked, slept, awakened and lived with you
Where you are with me when you're elsewhere,
Lover and friend, in the ways we've chosen.

Marilyn Hacker
"For K. J. Between Anniversaries"

Writing this memoir has evoked many old, almost forgotten memories of people, places, and events. It has focused me on both the successes and the failures of my personal and professional life and reminded me of how lucky I was to grow up in my particular family.

What did I think about when I was a kid? What did I want? Did I have a vision of what I could become?

I know that I felt hemmed in when we lived in the city. We were separate from the kids in the neighborhood—whites did not play with African-Americans in those days, with schools separate. The fact that we had a store, where the neighbors shopped, also discouraged fraternizing.

But it is true that my brother Leon had boys he played with, kids he knew from school. There were girls in the neighborhood and in my class I could have played with, but somehow I did not.

I picked up from my mother a sense of dissatisfaction with living where we were. So I dreamed about the country, where there would be trees, grass, streets I could walk on.

❧

The reading I did was much more adventurous than I was and included Robin Hood, the Nesbit books, and Robert Louis Stevenson. I loved reading about children in England, and my love of British culture just grew and grew. In retrospect, I am not sure why this was so.

One might have thought that I would have become acculturated to Russian literature because of my mother's influence. But as I was introduced to English literature, it really grabbed me. In school, of course, we learned Eng-

lish history as a prelude to American history, and this also influenced me.
Maybe it was the result of my need, a reflection of my mother's, to develop
high-toned social surroundings.

ෂංෂ

When we moved to the suburbs, I had just turned eleven and was in the sixth
grade. The experience felt freeing to me. I was able to walk in the neighborhood by myself, wandering down alleys and into wooded areas. I came to
know the other children. After I learned to ride a two-wheeled bike, I roamed
all over the neighborhood and to the city parks at some distance.

My English teachers were superb in junior and senior high school, and I
began to read adult English novels, particularly of the nineteenth century. At
some point, my Dad had acquired a second-hand set of Dickens's books with
the original drawings, and I began reading them. I still read a lot of fiction. I
also began to memorize poetry beyond *A Child's Garden of Verse*.

I joined the staff of the newspaper in junior high and enjoyed the putting
together of the whole paper once a week. This newspaper obsession lasted
through college. I enjoyed interviewing people for a story or writing up an
event. I remember in college interviewing our dean, my chemistry Professor
Louise Kelley, about what she thought of the sorority system; then I wrote an
article for the paper about the divisiveness of the system. I overheard another
student saying about me, after the paper came out, "She's just jealous because
she's Jewish." A little bit of anti-Semitism in college.

ෂංෂ

If I thought about the future, it was never ever about marriage and children. It
was about traveling and writing, journalism of the highest order, of course. I
don't remember thinking about becoming "famous" or "successful."

ෂංෂ

My father was the permissive one. He had more tolerance for the way people
chose to do things than Mom did. Mother had very tight standards: how to
dress, how to look, how to behave (so as not to attract attention).

My behavior toward potential lovers mirrored my father's style; unfortunately, my behavior toward live-in partners mirrored Mother's. I wasn't
easy to live with because I had deeply ingrained ideas about how to do things,
even silly things like how to slice a tomato! I even had my own ideas about
how people should dress! Claire took care of that—she has the artist's eye for
dressing in splashy style and laughs when I comment about it.

৯৯৯

In college, my fascination with the English literature of the nineteenth century grew, particularly novels from this period. Disenchantment with literary criticism set in, however, and I recognized that I did not have any novels or poetry inside me. Seeing "Wit" recently reminded me of how I began to see the literary/scholarly life while I was in college. It seemed so narrow. (With increasing emphasis on deconstructing dead authors, this has seemed more and more pointless to me.)

If I did not want to be a critic and couldn't be an author, could I become a journalist? Did I want that? It seemed to me to be once removed from the real action ultimately, and so I let that dream die.

৯৯৯

Discovering physiology was a godsend. I did not think of it as a potential "career." I never dreamed about a Nobel Prize or membership in an honorary academy. I just wanted to do it.

It took time for me to recognize that I was being successful as a scientist. Sure, I did not always get a grant when I wanted it, or have an article published without a lot of changes being made to it, or get the results I had hoped for from a particular experiment. But the doing of science was so exciting and ultimately so rewarding.

Since I started my academic career in a non-elite school (University of Illinois College of Medicine), I became a professor fairly quickly. But I recognized that I was treated differently than some of my male colleagues when assertiveness worked for them but got me into trouble. My sense of fairness made me angry, so I became an activist for women in science. I realize in retrospect, that while I never thought I would be famous or very successful, it also never occurred to me that I would not be able to succeed as an independent investigator, a good teacher, or as an officer in a professional society. Where did that confidence come from?

In reading *The Frame of the Door* about the career of some female members of the National Academy of Science, an honor I have not achieved, I have been struck by the overall confidence in their ability these women show. The married ones talk about the difficulty of simultaneously teaching, doing research, being active in professional societies, and having children. Many of them chose a straightforward focus on a research career without teaching or much participation in administration, so that they could raise their children, and this is an understandable choice. I never had to make that choice and would have felt deprived if I had not taught. In fact, I have also enjoyed my administrative work at the university and in professional societies.

But *confidence* in myself, I believe, is the major reason I succeeded in being a successful scientist, a good university citizen, and an effective participant in professional society affairs. Confidence needs to be part of every successful woman's make-up.

Where does confidence come from? For me, it came from my family, where I was treated like an equal and was listened to, even when I was being argumentative. People in the family were a stubborn bunch. I still remember the day when Alicia was visiting my house for supper and my Dad came home from work with a box of plates, which his wholesale business was selling to stores.

He said, "These are new—they're unbreakable."

He pulled one from the box and threw it against the wall and it smashed to pieces. Mother came running out of the kitchen, and Leon and Pearl ran in from the backyard, all gathering in our small breakfast room.

He got red and said, "Well that one was bad," and proceeded to toss another one at the wall; it also fell in pieces.

By this time we were all laughing, except for Alicia, who was looking alarmed. We all pitched in and tested all six plates and they were all "bad." My family was stubborn, but they also had a funny streak with it all.

My parents encouraged me in school. Girls need to be actively encouraged to do what they want to, certainly not discouraged from taking math and science. Having female scientists as role models in college was helpful too. This has been a major argument in the movement to increase female faculty in science departments.

What accounts for my assertiveness, my determination, my self-confidence? Neither my mother nor my father was timid. We children did not always get our way, but they always listened to us. I never felt that I should not express an opinion within the family, even if it contradicted what someone else thought and said. We did not always agree, and I argued with my Dad a lot, but anger did not linger on anybody's part.

Certainly learning was valued above just about everything else.

ตดต

Part of the credit for my need to learn should be given to my Grandfather, Tzadik Shulman, who lived with us from 1935 until 1948. He paid a lot of attention to Pearl, Leon, and me and taught us to read Hebrew and speak Yiddish. He was extraordinarily sensitive to my father's role as "head of the house"; he made sure that there was never a question about this. He read to us in Yiddish when we were little, marvelous stories from the Old Testament and from Sholem Aleichem. He told us about the Jewish religion when we asked. I remember, at the age of eleven, the first time I was asked to dinner at the home of a Gentile friend, I asked him what to do if her mother served unkosher food.

He said: "Eat it. It is more of a sin to insult a woman in her home than to eat something that is not kosher."

I guess that expresses my feelings about religion as well. My grandfather's capacity for tolerance and openness was a guiding light for all of us.

৯৽৹৶

Four times during my life I was given important advice, which I did *not* take, and the not taking has had important consequences. It is characteristic of me to be stubborn and independent, and while I was not always right, this seemed to be the way I had to do things. The first time was at the end of my sophomore year in high school, when my math teacher discovered I had not signed up for junior year math

She stopped me in the hall and asked, "Why haven't you signed up for math next year? You are making a mistake."

"I want to major in English in college and won't need more math or science," I said.

As a result, I had trouble switching to science in college and had to take calculus in graduate school at night, which was costly in time and money.

The second advice not taken occurred while I was in my senior year in high school when my mother, after discovering the letter from my female lover, said, "Don't stay in this lifestyle—you will never be happy." Obviously, I ignored her well intentioned advice, and being lesbian has shaped my whole life. Was she right? I don't think so.

In 1972, after the FASEB meeting at which AWIS was formed, I returned to the University of Illinois from the meeting, charged up with enthusiasm. I met a female colleague in the hall and told her about it. She said, "It's not worth wasting your time on losers. If they are any good, they'll make it."

This was the third piece of advice I ignored. I was disappointed in her attitude, but not surprised. She was a tenured professor in another basic science department and was married to a famous male scientist. Many women scientists failed to join AWIS, WE, or other women's groups. It is sad that this is true, but what she said was not true. Many women who are "good" never make it because of prejudice. I have never regretted the time I have spent helping other women.

The fourth piece of advice I did not take was in 1978 after I presented my first talk on inhibin from ovarian follicles at a FASEB meeting. A valued older male colleague called me on the phone.

"You will ruin your career if you continue to study this non-existent hormone. Get out of this field," he told me.

He was reflecting the current wisdom, which was based on more than forty years of experience looking for this hormone in the testes. Many scientists had searched in vain for FSH-suppressing activity. He was (and is still) a friend and was trying to protect me. I did not take his advice, and my research career took off in this new direction. The work on inhibin not only became a major focus for my lab, in working out the physiology of FSH and the ovary, but molecular biologists followed our lead with the delineation of a whole new family of proteins, the TGF-b group, and a new family of receptors for these proteins.

಄಄

As I have written these memoirs and gone back through my diary, I have also been painfully reminded of how incapacitating my depression was for a long time. I have recently read Kay Redfield Jamison's *An Unquiet Mind: A Memoir of Moods and Madness* about her life with manic-depressive disease, before and after lithium. She says at one point, speaking about a conversation she had with a colleague:

> I began to feel the usual discomfort I tend to experience whenever a certain level of friendship or intimacy has been reached in a relationship and I have not mentioned my illness. It is after all, not just an illness, but something that affects every aspect of my life: my temperament, my work, and my reaction to almost everything that comes my way.

I felt this same way about my lesbianism, which is why I started this memoir off by telling about it. But I now wonder, in retrospect, whether the depression I have suffered is also not an important sub-plot to my life and work. It has certainly had a negative impact on my relationships with lovers because of the anger which often accompanies it. I am prickly to live with.

The depression frequently also interfered with my relations with my lab colleagues, leaving me sometimes hovering in my office rather than engaging with my students and technicians. It has left me unable to work efficiently on many occasions.

Like Jamison's manic-depression, depression is strongly familial. As I think back on my nuclear family, and my extended kin, I can see the signs of it in many of us. But there is also something seductive about it. It makes one feel "special" or superior to others because they can't seem to see the futility of life. As I would move away from a deep depression under medication, I could feel the tug back, and it was always tough to resist.

> Oh, no no no, it was too cold always
> I was much too far out all my life
> And not waving but drowning.
> —Stevie Smith, "Not Waving but Drowning"

After writing the preceding paragraph, and reflecting more about the depression, which has certainly made me unhappy and despairing many times, I again went back to my depression journal. The depression certainly did not interfere with the publication output of the lab. I interpret this as indicating not only how good my technicians, students, and fellows were, but also to my ability to compartmentalize my life. Maybe the compartmentalization skills I learned as a lesbian helped me work at science in spite of personal feeling of despair.

જે-જી

In January 1999, my department gave me a retirement party. My brother and sister and their spouses came to Evanston from California and Maryland. My two nieces came, each with a baby less than three months old. My nephew Howard came. My cousin Bernie came with a son and grandchild. Some of my friends, straight and gay, came. My partner Claire did an audiotape of the event. Many of my former graduate students and post-docs joined us. In a way, most of the important people in my life were in one place. My colleagues held an elaborate "symposium," which spoofed my seminar style and my modeling. Kelly Mayo updated the model I presented in 1968 at the Laurentian Hormone Conference with a new version, which included searching for inhibin, sailing in Door County, and traveling around the world!

જે-જી

My beloved brother Leon died in April 2003. We will no longer walk together on the Back Bay of Newport Beach, spotting birds competitively and talking, talking, talking. Our sister Pearl called him "my hero," and I feel that way about him too. In his non-assuming way, he moved from the National Aeronautics and Space Administration to the National Science Foundation to NIH and then to the new University of California, Irvine campus, where he was vice-chancellor in charge of administration and developed an enviable record of mentoring and compassionate administration. My sister and I have always been close, but Leon's death has made us even closer.

જે-જી

The house *At Beigh* is still a refuge and a delight. I am so used to working up there, interspersed with hikes, swimming, and reading for pleasure that it is not possible just to do nothing there. This book, for the most part, has been written there.

જે-જી

Since retiring from my lab, I have done some undergraduate teaching to small classes. I continued to serve as director of the Center for Reproductive Science for several years, and with more time on my hands, I started a Newsletter and website for the center. The newsletter was a fun experience that took me back to my high school and college days as a journalist. I agreed to stand for election for the executive board of AAAS and won. Being involved with AAAS has been rewarding as I have pursued the "teaching of science" pathways within the society, as well as activities involved with creating more equal opportunities.

I am still reviewing papers for several journals and enjoying it. It does induce me to keep up with newer ideas and techniques. I am convinced that the only way to keep my brain reasonably functional is to keep using it.

Along this line, I keep doing crosswords and some computer games. I am still being asked to give talks on biology/gender, women in science, or teaching of endocrinology, instead of on-cutting-edge science. Until 2001, I was funded on our program project grant for studies on progesterone receptors and FSH secretion, but I had to depend on others' hands in Jon Levine's lab. He and I were co-principal investigators on a project within the grant. The work went slowly because I had to wait in line for resources, but I am attending his lab meetings and enjoying that interaction with his grad students.

Now, I am the consummate insider in the university and in my professional societies. As I look back, it does not seem to me that I was ever actually angry about my outsider status in the way I was angry when my dean fired me from the chair, or when my department head at Illinois humiliated me in front of foreign visitors. It is as though I just felt, "This is unfair."

❧❧

With respect to being lesbian, I wasn't angry about having to hide my lifestyle; I was, for much of my life, too consumed with guilt about doing something unacceptable.

What has it meant to be a lesbian who has spent much of her life "passing"? I think of this as being seen only from one side, always turning that face to the public, the camera. But I realize now that I didn't have to pass in my private sanctuary: the lab. My lab colleagues always met my current live-in partner because of our parties and pot-lucks. I never felt judged by them. Obviously, they recognized the relationship, though we did not talk about it ever. What did this cost? I will probably never know. Have I made a mistake in coming out so visibly in this book? Maybe, but was there a choice?

❧❧

Claire and I have taken two cruises with Olivia, a travel agency that specializes in planning lesbian vacations. Taking some vacations with other lesbians has been an incredible experience. We are surrounded by women, young and old, some overweight like us, some slim, some wearing lipstick, well coiffed and fashionably dressed. There are the young butches, whose hair is close cropped, and the middle-aged women, with short, elegant hairdos and resort quality leisure clothing—and the old ones like us, grey or graying and looking a little surprised to be here.

We introduce ourselves by first names. The first question is, "Where are you from?" Then, after more chat, "How long have you been together?" and "How did you meet?" Then start the coming-out stories. It doesn't feel like the real world to me, and it isn't. It is an artificial safe space, set aside for people who, in the main, don't ask or tell within their work spaces or even with their families. But that is the way *I* feel about it, because of how and when I grew up. While it feels good to be accepted and accepting, it is just too late for me to feel natural or real about it. But it is fun, and I have loved it.

By now, lesbianism is *in*, I have been President of both the SSR and the Endocrine Society, and have won several awards. Reproductive science is *in* because there is so much money to be made from it nowadays by clinics and pharmaceutical companies. I have become a senior statesperson in my field. But not having a lab of my own lowers my status tremendously, or at least it seems so to me.

❧

I suspect I am still useful to colleagues because of my integrative view of physiology in general and reproductive endocrinology in particular. Unfortunately, it is difficult to get funding for pure systems physiology these days. But it is also necessary to learn enough molecular biology to understand what it can enable you to understand.

I am reminded of the time I was confronted by an endocrinologist of my generation as I walked into an Endocrine Society meeting in the late 1980s. By that time, the papers being given at the meeting were shifting to a preponderance of cell and molecular emphasis. He said that he had heard I was taking a year in Jack Gorski's lab to do some molecular endocrinology. When I replied that I was really excited by the prospect, he told me, "You are selling out. It isn't real endocrinology." It scares me that I might start thinking that way too.

This shift in the biological sciences to the study of events inside the cells, rather than in groups of cells, was very obvious to me as the twenty-first annual minisymposium sponsored by the Center for Reproductive Science was being planned in 1999. I sat with the five graduate students who were the planning committee, putting the program together. They were classifying the submitted abstracts into like categories, and I realized as I sat with them that only one of the present categories was represented in the first few years of the symposium. All the others were new—a striking example of how much reproductive science has changed. I did not tell the committee what I was thinking. I was mourning the loss of a more holistic, less fractured approach to biology. Sad to say, I was also somewhat resentful of how quickly people forget what one has done.

જ⊷∽

Does someone ever stop being a scientist? Thank goodness I have not. I love the way a scientist thinks. But as the field I was in changes, I don't have the same energy to keep up. I'm proud that the integrative science I did was important in dissecting the events of the rat estrous cycle, and many of these ideas spilled over to work on other species. The science we accomplished on the separation of the regulation of FSH from LH has had a major impact in the field, far beyond anything I could have imagined when we started.

Some battles persist. An interesting sequence of articles relevant to feminism, science and diversity appeared in the journal *Science* on July and August of 1999. Florence Haseltine, director of the Center for Population Research at the Institute for Child Health and Human Development, and senior editor of the *Journal of Women's Health* reviewed Linda Scheibinger's book *Has Feminism Changed Science?* In a generally favorable review of the book, Haseltine said, "Within her discussions of these disciplines, she interweaves many different themes. The interwoven discussion made perfect sense to me until a high-level science policy wonk I could not ignore asked me, "What contributions have women made in science that a man could not have made?" Scheibinger responded (1999):

> This is precisely what the book argues against. The whole point of my book was to argue that it is wrong to imagine that women do science differently simply because they are women. My claim is that "feminism" is a broad-based social movement and an academic theoretical perspective and that "feminists"—both men and women—have changed science.

Vera Rubin, an astronomer who is in the National Academy of Science, also responded to Haseltine's review (1999). "Why not ask, 'What contributions have men made to science that a woman could not have made?'" Rubin goes on to say:

> In speaking to science students, I often pose the following experiment. Listen carefully as you say, "there is no science problem that has been solved by a man that could not be solved by a woman." Then say, "There is no science problem that has been solved by a woman that could not be solved by a man." Do they mean the same thing? And the students often answer, "No. The first seems to say that a woman scientist can be as good as a man. In contrast, the second seems to say that women solve only simple problems, which of course a man could solve."

✌

Diversity among female scientists was again revealed in the 6 December 2002 issue of *Science* when two letters from female scientists appeared. The first, from a female oceanographer, said, "Affirmative action may serve to broaden the pool of female scientists, but it will also weaken it [as] lower requirements naturally mean lower quality." The second letter, from a female science consultant, said of women:

> They will achieve parity once they are provided with a 'level playing field' upon which they can compete directly with men. My observation is that scientific contributions of female scientists tend to be undervalued by men.

Then in 2005, Lawrence Summers, then president of Harvard, weighed in with the nonsense about "studies" showing that women are not as skilled in math and science as men. He cited this as a reason why there are fewer women than men in science departments (especially at Harvard!). I gave several media interviews on the subject and a talk at the AAAS meeting. But it was disheartening to me and other women I know well.

✌

Life goes on. Claire has also retired, although she continues writing papers and doing some part-time teaching. Our house in Evanston has become something of a burden because I have a knee problem which makes stair-climbing difficult, but the house is so beautiful, so close to the lake and near enough to Chicago to make getting to the opera and symphony easy. Door County beckons at every season. But both of us like to travel, and we hope to continue to do this.

✌

I have been asked if it is okay if the annual lecture at our mini-symposium is named after me. This is startling to contemplate. The twenty-fifth anniversary of this annual event occurred in the autumn of 2004. It was celebrated with talks by five alumnae of our training program, in addition to the usual trainee presentations. It was a wonderful celebration.

✌

While I was chair of Biological Sciences in 1975, a graduate student came into my office to chat. She asked me what all the papers were scattered across my desk.

"A grant application," I said wearily.

"Why do you go on doing it?" she asked.

"I need to keep writing grants in order to keep doing science."

"Why keep doing science?"

I looked up surprised. "Why, it's the only game in town," I said.

How lucky I was to play that game for so many years.

Study Questions

(1) Discuss, based on what you have read, whether you would like to meet Neena on a personal basis, professional basis, both, or not particularly.
  - Give you reasons based on values she evinces.

(2) Compare and contrast your values with those shown by Neena in the personal sphere, with regard to work ethic, academic achievement, mentoring, professionalism, and political activism.
  - Discuss whether your views or goals have changed based on reading about her life.

(3) Had you the opportunity to mentor Neena, at what age would you wish to touch her life, and in what way?
  - What advice would you have given her?

(4) Reviewing this entire volume, would you judge Neena's relationship to her career to be more personal, professional, both, or other?
  - Cite specific places in the book that support your judgment and give your reasons.
  - Using whatever judgment you made (e.g., more professional than personal) discuss whether you believe other Professors with whom you have worked have had a similar or different relationship based on the same factors you chose to support your claims.
  - Discuss the advantages or disadvantages—regarding personal or professional results—of the relationships you have discussed. Give examples or, if you lack experience, postulate reasons.

(5) Repeat the exercises in (4), this time considering Neena's relationships with family, friends, colleagues.

FOR FURTHER READING

* Entries marked with asterisks were cited in the text.
** Annotations offered for works whose theme is not apparent from the title.
*** For an extensive treatment of the scientific topics discussed, please refer to Appendix
  B: Chronology: Neena B. Schwartz, which lists all of her publications.

Abir-Am, Pnina G.,and Dorinda Outram. (1987) *Uneasy Careers and Intimate Iives: Women in Science, 1789–1979.* New Brunswick: Rutgers University Press.

Aldrich, Robert. (2006) *Gay Life and Culture: A World History.* New York: Universe.

Ambrose, Susan A. (1997) *Journeys of Women in Science and Engineering: No Universal Constants.* Philadelphia: Temple University Press.

*Angier, Natalie. (1999) *Woman: An Intimate Geography.* Boston: Houghton Mifflin.

Anzaldua, G. (1999) *Borderlands. La Frontera.* 2nd Edition. San Francisco: Aunt Lute Books.

Appel, T.A. (1999) "Physiology in Women's Colleges: The Rise and Decline of a Female Subculture." In *History of Women in the Sciences: Readings from Isis.* Edited by S. G. Kohlstedt. Chicago: University of Chicago Press.

*Arnold, A.P., and Burgoyne, P.S. (2004) Are XX and XY brain cells intrinsically different? *Trends Endocrinol Metab* 15:6–11.

Astin, Helen S., and Carole Leland. (1991) *Women of Influence, Women of Vision: A Cross-Generational Study of Leaders and Social Change.* San Francisco.

*Bailey, J.M., and Pillard, R. (1995) Genetics of human sexual orientation. *Annual Review of Sex Research* 6: 126–150.

Bailey, Martha J. (1994) *American Women in Science: A Biographical Dictionary.* Santa Barbara, Calif.: ABC-CLIO.

Barr, Jean, and Lynda I. A. Birke. (1998) *Common Science? Women, Science, and Knowledge.* Bloomington: Indiana University Press.

Barrington, J. (1991) An *Intimate Wilderness: Lesbian Writers on Sexuality.* Portland, Ore.: Eighth Mountain Press.

*Bauer-Dantoin, A.C., and Hanke, C. J. (2007) Using a classic paper by I. E. Lawton and N. B. Schwartz to consider the array of factors that control luteinizing hormone production. *Advan. Physiol. Edu.* 31: 318–322.

Benkov, Laura. (1994) Reinventing the Family: The Emerging Story of Lesbian and Gay Parents. New York: Crown Publishers.

Birke, L. (1980) "From Zero to Infinity: Scientific Views of Lesbians," pp. 108–123. In *Alice Through the Microscope: The Power of Science Over Women's Lives.* London, Virago Press.

Bittencourt, S., and Martinac, P. (2003) *My Road to Microsoft: One Woman's Success Story.* New York: XLibris.

Bleier, Ruth. (1984) *Science and Gender: A Critique of Giology and Its Theories on Women.* New York: Pergamon Press.

————. (1991) *Feminist Approaches to Science.* New York: Pergamon Press.

*Blum, Deborah. (1997) *Sex on the Brain: The Biological Differences between Men and Women.* New York: Viking.

Boxer, Marilyn J., and Jean H. Quataert. (1987) *Connecting Spheres: Women in the Western World, 1500 to the Present.* New York: Oxford University Press.

Brobeck, J. R., Reynolds, O.E., and Appel, T.A. (1987) *History of the American Physiological Society: The First Century, 1887–1987.* Bethesda Md., American Physiological Society.

Brown, Rita Mae. (1993) *Venus Envy.* New York: Bantam Books.
Brown, author and social activist, writes this novel about a beautiful, successful thirty-five-year-old businesswoman who has achieved her professional status at the expense of her personal happiness and integrity, as she has been hiding her lesbianism from everyone save her closest friend, Billy Cicero, a rich, fast-living, gorgeous gay man who is also firmly in the closet.

*Buchan, John. (1924) *John Mcnab.* Boston: Houghton Mifflin.
Each of the three heroes of John Macnab is a leader in his field and each is suffering from boredom and lethargy in London. They decide to emulate and extend the exploits of a famous gentleman-poacher in the Scottish Highlands by issuing a challenge to three estates that they will successfully poach from them two stags and a salmon, and then return them undetected.

————. (1930) *The Four Adventures of Richard Hannay* [Containing: *The Thirty-Nine Steps*; *Greenmantle*; *Mr. Standfast*; *The Three Hostages*] London: n.p.
Richard Hannay has WWI experiences in Greenmantle (1916) and Mr Standfast (1919), and then battles German spies across England and Scotland in The Thirty Nine Steps (1915) and The Three Hostages (1924).

*Bucher, Rue, and Joan G. Stelling. (1977) *Becoming Professional.* Beverly Hills, Calif.: Sage.
Examines theoretical frameworks and institutional practices with regard to training professionals. Considers role models and self-evaluation.

Bug, A. (2003) Has feminism changed physics? *Signs* 28:881–899.

Burr, C. (1996) *A Separate Creation: The Search for the Biological Origins of Sexual Orientation.* New York: Hyperion.

Butler, J. P. (1993) *Bodies That Matter: On the Discursive Limits of "Sex."* New York: Routledge.

Carter-Su, C. (2005) Mentoring for success in physiology. *The Physiologist* 48:167–178.

Castle, Terry. (1993) *The Apparitional Lesbian: Female Homosexuality and Modern Culture.* New York: Columbia University Press.

Ceci, Stephen J., and Wendy M. Williams. (2007) *Why Aren't More Women in Science? Top Researchers Debate the Evidence.* Washington, D.C.: American Psychological Association.

Clarke, A. (1998) *Disciplining Reproduction: Modernity, American Life Sciences, and "The Problems of Sex."* Berkeley: University of California Press.

Clunis, D.M., Fredriksen-Goldsen, K.I., Freeman, P.A., and Nystrom, N. (2005) *Lives of Lesbian Elders: Looking Back, Looking Forward*. Binghamton, N.Y.:The Hayworth Press.

*Colapinto, J. (2001) *As Nature Made Him*. New York: Perennial Press.

Cole, Jonathan R. (1979) *Fair Science: Women in the Scientific Community*. New York: Free Press.

Committee on Maximizing the Potential of Women in Acadademic Science and Engineering. (2007) *Beyond Bias and Barriers: Fulfilling the Potential of Women in Academic Science and Engineering*. Washington, D.C.: Natl. Acad. Press.

Conkey, M.W. (2003) Has feminism changed archaeology? *Signs* 28:867–880.

Conley, F. K. (1998) *Walking Out On the Boys*. New York: Farrar, Straus & Giroux.

*Conway, Jill K. (1994) *True North: A Memoir*. New York: Knopf.

———. (2001) *A Woman's Education:The Road to Coorain Leads to Smith College*. New York: Alfred A. Knopf: Distributed by Random House.

Creese, Mary R. S., and Creese, Thomas M. (1998) *Ladies in the Laboratory? American and British Women in Science, 1800–1900: A Survey of Their Contributions to Research*. Lanham, Md.: Scarecrow Press.

Crew, Louie,and Ellen M. Barrett. (1978) *The Gay Academic*. Palm Springs, Calif.: ETC Publications.

*Diamond, M., and Sigmundson, H.K. (1997) Sex reassignment at birth: a long term review and clinical implications. *Arch Pediatrics and Adolescent Medicine* 151: 298–304.

Ding,W.W., Murray, F., and Stuart, T.E. (2006) Gender differences in patenting in the academic life sciences. *Science* 313:665–667.

Driscoll, Dawn-Marie, and Carol R. Goldberg. (1993) *Members of the Club: The Coming of Age of Executive Women*. New York: Free Press.
    Argues the "glass ceiling" is a myth and this is a period of opportunities for women. Presents analyses of closed "clubhouse" and "old-boy networks."

Duberman, M. B., Vicinus, M., and Chauncey, G., Jr. (1989) *Hidden from History: Reclaiming the Gay and Lesbian Past*. New York: New American Library.

Eisenhart, Margaret A., and Elizabeth Finkel. (1998) *Women's Science: Learning and Succeeding from the Margins*. Chicago, Ill: University of Chicago Press.

Etzkowitz, Henry, Carol Kemelgor, and Brian Uzzi. (2000) *Athena Unbound: The Advancement of Women in Science and Technology*. New York: Cambridge University Press.

*Eugenides, J. (2002) *Middlesex*. New York: Farrar, Straus and Giroux.

*Everett, J.W., and Sawyer, C.H. (1950) "A 24-hour periodicity in the LH-release apparatus of female rats, disclosed by barbiturate sedation." *Endocrinology* 47: 198–218.

Faderman, Lillian. (1991) *Odd Girls and Twilight Lovers: A History of Lesbian Life in Twentieth-Century America*. New York: Columbia University Press.

*———. (1999) *To Believe in Women: What Lesbians Have Done for America: A History*. Boston: Houghton Mifflin.

*———. (2003) *Naked in the Promised Land.* Boston: Houghton Mifflin.

*Fausto-Sterling, A. (1981) "Women and Science" *Women's Studies Int. Quart.* 4:41–50.

*———. (1992) *Myths of Gender: Biological Theories about Women and Men.* New York: Basic Books.

*———. (2000) *Sexing the Body: Gender Politics and the Construction of Sexuality.* New York: Basic Books.

Ferry, G. (1998) *Dorothy Hodgkin: A Life.* Cold Spring Harbor, N.Y., Cold Spring Harbor Press.

*Fort, D.C., Ed. (1995) *A Hand Up: Women: Mentoring Women in Science.* Washington D.C.: Association of Women in Science.

Friedman, A. (2000) "Remembrance II: The Growth and Development of the Endocrine Society." *Endocrinology* 141: 3–4.

Frisch, R.E. (2002) *Female Fertility and the Body Fat Connection.* Chicago, Ill. University of Chicago Press

Gibson, Michelle, and Deborah T. Meem. (2005) *Lesbian Academic Couples.* New York: Harrington Park Press.

*Glickman, S.E., Cunha, G.R., Drea, C.M., Conley, A.J., and Plao, N.J. (2006) Mammalian sexual differentiation: lessons from the spotted hyena. *Trends Endocrinol Metab* 17: 349–356.

*Gooren . L. (1986) The neuroendocrine response of Luteinizing Hormone to estrogen administration in the human is not sex specific but dependent on hormonal environment. *Journal Clinical Endocrinology and Metabolism* 63:559–593.

Gornick, Vivian. (1983) *Women in Science: Portraits from a World in Transition.* New York: Simon and Schuster.

Gowaty, P.A. (2003) Sexual natures: how feminism changed evolutionary biology? *Signs* 28:867–880.

*Greenberg, A.S., and Bailey, J.M. (2001) Parental selection of children's sexual orientation." *Arch Sexual Behavior* 30:423–437.

*Hall, Radclyffe. (1938) *The Well of Loneliness.* Leipzig: The Albatross.

———.(2006) "Why Did I Write The Well of Loneliness?" In *American Queer, Now and Then.* Edited by David Shneer and Caryn Aviv. Boulder, Colo.: Paradigm Publishers.

*Halliburton, Richard. *New Worlds to Conquer.* Indianapolis, Ind.: Bobbs-Merrill, 1929. Details Halliburton's exploration of South America.

*Hamer, D.H., Hu, S., Magnuson, V.L., Hu, N., and Pattatucci, A.M.L. (1993) "A linkage between DNA markers on the X chromosome and male sexual orientation." *Science* 261: 321–327.

Harding, Sandra G. (1991) *Whose science? Whose knowledge?: Thinking from Women's Lives.* Ithaca, N.Y.: Cornell University Press.

Heilbrun, C.G. (1997) *The Last Gift of Time: Life Beyond Sixty.* New York: Dial Press.

*Hodges, A. (1983) *Alan Turing: The Enigma.* New York: Simon and Schuster.

*Hollander, J. (1999) *Reflections on Espionage.* New Haven:: Yale University Press.

Hornig, L.S. (2003) *Equal Rites, Unequal Outcomes: Women in American Research Universities.* New York: Kluwer Academic.

Howard, Kim, and Annie Stevens. (2000) *Out & About Campus: Personal Accounts by Lesbian, Gay, Bisexual & Transgendered College Students.* Los Angeles: Alyson Books.

Inness, Sherrie A. (1997) *The Lesbian Menace: Ideology, Identity, and the Representation of Lesbian Life.* Amherst, Mass.: University of Massachusetts Press.

*Ishiguro, Kazuo. (2005) *Never Let Me Go.* London: Faber.
    This novel describes the life of Kathy H., a young woman of 31, focusing at first on her childhood at an unusual boarding school and eventually her adult life. The story takes place in a dystopian Britain, in which human beings are cloned to provide donor organs for transplants. Kathy and her classmates have been created to be donors, though the adult Kathy is temporarily working as a "carer," someone who supports and comforts donors as they are made to give up their organs and, eventually, submit to death.

*Jagsi, R., Guancial, E.A., and Worobey, C.C. (2006) "The 'gender gap' in authorship of academic medical literature: a 35-year perspective." *N. Engl. J. Med* 355:281–287.

*Jamison, K.R. (1996) *An Unquiet Mind: A Memoir of Moods and Madness.* New York: Vintage Books.

*Jay, Karla. (1999) *Tales of the Lavender Menace: A Memoir of Liberation.* New York: Basic Books.

Jennings, Kevin, and Patricia Gottlieb Shapiro. (2003) *Always My Child: A Parent's Guide to Understanding Your Gay, Lesbian, Bisexual, Transgendered, or Questioning Son or Daughter.* New York: Simon & Schuster.

Johnson, L.L., and Granholm, N.H. (1978) In vitro analysis of pre- and early postimplantation development of lethal yellow (Ay/Ay) mouse embryos. *J. Exp. Zool.* 204: 381–390.

Josselson, Ruthellen. (1987) *Finding Herself: Pathways to Identity Development in Women.* San Francisco: Jossey-Bass.

Kass-Simon, G., and Patricia Farnes. (1990) *Women of Science: Righting the Record.* Bloomington: Indiana University Press.

Keller, E.F. (1983) *A Feeling for the Organism: The Life and Work of Barbara McClintock.* San Francisco: W.H. Freeman.

———. (1985) *Reflections on Gender and Science.* New Haven, Conn.: Yale University Press.

*———, and Longino, H.E. (1996) *Feminism and Science.* New York: Oxford University Press.

Kent, Kathryn R. (2003) *Making Girls into Women: American Women's Writing and the Rise of Lesbian Identity.* Durham, N.C.: Duke University Press.

Kissen, Rita M. (1996) *The Last Closet: The Real Lives of Lesbian and Gay Teachers.* Portsmouth, N.H.: Heinemann.

*Kohlstedt, S.G.L., and Longino, H.E. (1997) *Women, Gender, and Science: New Directions.* Chicago, Ill.: University of Chicago Press.

Koprowska, Irena. (1997) *A Woman Wanders through Life and Science*. Albany: State University of New York Press.

    Irena Koprowska is a Polish-born pathologist, cytologist, and cancer research pioneer. Tells of competing pulls of war, marriage, motherhood, and career. Sexism more than nationality has posed the greatest barrier to Koprowska's personal and professional happiness. Began her career anew to follow her husband for a job.

*Krafft-Ebing, Rudolf von. (1965/1922) *Psychopathia Sexualis: A Medico-Forensic Study*. New York: Putnam.

Kundsin, R.B., Ed. (1973) Successful Women in the Sciences: An Analysis of Determinants. Conference 11–13 May 1972. Ann. N.Y. Acad Sci 208. *JAMA* 225(11):1392–1393.

Larkin, Joan. (1999) *A Woman Like That: Lesbian and Bisexual Writers Tell Their Coming Out Stories*. New York: Avon Books.

Latour, B.W.S. (1986) *Laboratory Life: The Construction of Scientific Facts*. Beverly Hills, Calif.: Sage Press.

Lear, L.J. (1997) *Rachel Carson: Witness for Nature*. New York: H. Holt.

Levay, S. (1993) *The Sexual Brain*. Cambridge, Mass.: MIT Press.

Levi-Montalcini, Rita. (1988) *In Praise of Imperfection: My Life and Work*. New York: Basic Books.

    Levi-Montalcini is Italian neurologist who, with Stanley Cohen, received the 1986 Nobel Prize in Physiology or Medicine for discovery of Nerve Growth Factor (NGF). During World War II, she conducted experiments from a home laboratory, studying the growth of nerve fibers in chicken embryos which laid the groundwork for much of her later research. Her first genetics laboratory was in her bedroom at her home. Today she is the oldest living Nobel laureate and the first ever to reach the 100th birthday.

Levithan, David, and Billy Merrell, Billy. (2006) *The Full Spectrum: A New Generation of Writing about Gay, Lesbian, Bisexual, Transgender, Questioning, and Other Identities*. New York: Knopf.

*Lewin, E., and Leap, W.L. (1996) *Out in the Field*. Urbana: University of Illinois Press.

*Long, C.N.H., and Evans, H.M. (1922) The œstrous cycle in the rat and its associated phenomena. *Mem. Univ. Calif.* 6, 1.

Maddox, B. (2002) *Rosalind Franklin: The Dark Lady of DNA*. New York: Harper Collins.

Malakoff, D. (2000) The rise of the mouse, biomedicine's model mammal. *Science* 288: 248–253.

Mann, Thomas. (1936) *Stories of Three Decades*. Translated by H. T. Lowe-Porter. New York: A. A. Knopf.

*Margolis, Jane. (2002) *Unlocking the Clubhouse: Women in Computing*. Cambridge, Mass.: MIT Press.

McCarthy, M.M., and Konkle, A.T.M. (2005) When is a sex difference not a sex difference? *Frontiers in Neuroendocrinology*. 26:85–102.

*McClintock, M. (1971) Menstrual synchrony and suppression. *Nature* 229: 244–245.

McGarry, Molly, and Fred Wasserman. (1998) *Becoming Visible: An Illustrated History of Lesbian and Gay Life in Twentieth-Century America.* New York: Penguin Studio.

McGrayne, Sharon Bertsch. (1993) *Nobel Prize Women in Science: Their Lives, Struggles, and Momentous Discoveries.* Secaucus, N.J.: Carol Pub. Group.

McKay, A. (1993) *Wolf Girls at Vassar: Lesbian & Gay Experiences, 1930–1990.* New York: St. Martin's Press.

McNaron, Toni A. H. (1997) *Poisoned Ivy: Lesbian and Gay Academics Confronting Homophobia.* Philadelphia: Temple University Press.

Medvei, V. C. (1982) *A History of Endocrinology: A Comprehensive Account of Endocrinology from Earliest Times to the Present Day.* Boston: MTP Press.

*Meyer-Bahlburg, H.F.L., Dolezal, C., Baker, S.W., and New, M.J. (2005) Sexual orientation in women with classical or non-classical congenital adrenal hyperplasia as a function of degree of prenatal androgen excess. *Arch Sex Behav* 37:85–99.

Meyerowitz, Joanne J. (1994) *Not June Cleaver: Women and Gender in Postwar America, 1945–1960.* Philadelphia, Pa.: Temple University Press.

Miller, Neil. (1995) *Out of the Past: Gay and Lesbian History from 1869 to the Present.* New York: Vintage Books.

Morantz-Sanchez, Regina Markell. (1985) *Sympathy and Science: Women Physicians in American Medicine.* New York: Oxford University Press.

Muller, Ann. (1987) *Parents Matter: Parents' Relationships with Lesbian Daughters and Gay Sons.* Tallahassee, Fla.: Naiad Press.

Nequin, L.G., Alvarez, J.A., and Campbell, C.S. (1975) Alterations in steroid and gonadotropin release resulting from surgical stress during the morning of proestrus in 5-day cyclic rats. *Endocrinology* 97:718–724.

*Newton, Esther. (2000) *Margaret Mead Made Me Gay: Personal Essays, Public Ideas.* Durham, N.C.: Duke University Press.

Ogilvie, Marilyn Bailey. (1986) *Women in Science: Antiquity through the Nineteenth Century: A Biographical Dictionary with Annotated Bibliography.* Cambridge, Mass.: MIT Press.

———., and Joy Dorothy Harvey. (2000) *The Biographical Dictionary of Women in Science: Pioneering Lives from Ancient Times to the Mid-20th Century.* New York: Routledge.

*Pert, C. (2003) *Molecules of Emotion.* New York: Scribner

*Peters, Margot. (1997) *May Sarton: A Biography.* New York: Random House. May Sarton is the pen name of Eleanore Marie Sarton (3 May 1912–16 July 1995), an American poet, novelist, and memoirist. Many of her works reflect the lesbian experience.

*Pillard, R.C., and Bailey, J.M. (1998) Human sexual orientation has a heritable component. *Human Biology* 70(2): 347–365.

Polk, Milbry, and Mary Tiegreen. (2001) *Women of Discovery: A Celebration of Intrepid Women Who Explored the World*. New York: C. Potter.
  Readers feel they are witnesses to history thanks to well-chosen, first-person observations and ample visual contents such as contemporary maps, memorabilia, photos, and art; includes aristocrats and paupers, ancient Vikings and modern scientists.

Pollack, Rachel, and Cheryl Schwartz. (1995) *The Journey Out: A Guide For and About Lesbian, Gay and Bisexual Teens*. New York, N.Y.: Viking.

*Ramey, E.R. (1971) "What did happen at the Bay of Pigs?" *McCall's* (January).

*Rice, G., Anderson, C., Risch, N., and Ebers, G. (1999) Male homosexuality: absence of linkage to microsatellite markers at Xq28. *Science* 284: 665–667.

*Rich, A. (1989) "Split at the Root." In *Nice Jewish Girls: A Lesbian Anthology*. Edited by E. T. Beck. Boston: Beacon Press.

Rimmerman, Craig A. (2001) *From Identity to Politics: The Lesbian and Gay Movements in the United States*. Philadelphia, Pa.: Temple University Press.

Rosser, Sue Vilhauer. (1988) *Feminism within the science and health care professions : overcoming resistance*. New York : Pergamon Press.

*———. (1990) *Female-Friendly Science: Applying Women's Studies Methods and Theories to Attract Students*. New York: Pergamon Press.

———. (1992) *Biology & Feminism: A Dynamic Interaction*. New York: Twayne.

———. (1995) *Teaching the Majority: Breaking the Gender Barrier in Science,Mathematics, and Engineering*. New York: Teachers College Press.

———. (2000) *Women, Science, and Society: The Crucial Union*. New York: Teachers College Press.

Rossiter, M.W. (1995) *Women Scientists in America: Before Affirmative Action, 1940–1972*. Baltimore, Johns Hopkins University Press.

*Runner, M.N., and Ladman, A.J. (1950) The time of ovulation and its diurnal regulation in the post-parturitional mouse. *Anat. Rec.* 108: 343–361.

Savin-Williams, Ritch C. (2001) *Mom, Dad, I'm Gay: How Families Negotiate Coming Out*. Washington, D.C.: American Psychological Association.

Sayre, A. (1975) *Rosalind Franklin and DNA*. New York: Norton.

Schiebinger, Londa L. (1989) *The Mind Has No Sex?: Women in the Origins of Modern Science*. Cambridge, Mass.: Harvard University Press.

*———. (1999) *Has Feminism Changed Science?* Cambridge, Mass.: Harvard University Press.

———. (1999) How women contribute. *Science* 285:835.

Seidman, Steven. (2002) *Beyond the Closet: The Transformation of Gay and Lesbian Life*. New York: Routledge.

Signorile, Michelangelo. (1995) *Outing Yourself: How to Come Out as Lesbian or Gay to your Family, Friends, and Coworkers*. New York: Random House.

*Solomon, M. (2003) The whiptail lizard revisited. *Perspectives on Science* 113:318–325.

*Stern, K., and McClintock, M. (1998) Regulation of ovulation by human phero- mones. *Nature* 392: 177–179.

*Straus, E. (1998) *Rosalyn Yalow, Nobel Laureate: Her Life and Work in Medicine: A Biographical Memoir*. New York: Plenum Trade.

Suiter, M. (2006) Wisdom on mentoring- sharing the methods of exemplary science and engineering mentors. *AWIS Magazine* 35:17- 25.

Suleebka, K. P. (1996) *Role of Women in Science: Society Interaction*. Proceedings, VII. All India Meeting of Women in Science. Roorkee, India: Ajay Printers & Publishers.

Sutton, Roger, and Lisa Ebright. (1994) *Hearing Us Out: Voices from the Gay and Lesbian Community*. Boston: Little, Brown.

Thompson, Mark. (1994) *Long Road to Freedom: The Advocate History of the Gay and Lesbian Movement*. New York: St. Martin's Press.

Turgeon, J.L., Carr, M.C., Maki, P.M., Mendelsohn, M.M., and Wise, P.M. (2006) Complex actions of sex steroids in adipose tissue, the cardiovascular system and brain: insights from basic science and clinical studies. *Endo. Rev.* 27:575–605.

Ulrich, L.T. (2007) *Well-Behaved Women Seldom Make History*. New York: A. Knopf.

Vaid, Urvashi. (1995) *Virtual Equality: The Mainstreaming of Gay and Lesbian Libe- ration*. New York: Anchor Books.

Valian, V. (1998) *Why So Slow? The Advancement of Women*. Cambridge, Mass.: MIT Press.

Van Gelder, Lindsy, and Pamela Robin Brandt. (1996) *The Girls Next Door: Into the Heart of Lesbian America*. New York: Simon & Schuster.

Walters, Suzanna Danuta. (2001) *All the Rage: The Story of Gay Visibility in America*. Chicago: University of Chicago Press.

*Wasserman, Elga. (1999) *The Door in the Dream: Conversations with Eminent Women in Science*. Washington, D.C.: Joseph Henry Press.

———., and Arie Y. Lewin. (1975) *Women in Academia: Evolving Policies toward Equal Opportunities*. New York: Praeger Publishers.

Wennstrom, K.L., and Crews, D. (1995) Making males from females: the effects of aromatase inhibitors on a parthenogenetic species of whiptail lizard. *Gen and Comp Endocrinology* 99:316–322.

*Wilson, J. (1999) The role of androgens in male gender role behavior. *Endocrine Reviews* 20: 726–737.

*Wolfe, Thomas. (1957/1929) *Look Homeward Angel: A Story of the Buried Life*. New York: Scribner.

*Woolf, V. (1929) *A Room of One's Own*. London: Hogarth Press.

*Yalow, R. (1980) Presidential address: reflections of a non-establishmentarian. *En- docrinology* 106: 412–414.

Family in Evanston for Retirement Dinner, 1999. Standing l-r: Howard Schwartz, nephew; Nancy Imber Sellman, neice; Susan Imber Smith, niece, holding Carly Smith, grand-niece; Bernard Imber, brother-in-law. Seated l-r: Neena; Pearl Imber, sister, holding Olivia Sellman, grand-niece; Joan and Leon Schwartz.

80th birthday party, 2006 given by Northwestern University Center for Reproductive Science.

CHRONOLOGY
NEENA B. SCHWARTZ

*Experiences that span multiple years are listed under the earliest date of occurrence or affiliation.

1926–1939

Born December 10, 1926, Baltimore, Maryland, to Paul Schwartz (nee 1903) and Ethyl "Pep" Shulman Schwartz (nee 1903).

Bennett Place, home connected to parents' grocery store, 1931–1937.

Lived in northwest Baltimore; Liberty Heights, 1937–1948.

Garrison Junior High School, 1938–1941.

1940–1949

Forest Park High School, 1941–1944; recognized herself to be lesbian.

Goucher College, Baltimore, Maryland, AB, 1944–1948, graduated with honors, Phi Beta Kappa, Lillian Welsh Prize in physiology.

Worked in Curt Richter's lab at Johns Hopkins, summer 1946.

Jackson Memorial Laboratory, Bar Harbor, Maine, Research Assistant to Meredith Runner, summers, 1947, 1948.

Northwestern Medical School, Graduate student in physiology, 1948–1952; MS Physiology, thesis, "Studies on the Microanalysis of Organically Bound Iodine," 1950; Sigma XI, 1952.

1950–1959

United States Public Health Service, Postdoctoral Research Fellowship, 1952 (not activated at request of recipient).

Northwestern Medical School, PhD, June 1953; dissertation, "The Influence of Thyroid Hormone on Skeletal Muscle Function."

Instructor, then Assistant Professor, Physiology, University of Illinois, College of Medicine, 1953–1957.

NIH R01 AM 3801 Research Grant, "Thyroid Status and Neuromuscular Function," Principal Investigator, 1955–1969.

Michael Reese Hospital, Chicago, Illinois, Institute for Psychosomatic and Psychiatric Research and Training, Director of Biology Laboratories, 1957–1961.

Publications:

Lein, A., & **Schwartz, N.B.** (1951) Ceric sulfate-arsenous acid reaction in microdetermination of iodine. *Anal. Chem.* 23:1507–1510.

Schwartz, N.B. (1953) Relationship between body weight and gastrocnemius-soleus muscle weight in growing rats. *Growth* 17:123–126.

Schwartz, N.B., Shirky, L.E., & Steck, I.E. (1955) Pituitary-adrenal function during pseudopregnancy and early pregnancy in rats. *Endocrinology* 57:114–119.

Schwartz, N.B., & Lein, A. (1955) Effects of thyroxin on skeletal muscle function. *Am. J. Physiol.* 182:5–11.

Schwartz, N.B., Hammond, G.E., & Gronert, G.A. (1957) Interaction between thyroxine and dibensyline on metabolic rate. *Am. J. Physiol.* 191:573–576.

Schwartz, N.B., & Boswell, L.S. (1958) Independence of LH and ACTH release from the rat pituitary. *Endocrinology* 63:319–322.

1960–1969

University of Illinois, College of Medicine, Associate, then Full Professor of Physiology, 1961–1969, Assistant Dean for Faculty, 1968–1970.

American Physiological Society, Program Committee, 1965–1968; Committee on Committees, 1978–1982.

Mild heart attack, 1966.

Built house in Wisconsin, 1967.

Laurentian Hormone Conference, Pincus Memorial Talk, 1968.

University of Illinois, College of Medicine faculty, General Research Support Grant, Administrator, 1968–1970.

University of Illinois, Cardiovascular Undergraduate Training Grant, Principal Investigator, 1968–1970.

NIH R01-HD07504 Research Grant, "Hormonal and Environmental Interplay in Control of Ovulation," Principal Investigator, 1968–1997.

Society for Study of Reproduction, Membership Committee, 1968–1969; Nominating Committee, 1970–1971, 1987–1988, 1994–1995; Awards Committee, 1972–1973; Publications Committee, 1974–1976; Board of Directors, 1975–1976; Executive Vice-President, 1976–1977; President, 1977–1978; Emeritus Committee, 2002–2010.

Publications:

Schwartz, N.B., & Kling, A. (1960) Stress-induced adrenal ascorbic acid depletion in the cat. *Endocrinology* 66:308–310.

Schwartz, N.B., Ingold, A.H., Hammond, G.E., & Gronert, G.A. (1960) Role of temperature in determining the effects of thyroxin and propylthiouracil on the motor unit. *Am. J. Physiol.* 198:456–462.

Kling, A., Orbach, J., **Schwartz, N.B.**, & Towne, J.C. (1960) Injury to the limbic system and associated structures in cats: Chronic behavioral and physiological effects. *Arch. Gen. Psych.* 73:391–420.

Oken, D., Grinker, R.R., Heath, H.A., Sabshin, M., & **Schwartz, N.B.** (1960) Stress response in a group of chronic psychiatric patients. *Arch. Gen. Psych.* 3:451–466.

Schwartz, N.B. (1961) Changing size, composition, and contraction strength of gastrocnemius muscle. *Am. J. Physiol.* 201:164–170.

Mills, J.M., & **Schwartz, N.B.** (1962) Ovarian ascorbic acid as an endogenous assay for cyclic proestrous LH release. *Endocrinology* 69:844–850.

Schwartz, N.B. (1962) Effect of dibensyline on the metabolic actions of epinephrine and thyroxine. *Am. J. Physiol.* 203:525–531.

Oken, D., Grinker, R.R., Heath, H.A., Herz, M., Kordin, S.J., Sabshin, M., & **Schwartz, N.B.** (1962) Relation of physiological response to affect expression. *Arch. Gen. Psychiat.* 6:336–351.

Schwartz, N.B., & Bartosik, D. (1962) Changes in pituitary LH content during the rat estrous cycle. *Endocrinology* 71:756–762.

Schwartz, N.B., & Kling, A. (1964) The effect of amygdaloid lesions on feeding, grooming and reproduction in rats. *Acta Neuroveg.* 26:12–34.

Schwartz, N.B., & Rothchild, I. (1964) Changes in pituitary LH concentration during pseudopregnancy in the rat. *Proc. Soc. Exp. Biol. Med.* 116:107–110.

Schwartz, N.B. (1964) Acute effect of ovariectomy on pituitary LH, uterine weight and vaginal cornification. *Am. J. Physiol.* 207:1251–1259.

Rothchild, I., & **Schwartz, N.B.** (1965) The corpus-luteum-pituitary relationship: The effects of progesterone and estrogen on the secretion of luteotrophin and luteinizing hormone in the rat. *Acta Endocrin.* 49:120–137.

Lawton, T.E., & **Schwartz, N.B.** (1965) Effect of LH on ovarian ascorbic acid over a 24-hour period. *Endocrinology* 76:276–281.

Hoffmann, J.C., & **Schwartz, N.B.** (1965) Timing of post-partum ovulation in the rat. *Endocrinology* 76:620–626.

Hoffmann, J.C., & **Schwartz, N.B.** (1965) Timing of ovulation following progesterone withdrawal in the rat. *Endocrinology* 76:626–631.

Schwartz, N.B., & Calderelli, D. (1965) Plasma LH in cyclic female rats. *Proc. Soc. Exp. Biol. Med.* 119:16–20.

Lawton, T.E., & **Schwartz, N.B.** (1965) Pituitary LH content in rats exposed to continuous illumination. *Endocrinology* 77:1140–1142.

Schwartz, N.B., & Talley, W. (1965) Effect of acute ovariectomy on mating in the cyclic rat. *J. Reprod. Fert.* 10:463–466.

Orsini, M.W., & **Schwartz, N.B.** (1966) Pituitary LH content during the estrous cycle in female hamsters: Comparisons with males and cyclic females. *Endocrinology* 78:34–40.

Schwartz, N.B., & Hoffmann, J.C. (1966) A model for the control of the mammalian reproductive cycle. Symposium Paper. 2nd International Congress on Hormonal Steroids (Milan, 1966). *Excerpta Medica Int. Cong.*, No. 132, pp. 997–1003.

Schwartz, N.B., & Gold, J.J. (1967) Effect of a single dose of anti-LH-serum at proestrus on the rat estrous cycle. *Anat. Rec.* 157:137–149.

Lawton, I.E., & **Schwartz, N.B.** (1967) Pituitary-ovarian function in rats exposed to constant light: A chronological study. *Endocrinology* 81:497–508.

Schwartz, N.B., & Talley, W. (1968) Daily measurement of pituitary LH content during pregnancy in the rat. *J. Reprod. Fert.* 15:39–45.

Schwartz, N.B., & Lawton, I.E. (1968) Effects of barbiturate injection on the day before proestrus in the rat. *Neuroendocrinology* 3: 9–17.

Lawton, I.E., & **Schwartz, N.B.** (1968) A circadian rhythm of luteinizing hormone secretion in ovariectomized rats. *Am. J. Physiol.* 214:213–217.

Shirley, E., Wolinsky, J., & **Schwartz, N.B.** (1968) Effects of a single injection of an estrogen antagonist on the estrous cycle of the rat. *Endocrinology* 82:959–968.

McClintock, J.A., & **Schwartz, N.B.** (1968) Changes in pituitary and plasma follicle stimulating hormone concentrations during the rat estrous cycle. *Endocrinology* 83:433–441.

Brom, G., & **Schwartz, N.B.** (1968) Acute changes in the estrous cycle following ovariectomy in the golden hamster. *Neuroendocrinology* 3:366–377.

Schwartz, N.B. (1968) Newer concepts of gonadotrophin and steroid feedback mechanisms, pp. 35–50. In *Textbook of Gynecologic Endocrinology*. Edited by J.J. Gold. Hoeber Medical Division, Harper & Row. (3rd Edition, revised, 1980).

Schwartz, N.B., & Ely, C.A. (1968) Temporal dissection of pituitary and ovarian events in the rat estrous cycle, pp. 1005–1011. *Excerpta Medica* Symposium paper. 3rd Int. Cong. Endocrinol., Mexico City. New York: Raven Press.

Bingel, A.S., & **Schwartz, N.B.** (1969) Pituitary LH content, and reproductive tract changes during the mouse oestrous cycle. *J. Reprod. Fert.* 19:215–222.

Bingel, A.S., & **Schwartz, N.B.** (1969) The timing of LH release and ovulation in the cyclic mouse. *J. Reprod. Fert.* 19:223–229.

Bingel, A.S., & **Schwartz, N.B.** (1969) Timing of LH release and ovulation in the postpartum mouse. *J. Reprod. Fert.* 19:231–237.

Schwartz, N.B. (1969) Modeling and control in gonadal function, pp. 229–255. (Presented at the Conference on Hormonal Control Systems in Health and Disease, Rancho Santa Fe, California, 1967). Math. Biosc. Suppl.

Schwartz, N.B. (1969) A model for the control of the rat estrous cycle. *Transactions of the American Society for Mechanical Engineers*, 91:321–324.

Schwartz, N.B. (1969) A model for the regulation of ovulation in the rat. *Recent Progress in Hormone Research*, 25:1–55, 1969. (Gregory Pincus Memorial Lecture, Laurentian Hormone Conference, 1968).

1970–1979

Professor of Neuroendocrinology, Department of Psychiatry, University of Illinois College of Medicine, 1970–1972; Faculty award, 1971.

Endocrine Society, Vice-President, 1970–1971; Program Committee, 1972–1973; Ad Hoc Committee on Animal Experimentation, Chair, 1972–1974; Membership Committee, 1972–1977, Chair, 1976–1977; Council Member, 1979–1982; President-elect, 1981–1982; President, 1982–1983; Nominating Committee, 1997–1998; Awards Committee, 2000–2004; History Task Force, Chair, 2006–2009.

University of Illinois Medical School, Freshman medical class' "Golden Apple" teaching award, 1971.

Laurentian Hormone Conference, Committee on Arrangements, 1971–1992.

Association of Women in Science, Co-President, 1971–1972; President, 1972–1973; Fellow, 1996; Task Force on Relation of Foundation to Society, 2009.

Associate Editor, *Biology of Reproduction*, 1971–1974.

NIH 70–2307 Research Contract, "A Simultaneous Theoretical and Empirical Approach to the Study of the Rat Estrous Cycle," Principal Investigator, 1972–1974.

Endocrinology, Editorial Board, 1972–1976, 1977–1978, 1993–1998.

National Institute of Child Health and Human Development, Population Research and Training Committee , 1972–1976; Chair, 1975–1976; Board of Scientific Counselors , 1976–1980, 1989–1993; National Centers for Infertility Research (Michigan, Harvard), Steering Committee, Chair, 1992–1995.

Northwestern University Medical School, Professor of Physiology, 1973–1974.

Northwestern University Medical School, House Staff Review Committee, 1973–1974.

Ford Foundation Project, "A Review of Reproductive Biology and Contraceptive Development," Advisory Committee, 1973–1975.

Women in Endocrinology, founding member, 1974.

Northwestern University Deering Professor of Biological Sciences, 1974–1999; Chair, 1974–1978; fired, 1978. *Department changed name to Neurobiology and Physiology in 1978.

Formation of Program for Reproductive Sciences, 1974; established annual minisymposium, 1979.

Northwestern University Honorary Degrees Committee, 1975–1976.

Northwestern University College of Arts and Sciences Promotions Committee, 1975–1977; 1986–1989; 1993–1995).

National Research Council, Commission on Human Resources, Committee on Education and Employment of Women in Science and Engineering, 1975–1981; Committee on Continuity in Academic Performance, 1979–1981.

Northwestern Univ. Medical School, Pharmacology Search Committee, 1976.

NIH 5 R01 HD 10050 Research Grant, "The Role of the Environment in Reproductive Rhythms," Principal Investigator, 1976–1982.

Northwestern University Task Force in the Life Sciences, 1977–1978.

Northwestern Univ. Budget and Resources Advisory Committee, 1978–1981.

Northwestern University Reappointment, Promotion and Tenure Appeals Committee, 1978–1981.

National Institute of Health, Pituitary Task Force, Endocrinology, 1978–1980.

NIH T32–HD07068 Training Grant, "Training Program in Reproductive Biology, Preceptor, 1978–2004.

Publications:

Orsini, M.W., & **Schwartz, N.B.** (1970) Uterine weight and pituitary LH content in the pseudopregnant hamster. *J. Reprod. Fert.* 21:431–441.

Schwartz, N.B., & Ely, C.A. (1970) Comparison of effects of hypophysectomy, anti-serum to ovine LH, and ovariectomy on estrogen secretion during the rat estrous cycle. *Endocrinology* 86:1420–1435.

Schwartz, N.B. (1970) Cybernetics of mammalian reproduction, pp. 97–111. From the 21st Mosbach Colloq., Edited by Gibian and Plotz. New York: Springer-Verlag.

Schwartz, N.B., & Waltz, P. (1970) Role of ovulation in the regulation of the estrous cycle. *Fed. Proc.* 29:1907–1912.

Schwartz, N.B. (1970) Control of rhythmic secretion of gonadotrophins, pp. 515–528. In *The Hypothalamus.* Edited by L. Martini, M. Motta, & F. Fraschini. New York: Academic Press.

Nequin, L.G., & **Schwartz, N.B.** (1971) Adrenal participation in the timing of mating and LH release in the cyclic rat. *Endocrinology* 88:325–331.

Dupon, C., & **Schwartz, N.B.** (1971) Prepubertal pituitary LH patterns in normal and testosterone-sterilized rats. *Neuroendocrinology* 7:236–248.

Bogdanove, E.M., **Schwartz, N.B.**, Reichert, L.E., Jr., & Midgley, A.R., Jr. (1971) Comparisons of pituitary: Serum luteinizing hormone (LH) in the castrated rat by radioimmunoassay and OAAD bioassay. *Endocrinology* 88:644–652.

Ely, C.A., & **Schwartz, N.B.** (1971) Elucidation of the role of the luteinizing hormone in estrogen secretion and ovulation by use of antigonadotropic sera. *Endocrinology* 89:1103–1108.

Schwartz, N.B. (1971) Review of Bardwick's "Psychology of Women: A Study of Biocultural Conflicts." *J. Marriage and the Family*, August.

Rodgers, C.H., & **Schwartz, N.B.** (1972) Diencephalic regulation of plasma LH, ovulation and sexual behavior in the rat. *Endocrinology* 90:461–465.

Schwartz, N.B. (1972) Letter to the Editor. *Science.* 1 December, p 934.

Hoffmann, J.C., & **Schwartz, N.B.** (1972) Ovulation: Basic aspects. In *Reproductive Biology*, Balin & Glasser (eds.), *Excerpta Medica*, pp. 438–476.

Schwartz, N.B., & McCormack, C.E. (1972) Reproduction: Gonadal function and its regulation. *Ann. Rev. Physiol.* 34:425–472.

Orsini, M.W., & **Schwartz, N.B.** (1973) Organ weight changes and pituitary LH content during pregnancy and the early postpartum period in the hamster. *Biol. Reprod.* 8:515–522.

Beattie, C.W., Campbell, C.S., Nequin, L.G., Soyka, L.F., & **Schwartz, N.B.** (1973) Barbiturate blockade of tonic LH secretion in the male and female rat. *Endocrinology* 92:1634–1638.

Schwartz, N.B., Krone, K., Talley, W.L., & Ely, C.A. (1973) Administration of anti-serum to ovine FSH in the female rat: Failure to influence immediate events of the cycle. *Endocrinology* 92:1165–1174.

Beattie, C.W., & **Schwartz, N.B.** (1973) Blockade of the proestrous LH surge in cyclic rats by barbiturate administration on diestrus. *Proc. Soc. Exp. Biol. Med.* 142:933–935.

Rodgers, C.H. & **Schwartz, N.B.** (1973) Serum LH and FSH levels in mated and un-mated proestrous rats. *Endocrinology* 92:1475–1979.

Schwartz, N.B. (1973) Why women form their own professional organizations. *J. Am. Med. Women's Assoc.* 28:12–15.

Schwartz, N.B. (1973) Mechanisms controlling ovulation in small mammals, pp. 125–141. *Handbook of Physiology, Endocrinology Section: The Female Reproductive System.* Part I. Edited by R.O. Greep. Washington, D.C.: American Physiological Soc.

Schwartz, N.B., Cobbs, S.B., & Ely, C.A. (1973) What is the function(s) of the proestrous FSH surge in the rat? *Excerpta Medica* Symposium paper. 5th Int. Cong. Endocrinol. ICS No. 273, pp. 897–902.

Mann, B.G., Talley, W.L., Proudfit, C.M., & **Schwartz, N.B.** (1973/1974) Examination of pituitary and ovarian variables during a twenty-four hour period in rats after prolonged exposure to continuous light. *Neuroendocrinology* 13:139–150.

Proudfit, C.M., & **Schwartz, N.B.** (1974) Reversal of pentobarbital blockade of ovulation after cardiac puncture. *Endocrinology* 94:526–531.

Nequin, L.G., Talley, W.L., Mann, B.G., & **Schwartz, N.B.** (1974) Measurement of serum LH during the proestrous critical period in rats exhibiting four- or five-day cycles. *Neuroendocrinology* 14:65–714.

Rodgers, C.H., & **Schwartz, N.B.** (1974) The effect of mating on the afternoon of proestrus on serum LH (and FSH) and ovulation in the rat. *Proc. Soc. Exp. Biol. Med.* 147:148–150.

Schwartz, N.B., Anderson, C.H., Nequin, L.G., & Ely, C.A. (1974) Follicular maturation, pp. 367–381. In *The Control of Onset of Puberty.* Edited by Grumbach, Grave, & Mayer. New York: John Wiley & Sons.

Schwartz, N.B. (1974) The role of FSH and LH and of their antibodies on follicle growth and on ovulation Symposium. *Biol. Reprod.*, 10:236–272.

Rodgers, C.H., **Schwartz, N.B.**, & Nequin, L.G. (1974) Interaction between the ovarian and adrenocortical regulating systems: Occurrence of ovulation, pp. 241–252. In *Biological Rhythms in Neuroendocrine Activity.* Edited by M. Kawakami. Tokyo: Iagu Shoin Ltd.

Schwartz, N.B., & Ely, C.A. (1974) Role of gonadotrophins in ovulation, pp. 237, 252. In *Gonadotropins and Gonadal Function.* Edited by N.R. Moudgal. New York: Academic Press.

Schwartz, N.B., Cobbs, S.B., Talley, W.L., & Ely, C.A. (1975) Induction of ovulation by LH and FSH in the presence of anti-gonadotrophic sera. *Endocrinology* 96:1171–1178.

Nequin, L.G., Alvarez, J., & **Schwartz, N.B.** (1975) Steroid control of gonadotropin release. *J. Steroid Biochem,* 6:1007–1012.

Anderson, C.H., **Schwartz, N.B.**, Nequin, L.G., & Ely, C.A. (1976) Effects of early treatment with anti-serum to ovine FSH and LH on gonadal development in the rat. *Fert. Steril.* 27:47–58.

Balin, M.S., & **Schwartz, N.B.** (1976) Effects of mating on serum LH, FSH and prolactin and accessory tissue weight in male rats. *Endocrinology* 98:522–526.

Campbell, C.S., Ryan, K.D., & **Schwartz, N.B.** (1976) Estrous cycles in the mouse: Relative influence of continuous light and the presence of a male. *Biol. Reprod.* 14:292–299.

Rodgers, C.H., & **Schwartz, N.B.** (1976) Differentiation between neural and hormonal control of sexual behavior and gonadotrophin secretion in the female rat. *Endocrinology* 98:778–786.

Schwartz, N.B. (1976) Comment on "Brenner and de Kretzer's 'Contraceptives for Males.'" *Signs,* 2:247–248.

Moss, R.L., Dudley, C.A., & **Schwartz, N.B.** (1977) Coitus-induced release of luteinizing hormone in the proestrous rat: Fantasy or fact? *Endocrinology* 100:394–397.

Campbell, C.S., **Schwartz, N.B.**, & Firlit, M.G. (1977) The role of adrenal and ovarian steroids in the control of serum LH & FSH. *Endocrinology* 101:162–172.

Schwartz, N.B., & Justo, S.N. (1977) Acute changes in serum gonadotrophins and steroids following orchidectomy in the rat: Role of adrenal gland. *Endocrinology* 100:1550–1556.

Firlit, M.G., & **Schwartz, N.B.** (1977) Uncoupling of vaginal opening and the first ovulation—an indication of an alteration in the pituitary-gonadal axis. *Biol. Reprod.* 16:441–444.

Ryan, K.D., & **Schwartz, N.B.** (1977) Grouped female mice: Demonstration of pseudo-pregnancy. *Biol. Reprod.* 17:578–583.

Marder, M.L., Channing, C.P., & **Schwartz, N.B.** (1977) Suppression of serum follicle stimulating hormone in intact and acutely ovariectomized rats by porcine follicular fluid. *Endocrinology* 101:1639–1642.

Schwartz, N.B., & Channing, C.P. (1977) Evidence for ovarian "inhibin" suppression of the secondary rise in serum follicle stimulating hormone levels in proestrous rats by injection of porcine follicular fluid. *Proc. Nat. Acad. Science* 74:5721–5724.

Schwartz, N.B., Dierschke, D.J., McCormack, C.E., & Waltz, P.W. (1977) Feedback regulation of reproductive cycles in rats, sheep, monkeys and humans, with particular attention to computer modeling, pp. 55–89. In *Frontiers in Reproduction and Fertility Control.* Edited by Greep, Koblinsky, & Jaffe. Boston: MIT Press.

Campbell, C.S. & **Schwartz, N.B.** (1977) Steroid feedback regulation of luteinizing hormone and follicle stimulating hormone secretion rates in male and female rats. *J. Toxicol. Envir. Health*, 3:61–95.

Schwartz, N.B., & Talley, W.L. (1978) Effects of exogenous LH or FSH on endogenous FSH, progesterone and estradiol secretion. *Biol. Reprod.* 18:820–828.

Lorenzen, J.R., Channing, C.P., & **Schwartz, N.B.** (1978) Partial characterization of FSH-suppressing activity (folliculostatin) in porcine follicular fluid using the metestrous rat as an *in vivo* model. *Biol. Reprod.* 19:635–640.

Lorenzen, J.R., & **Schwartz, N.B.** (1978) The suppression of serum FSH by a non-steroidal factor from porcine follicles: Some properties of the inhibitor, pp. 339–353. In *Novel Aspects of Reproductive Physiology.* 7th Brook Lodge Workshop. Edited by Spilman & Wilks. New York: Spectrum Publications.

Nequin, L.G., Alvarez, J., & **Schwartz, N.B.** (1979) Measurement of serum steroid and gonadotrophin levels, and uterine and ovarian variables throughout the 4-day and 5-day estrous cycles in the rat. *Biol. Reprod.* 20:659–670.

Campbell, C.S., & **Schwartz, N.B.** (1979) Time course of serum FSH suppression in ovariectomized rats injected with porcine follicular fluid (folliculostatin): Effect of estradiol treatment. *Biol. Reprod.* 20:1093–1098.

Hoffmann, J.C., Lorenzen, J.R., Weil, T., & **Schwartz, N.B.** (1979) Selective suppression of the primary surge of follicle stimulating hormone in the rat: Further evidence for folliculostatin in porcine follicular fluid. *Endocrinology* 105:200–203.

Lagace, L., Labrie, F., Lorenzen, J.R., **Schwartz, N.B.**, & Channing, C.P. (1979) Selective inhibitory effect of porcine follicular fluid on FSH secretion in anterior pituitary cells in culture. *Clin. Endocrinol.* 10:401–406.

Lorenzen, J.R., & **Schwartz, N.B.** (1979) The differential ability of porcine follicular fluid to suppress serum FSH in female rats from 6 days of age to adulthood. *Ovarian Follicular and Corpus Luteum Function. Adv. Exp. Med. Biol.* 112:375–381.

1980–1989

NIH IR13–HD 14570 Research Grant, "Workshop on Physiologic Cessation of Ovarian Function," Principal Investigator, 1980–1981.

Northwestern University College of Arts and Sciences, Committee on Committees, 1980–1983.

Ford-Mellon-Rockefeller Program for Targeted Research in Reproduction, "Purification and Characterization of Folliculostatin,an Inhibitor of Gonadal Origin," Principal Investigator, 1981–1982.

Honorary Doctor of Science, Goucher College, 1982.

Northwestern University University Medical & Dental Schools, Provost's Committee to Study Tenure Policy, 1982–1983.

Endotronics, Inc., Scientific Advisory Board, 1982–1985.

National Hormone and Pituitary Program, Medical Advisory Board, 1983–1986.

Endocrine Society, Williams Service Award, 1985.

Office of Technology Assessment of the Congress of the United States, Advisory Panel, Reproductive Hazards in the Workplace, 1984–1985.

Mother died, 1985.

Friend, Rue Bucher, significant other, died, 1985.

Northwestern University Search Committee for Vice-President of Research, 1985–1986.

NIH Endocrinology Study Section 1985–1989

Northwestern University Research Policies Advisory Committee, 1986–1988.

Northwestern University Committee on Evanston Campus Life Science Development, 1986–1990.

NIH 2P01–HD21921 Program Project Research Grant, "Follicle Stimulating Hormone: Control and Action," 1986–2003; Director, 1986–1998.

Northwestern University Alumnae Award, 1987.

National Research Council, Commission on Life Sciences, Committee on Biological Markers, Reproductive and Developmental Toxicology Panel, Board on Environmental Studies and Toxicology, 1986–1987.

American Association for the Advancement of Science, Fellow, 1986; Executive Board, 1998–2002; Committee on Opportunities, 1998–2004.

Northwestern Center for Reproductive Science, Director, 1987–2003.

Northwestern Life Sciences Advisory Board, 1989–1992; Chair, 1995.

Publications:

Ryan, K.D., & **Schwartz, N.B.** (1980) Changes in serum hormone levels associated with male induced ovulation in group-housed female mice. *Endocrinology* 106:959–966.

Lorenzen, J.R., Schlepphorst, C., & **Schwartz, N.B.** (1980) The interaction of castration and adrenalectomy on pituitary responses to loss of target gland negative feedback in the male rat. *Endocrinology* 106:592–599.

Campbell, C.S., & **Schwartz, N.B.** (1980) The impact of constant light on the estrous cycle of the rat. *Endocrinology* 106:1230–1238.

Ramaley, J.A., & **Schwartz, N.B.** (1980) The pubertal process in the rat: The effect of chronic corticosterone treatment. *Neuroendocrinology* 30:213–219.

Savoy-Moore, R.T., **Schwartz, N.B.**, Duncan, J.A., & Marshall, J.C. (1980) Pituitary gonadotropin-releasing hormone receptors during the rat estrous cycle. *Science* 209:942–944.

Hoak, D., & **Schwartz, N.B.** (1980) Blockade of recruitment of ovarian follicles by suppression of the secondary surge of follicle stimulating hormone with folliculostatin. *Proc. Nat. Acad. Sciences* 77:4953–4956.

Savoy-Moore, R.T., & **Schwartz, N.B.** (1980) Differential control of FSH and LH secretion, pp. 203–248. In *Reproductive Physiology III*. Int. Rev. Physiol. Series. Edited by R.O. Greep., Baltimore, Md.: University Park Press.

Lorenzen, J.R., Dworkin, G.H., & **Schwartz, N.B.** (1981) Specific FSH suppression in the male rat by porcine follicular fluid. *Am. J. Physiol.* 240:E209–E215.

Savoy-Moore, R.T., **Schwartz, N.B.**, Duncan, J.A., & Marshall, J.C. (1981) Pituitary GnRH receptors on proestrus: Effect of pentobarbital blockade of ovulation in the rat. *Endocrinology* 109:1360–1364.

Summerville, J.W., & **Schwartz, N.B.** (1981) Suppression of serum gonadotropin levels by testosterone and porcine follicular fluid in castrate male rats. *Endocrinology* 109:1442–1447.

Schwartz, N.B. (1981) Inhibin (folliculostatin) in the female, pp. 139–146. In *Oligozoospermia: Recent Progress in Andrology*. Edited by G. Frajese, E.S.E. Hafez, C. Conti & A. Fabbrini. New York: Raven Press.

Grady, R.R., Savoy-Moore, R.T., & **Schwartz, N.B.** (1981) Selective suppression of follicle stimulating hormone by folliculostatin, a proposed ovarian hormone. In *Bioregulators of Reproduction*, pp. 359–369. Edited by G. Jagiello & H.J. Vogel. New York: Academic Press.

Grady, R.R., & **Schwartz, N.B.** (1981) Role of gonadal feedback in the differential regulation of LH and FSH in the rat. pp. 377–392. In *Intragonadal Regulators of Reproduction*. Edited by P. Franchimont & C.P. Channing. London: Academic Press.

Schwartz, N.B., & M. Hunzicker-Dunn, Eds. (1981) *Dynamics of Ovarian Function*. New York: Raven Press.

Childs, G.V., Ellison, D.G., Lorenzen, J.R., Collins, T.J., & **Schwartz, N.B.** (1982) Immunocytochemical studies of gonadotropin storage in developing castration cells. *Endocrinology* 111:1318–1328.

Schwartz, N.B. (1982) Role of ovarian inhibin (folliculostatin) in regulating FSH secretion in the female rat. In *Intra-Ovarian Control Mechanisms*, C.P. Channing & S. Segal (eds.), Plenum Press, pp. 15–36.

Schwartz, N.B. (1982) Novel peptides in ovarian follicular fluid: Implications for contraceptive development. *Research Frontiers in Fertility Regulation*, 2:2.

Grady, R.R., Charlesworth, M.C., & **Schwartz, N.B.** (1982) Characterization of the FSH-suppressing activity in follicular fluid, pp. 409–456. *Rec. Prog. Horm. Res.* Edited by R.O. Greep. New York: Academic Press.

Childs, G.V., Ellison, D.G., Lorenzen, J.R., Collins, T.J., & **Schwartz, N.B.** (1983) Retarded development of castration cells following adrenalectomy or sham adrenalectomy. *Endocrinology* 113:166–177.

Shih-Hoellwarth, A., Lee, C., & **Schwartz, N.B.** (1983) Endocrine consequences of portacaval anastomosis in female rats. *Am. J. Physiol.* 245:E288–E293.

Ringstrom, S., & **Schwartz, N.B.** (1983) Differential control of LH and FSH in male rats, pp. 171–181. *II Pan-American Congress of Andrology Symposium*, Mexico City, Mexico. New York: Raven Press.

Charlesworth, M.C., Grady, R.R., & **Schwartz, N.B.** (1983) The effect of GnRH on the specificity of gonadotropin response to follicular fluid *in vivo*, pp. 169–173. In *Factors Regulating Ovarian Function*. Edited by Greenwald & Terranova. New York: Raven Press.

Schwartz, N.B. (1983) Selective control of FSH secretion, pp. 193–213. In *Role of Peptides and Proteins in Control of Reproduction*. Edited by McCann & Dhindsa. Elsevier Press.

Charlesworth, M.C., Grady, R.R., Shin, L., Vale, W.W., Rivier, C., Rivier, J., & **Schwartz, N.B.** (1984) Differential suppression of FSH and LH secretion by follicular fluid in the presence or absence of GnRH. *Neuroendocrinology* 38:199–205.

Ringstrom, S.J., & **Schwartz, N.B.** (1984) Examination of prolactin and pituitary adrenal axis components as intervening variables in the adrenalectomy-induced inhibition of gonadotropin response to castration. *Endocrinology* 114:880–887.

Jorgenson, K.L., & **Schwartz, N.B.** (1984) The effect of steroid treatment on tonic and surge secretion of LH and FSH in the female golden hamster: Effect of photoperiod. *Neuroendocrinology* 39:549–554.

Schwartz, N.B. (1984) Endocrinology as paradigm, endocrinology as authority. Presidential Address of the Endocrine Society 65th Annual Meeting. *Endocrinology* 114:308–313.

Suter, D.E., Goldberg, E., Wheat, T.E., Bahr, J.M., Dzuik, P.J., & **Schwartz, N.B.** (1984) FolliculostatIn biochemical studies and quantitation in porcine follicular fluid, pp. 97–110. In *Gonadal Proteins and Peptides and Their Biological Significance*. Edited by Sairam & Atkinson. World Scientific Publ. Co., Singapore.

Charlesworth, C., & **Schwartz, N.B.** (1984) Novel peptides in human follicular fluid: Contraceptive implications, pp. 77–88. In 5th International Meeting on Fertility Control, Genoa, Italy, March 1–3, 1984. Edited by Sciarra, Pescetto, Martini, De Cecco. Monduzzi Editore, Bologna, Italy.

Grady, R.R., Shin, L., Charlesworth, M.C., Cohen-Becker, I.R., Smith, M., Rivier, C., Rivier, J., Vale, W.W., & **Schwartz, N.B.** (1985) Differential suppression of follicle stimulating hormone and luteinizing hormone secretion *in vivo* by a gonadotropin releasing hormone antagonist. *Neuroendocrinology* 40:246–252.

Schwartz, N.B., Rivier, C., Rivier, J., & Vale, W.W. (1985) Effect of gonadotropin-
-releasing-hormone antagonists on serum follicle stimulating hormone and
luteinizing hormone under conditions of singular follicle stimulating
hormone secretion. *Biol. Reprod.* 32:391–398.

Jorgenson, K.L., & **Schwartz, N.B.** (1985) Shifts in gonadotropin and steroid levels
that precede anestrus in female golden hamsters exposed to a short
photoperiod. *Biol. Reprod.* 32:611–618.

Ringstrom, S., & **Schwartz, N.B.** (1985) Cortisol suppresses the LH, but not the FSH,
response to gonadotropin-releasing hormone after orchidectomy. *Endocrinology*
116:472–474.

Suter, D.E., & **Schwartz, N.B.** (1985) Effects of glucocorticoids on secretion of
luteinizing hormone and follicle-stimulating hormone by female rat pituitary
cells *in vitro. Endocrinology* 117:849854.

Suter, D.E., & **Schwartz, N.B.** (1985) Effects of glucocorticoids on responsiveness of
luteinizing hormone and follicle-stimulating hormone to gonadotropin-releasing
hormone by male rat pituitary cells *in vitro. Endocrinology* 117:855–859.

Charlesworth, M.C., & **Schwartz, N.B.** (1986) Estrogen inhibition of LH and FSH secretion: Effects of a GnRH antagonist. *Am. J. Physiol. (E & M)* 250:E341–E345.

Savoy-Moore, R.T., Grady, R.R., & **Schwartz, N.B.** (1986) Detection of folliculostatin: A
sensitive & specific bioassay using the female rat. *Life Science* 38:1281–1288.

Suter, D.E., J.M. Bahr, P.J. Dziuk & **Schwartz, N.B.** (1986) Effect of stage of the porcine
estrous cycle and method of collection on folliculostatin in porcine follicular
fluid. *Animal Reprod. Sci.* 11:43–49.

Dalterio, S.L., Suter, D.E., **Schwartz, N.B.**, Mayfield, D., & Rettori, V.B. (1986) Differential effects of follicle-stimulating and luteinizing hormones on testosterone
production by mouse testes. *J. Steroid Biochem.* 25:149–156.

Schwartz, N.B. (1986) Mechanisms of Stress-inhibition of reproduction: An endocrinological inquiry at many levels, pp. 128–142. In *III. Bi-National Colloquium for
Humboldt Awardees.* Edited by H. Hanle. Alexander von-Humboldt Foundation, Bonn, W. Germany.

Jorgenson, K.L., & **Schwartz, N.B.** (1987) Dynamic pituitary & ovarian changes occurring during the anestrus to estrus transition in the golden hamster.
Endocrinology 120:34–42.

Kartun, K., & **Schwartz, N.B.** (1987) Effects of a potent antagonist to gonadotropin-
releasing hormone on male rats: Luteinizing hormone is suppressed more
than follicle stimulating hormone. *Biol. Reprod.* 36:103–108.

Hiatt, E.S., Valadka, R.J., & **Schwartz, N.B.** (1987) Sex differences following
gonadectomy in basal gonadotropin secretion rate of rat pituitary fragments
in vitro. Biol. Reprod. 37:1114–1129.

Schwartz, N.B., Milette, J.J., & Cohen, I.R. (1987) Animal models which
demonstrate divergence in secretion or storage of FSH and LH, pp. 239–
252. In *InhibIn Non-Steroid Regulation of FSH Secretion.* Symposia
Publications. Volume 42. Edited by H.G. Burger, D.M. deKretser, J.K.
Findlay, & M. Igarashi Serono. New York: Raven Press.

Waites, G.M.H., Bialy, G., Gordon, W.L., Findlay, J.K., de Jong, F.H., Robertson, D.M.,
Schwartz, N.B., & P.L. Storring. (1987) International research standard for
inhibin, pp. 281–287. In *InhibIn Non- Steroidal Regulation of FSH Secretion.*
Serono Symposia Publications. Volume 42. Edited by H.G. Burger, D.M.
deKretser, J.K. Findlay & M. Igarashi. New York: Raven Press.

Ringstrom, S.J., & **Schwartz, N.B.** (1987) Differential effect of glucocorticoids on synthesis and secretion of luteinizing hormone (LH) and follicle stimulating hormone (FSH). *J. Steroid Biochem.* 27:625–630.

Woodruff, T.K., D'Agostino, J.B., **Schwartz, N.B.**, & Mayo, K.E. (1988) Dynamic changes in inhibin mRNAs in rat ovarian follicles during the reproductive cycle. *Science* 239:1296–1299.

Milette, J.J., **Schwartz, N.B.**, & Turek, F.W. (1988) The importance of follicle stimulating hormone in the initiation of testicular growth in photostimulated Djungarian hamsters. *Endocrinology*, 122:1060–1066.

Suter, D.E., **Schwartz, N.B.**, & Ringstrom, S.J. (1988) Dual role of glucocorticoids in regulation of pituitary content and secretion of gonadotropins. *Am. J. Physiol.*, 254:E595–599.

Spitzbarth, T.L., Horton, T.H., Lifka, J., & **Schwartz, N.B.** (1988) Pituitary gonadotropin content in gonadectomized rats: Immunoassay measurements influenced by extraction solvent and testosterone replacement. *J. Androl.*, 9:294–304.

D'Agostino, J.B., Woodruff, T.K., Mayo, K.E., & **Schwartz, N.B.** (1989) Unilateral ovariectomy increases inhibin mRNA levels in newly recruited follicles. *Endocrinology*, 124:310–317.

Woodruff, T.K., D'Agostino, J., **Schwartz, N.B.**, & Mayo, K.E. (1989) Decreased inhibin gene expression in pre-ovulatory follicles requires the primary gonadotropin surges. *Endocrinology*, 124:2193–2199.

Fallest, P.C., Hiatt, E.S., & **Schwartz, N.B.** (1989) Effects of gonadectomy on the *in vitro* and *in vivo* gonadotropin responses to GnRH in female and male rats. *Endocrinology*, 124:1370–1379.

Hiatt, E.S., & **Schwartz, N.B.** (1989) Suppression of basal and GnRH-stimulated gonadotropin secretion rate *in vitro* by GnRH antagonist. Differential effects on metestrous and proestrous pituitaries. *Neuroendocrinology*, 50:158–164.

1990–1999

Jack Gorski Lab, Departments of Animal Sciences and Biochemistry, Madison, Wisconsin, Sabbatical, 1990.

Institute of Medicine, Committee on Oral Contraceptives and Breast Cancer, 1990; Workshop on Contraceptive Research and Development and the Frontiers of Contemporary Science, 1994–1995.

Northwestern Univ. Program Review Council, 1990–1994; Chair, 1993–1994.

Society for the Study of Reproduction, Carl Hartman Award, 1992.

American Academy of Arts and Sciences, Member, 1992.

World Book Science Annual, Advisory Board, 1996–1999.

American Menopause Foundation, Advisory Board, 1997–1999.

Stevenson Lecture Award, University of Western Ontario, 1994.

Geschwind Memorial Lecture, University of California, Davis, 1994.

Nalbandov Memorial Lecture, University of Illinois, Champaign-Urbana, 1994.

Northwestern University Task Force Concerning Women in the Academic Workplace, 1994–1995.

Northwestern University Excellence in Teaching Award, 1995.

Father died, 1995.

Nothwestern University Faculty Honors Committee, 1995–2000.

CAS, Northwestern University, Acting Dean, 1996–1997.

NIH P30 Research Grant, Center for Research on Fertility and Infertility, "Hormone and Neurotransmitter Measurement Core," Director, 1996–2001.

Northwestern University Faculty Women Award, 1997.

Women in Endocrinology Mentor Award, 1997.

Endocrine Society, Distinguished Educator Award, 1998

Northwestern University William Deering Professor Emerita of Biological Sciences, 1999.

Publications:

Ackland, J.F., D'Agostino, J.B., Ringstrom, S.J., Hostetler, J.P., Mann, B.G., & **Schwartz, N.B.** (1990) Circulating radioimmunoassayable inhibin during periods of transient FSH rise: Secondary surge and unilateral ovariectomy. *Biology of Reproduction*, 43:347–352.

D'Agostino, J.B., Valadka, R.J., & **Schwartz, N.B.** (1990) Differential effects of *in vitro* glucocorticoids on LH and FSH secretion: dependence on sex of pituitary donor. *Endocrinology*, 127:891–899.

Fallest, P.C., & **Schwartz, N.B.** (1990) Pituitary LH and FSH responses to GnRH during the rat estrous cycle: an increased ratio of FSH:LH is secreted during the secondary FSH surge. *Biology of Reproduction*, 43:977–985.

Hollingsworth, D., Hotchkiss, J., Kaplan, S.L., Koppelman, M.C., Nikitovitch-Winer, M.B., Richards, G.E., Rosemberg, E., **Schwartz, N.B.**, Turgeon, J.L., & Wise, P.M. (1990) The contraception/abortion issue: should we get involved? *Endocrinology* 127:1559–1560.

Fallest, P.C., & **Schwartz, N.B.** (1991) Acute inhibitory effects of 17ß-estradiol are observed on gonadotropin secretion from perifused pituitary fragments of metestrous but not proestrous rats. *Endocrinology*, 128:273–279.

Woodruff, T.K., Ackland, J.F., Rahal, J.O., **Schwartz, N.B.**, & Mayo, K.E. (1991) Expression of ovarian inhibin during pregnancy in the rat. *Endocrinology*, 128:1647–1654.

Ackland, J.F., & **Schwartz, N.B.** (1991) Changes in immunoreactive inhibin and FSH during gonadal development in the rat. *Biol. Reprod.*, 45:295–300.

Jetton, A.E., Fallest, P.C., Dahl, K.D., **Schwartz, N.B.**, & Turek, F.W. (1991) Photoperiodic differences in *in vitro* pituitary gonadotropin basal secretion and GnRH responsiveness in the golden hamster. *Endocrinology*, 129:1025–1032.

Luderer, U., & **Schwartz, N.B.** (1991) Sex differences in acute LH responses to gonadectomy remain after progesterone antagonist and dopamine agonist treatment. *Biology of Reproduction*, 45:918–926.

Ringstrom, S.J., McAndrews, J.M., Rahal, J.O., & **Schwartz, N.B.** (1991) Cortisol *in vivo* increases FSHB mRNA selectively in pituitaries of male rats. *Endocrinology*, 129:2793–2795.

Schwartz, N.B. (1991) Remembrance: Why I was told not to study inhibin and what I did about it. *Endocrinology*, 129:1690–1691.

Knox, K.L., & **Schwartz, N.B.** (1992) RU486 blocks the secondary surge of FSH in the rat without blocking the drop in serum inhibin. *Biology of Reproduction*, 46:220–225.

Ringstrom, S.J., Suter, D.E., Hostetler, J.P., & **Schwartz, N.B.** (1992) Cortisol regulates secretion and pituitary content of the two gonadotropins differentially in female rats: effects of GnRH antagonist. *Endocrinology*, 130:3122–3128.

Kirby, J.D., Jetton, A.E., Cooke, P.S., Hess, R.A., Bunick, D., Ackland, J.F., Turek, F.W., & **Schwartz, N.B.** (1992) Developmental hormonal profiles accompanying the neonatal hypothyroidism induced increase in adult testis size and sperm production in the rat. *Endocrinology* 131:559–565.

Woodruff, T.K., D'Agostino, J., **Schwartz, N.B.**, & Mayo, K.E. (1992) Modulation of rat inhibin mRNAs in pre-ovulatory and atretic follicles. VIIth Ovary Workshop Proceedings, Paracrine Communications in the Ovary, Plenum Press, pp. 291–295.

Ringstrom, S.J., Suter, D., D'Agostino, J., Hostetler, J.P., & **Schwartz, N.B.** (1992) Effects of glucocorticoids on the hypothalamic-pituitary-gonadal axis. *Proceedings of the International Congress on Stress and Related Disorders, Modena, Italy.* Parthenon Publishing, pp. 297–305.

Luderer, U., & **Schwartz, N.B.** (1992) Regulation and actions of FSH, pp 1–28. In Hunzicker-Dunn M, Schwartz NB, Eds. *Follicle-Stimulating Hormone: Regulation of Secretion and Molecular Mechanisms of Action.* Serono Symposia USA. New York: Springer-Verlag.

Turek, F.W., & **Schwartz, N.B.** (1992) Photoperiodic control of reproduction in male hamsters: role of FSH in early stages of photostimulation, pp. 83–94. In *Follicle-Stimulating Hormone: Regulation of Secretion and Molecular Mechanisms of Action.* Edited by M. Hunzicker-Dunn & N.B. Schwartz. Serono Symposia USA. Serono Symposia, USA.

Hunzicker-Dunn, M., & **Schwartz, N.B.**, Eds. (1992) *Follicle-Stimulating Hormone: Regulation of Secretion and Molecular Mechanisms of Action.* Serono Symposia USA. New York: Springer-Verlag.

Ackland, J.F., **Schwartz, N.B.**, Mayo, K.E., & Dodson, R.E. (1992) Nonsteroidal signals originating in the gonads. *Physiological Reviews*, 72:731–787.

Knox, K.L., & **Schwartz, N.B.** (1993) Pituitary in vitro LH and FSH secretion after administration of the anti-progesterone RU486 in vivo. In *Recent Progress in Hormone Research*, 48:523–530.

Strobl, F.J., Luderer, U., Besecke, L., Wolfe, A., **Schwartz, N.B.**, & Levine, J.E. (1993) Differential gonadotropin responses to N-methyl-D,L aspartate in intact and castrate male rats. *Biology of Reproduction* 48:867–873.

Luderer, U., Strobl, F.J., Levine, J.E., & **Schwartz, N.B.** (1993) Differential gonadotropin responses to N-methyl-D,L aspartate in metestrous, proestrous and ovariectomized rats. *Biology of Reproduction* 48:857–8663.

Knox, K.L., Ringstrom, S.J., & **Schwartz, N.B.** (1993) RU486 blocks effects of inhibin antiserum or luteinizing hormone on the secondary FSH surge. *Endocrinology* 133:277–283.

Kirby, J.D., Jetton, A.E., Ackland, J.F., Turek, F.W., & **Schwartz, N.B.** (1993) Changes in serum immunoreactive inhibin-α during photoperiod-induced testicular regression and recrudescence in the golden hamster. *Biology of Reproduction* 49:483–488.

Bauer-Dantoin, A.C., Knox, K.L., **Schwartz, N.B.**, & J.E. Levine. (1993) Estrous cycle state-dependent effects of neuropeptide Y (NPY) on LHRH-stimulated LH and FSH secretion from anterior pituitary fragments *in vitro*. *Endocrinology* 133:2413–2417.

Ackland, J.F., Mann, B.G., & **Schwartz, N.B.** (1993) Release of immunoreactive inhibin from perifused rat ovaries: effects of forskolin and gonadotropins during the estrous cycle. In *Recent Progress in Hormone Research*, 48:531–537.

McAndrews, J.M., Ringstrom, S.J., Dahl, K.D., & **Schwartz, N.B.** (1994) Corticosterone *in vivo* increases pituitary FSHß mRNA Content and Serum FSH bioactivity selectively in female rats. *Endocrinology* 134:158–163.

Luderer, U., & **Schwartz, N.B.** (1994) Acute changes in pulsatile LH and FSH secretion after ovariectomy in rats: suppression of LH, but not FSH, by treatment with oestradiol for at least 48 h. *Journal of Reproduction & Fertility* 100(2):613–621.

Jetton, A.E., Turek, F.W., & **Schwartz, N.B.** (1994) The effects of melatonin and time of day on *in vitro* pituitary gonadotropin basal secretion and GnRH responsiveness in the male golden hamster. *Neuroendocrinology*, 60:527–534.

Ackland, J.F., Knox, K.L., Elskus, A.A., Fallest, P.C., Hiatt, E.S., & **Schwartz, N.B.** (1994) Use of an *in vitro* perifusion system to study the effects of pulsatile hormone administration on the control of the hypothalamic-pituitary-ovarian axis, pp 466–487. In *Methods in Neurosciences*: Pulsatility in Neuroendocrine Systems. Volume 20. Edited by J.E. Levine. San Diego: Academic Press.

McAndrews, J.M., Ringstrom, S.J., Dahl, K.D., & **Schwartz, N.B.** (1995) Effects of corticosterone and testosterone on pituitary gonadotropin content, secretion, bioactivity and messenger RNA levels in the presence or absence of GnRH in male rats. *Endocrine*, 3:13–20.

Knox, K.L., Bauer-Dantoin, A.C., Levine, J.E., & **Schwartz, N.B.** (1995) Unmasking of Neuropeptide-Y inhibitory effects on in vitro gonadotropin secretion from pituitaries of metestrous, but not proestrous, rats. *Endocrinology*, 136:187–194.

Elskus, A.A., Phelps, A.F., & **Schwartz, N.B.** (1995) Acute sex differences in serum LH levels in gonadectomized rats: investigation of pituitary response to GnRH pulse frequency and prolactin secretion as etiological agents. *Neuroendocrinology*, 61:301–309.

Aloi, J.A., Dalkin, A.C., **Schwartz, N.B.**, Yasin, M., Mann, B., Haisenleder, D.J., & Marshall, J.C. (1995) Ovarian inhibin subunit gene expression: regulation by gonadotropins and estradiol. *Endocrinology* 136: 1227–1232.

Elskus, A.A., & **Schwartz, N.B.** (1995) Pituitary and hypothalamic regulation of sex differences in serum-luteinizing hormone levels in gonadectomized rats: in virto perifusion studies, pp 397–401. In *Recent Progress in Hormone Research*. Volume 50. New York: Academic Press.

Lobotsky, J., & **Schwartz, N.B.** (1995) Channing, Cornelia P. (biosketch), pp.86–87. In *Zur Geschichte der Endokrinologies und Reproduktions-medizin*. Edited by G. Bettendorff.

Schwartz, N.B. (1995) Schwartz, Neena B. (biosketch), pp. 502–504. In *Zur Geschichte der Endokrinologies und Reproduktions-medizin*. Edited by G. Bettendorft.

Schwartz, N.B. (1995) Follicle stimulating hormone and luteinizing hormone: a tale of two gonadotropins. *Can. J. Physiol. Pharmacol.*, 73(6):675–684.

Szabo, M., Knox, K.L., Ringstrom, S.J., Perlyn, C.A., Sutandi, S., & **Schwartz, N.B.** (1996) Mechanism of the inhibitory action of RU486 on the secondary follicle-stimulating hormone surge. *Endocrinology*, 137:85–89.

Knox, K.L., Ringstrom, S.J., Szabo, M., Perlyn, C.A., Sutandi, S., & **Schwartz, N.B.** (1996) RU486 on an estrogen background blocks the rise in serum follicle-stimulating hormone induced by antiserum follicle-stimulating hormone induced by antiserum to inhibin or ovariectomy. *Endocrinology*, 137:1226–1232.

Kilen, S.M., Szabo, M., Strasser, G.A., McAndrews, J.M., Ringstrom, S.J., & **Schwartz, N.B.** (1996) Corticosterone selectively increases FSHß subunit in primary anterior pituitary cell culture without affecting its half-life. *Endocrinology* 137:3802–3807.

Woodruff, T.K., Besecke, L.M., Groome, N., Draper, L.B., **Schwartz, N.B.**, & Weiss, J. (1996) Inhibin A and inhibin B are inversely correlated to follicle-stimulating homone, yet are discordant during the follicular phase of the rat estrous cycle, and inhibin A is expressed in a sexually dimorphic manner. *Endocrinology*, 137:5463–5467.

Ringstrom, S.J., Szabo, M., Kilen, S.M., Saberi, S., Knox, K.L., & **Schwartz, N.B.** (1997) The antiprogestins RU486 and ZK98299 affect follicle-stimulating hormone secretion differentially on estrus, but not on proestrus, *Endocrinology*, 138:2286–2290.

Szabo, M., Kilen, S.M., Saberi, S., Ringstrom, S.J., & **Schwartz, N.B.** (1998) Antiprogestins suppress basal and activin-stimulated follicle-stimulating hormone secretion in an estrogen-dependent manner. *Endocrinology* 139:2223–2228.

Schwartz, N.B., Szabo, M., Verina, T., Wei, J.J., Dlouhy, S., Won, L., Heller A., Hodes, M.E., & Ghetti, B. (1998) The hypothalamic-pituitary-gonadal-axis in the mutant weaver mouse. *Neuroendocrinology*, 68:374–385.

Schwartz, N.B. (1999) Gonadotropins, pp 837–839. In *The Encyclopedia of Neuroscience,* 2nd Edition (*Article on CD-ROM*). Edited by G. Adelman & B.H. Smith. Amsterdam: Elsevier Science.

Kilen, S.M., & **Schwartz, N.B.** (1999) Estrous cycle, pp. 127–136. In *Encyclopedia of Reproduction.* Volume 2. Edited by E. Knobil & J.D. Neill. San Diego: Academic Press.

Schwartz, N.B. (1999) Neuroendocrine regulation of reproductive cyclicity, pp. 135–145. In *Neuroendocrinology in Physiology and Medicine.* Edited by P.M. Conn & M.E. Freeman. Totowa, N.J.: Humana Press Inc.

2000–present

Rush Medical School, Chicago, Illinois, Workshop on Teaching of Physiology, Lecture: Sex Difference in Gonadal Negative Feedback: Science and Sound Bites, 16 September, 2000.

St. Louis University, St. Louis, Missouri, Women and Gender in Science, Medicine, and Technology, Lecture: My Career in Science, 13 October 2000.

Goucher College Visiting Committee, 2000–2009.

American Physiological Society Symposium on the Mentoring Process; Federation of American Societies for Experimental Biology, New Orleans, Louisiana, Lecture: How to Become a Good Mentor/ Mentee, April 2002.

Fourteenth Ovarian Workshop, Baltimore, Maryland, Keynote Speaker, Lecture: Greatest Discoveries of the Ovary/The Illegitimacy of Our Science, 25 July 2002.

Department of Health and Human Services Peer Review Panel, Toxicology
Profile for Methoxychlor, 2002.

Northwestern University Specialized Center of Research Advisory Committee, Chair (Andrea Dunaif, Principal Investigator), 2002–2010.

American Association for the Advancement of Science, Lifetime Mentor
Award, 2003.

University of Maryland Medical School, BIRCH Grant, External Advisory
Board, 2003–2010.

Northwestern University College of Medicine Alumni Award, 2004.

Feinberg School of Medicine, Northwestern University, Chicago. Illinois, Annual Distinguished Women in Medicine and Science Lecture, Lecture: Why
I Was Told Not to Study Inhibin, and What I Did About It, 21 April 2004.

Cornell University, Ithaca, New York, 2005 Sidney A. Asdell Lecture: Greatest Discoveries of the Ovary/The Illegitimacy of Our Science, 28 September 2005.

Northwestern University U54 Advisory Committee, Chair (Teresa K. Woodruff, Principal Investigator), 2005–2010.

Frontiers in Reproduction Pioneer Award, 2007.

Marine Biological Laboratory, Pioneer Lecture, Woods Hole, Massachusetts,
Lecture: A Lab of Her Own: Catching Up With the Boys, June 2007.

Endocrine Society History Task Force, Oral History, Video Interview, 2008.

Endocrine Society Annual Meeting, San Francisco, California, Clark Sawin
Memorial Lecture: A Lab of Our Own: Historical Perspectives on the Contribution of Women in Endocrinology, June 2008.

Junior Science Café, Evanston, Illinois, Lecture: Hormones, Dwarfs and Giants,
8 November, 2008.

Federation of American Societies for Experimental Biology, Excellence in
Science Committee, 2008–2011.

Publications:

Szabo, M., Kilen, S.M., Nho, J., & **Schwartz, N.B.** (2000) Progesterone receptor A
and B messenger ribonucleic acid levels in the anterior pituitary of rats are
regulated by estrogen. *Biol. Reprod.,* 62:95–102.

Bohnsack, B.L., Kilen, S.M., Tam, D.H.Y., & **Schwartz, N.B.** (2000) Follistatin
suppresses steroid-enhanced follicle-stimulating hormone release in vitro.
Biol. Reprod., 62:636–641.

Hood, S.C.H., & **Schwartz, N.B.** (2000) Sex difference in serum luteinizing hormone
postgonadectomy in the rat. *Endocrine,* 12:35–40.

Schwartz, N.B. (2001) Perspective: reproductive endocrinology and human health in
the 20th century: A personal retrospective. *Endocrinology* 142:2163–2166.

Foeking, E.M., Szabo, M., **Schwartz, N.B.,** & Levine, J.E. (2005) Neuroendocrine
consequences of prenatal androgen exposure in the female rat: absence of

LH surges, suppression of progesterone receptor gene expression, and acceleration of the GNRH pulse generator. *Biol. Reprod.* 72:1475–1483.

Schwartz, N.B. (2005) Reproduction and Fertility. In *Endocrinology: Basic and Clinical Principles.* 2nd Edition. Edited by Melmed & Conn. Totowa, N.J.: Humana Press.

Schwartz, N.B., & Levine, J. (2006) Ontogeny of gonadotropin-releasing hormone neurons: fishing for clues in Medaka. Endocrinology 147:1074–1075.

Schwartz, N.B. (2008) A lab of our own: historical perspectives on the contribution of women to endocrinology. Clark T. Sawin Memorial Lecture. *Endocrine News* (August), pp. 38–40.

Schwartz, N.B. (2008) Genes, Hormones and Sexuality. *Harvard Gay and Lesbian Review.* January.

Recorder concert at Music Institute of Chicago, 2008; L-R: Lise Weisberger, Neena, Kate Todd, Paloma Larramendi, Patrick O'Malley, Instructor

Appendix A

THE ENVIRONMENT/BRAIN/PITUITARY/ TARGET GLAND AXIS

This figure summarizes the cascade of signals linking the environment, acting through our sense organs, to the target cells in the body which regulate growth, sexual activity, and metabolism.

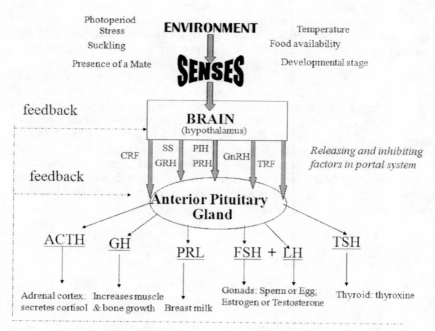

Figure App. 1. Cascade of signals linking the environment to the anterior pituitary gland and the pituitary gland to the rest of the body.

Specific cells in the hypothalamus respond to incoming impulses from the sense organs and to feedback information from hormones. These cells secrete specific releasing and inhibiting factors into the portal system, which flows directly to the anterior pituitary gland. Specific cells within the anterior pituitary gland have receptors to these factors and release their hormones (ACTH, GH, PRL, FSH, LH, and TSH) into the bloodstream where they are exposed to every cell in the body.

Releasing and inhibiting factors (small peptides): CRF = corticotrophin releasing factor, causes ACTH secretion. GRH = growth hormone releasing factor. SS = somatostatin or growth hormone inhibiting factor. PIH = prolactin inhibiting factor (dopamine is one such factor). PRH = prolactin releasing hormone. GnRH = gonadotropin releasing hormone acts on the gonadotrope cells to trigger secretion of LH and FSH. TRF = TSH releasing factor.

Anterior Pituitary Hormones (large proteins): ACTH = adrenocorticotropic hormone acts on the adrenal cortex cells to cause secretion of cortisol. GH = growth hormone which acts on muscle and bones to induce growth. PRL = prolactin, which acts on mammary tissue to induce milk synthesis. FSH and LH = follicle stimulating hormone and luteinizing hormone act on the ovaries and testes to cause sperm and egg maturation and steroid (estrogen, progesterone, testosterone) secretion. TSH = thyroid stimulating hormone which acts on the thyroid gland to cause secretion of thyroxin and triiodothyronine.

Feedback: Cortisol can act at the level of the brain or the pituitary cells to suppress CRF or ACTH secretion. Amino acids, which are synthesized into proteins under the influence of GH, can act as feedback signals to the brain altering GRH and SS secretion. Estrogen acts at the hypothalamus to elicit GnRH secretion midcycle to elicit the preovulatory LH secretion. Progesterone in steady high doses feeds back on the brain to suppress GnRH. All three steroids act at the brain and pituitary to suppress LH secretion. Testosterone can act at the pituitary level to enhance FSH secretion. It should also be remembered that the sex steroids act at brain sites other than the hypothalamus to influence behavior and affect.

ABOUT THE AUTHOR

NEENA B. SCHWARTZ was an honors graduate (AB) of Goucher College in Baltimore, Maryland. She earned the MS and PhD in Physiology from Northwestern University (1950 and 1953 respectively). Although awarded a United States Public Health Service postdoctoral fellowship in 1952, she chose not to activate it, instead taking a position as an instructor and assistant professor in Physiology at the University Of Illinois College Of Medicine in Chicago for four years. She was then Director of the Biological Laboratories at Michael Reese Hospital Institute for Psychosomatic and Psychiatric Research and Training (1957–1961), after which she returned to the University of Illinois as Associate Professor of Physiology. She remained there until 1972, rising to full professor of Physiology in 1967 and serving as Assistant Dean of Faculty Affairs for three years. In 1973, Schwartz moved to the Northwestern University Medical School. In 1974, she was named Deering Professor of Biological Sciences in the College of Arts and Sciences, and served as Department Chair from 1974 to 1978. She served for seven years as Director of the Program for Reproductive Research, and in 1987 became Director of the Center for Reproductive Science at Northwestern. NIH funded her research on the factors that establish reproductive cycles in mammals, including the role of ovarian inhibin, for more than forthy years. She served on several research committees at the NIH, and has been on numerous national study boards and government advisory panels concerned with public health or research policy, including those of the National Research Council and the National Science Foundation. She has served on the editorial boards of Endocrinology and Biology of Reproduction and was President of the Society for the Study of Reproduction and of the Endocrine Society.

NAME INDEX

SUBJECT INDEX

Woman: Intimate Geography (Angier), 214
Women in Endocrinology (WE), 116–
    120, 217, 221, 224, 223, 229,
    233, 249
Women in Science, 113, 195
Women's Equity Action League, 111

"Writing the Past, Claiming the Future," 195
Xq28, 209, 210

Yiddish, 17, 18, 23, 151, 183–185, 248
Young Women's Hebrew Association
    (YWHA), 26

VIBS

The **Value Inquiry Book Series** is co-sponsored by:

Titles Published

188.   Gail M. Presbey, Editor, *Philosophical Perspectives on the "War on Terrorism."* A volume in **Philosophy of Peace**

189.   María Luisa Femenías, Amy A. Oliver, Editors, *Feminist Philosophy in Latin America and Spain.* A volume in **Philosophy in Latin America**

190.   Oscar Vilarroya and Francesc Forn I Argimon, Editors, *Social Brain Matters: Stances on the Neurobiology of Social Cognition.* A volume in **Cognitive Science**

191.   Eugenio Garin, *History of Italian Philosophy.* Translated from Italian and Edited by Giorgio Pinton. A volume in **Values in Italian Philosophy**

192.   Michael Taylor, Helmut Schreier, and Paulo Ghiraldelli, Jr., Editors, *Pragmatism, Education, and Children: International Philosophical Perspectives.* A volume in **Pragmatism and Values**

193.   Brendan Sweetman, *The Vision of Gabriel Marcel: Epistemology, Human Person, the Transcendent.* A volume in **Philosophy and Religion**

194.   Danielle Poe and Eddy Souffrant, Editors, *Parceling the Globe: Philosophical Explorations in Globalization, Global Behavior, and Peace.* A volume in **Philosophy of Peace**

195.   Josef Šmajs, *Evolutionary Ontology: Reclaiming the Value of Nature by Transforming Culture.* A volume in **Central-European Value Studies**

196.   Giuseppe Vicari, *Beyond Conceptual Dualism: Ontology of Consciousness, Mental Causation, and Holism in John R. Searle's Philosophy of Mind.* A volume in **Cognitive Science**

197.   Avi Sagi, *Tradition vs. Traditionalism: Contemporary Perspectives in Jewish Thought.* Translated from Hebrew by Batya Stein. A volume in **Philosophy and Religion**

198.   Randall E. Osborne and Paul Kriese, Editors, *Global Community: Global Security.* A volume in **Studies in Jurisprudence**

199.   Craig Clifford, *Learned Ignorance in the Medicine Bow Mountains: A Reflection on Intellectual Prejudice.* A volume in **Lived Values: Valued Lives**